Public Administration in Canada
Selected Readings

third edition

Methuen: Canadian Politics and Government

Public Administration in Canada
Selected Readings
third edition

edited by

Kenneth Kernaghan

Brock University

Methuen

Toronto • London • Sydney • Wellington

Canadian Cataloguing in Publication Data

Main entry under title:

Public administration in Canada

Texts of cases cited in this work may be found in a companion volume, Canadian cases in public administration, by W.D.K. Kernaghan.

Includes bibliographies.
ISBN 0-458-92410-5

1. Public administration — Addresses, essays, lectures. 2. Canada — Politics and government — Addresses, essays, lectures. I. Kernaghan, W.D.K., 1940-

JL108.P82 1977   354'.71   C77-001130-6

Printed and bound in Canada

3   4   5   81   80

CONTENTS

PREFACE

The articles in this third edition have been selected and organized to provide a book for use either as a text or as a book of readings on public administration in Canada. Brief introductory notes to each chapter are designed to explain the content of the chapters and to link them in a coherent whole.

This edition differs from the second edition in several important ways. Recent developments in the study and practice of public administration have required the inclusion of many new articles and the revision and updating of most of the others. New Canadian material has been included on such subjects as the political and policy roles of public servants, management development, the Operational Performance Measurement System, the Auditor General, citizen participation, administrative responsibility and ethical conduct. In addition, essays have been written especially for this book on the subjects of crown corporations, regulatory agencies, bilingualism, collective bargaining and federal-provincial administrative relations.

It is worth noting that a book of case studies, entitled *Canadian Cases in Public Administration*, has recently been published as a companion volume to this book of readings. The casebook contains twenty-four cases related to the essays in this book. At the end of each chapter of this book, preceding the bibliography, the cases most relevant to the essays in that chapter are listed. To assist teachers who wish to select a case related to a specific topic or problem, the casebook contains a subject index of the primary political-administrative issues covered by the cases. The use of the casebook in conjunction with this book of readings and formal lectures allows students to relate theoretical and descriptive material to actual administrative situations. Reference is also made, in the list of cases, to those cases and simulations published in the *Case Program in Canadian Public Administration* by the Institute of Public Administration of Canada.

Bibliographies at the end of each chapter supply valuable references for further reading on particular subjects. For a comprehensive bibliography on Canadian public administration, students should consult W.E. Grasham and Germain Julien, *Canadian Public Administration Bibliography*, including supplements 1 and 2.

The main purpose of this book is to provide a description and analysis of the institutions, processes and problems of Canadian public administration with a view to promoting better understanding and further study of the subject. It is hoped that students will come to understand the unique elements of administration in the public sector and to appreciate the challenges and opportunities of a career in Canadian government. The book is also intended to meet the needs of the increasing number of public officials engaged in training and development courses at all levels of government.

The choice of articles is based on an extensive search of the literature on public administration, and the articles are taken from a variety of sources. A broadly representative selection of concepts, issues and developments in modern public administration has been provided. The large percentage of essays written by Canadian scholars and public servants reflects the recent increase in Canadian public administration literature. Although the articles relate primarily to the federal public service, much of the material is also relevant to the concerns of provincial and municipal public employees.

In Chapter 1, an explanation of the meaning and development of public administration is based on a description of the evolution of organization theory.

This theoretical foundation prepares the reader for an inquiry into government organization and management functions which is provided in the next several chapters. Chapter 2 focuses on the study of Canadian public administration and on the unique environment and the complex political, legal and administrative structures within which the Canadian public services operate.

Chapter 3 is concerned with the intimately related management issues of motivation, leadership, decision making, communications and efficiency. Chapter 4 centres on planning and finance. An account of recent management improvement systems is followed by a discussion of parliamentary and administrative control over financial management and the role of the Auditor General. Chaper 5 contains an evaluation of the major elements of public personnel administration and includes an analysis of collective bargaining by federal employees.

Chapters 6 and 7 treat the critical issues of the politics and control of contemporary public services. Chapter 6 explores the political milieu within which public administrators work and the close relationship between policy and administration. Chapter 7 examines the concept of administrative responsibility and outlines existing and potential instruments of control designed to preserve and promote responsible administrative behaviour.

I wish to acknowledge my indebtedness to the authors and publishers who permitted their material to be printed in this volume. I express particular gratitude to the Institute of Public Administration of Canada for permission to reprint several articles from its journal, *Canadian Public Administration*, and to those authors who wrote original essays for this book.

K.K.

CHAPTER 1
PUBLIC ADMINISTRATION
AND ORGANIZATION THEORY

The scope of the study of public administration has broadened so greatly during the post-war period that a brief definition of the subject is now impracticable. The difficulty of delimiting the content of the field of public administration is compounded by an increasing number of interdisciplinary research contributions which continue to expand its boundaries. The study of public administration is also closely related to developments in the broad field of organization theory.

In the first essay of this chapter James L. Gibson traces the evolution of organization theory and its relation to the nature of organizational man by analyzing the mechanistic tradition, the humanistic challenge and the realistic synthesis. This essay provides a basis for Nicholas Henry's account of the intellectual development of public administration and the relation of this development to organization theory. Henry reviews the history of public administration's identity crisis by describing five major stages in the evolution of the study of public administration, including public administration as political science and as administrative science. The fifth and, in his view, the current stage of "public administration as public administration" is based on his contention that public administration is a unique field which is distinct from both political science and administrative science.

1

Organization Theory and the Nature of Man*

James L. Gibson

This essay seeks to add to the literature on the philosophy of organizations by emphasizing the value premises which underlie some of the major strands of thought.

The vehicle used to develp the literature is a classification system of three categories: the *mechanistic tradition*; the *humanistic challenge*; and the *realistic synthesis*. An essential feature of literature classified in the mechanistic tradition category is the view of man as a constant without peculiar features and malleable without incident into the organization structure; man is characterized as a machine—predictable, repairable, and replaceable. The literature of the humanistic challenge is characterized by an awareness of man as a unique element in the organization structure; man is viewed as having a need structure and individual differences are tolerated. The literature of the realistic synthesis is not easily characterized, but its essential feature is to treat man as one of a number of variables in the organization all of which are interdependent and interacting. Man is seen as being acted upon and as acting on the organization environment.

THE MECHANISTIC TRADITION

The writers of the mechanistic tradition focused on *two* aspects of organization theory.

At *one level*, Frederick W. Taylor and others analyzed the basic tasks of the individual members. The objective of Taylor and his followers was to reduce the contributions of each workman to the smallest, most specialized unit of work possible and to eliminate any uncertainty about the expect outcome. Elementary to such analysis were (and are) work simplification studies which break down manual labor tasks into definite repetitive movements and motion and time studies which establish time standards for the accomplishment of each movement. As Taylor himself said:

> Perhaps the most prominent single element in modern scientific management is the task idea. The work of every workman is fully planned out by the management at least one day in advance, and each man receives in most cases complete written instructions, describing

---

*Reprinted by permission from James L. Gibson, "Organization Theory and the Nature of Man," *Academy of Management Journal*, vol. 9, no. 3 (September 1966), pp. 233-245.

in detail the task which he is to accomplish, as well as the means to be used in doing the work. And the work planned in advance in this way constitutes a task which is to be solved, as explained above, not by the workman alone, but in almost all cases by the joint effort of the workman and the management. This task specifies not only what is to be done but how it is to be done and the exact time allowed for doing it.[1]

To assure that each task is performed according to the plan, the worker is paid on an incentive basis which rewards him for meeting the expectations of the organization and punishes him if he does not. The application of scientism tended to reduce the skills of craftsmen to routine, procedural, predictable sequences of movement; workers were to be as interchangeable as the cogs in Eli Whitney's cotton gin.

Underlying the procedural prescriptions of scientific management were definite assumptions about the nature of man. Taylor said:

A reward, if it is to be effective in stimulating men to do their best work, must come soon after the work has been done. But few men are able to look forward for more than a week or perhaps at most a month, and work hard for a reward which they are to receive at the end of this time.[2]

Later, in discussing the reasons for the failure of profit share schemes, he said: "Personal ambition always has been and will remain a more powerful incentive to exertion than a desire for the general welfare."[3] The view that man is motivated soley and predictably by economic considerations and is an isolated factor of production dependent of social and group pressures guided the development of scientific management theories and practices.

The postulates of scientific management were quite appealing to those who were concerned with administrative aspects of organizations — the *second level* of analysis.

Wolin suggests that Saint-Simon[4] laid the foundations of organization theory "with the conscious intent of establishing a defense against political instability and social disorder" in the aftermath of the French Revolution.[5] However, it was one hundred years later before a theory of organization structuring was articulated.

The most prominent writers of what is often called "Classical Organization Theory" were Luther Gulick,[6] Henri Fayol,[7] James D.

[1]Frederick W. Taylor, *Scientific Management* (New York: Harper and Brothers, 1911), p. 39.
[2]*Ibid.*, p. 94.
[3]*Ibid.*, p. 95
[4]See Henri de Saint-Simon, *Social Organization, The Science of Man, and other Writings*, edited and translated by Felix Markham (New York: Harper and Row, 1965).
[5]Sheldon S. Wolin, *Politics and Vision* (Boston: Little, Brown, and Co., 1960), p. 376.
[6]Luther Gulick and L. Urwick (eds.), *Papers on the Science of Administration* (New York: Institute of Public Administration, 1937).
[7]Henri Fayol, *General and Industrial Mangement* (London: Sir Isaac Pitman and Sons, 1949).

Mooney and A.C. Reiley,[8] and L. Ruwick[9] all of whom wrote from the perspective of business or military organizations. These writers owe an intellectual debt to Max Weber who provided the "ideal type" of administrative organization which he called a bureaucracy.[10] Even though Weber's model is based primarily on the European methods of organizing civil servants (chiefly the Prussian experience), the characteristics of his "ideal type" are illustrative of the main features of classical organization theory.

According to Weber, the essential characteristics of the "ideal type" are as follows:[11]

1.   All tasks necessary for the accomplishment of the goals are broken down into the smallest possible unit; the division of labor is carried out to the extent that specialized experts are responsible for the successful performance of specified duties.
2.   Each task is performed according to a "consistent system of abstract rules"[12] to assure uniformity and coordination of different tasks. This uncertainty in the performance of tasks due to individual differences is theoretically eliminated.
3.   Each member or office of an organization is accountable to a superior for his or its decisions as well as for his or its subordinates. The authority is based on expert knowledge and is sanctioned and made legitimate by the ultimate source of authority—the chief official at the top of the hierarchial pyramid.
4.   Each official in the organization conducts the business of his office in an impersonal, formalistic manner. He maintains a social distance between himself and his subordinates and between himself and the clients of the organization. The purpose of this impersonal detachment is to assure that personalities do not interfere with the efficient accomplishment of the mission.
5.   "Employment in the bureaucratic organization is based on technical

---

[8]J.D. Mooney and A.C. Reiley, *Principles of Organization* (New York: Harper and Brothers, 1939).

[9]L. Urwick, *The Elements of Administration* (New York: Harper and Brothers, 1943).

[10]Max Weber, *The Theory of Social and Economic Organization*, translated by A.M. Henderson and Talcott Parsons (New York: Oxford University Press, 1947). Michel Crozier in *The Bureaucratic Phenomenon* (Chicago: University of Chicago Press, 1964), a study of the French experience in organization of the civil service, points out three usages of the term bureaucracy: (1) The "traditional usage" is the political science concept of government by bureaus but without participation by the governed; (2) the Weberian usage is the sociological concept of rationalization of collective activities; and, (3) the vulgar usage is the laymen's concept which implies the dysfunctional nature of "bureaucratic" organizations, i.e., red tape, procedural delays, frustrations of agents and clients, p. 3.

[11]Weber, *ibid.*, pp. 329-340. For more reflective analyses of the "ideal type" see Peter M. Blau, *Bureaucracy in Modern Society* (Chicago: University of Chicago Press, 1956), pp. 27-56 and Victor A. Thompson, *op. cit.*, pp. 12-21.

[12]Weber, *ibid.*, p. 330.

qualifications and is protected against arbitrary dismissal."[13] Promotions are based on seniority and achievement. Because employment is considered a career and the vagaries of making a living are eliminated, a high degree of loyalty for the organization is engendered in the members.

The inherent logic of the bureaucratic structure led Weber to believe that the bureaucratic form of administration is "superior to any other form in precision, in stability, in the stringency of its discipline, and in its reliability. It thus makes possible a particularly high degree of calculability of results for the heads of the organization and for those acting in relation to it."[14] Thus Weber presented the case for bureaucratic administration on precisely the same grounds that the Taylorites presented the case for Scientific Manager. In fact Weber himself drew the analogy: "The fully developed bureaucratic mechanism compares with other ogranizations exactly as does the machine with nonmechanical modes of production."[15]

The bureacratic form of organization was (and is) prominent in business practice. The proponents of its use in this context formulated "principles" which are obviously in the Weberian tradition. Haynes and Massie have codified these principles as follows:[16]

1. The Unity of Command principle: No member of an organization should report to more than one superior.
2. The Span of Control principle: No superior should have responsibility for the activities of more than five to eight subordinates.
3. The Exception principle: A superior should delegate responsibility for routine matters to subordinates.
4. The Scalar principle: Every organization should have a well defined hierarchial structure.

One is struck by the prescriptive nature of these principles, by their similarity to the characteristics of Weber's ideal type, and by their concern for order and certainty in carrying on the activities of the organization.

The evidence supplied in the foregoing discussion suggests the assumptions regarding the nature of man underlying scientific manage-

---

[13]Blau, op. city., p. 30.
[14]Weber, op. cit., p. 334.
[15]From Max Weber: Essays in Sociology, translated by H.H. Gerth and C. Wright Mills (New York: Oxford University Press, 1946), p. 214 and quoted in Blau, op. cit., p. 31.
[16]W. Warren Haynes and Joseph L. Massie, Management (Englewood Cliffs, N.J.: Prentice-Hall, Inc., 1961), pp. 39-43. Other writers notably L. Urwick, op. cit., pp. 119-129 have lengthened the list, but the four here seem to be primary. Herbert A. Simon refers to such principles as "proverbs" in Administrative Behavior (New York: The Macmillan Co., 1945), pp. 20-36 because they have neither empirical verification nor universality of application.

ment and classical organization theory. March and Simon observe that two "views" of organization members are pervasive: "First, in general there is a tendency to view the employee as an inert instrument performing the tasks assigned to him. Second, there is a tendency to view personnel as a given rather than a variable in the system."[17] Mason Haire has been less polite: "These are the implicit assumptions about man on which classical organization theory seems to me to be based: He is lazy, short-sighted, selfish, liable to make mistakes, has poor judgment, and may even be a little dishonest."[18]

From another perspective, William F. Whyte argues that there are three assumptions underlying the theory: First, it is assumed that "man is a rational animal concerned with maximizing his economic gains," second, "each individual responds to economic incentives as an isolate individual," and third, "men, like machines, can be treated in a standardized fashion."[19]

THE HUMANISTIC CHALLENGE

It was only in the 1930's that these assumptions and their implications for organization theory and practice were seriously challenged. The body of concepts that developed during the initial thrust of the industrial revolution and which I have characterized as mechanistic was soon confronted with evidence that seriously challenged its validity. This challenge (which I call the humanistic challenge) came from two sources:

1. There were those who questioned the basic assumptions of the scientific management approach regarding the motivation of men; and,
2. There were those who questioned the efficiency of the bureaucratic form of organization.

Although two sources of challenge were seemingly unrelated, the emphasis of both was the same, namely: the participants of organizations are not constants and cannot be regarded as givens; and, a large mass of empirical evidence was soon available to show that participants adjust the environment to meet their individual and group needs. And part of this adjustment process is related to motivations, as some industrial engineers were to discover.

In 1924, engineers at the Hawthorne Works, a division of the

---

[17]James G. March and Herbert A. Simon, *Organizations* (New York: John Wiley and Sons, 1958), p. 29.
[18]George B. Strother (ed.), *Social Science Approaches to Business Behavior* (Homewood, Illinois: The Dorsey Press, Inc., 1962), p. 175.
[19]William F. Whyte, *Money and Motivation* (New York: Harper and Brothers, 1955), pp. 2-3.

Western Electric Company in Chicago, began a series of tests to determine the relationship between certain variables and the rate of production.[20] A number of frustrating experiments caused the scientists to reject their original hypothesis (that a high and positive correlation exists between working conditions and the rate of output) and they formulated alternative hypotheses. The major sources of data for testing the revised hypotheses were the voluminous recordings of interpersonal conversations that the experimenters had accumulated. These conversations between workers and the scientists revealed that the workers were members of closely knot work groups and that these work groups had established acceptable patterns of behavior for the members. These patterns of behavior, in turn, were based on the sentiments of the members of the group, but these sentiments were easily disguised and difficult to isolate. Nevertheless, the scientists discarded their statistical techniques and "denuded of their elaborate logical equipment"[21] they went into the shop to learn the things that were important to the workers.

The findings of the Hawthorne studies challenged the basic assumptions of earlier organization theory, namely the social isolation of the worker and the primacy of economic incentives. For these two assumptions, the human relations school substituted the view that man desires "first, a method of living in social relationship with other people, and, second, as part of this economic function for and value to the group."[22] Thus man (according to Mayo and his followers) "is a uniquely social animal who can achieve complete 'freedom' only by fully submerging himself in the group."[23] Based on the notion of man as a gregarious animal, the human relations school included in their ideology a view of a society in which man could best achieve his freedom. But the industrial society is not such a society and in fact the process of industrialization destroys the cultural traditions of former times which had enhanced social solidarity. The results of industrialization are social disorganization and unhappy individuals.

According to Mayo the responsibility for restoring the bases for social stability belongs to administrators of large industrial firms. With leadership that is human-oriented rather than production-oriented the

[20]The Hawthorne Studies are reported in T.N. Whitehead, *The Industrial Worker*, 2 volumes (Cambridge, Massachusetts: Harvard University Press, 1938), Fritz J. Roethlisberger and William J. Dickson, *Management and the Worker* (Cambridge, Massachusetts: Harvard University Press, 1947). Fritz J. Roethlisberger, *Management and Morale* (Cambridge, Massachusetts: Harvard University Press, 1941), and Elton Mayo, *The Human Problems of an Industrial Civilization* (New York: The Macmillan Co., 1933).

[21]F.J. Roethlisberger, *ibid.*, p. 16.

[22]Mayo, *op. cit.*, p. 18.

[23]Clark Kerr, *Labor and Management in Industrial Society* (Garden City, New York: Doubleday and Co., Inc., 1964), p. 54.

prospects for social stability and its concomitant, a meaningful life for the individual, are enhanced. In fact, Mayo has said: "If our social skills (that is, our ability to secure cooperation between people) had advanced step by step with our technical skill, there would not have been another European war."[24] Thus the ideology of the founders of the "human relations" approach consisted of three parts: (1) a view of man as a social animal, (2) a view of industrial society as incompatible with the basic nature of man, and (3) a view of the solution to man's dilemma as resting with industrial leaders.

The findings of the Hawthorne experiments were exceedingly important to those members of society primarily concerned with rational industrial supervision.[25] It had long been a mystery why workers would restrict output and produce far below standards established by exacting analyses. The Hawthorne studies provided both diagnosis and prescription. The practical application of human relations theory required careful consideration of the informal organization, work teams, and symbols that evoke worker response. Unions were viewed in a new dimension and were seen as making a contribution to effective organization rather than as the consequence of malfunctions in the organization.[26] Participative management, employee education, junior executive boards, group decisions and industrial counseling became important means for improving the performance of workers in the organization. Industrial leaders were spurred on by researchers whose findings indicated that "every human being earnestly seeks a secure, friendly, and supportive relationship and one that gives him a sense of personal worth in the face-to-face groups most important to him."[27] Thus, in practice, the "herd hypothesis" replaced the "rabble hypothesis."

The research methodology, the ideology, and the practice of human relations have been attacked on several points. The methodology of the supporting research is criticized for dealing with only immediate variables and for ignoring the external environment; the work is viewed as static and subject to little change over time. The findings of single case studies do not provide sufficient data for the construction of a rigorous theory of man and his organizations. But at a more fundamental level, the ideological view of man is attacked. "They (the human relations

---

[24]Elton Mayo, *The Social Problems of an Industrial Civilization* (Boston: Division of Research, Graduate School of Business Administration, Harvard University, 1947), p. 33.
[25]Burleigh B. Gardner, *Human Relations in Industry* (Chicago: Richard D. Irwin, Inc., 1945) is a "classic" of this tradition.
[26]See William F. Whyte, *Pattern for Industrial Peace* (New York: Harper and Brothers, 1951).
[27]Rensis Likert, *Motivation: The Core of Management* (New York: American Management Association, 1953). Reprinted in Harry Knudson, *Human Elements of Administration* (New York: Holt, Rinehart, and Winston, 1963), p. 81.

advocates) begin by saying that man dislikes isolation and end by consigning him to the care of the managerial elite for his own salvation."[28] Thus by losing his identity man becomes free or so assert the Mayo-ites.[29]

Critics of the practice of human relations have pointed to a number of defects. Most vehemently criticized has been the use of human relations techniques as means of manipulating workers to accept the superior's view of reality. Indeed, one has said: "I am totally unable to associate the *conscious practice of human relations skill* (in the sense of making people happy in spite of themselves or getting them to do something they don't think they want to do) with the *dignity of an individual person created in God's image*."[30]

This tendency toward manipulation is, at least in part, due to a misunderstanding of the purpose of the social sciences, "to the belief that the function of the social sciences is the same as that of the physical sciences, namely, to gain control of something outside."[31]

A second misunderstanding, and one springing directly from the ideology of human relations, is the belief that the business firm is a total institution which provides for all the needs of its members and that such an institution has the "right" to demand total loyalty. The attempt to gain total loyalty underlies much of personnel and human relations work; administrators frequently use the tags "loyal service" and "loyal employee" to describe the record of a retiring organization member. On this point Peter Drucker has said: "It is not only not compatible with the dignity of man, but it is not permissible to believe that the dignity of man can or should be realized totally in a partial institution."[32] The present state of human relations theory might be expressed as follows: "Let's treat people like people, but let's not make a big production of it."[33]

The findings of post-Weber studies of bureaucratic behavior are similar to the findings of the Hawthorne studies—the reaction of individuals to organizational factors is not always predictable.[34]

---

[28]Kerr, *op. cit.*, p. 57.

[29]It is not quite fair to say that Mayo "asserts" in this connection. In *Human Problems of an Industrial Civilization, op. cit.*, he analyzes various traditional cultures and presents as evidence of the social nature of man the many practices designed to achieve social integration, e.g., ritual custom, codes, family and tribal instincts.

[30]Malcolm P. McNair, "Thinking Ahead: What Price Human Relations?" *Harvard Business Review* (March-April, 1957), pp. 15-23. Reprinted in Harold Koontz and Cyril O'Donnell, *Readings in Management* (New York: McGraw-Hill Book Co., Inc., 1959), p. 279.

[31]Peter Drucker, "Human Relations: Where Do We Stand Today?" in Knudson, *op. cit.*, p. 364. The purpose of the social sciences is to gain understanding of one's self as Drucker explains.

[32]*Ibid.*, p. 364.

[33]McNair, *op. cit.*, p. 285.

[34]This discussion is based on March and Simon, *op. cit.*, pp. 36-47.

Merton,[35] Selznick,[36] and Gouldner[37] suggest that treating people as machines not only leads to unforeseen consequences but can actually reinforce the use of the "machine model." Each researcher studied some form of procedure designed to control the activities of the members of the organization.

Merton analyzed the organizational need for control and the consequent concern for reliability of members' behavior. In order to get the desired results, the organization implements standard rules and procedures. Control is achieved by assuring that the members are following the rules. Merton points out three consequences that result from concern for reliability of behavior: (1) officials react to individuals as representative of positions having certain specified rights and privileges; (2) rules assume a positive value as ends rather than as means to ends; and, (3) decision-making becomes routine application of tried and proven approaches and little attention is given to alternatives not previously experienced.[38] The organization becomes committed to activities that insure the status quo at the expense of greater success in achieving organization objectives.

Selznick studied the consequences of a second technique for achieving control and reliability—the delegation of authority. As intended, the specialized competence required to carry out the delegate tasks has the positive effect of achieving organization goals, but that are unintended consequences. Delegation of authority "results in depart-mentalization and an increase in the *bifurcation of interests* among the subunits in the organization."[39] Members of the organization become increasingly dependent upon the maintenance of subunits and there is a growing disparity between the goals of the subunit and the goals of the organization. The content of decisions is increasingly concerned with subunit objectives and decreasingly concerned with organization goals, except that there must not be too great a disparity between the two. Subunit officials seek to make legitimate their activities by squaring their decisions with precedent. Again there seems to be an inherent tendency in the bureaucratic structure toward conservatism and the maintenance of the status quo.[40]

---

[35]Robert K. Merton, "Bureaucratic Structure and Personality," *Social Forces,* Vol. 18, (1940), pp. 560-568.

[36]Philip Selznick, *TVA and the Grass Roots* (Berkeley: The University of California Press, 1949).

[37]Alvin W. Gouldner, *Patterns of Industrial Bureaucracy* (New York: The Free Press of Glencoe, 1954).

[38]March and Simon, *op. cit.,* pp. 38-39.

[39]*Ibid.,* p. 41.

[40]Such is the thesis of Robert Michels, *Political Parties* (Glencoe, Illinois: The Free Press, 1949), whose concept of the "iron law of oligarchy" is a classic description of the tendency of organization to become conservative as the demands for more specialized competence intensify.

Gouldner gives additional support to the thesis that organization techniques designed to implement control often entail unanticipated results. In his study of industrial organization he found, among other things, that the improvisation of rules to assure control results in the knowledge of *minimum acceptable levels of behavior* and that members of organizations gear their activities to these minimum levels of behavior if there is a high level of bifurcation of interest. As officials perceive this low performance, they react by increasing the closeness of supervision and by enacting additional rules and procedures. Again, the unintended consequences are increasing tension among members, increasing non-acceptance of organization goals, and increasing the use of rules to correct matters.[11]

To summarize, the essence of the humanistic challenge is that man in organizations is socially oriented and directed. He has multiple need which affect and are affected by the work environment; he reacts unpredictably, yet predictably, to stimuli encountered in the organization. The "unintended consequences" of bureaucratic methods imply that man may be incompatible with organization needs. The scene is set, then, for contemporary organization theorists to devise a synthesis of the two polar positions.

THE REALISTIC SYNTHESIS[42]

An important feature of modern organization theory[43] is the systems approach which treats organizations as complex sets of mutually dependent and interacting variables. In this framework the participants are one set of variables which act on all other variables. Because this paper is concerned only with the place of man in organization theory, I will outline the features of the systems approach (which I term the realistic synthesis) and then return to the discussion of man as a variable in the system.

The systems approach to organization theory presents the opportunity to view the organization as a totality. The emphasis is on the

---

[41]March and Simon, *op. cit.,* p. 45. Those studies are classics in the development of our knowledge of organizational behavior. It is obvious that many of Downs' hypotheses are suggested by this literature, particularly the hypotheses that organizations value status quo solutions and consensus and that the content of decisions is limited to precedents.

[42]Some third dimension as a basis for synthesis and the criteria for its selection are a concern to many students of organization theory. The work of Warren B. Bennis and many others could be cited. The focus of this paper, however, is on *values* more than the whole panorama.

[43]Some presentations of modern organization theory are March and Simon, *op. cit.;* Mason Haire (ed.), *Modern Organization Theory* (New York: John Wiley and Sons, 1959); Albert H. Rubenstein and Chadwick J. Haberstroh, *Some Theories of Organization* (Homewood, Illinois: The Dorsey Press, Inc., 1960); Joseph A. Litterer, *The Analysis of Organizations* (New York: John Wiley and Sons, 1965); and, Theodore Caplow, *Principles of Organizations* (New York: Harcourt, Brace and World, Inc., 1964).

parts of the system, the nature of interaction among the parts, the processes which link the parts, and the goals of the system.[44] The key parts are the individual and his unique personality, the formal structure of jobs, the informal groups, the status and role patterns within the groups, and the physical environment. Relating these parts are complex patterns of interactions which modify the behavior and expectations of each. The basic parts are linked together by certain organizational processes including structured roles, channels of communication, and decision making. These processes provide means for overcoming the centrifugal tendency of the parts[45] and for directing the parts toward the ultimate goals of the organization—growth, stability and social interaction.[46]

The systems approach is a realistic synthesis because it views the individual as only one of many parts, because it allows for modification of the parts, because it views conflict within the organization as a natural by-product of group endeavor, and because it anticipates dynamic rather than static patterns of interaction.

The realistic view of man in the organization acknowledges the contributions of the Hawthorne experiments, but it has added certain ideas that go beyond "human relations." The basic premise seems to be that man's needs and the organization's needs are inconsistent.[47] Man's behavior is seen to be motivated by a hierarchy of needs and once the most basic needs are satisfied, the individual turns to the ultimate source of satisfaction—self-actualization. But to achieve self-actualization requires that the healthy individual be "independent, creative . . . exercise autonomy and discretion, and . . . develop and express . . . unique personality with freedom."[48] The organization, however, presents barriers to this development of self-actualization and requires that the individual be dependent upon others for goal-setting and direction and conform to norms far below the level of his ability or expectations. The results of this conflict are immature behavior and frustration-oriented activities, the overt expression being determined by the unique personality of the individual. Argyris' studies indicate that an organization member experiencing frustration and conflict may behave in any one of the following ways.[49]

---

[44]William G. Scott, "Organization Theory: An Overview and an Appraisal," *Academy of Management Journal* (April 1961), pp. 7-26. Reprinted in Joseph A. Litterer (ed.), *Organizations: Structure and Behavior* (New York: John Wiley and Sons, 1963), p. 19.

[45]John M. Pfiffner and Frank P. Sherwood, *Administrative Organization* (Englewood Cliffs, N.J.: Prentice-Hall, Inc., 1960), pp. 116-117.

[46]Scott, *op. cit.*, p. 22.

[47]This view is developed by Chris Argyris in *Personality and Organization* (New York: Harper and Brothers, 1957) and more recently in *Integratiny the Individual and the Organization* (New York: John Wiley and Sons, 1964).

[48]George Strauss, "Some Notes on Power-Equalization" in Harold J. Leavitt, editor, *The Social Science of Organization* (Englewood Cliffs, N.J.: Prentice-Hall, Inc., 1963), p. 46.

a.   He may leave the organization.
b.   He may work hard and become president.
c.   He may adapt through the use of defense mechanisms.
d.   He may adapt by lowering his work standards and by becoming apathetic.

Other students of organizational behavior also perceive basic conflicts between the organization and the individual. Presthus argues that the reactions of members can be characterized by three bureaucratic types: the upward-mobiles; the indifferents; and, the ambivalents. The upward-mobiles are those who react positively to the organizational requirements and by adopting the sanctioned behavioral patterns succeed in it.[50] The indifferents are the great majority who view their jobs as means to secure off-work satisfactions and who neither seek nor expect on-job satisfaction.[51] The ambivalents are a small minority who are unable to play the organizationally defined role which would enable them to realize their ambitions.[52] The similarity between these three patterns of behavior and the adaptive responses which Argyris lists is evident.

Thus, the contemporary view of the nature of man in organizations recognizes the essential conflict that exists. Whereas: the mechanistic tradition considered conflict to be dysfunctional to organization purposes and felt that it could be neutralized by monetary payments; and, the humanist challenge viewed conflict as dysfunctional but believed that human relations techniques could control it; the realistic synthesis assumes that conflict is a normal aspect of organization life.

The problem posed then is how to harness the energies of conflict such that both organizational and individual needs are realized. Given the problem, we can accept at the outset that neither will be met perfectly—this being the essence of the conflict.[53] And whether conflict or cooperation is the *essential* nature of man does not seem to be relevant,[54] since research indicates that many organization members are *in fact in conflict* with the requirements of the organization.

I offer no final conclusions as to where recent efforts in organization theory and organization structuring will lead us;[55] all the evidence is not

---

[49]*Personality and Organization* ... pp. 78-79.
[50]Robert Presthus, *The Original society (New York: Alfred A. Knopf, 1962)* pp. 164-204.
[51]*Ibid.,* pp. 205-256.
[52]*Ibid.,* pp. 257-285.
[53]Conflict and struggle for power in organizations lead to patterns of behavior that are political in nature. Melville Dalton in *Men Who Manage* (New York: John Wiley and Sons, 1959) analyzes organizational politics.
[54]Nor is there a final answer since some men (e.g. Thomas Hobbes) have viewed the essence of man to be conflict while others (e.g. John Locke) have viewed man as essentially cooperative. Realization of the individual through the group is not characteristic of Rousseau.

in and final arguments have not been heard. However, it is not difficult to concur with Haire's statement:

> Whenever we try to plan what an organization should be like, it is necessarily based on an implicit concept of man. If we look ... at the outline of a "classical" organization theory and some more modern alternatives, we begin to see the change in the concept of man.[56]

2
The Intellectual Development of Public Administration*

Nicholas Henry

The study and practice of public bureaucracy is called public administration. Phrased more specifically, public administration is a broad-ranging and amorphous combination of theory and practice designed to promote a superior understanding of government and its relationship with the society it governs, as well as to encourage public policies more responsive to social needs and institute managerial practices on the part of the public bureaucracies that are substantially attuned to effectiveness, efficiency and, increasingly, the deeper human requisites of the citizenry. Admittedly, the preceding sentence is itself rather broad-ranging and amorphous, but for the purposes of this essay it will suffice. There are, however, additional characteristics of public administration.

As Stephen K. Bailey has noted, public administration is (or should be) concerned with the development of four kinds of theories:

1. "descriptive theory," or descriptions of hierarchical structures and relationships with their sundry task environments;
2. "normative theory," or the "value goals" of the field, that is, what public administrators (the practitioners) ought to do given their realm of decision alternatives, and what public administrationists (the scholars) ought to study and recommend to the practitioners in terms of policy;

[55]See William W. Cooper, Harold J. Leavitt, and Maynard W. Shelly, *New Perspectives in Organization Research* (New York: John Wiley and Sons, Inc., 1964) for some indications.
[56]Strother, *op. cit.*, pp. 170-171.

*Reprinted by permission from Nicholas Henry, *Public Administration and Public Affairs* (Englewood Cliffs, N.J.: Prentice-Hall, Inc., 1975), pp. 4-18, 22.

3. "assumptive theory," or a rigorous understanding of the reality of administrative man, one that assumes neither angelic nor satanic models of the public bureaucrat;
4. "instrumental theory," or the increasingly refined managerial techniques for the efficient and effective attainment of public objectives.

Taken together, Bailey's quartet of "theories" form three defining pillars of public administration: organizational behavior and the behavior of people in public organizations; the technology of management; and the public interest as it relates to individual ethical choice and public affairs.

In this essay we review the successive definitional crises of public administration—that is, how the field has "seen itself" in the past. These paradigms of public administration are worth knowing about because, first, one must know where the field has been in order to comprehend it. It is contended that public administration is unique, a field significantly different from both political science (public administration's "mother discipline") and administrative science (public administration's traditional alter ego) in terms of developing certain facets of organization theory and techniques of management). Public administration differs from political science in its emphasis on bureaucratic structure and behavior and in its methodologies. Public administration differs from administrative science in that the evaluative techniques used by non-profit public organizations are not the same as those used by for-profit private organizations, and because profit-seeking organizations are considerably less constrained in considering the public interest in their decision-making structures and the behavior of their administrators.

THE INTELLECTUAL DEVELOPMENT OF PUBLIC ADMINISTRATION

In terms of public administration's development as an academic field, there have been a succession of five overlapping paradigms. As Robert T. Golembiewski has noted in a perceptive essay on the development of the field, each phase may be characterized according to whether it has "locus" or "focus." *Locus* is the institutional "where" of the field. A recurring locus of public administration is the government bureaucracy, but this has not always been the case and often this traditional locus has been blurred. *Focus* is the specialized "what" of the field. One focus of public administration has been the study of certain "principles of administration," but, again, the foci of the discipline have altered with the changing paradigms of public administration. As Golembiewski observes, the paradigms of public administration may be understood in terms of locus or focus; when one has been relatively sharply defined, the other has been conceptually ignored in academic circles and vice-versa. We shall use the notion of loci and foci in reviewing the intellectual development of public administration.

The Beginning

Woodrow Wilson largely set the tone for the early study of public administration in an essay entitled "The Study of Administration," published in the *Political Science Quarterly* in 1887. In it, Wilson observed that it "is getting harder to *run* a constitution than to frame one," and called for the bringing to bear of more intellectual resources in the management of the state. Wilson's seminal article has been interpreted by later scholars in a number of differing ways. Some have insisted that Wilson was the originator of the "politics/administration dichotomy," or the naive distinction between "political" activity and "administrative" activity in public organizations that would plague the field for years to come. Other scholars have countered that Wilson was well aware that public administration was innately political in nature, and made this point clear in his article. The reality of the matter appears to be that Wilson himself was ambivalent about what public administration really was. As Richard J. Stillman, II, concluded in a thorough and timely reconsideration of "The Study of Administration," Wilson failed to amplify what the study of administration actually entails, what the proper relationship should be between the administrative and political realms, and whether or not administrative study could ever become an abstract science akin to the natural sciences." Nevertheless, Wilson unquestionably posited one unambiguous thesis in his article that has had a lasting impact on the field: Public administration was worth studying. Political scientists later on would create the first indentifiable paradigm of public administration around Wilson's contention.

Paradigm 1: The politics/administration dichotomy, 1900-1926

Our benchmark date for the Paradigm 1 period corresponds to the publication of books written by Frank J. Goodnow and Leonard D. White; they are, as are the years chosen as marking the later periods of the field, only rough indicators. In *Politics and Administration* (1900), Goodnow contended that there were "two distinct functions of government," which he identified with the title of his book. Politics, said Goodnow, "has to do with policies or expressions of the state will," while administration "has to do with the execution of these policies." Separation of powers provided the basis of the distinction; the legislative branch, aided by the interpretive abilities of the judicial branch, expressed the will of the state and formed policy, while the executive branch administered those policies impartially and apolitically.

The emphasis of Paradigm 1 was on locus—where public administration should be. Clearly, in the view of Goodnow and his fellow public administrationists, public administration should center in the government's bureaucracy. While, admittedly, the legislature and judiciary had their quanta of "administration," their primary responsibility and function remained the expression of the state will. The initial conceptual legitimation of this locus-centered definition of the field, and one that would wax increasingly problematic for academics and practitioners alike, became known as the politics/administration dichotomy.

The phrase that came to symbolize this distinction between politics and administration was, "there is no Republican way to build a road," the reasoning being that there could only be one "right" way to spread tarmac—the administrative engineer's way. What was ignored in this statement, however, was that there was indeed a Republican way to decide whether the road needed building, a Republican way to choose the location for the road, a Republican way to purchase the land, a Republican way to displace the people living in the road's way, and most certainly a Republican way to let contracts for the road, There was also, and is, a Democratic way, a Socialist way, a Liberal way, even an Anarchist way to make these "administrative" decisions as well. The point is that, in reality, the politics/administration dichotomy posited by Goodnow and his academic progeny was, at best, naive. But many years would pass before this would be fully realized within public administration's ranks.

Public administration received its first serious attention from scholars during this period largely as a result of the "public service movement" that was taking place in American universities in the early part of this century. Political science, as a report issued in 1914 by the Committee on Instruction in Government of the American Political Science Association stated, was concerned with training for citizenship, professional preparations such as law and journalism, training "experts and to prepare specialists for governmental positions," and educating for research work. Public administration, therefore, was a clear and significant subfield of political science. In 1912, a Committee on Practical Training for Public Service was established under the auspices of the American Political Science Association, and in 1914 its report recommended, with unusual foresight, that special "professional schools" were needed to train public administrators, and that new technical degrees might be necessary as well for this purpose. This Committee formed the nucleus of the Society for the Promotion of Training for the Public Service, founded in 1914—the forerunner of the American Society for Public Administration, which was established in 1939 when public administration was at its most "separatist" stage of development in terms of political science.

Public administration began picking up academic legitimacy in the 1920s; notable in this regard was the publication of Leonard D. White's *Introduction to the Study of Public Administration* in 1926, the first textbook devoted *in toto* to the field. As Dwight Waldo has pointed out, White's text was quintessentially American Progressive in character and, in its quintessence, reflected the general thrust of the field: Politics should not intrude on administration; management lends itself to scientific study; public administration is capable of becoming a "value-free" science in its own right; the mission of administration is economy and efficiency, period.

The net result of Paradigm 1 was to strengthen the notion of a distinct politics/administration dichotomy by relating it to a corresponding value/fact dichotomy. Thus, everything that public administrationists scrutinized in the executive branch was imbued with the colorings and legitimacy of being somehow "factual" and "scientific," while the study of public policy-making and related matters was left to the political scientists. The carving up of analytical territory between public administrationists and political scientists during this locus-oriented stage can be seen today in political science departments: it is the public administrationists who teach organization theory, budgeting, and personnel, while political scientists teach such subjects as American government, judicial behavior, the Presidency, state and local politics, and legislative process, as well as such "non-American" fields as comparative politics and international relations. A secondary implication of this locus-centered phase was the isolation of public administration from other fields as well, such as business administration, which had unfortunate consequences later when these fields began their own fruitful explorations into the nature of organizations. Finally, largely because of the emphasis on "administration" and "facts" in public administration, and the substantial contributions by public administrationists to the emerging field of organization theory, a foundation was laid for the later "discovery" of certain scientific "principles" of administration.

Paradigm 2: The principles of administration, 1927-1937

In 1927, W.F. Willoughby's book, *Principles of Public Administration*, was published as the second full-fledged text in the field. While Willoughby's *Principles* was as fully American Progressive in tone as White's *Introduction*, its title alone indicated the new thrust of public administration: that certain scientific principles of administration were "there," that they could be discovered, and that administrators would be expert in their work if they learned how to apply these principles.

It was during the phase represented by Paradigm 2 that public administration reached its reputational zenith. Public administrationists were in high demand during the 1930s and early 1940s for their managerial knowledge, courted by industry and government alike. Thus the focus of the field—its essential expertise in the form of administrative principles—waxed, while no one thought too seriously about its locus. Indeed, the locus of public administration was everywhere, since principles were principles, and administration was administration, at least according to the perceptions of Paradigm 2. By the very fact that the principles of administration were indeed *principles*—that is, by definition, they "worked" in any administrative setting, regardless of culture, function, environment, mission, or institutional framework and without exception—it therefore followed that they could be applied successfully anywhere. Furthermore, because public administrationists had contributed as much if not more to the formulation of "administrative principles" as had researchers in any other field of inquiry, it also followed that public administrationists should lead the academic pack in applying them to "real-world" organizations, public or otherwise.

Among the more significant works relevant to this phase were Mary Parker Follett's *Creative Experience* (1924), Henri Fayol's *Industrial and General Management* (1930), and James D. Mooney and Alan C. Reiley's *Principles of Organization* (1939), all of which delineated varying numbers of overarching administrative principles. Organization theorists often dub this school of thought "administrative management," since it focussed on the upper hierarchical echelons of organizations. A related literature that preceded the work in administrative management somewhat in time, but which was under continuing development in business schools, focussed on the assembly line. Often called "scientific management," researchers in this stream (notably Frederick W. Taylor's *Principles of Scientific Management* [1911] and various works by Frank and Lillian Gilbreth) developed "principles" of efficient physical movement for optimal assembly-line efficiency. While obviously related in concept, scientific management had little effect on public administration during its principles phase because it focussed on lower-level personnel in the organization.

The "high noon of orthodoxy," as it often has been called, of public administration was marked by the publication in 1937 of Luther H. Gulick and Lyndall Urwick's *Papers on the Science of Administration*. This landmark study also marked the high noon of prestige for public administration. Gulick and Urwick were confidantes of President Franklin D. Roosevelt and advised him on a variety of matters managerial; their *Papers* were a report to the President's Committee on Administrative Science.

Principles were important to Gulick and Urwick, but where those principles were applied was not; focus was favored over locus, and no bones were made about it. As they said in the *Papers*,

> It is the general thesis of this paper that there are principles which can be arrived at inductively from the study of human organization which should govern arrangements for human association of any kind. These principles can be studied as a technical question, irrespective of the purpose of the enterprise, the personnel comprising it, or any constitutional, political or social theory underlying its creation.

Gulick and Urwick promoted seven principles of administration and, in so doing, gave students of public administration that snappy anagram, POSDCORB. POSDCORB was the final expression of administrative principles. It stood for:

P	lanning
O	rganizing
S	taffing
D	irecting
C }	ordinating
O	
R	eporting
B	udgeting

That was public administration in 1937.

The challenge, 1938-1947

In the following year, mainstream, top-of-the-heap public administration received its first real hint of conceptual challenge. In 1938, Chester I. Barnard's *The Functions of the Executive* appeared. Its impact on public administration was not overwhelming at the time, but it later had considerable influence on Herbert A. Simon when he was writing his devastating critique of the field, *dministrative Behavior*. The impact of Barnard's book may have been delayed because, as a former president of New Jersey Bell Telephone, he was not a certified member of the public administration community.

Dissent from mainstream public administration accelerated in the 1940s and took two, mutually reenforcing directions. One was the objection that politics and administration could never be separated in any remotely sensible fashion. The other was that the principles of administration were logically inconsistent.

Although inklings of dissent began in the 1930s, a book of readings in the field, *Elements of Public Administration*, edited in 1946 by Fritz von Morstein-Marx, was one of the first major volumes which questioned the assumption that politics and administration could be dichotomized.

All the fourteen articles were written by practitioners and indicated a new awareness that what often appeared to be value-free "administration" actually was value-laden "politics." Was a "technical" decision on a budgetary emphasis or a personnel change really impersonal and apolitical, or was it actually highly personal, highly political, and highly preferential? Was it ever possible to really discern the difference? Was it even worth attempting to discern the difference between politics and administration because, in reality, there was none? Was the underpinning politics/administration dichotomy of the field, at best, naive? Perhaps the frontal answer to these questions was published in 1950: John Gaus penned in the *Public Administration Review* his oft-quoted dictum, "A theory of public administration means in our time a theory of politics also." The die was cast.

Arising simultaneously with the challenge to the traditional politics/administration dichotomy of the field was an even more basic contention: that there could be no such thing as a "principle" of administration. In 1946, Simon gave a foreshadowing of his *Administrative Behavior* in an article entitled, appropriately, "The Proverbs of Administration," published in *Public Administration Review*. The following year, Robert A. Dahl published a searching piece in the same journal, "The Science of Public Administration:Three Problems," in which he argued that the development of universal principles of administration was hindered by the obstructions of values contending for preeminence in organizations, differences in individual personalities, and social frameworks that varied from culture to culture. Waldo's work also reflected this theme. His *The Administrative State: A Study of the Political Theory of American Public Administration* (1948) attacked the notion of immutable principles of administration, the inconsistencies of the methodology used in determining them, and the narrowness of the "values" of economy and efficiency that dominated the field's thinking.

The most formidable dissection of the principles notion also appeared in 1947: Simon's *Administrative Behavior: A Study of Decision-Making Processes in Administration Organization*. Simon showed that for every "principle" of administration there was a counter-principle, thus rendering the whole idea of principles moot. For example, the traditional administrative literature argued that bureaucracies must have a narrow "span of control" if orders were to be communicated and carried out effectively. Span of control meant that a manager could "control" properly only a limited number of subordinates; after a certain number was exceeded (authorities differed on just what the number was), communication of commands became increasingly garbled and control became increasingly ineffective and "loose." An organization that followed the principle of narrow span of control would have a "tall" organization chart (see Figure 1).

Span of control made sense up to a point. Yet, as Simon observed, the

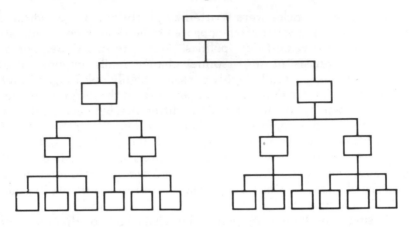

Figure 1
The "Principle" of Narrow Span of Control

literature on administration argued with equal vigor for another principle: that for organizations to maximize effective communications and to reduce distortion (thereby enhancing responsiveness and control), there should be as few hierarchical layers as possible; that is, a "flat" hierarchical structure. The logic behind this principle was that the fewer people who had to pass a message up or down the hierarchy, the more likely it would be that the message would arrive at its appointed destination relatively intact and undistorted. This, too, made sense up to a point. The "flat" hierachy required to bring the bureaucracy in accord with this principle of administration would have an organization chart like that in Figure 2.

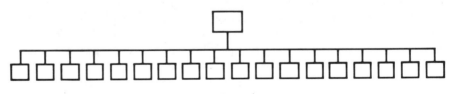

Figure 2
The "Principle" of Maximized Communications

Obviously, to Simon and now to us, the two "principles" were mutually contradictory and therefore could not be principles by definition. This dilemma encompassed the whole of the traditional public administration literature, but it was never more than suspected of being so stark a case until Simon published his book.

By mid-century, the two defining pillars of public administration—

the politics/administration dichotomy and the principles of administration — had been abandoned by creative intellects in the field. This abandonment left public administration bereft of a distinct epistemological identity. Some would argue that an identity has yet to be found.

Reaction to the challenge, 1947-1950

In the same year that Simon decimated the traditional foundations of public administration in *Administrative Behavior*, he offered an alternative to the old paradigms in an essay entitled "A Comment on 'The Science of Public Administration' " and published in the *Public Administration Review*. For Simon, a new paradigm for public administration meant that there ought to be two kinds of public administrationists working in harmony and reciprocal intellectual stimulation: those scholars concerned with developing "a pure science of administration" based on "a thorough grounding in social psychology," and a larger group concerned with "prescribing for public policy." This latter enterprise was far-ranging indeed. In Simon's view, prescribing for public policy "cannot stop when it has swallowed up the whole of political science; it must attempt to absorb economics and sociology, as well." Nevertheless, both a "pure science of administration" and "prescribing for public policy" would be mutually reenforcing components: "there does not appear to be any reason why these two developments in the field of public administration should not go on side by side, for they in no way conflict or contradict."

Despite a proposal that was both rigorous and normative in its emphasis, Simon's call for a "pure science" put off many scholars in public administration. For one thing, there already existed a growing irritation in the field with POSDCORB on the basis of its "pure science" claims; the challengers of the late 1940s had shown that the "principles of administration" were hardly the final expression of science, and consequently public administrationists were increasingly skeptical that the administrative phenomenon could be understood in wholly scientific terms. Second, Simon's urging that social psychology provided the basis for understanding administrative behavior struck many public administrationists as foreign and discomforting; most of them had no training in social psychology. Third, since science was perceived as being "value-free," it followed that a "science of administration" logically would ban public administrationists from what many of them perceived as their richest sources of inquiry: normative political theory, the concept of the public interest, and the entire spectrum of human values. While this interpretation may well have rested on a widespread misinterpretation of Simon's thinking (understandable, perhaps, given the wake of *Administrative Behavior*), as Golembiewski contends, the reaction nonetheless was real.

The threat posed by Simon and his fellow challengers of the traditional paradigms was clear not only to most political scientists but to many public administrationists as well. For their part, the public administrationists had both a carrot and a stick as inducements not only to remain within political science but to strengthen the conceptual linkages between the fields. The carrot was the maintenance of the logical conceptual connection between public administration and political science: that is, the public policy-making process. Public administration considered the "internal" stages of that process: the formulation of public policies within public bureaucracies and their delivery to the polity. Political science was perceived as considering the "external" stages of the process: the pressures in the polity generating political and social change. There was a certain logic in retaining this linkage in terms of epistemological benefits to both fields. The stick, as we have noted, was the worrisome prospect of retooling only to become a technically-oriented "pure science" that might lose touch with political and social realities in an effort to cultivate an engineering mentality for public administration.

Political scientists, for their part, had begun to resist the growing independence of public administrationists and to question the field's action orientation as early as the mid-1930s. Political scientists, rather than advocating a public service and executive preparatory program as they had in 1914, began calling for, in the words of Lynton K. Caldwell, "intellectualized understanding" of the executive branch, rather than "knowledgeable action" on the part of public administrators. In 1952, Roscoe Martin wrote an article appearing in the *American Political Science Review* calling for the continued "dominion of political science over public administration."

By the post-World War II era, political scientists were well under the gun, and could ill afford the breakaway of their most prestigious subfield. The discipline was in the throes of being shaken conceptually by the "behavioral revolution" that had occurred in other social sciences. The American Political Science Association was in some financially tight straits. Political scientists were aware that not only public administrationists had threatened secession in the past, now other subfields, such as international relations, were restive. And, in terms of science and social science both, it was increasingly evident that political science was held in low esteem by scholars in other fields. The formation of the National Science Foundation in 1950 brought the message to all who cared to listen that the chief federal science agency considered political science to be the distinctly junior member of the social sciences, and in 1953 David Easton confronted this lack of status directly in his influential book, *The Political System*.

Paradigm 3: Public administration as political science, 1950-1970

In any event, as a result of these concerns and icy conceptual critiques of the field, public administrationists leaped back with some alacrity into the mother discipline of political science. The result was a renewed definition of locus—the governmental bureaucracy—but a corresponding loss of focus. Should the mechanics of budgets and public personnel policies be studied exclusively? Or should public administrationists consider the grand philosophic schemata of the "administrative Platonists" (as one political scientist called them), such as Paul Appleby? Or should they explore quite new fields of inquiry, as urged by Simon, such as sociology, business administration, and social psychology, as they related to the analysis of organizations and decision-making? In brief, this third phase of definition was largely an exercise in reestablishing the conceptual linkages between public administration and political science. But the consequence of this exercise was to "define away" the field, at least in terms of its analytical focus, its essential "expertise." Thus, writings on public administration in the 1950s spoke of the field as an "emphasis," an "area of interest," or even as a "synonym" of political science. Public administration, as an identifiable field of study, began a long, downhill spiral.

Things got relatively nasty by the end of the decade and, for that matter, well into the 1960s. In 1962, public administration was not included as a subfield of political science in the report of the Committee on Political Science as a Discipline of the American Political Science Association. In 1964, Albert Somit and Joseph Tanenhaus's major survey of political scientists indicated a decline in faculty interest in public administration generally. In 1967, public administration disappeared as an organizing category in the program of the annual meeting of the American Political Science Association. Waldo wrote in 1968 that "many political scientists not identified with Public Administration are indifferent or even hostile; they would sooner be free of it," and added that the public administrationist has an "uncomfortable" and "second-class citizenship." Between 1960 and 1970, only four percent of all the articles published in the five major political science journals dealt with public administration. In the 1960s, "P.A. types" as they often were called in political science faculties, pretty much shuffled through political science departments.

Paradigm 4: Public administration as administrative science, 1956-1970

Partly because of their second-class citizenship status in a number of political science departments, some public administrationists began searching for an alternative. Although Paradigm 4 occurred roughly concurrently with Paradigm 3 in time, it never has received the broadly-based favor that political science has garnered from public administrationists as a paradigm (although its appeal is growing). Nonetheless, the administrative science option is a viable alternative for a significant number of scholars in public administration. But in both the political science and administrative science paradigms, the essential thrust was one of public administration losing its identity and its uniqueness within the confines of some "larger" concept.

"Administrative science" is used here as a catch-all phrase for studies in organization theory and management science. Organization theory draws primarily on the works of social psychologists, business administrationists, and sociologists, as well as public administrationists to better understand organizational behavior, while management science relies chiefly on the research of statisticians, systems analysts, computer scientists, and economists, as well as public administrationists, in order to measure program effectiveness more precisely and increase managerial efficiency. As a paradigm, administrative science provides a focus but not a locus. It offers techniques, often highly sophisticated techniques, that require expertise and specialization, but in what institutional setting that expertise should be applied is undefined. As in Paradigm 2, administration is administration wherever it is found; focus is favored over locus.

A number of developments, often stemming from the country's business schools, fostered the alternative paradigm of administrative science. In 1956, the important journal *Administrative Science Quarterly* was founded by a public administrationist on the premise that public, business, and institutional administration were false distinctions, that administration was administration. Public administrationist Keith M. Henderson, among others, argued in the mid-1960s that organization theory was, or should be, the overarching focus of public administration. And, it cannot be denied that such works as James G. March and Simon's *Organizations* (1958), Richard Cyert and March's *A Behavioral Theory of the Firm* (1963), March's *Handbook of Organizations* (1965), and James D. Thompson's *Organizations in Action* (1967) gave solid theoretical reasons for choosing administrative science as the paradigm of public administration.

In the early 1960s, "organization development" began its rapid rise as a specialty of administrative science. As a focus, organization development represented a particularly tempting alternative to political science for many public administrationists. Organization development as a field is grounded in social psychology and values the "democratization" of bureaucracies, whether public or private, and the "self-actualization" of individual members of organizations. Because of these values, organization development was seen by many younger public administrationists as offering a very compatible area of research within the framework of administrative science: democratic values could be considered, normative concerns could be broached, and intellectual rigor and scientific methodologies could be employed. Yale University became a major promoter of the organization development idea in public administration; its graduates often emerged with Ph.D.'s in political science but with transcripts heavy with industrial management courses.

But there was a problem in the administrative science route, and a real one. If it were selected as the sole focus of public administration, could one continue to speak of *public* administration? After all, administrative science, while not advocating universal principles, nevertheless did and does contend that all organizations and managerial methodologies have certain characteristics, patterns, and pathologies in common. If administrative science alone defined the field's paradigm, then public administration would exchange, at best, being an "emphasis" in political science departments for being, at best, a subfield in schools of administrative science. This often would mean in practice that schools of business administration would absorb the field of public administration. Whether profit-conscious "B-school types" could adequately appreciate the vital value of public interest as an aspect of administrative science was a question of genuine importance to public administrationists, and one for which the probable answers were less than comforting.

Part of this conceptual dilemma, but only part, lay in the traditional distinction between "public" and "private" spheres of American society. What is *public* administration, what is everything else (*i.e.,* "private" administration), and what is the dividing line between the two types has been a gnawing dilemma for a number of years.

"Real-world" phenomena are making the public/private distinction an increasingly difficult one to define empirically, irrespective of academic disputations. The research and development contract, the "military-industrial complex," the roles of the regulatory agencies and their relations with industry, and the growing expertise of government agencies in originating and developing advanced managerial techniques that influence the "private sector" in every aspect of American society, all conspired to make *public* administration an elusive entity in terms of determining its proper paradigm. This dilemma is not yet fully resolved. Consider the conceptual problems presented by the R & D contract alone, which is essentially a post-World War II phenomenon. Recently, each one of five "private" companies spent, as contractors, more than one billion dollars of federal funds in a year, a sum exceeding that expended by any one of five cabinet-level departments. In the same year, the 100 corporations with the top-funded military contracts spent more federal monies than all the civil agencies of the federal government combined, excluding interest on the national debt. Confusion about the *public* variety of the field of administration seems at least understandable; one scholar, in fact, has argued that we should begin talking about "publicadministration," since all kinds of managerial organizations increasingly find themselves relating to public, governmental, and political concerns due to the growing interrelatedness of technological societies.

As a result of these factors, public administrationists recently have begun to appreciate that the "public" in public administration no longer can be conceived in simply institutional terms, which have been the terms traditionally favored by the field. "Public" instead must be cast into philosophic, normative, and ethical terms; "public," then, becomes that which affects the public interest. Thus, rather than concentrating on the Department of Defense as its proper "public" locus, and leaving, say, Lockheed Corporation to students of business administration, public administrationists now would examine the Department's contractual and political relationships with Lockheed. Hence, the traditional definition of "public" (*e.g.,* the Department of Defense) is abandoned in favor of a more dynamic, normative definition (*e.g.,* the Department *and* its relations with Lockheed). The field is beginning to call this new dimension of the public interest, "public affairs."

The public/private, public interest/profit motive tensions represented by the administrative science paradigm do nothing to alleviate the problem of locus for public administration. Of these tensions, that of the public interest as it relates to public affairs is the most important. Without a sense of the public interest, administrative science can be used for *any* purpose, no matter how immoral. The concept of determining and implementing the public interest constitutes a defining pillar of public administration and a locus of the field that receives little if any attention within the context of administrative science, just as the focus of organization theory/management science garners scant support in political science. It would seem, therefore, that public administration should, and perhaps must, find a new paradigm that encourages both a focus and a locus for the field.

Paradigm 5: Public administration as public administration, 1970—?

Despite continuing intellectual turmoil, Simon's 1947 proposal for a duality of scholarship in public administration has been gaining a renewed validity. There is not yet a focus for the field in the form of a "pure science of administration," but at least organization theory primarily has concerned itself in the last two and a half decades with how and why organizations work, how and why people in them behave, and how and why decisions are made, rather than with how these things *should* happen. Additionally, considerable progress has been made in refining the applied techniques of management sciences, as well as developing new techniques, that often reflect what has been learned in the more theoretical realms of organizational analysis.

There has been less progress in delineating a locus for the field, or what the public interest, public affairs, and "prescribing for public policy" should encompass in terms relevant to public administrationists. Nevertheless, the field does appear to be zeroing in on certain fundamental social factors unique to fully developed countries as its proper locus. The choice of these phenomena may be somewhat arbitrary on the part of public administrationists, but they do share commonalities in that they have engendered cross-disciplinary interest in universities, require synthesizing intellectual capacities, and lean toward themes that reflect urban life, administrative relations among "public" and "private" organizations, and the interface between technology and society. The traditional and rigid distinction of the field between the "public sphere" and the "private sphere" appears to be waning as public administration's new and flexibly defined locus waxes. Furthermore, public administrationists have been increasingly concerned with the inextricably related areas of policy science, political economy, the public policy-making process and its analysis, and the measurement of policy outputs. This latter aspect can be viewed, in some ways, as a linkage between public administration's evolving focus and locus.

BIBLIOGRAPHY

Public Administration

Baker, R.S., *Administrative Theory and Public Administration*. London, Hutchinson, 1972.

Brown, R.G.S., *The Administrative Process in Britain*. London, Methuen and Company, 1970.

Caiden, Gerald E., *The Dynamics of Public Administration: Guidelines to Current Transformations in Theory and Practice*. New York, Holt, Rinehart & Winston, 1971.

Chapman, Brian, *The Profession of Government*. New York, The MacMillan Company, 1959.

Dimock, M.E. and Dimock, G.M., *Public Administration*. 4th ed., New York, Holt, Rinehart and Winston, 1969.

Dunsire, A., *Administration: The Word and the Science*. New York, John Wiley and Sons, 1973.

Dvorin, Eugene P. and Simmons, Robert H., *From Amoral to Humane Bureaucracy*. New York, Harper & Row, 1972.

Gaus, John M., *Reflections on Public Administration*. University, Ala., University of Alabama Press, 1947.

Heady, Ferrel, *Public Administration: A Comparative Perspective*. Englewood Cliffs, N J , Prentice-Hall, 1966.

Henry, Nicholas, *Public Administration and Public Affairs*. Englewood Cliffs, N.J., Prentice-Hall, 1975.

Hodgson, J.S., *Public Administration*. Toronto, McGraw-Hill Company, 1969.

Marini, Frank, ed., *Toward a New Public Administration: The Minnowbrook Perspective*. Scranton, Pa., Chandler, 1971.

Montgomery, John D. and Siffin, William J., *Approaches to Development: Politics, Administration and Change*. New York, McGraw-Hill Book Company, 1966.

Morstein Marx, F., ed., *Elements of Public Administration*. Englewood Cliffs, N.J., Prentice-Hall, 1965.
Mosher, Frederick C., *Democracy and the Public Service*. New York, Oxford University Press, 1968.
Nigro, Felix A. and Nigro, Lloyd A., *Modern Public Administration*. 3rd ed., New York, Harper and Row, 1973.
Ostrom, Vincent, *The Intellectual Crisis in American Public Administration*. University, Ala., University of Alabama Press, 1973.
Presthus, R.V., *Public Administration*. 6th ed., New York, Ronald Press, 1975.
Raphaeli, Nimrod, ed., *Readings in Comparative Public Administration*. Boston, Allyn and Bacon, 1967.
Redford, Emmette, *Ideal and Practice in Public Administration*. University, Ala., University of Alabama Press, 1966.
Rehfuss, John, *Public Administration as Political Process*. New York, Charles Scribner's Sons, 1973.
Ridley, F. and Blondel, J., *Public Administration in France*. New York, Barnes & Noble, 1965.
Self, Peter, *Administrative Theories and Politics*. London, George Allen and Unwin Ltd., 1972.
Sharkansky, Ira, *Public Administration*. 3rd ed., Chicago, Markham Publishing Company, 1975.
Simon Herbert A., Smithburg, D.W. and Thompson, V.A., *Public Administration*. New York, Alfred A. Knopf, 1950.
Stein, Harold, *Public Administration and Policy Development: A Casebook*. New York, Harcourt, Brace, 1952.
Van Riper, Paul P., *History of the United States Civil Service*. Evanston and White Plains, Row, Peterson & Company, 1958.
Waldo, Dwight, ed., *Public Administration in a Time of Turbulence*. Scranton, Pa., Chandler, 1971.
Waldo, Dwight, *The Administrative State: A Study of the Political Theory of American Public Administration*. New York, The Ronald Press Company, 1948.
Waldo, Dwight, *The Study of Public Administration*. New York, The Macmillan Company, 1955.
White, L.D., *Introduction to the Study of Public Administration*. New York, The Macmillan Company, 1955.
Willoughby, William F., *Principles of Public Administration*. Baltimore, Johns Hopkins Press, 1927.

Organization Theory

Argyris, Chris, *Integrating the Individual and the Organization*. New York, John Wiley & Sons, 1964.
Barnard, C.I., *Functions of the Executive*. Cambridge, Mass., Harvard University Press, 1938.
Bennis, Warren G., *Changing Organizations: Essays on the Development and Evolution of Human Organization*. New York, McGraw-Hill Book Company, 1966.
Blau, P.M., *Bureaucracy in Modern Society*. New York, Random House, 1956.
Blau, P.M., and Scott, W.R., *Formal Organizations: A Comparative Approach*. San Francisco, Chandler Publishing Company, 1962.
Crozier, Michel, *The Bureaucratic Phenomenon*. Chicago, University of Chicago Press, 1964.
Downs, Anthony, *Inside Bureaucracy*. Boston, Little, Brown & Company, 1967.
Etzioni, Amitai, *A Comparative Analysis of Complex Organizations*. Glencoe, Ill., Free Press, 1961.
Etzioni, Amitai, ed., *Complex Organizations: A Sociological Reader*. New York, Holt, Rinehart and Winston, 1961.
Fayol, H., *General and Industrial Management*. London, Pitman Publishing Corporation, 1949.
Fesler, J.W., *Area and Administration*. University, Ala., University of Alabama Press, 1949.
Follett, Mary Parker, *Dynamic Administration*. Edited by Henry C. Metcalf and L. Urwick, New York, Harper & Row Publishers, 1941.
George, Claude S. Jr., *The History of Management Thought*. Englewood Cliffs, N.J., Prentice-Hall, 1968.

Gross, Bertram M., *The Managing of Organizations*. 2 vols., New York, The Free Press of Glencoe, 1964.

Gulick, Luther and Urwick, Lyndall, eds., *Papers on the Science of Administration*. New York, Institute of Public Administration, Columbia University, 1937.

Katz, Daniel and Kahn, Robert L., *The Social Psychology of Organizations*. New York, John Wiley & Sons, 1966.

Likert, Rensis, *New Patterns of Management*. New York, McGraw-Hill Book Company, 1961.

Likert, Rensis, *The Human Organization: Its Management and Value*. New York, McGraw-Hill, 1967.

March, James G., ed., *Handbook of Organizations*. Chicago, Rand McNally & Company, 1965.

March, James G. and Simon, Herbert A., *Organizations*. New York, John Wiley & Sons, 1958.

Mayo, Elton, *The Human Problems of an Industrial Civilization*. New York, The Viking Press, 1933.

Merrill, Harwood F., *Classics of Management*. New York, American Management Association, 1960.

Merton, Robert K., ed., *Reader in Bureaucracy*. New York, Free Press of Glencoe, 1953.

Millett, J.D., *Organization for the Public Service*. Princeton, N.J., D. Van Nostrand Company, 1966.

Prethus, Robert, *The Organizational Society: An Analysis and a Theory*. New York, Vintage Books, 1965.

Roethlisberger, F.J., and Dickson, William J., *Management and the Worker*. Cambridge, Harvard University Press, 1939.

Scott, William G., *Organization Theory, A Behavioral Analysis for Management*. Homewood, Ill., Richard D. Irwin, 1967.

Simon, Herbert A., *Administrative Behavior: A Study of Decision-Making Processes in Administrative Organization*. 2nd ed., New York, Free Press of Glencoe, 1957.

Simon, Herbert A., *The Shape of Automation for Men and Management*. New York, Harper & Row Publishers, 1965.

Taylor, Frederick W., he Principles of Scientific Management. New York, Norton, 1967 (originally published in 1911).

Thompson, James D., *Organizations in Action*. New York, McGraw-Hill Book Company, 1967.

Thompson, Victor A., *Modern Organization*. New York, Alfred A. Knopf, 1961.

Weber, Max, *From Max Weber: Essays in Sociology*. Edited and translated by H.H. Gerth and C. Wright Mills, New York, Oxford University Press, 1946.

Weber, Max, *The Theory of Social and Economic Organization*. Translated by A.M. Henderson and Talcott Parsons, Fair Lawn, N.J., Oxford University Press, 1947.

CHAPTER 2

CANADIAN PUBLIC ADMINISTRATION
ENVIRONMENT AND FORMAL STRUCTURE

The unique social, political, economic and physical setting within which public administration has evolved in Canada has had an enormous impact both on the development of research and on the structure and operations of our public services.

The first essay in this chapter, by Kenneth Kernaghan, relates to Nicholas Henry's article in Chapter 1 in that it reviews the state of research in Canadian public administration and examines the question of public administration as political science and as administration within the Canadian context. In the second selection, J.E. Hodgetts outlines the major fixed and variable elements of the Canadian environment which have shaped and continue to shape this country's public services.

Next, A.M. Willms briefly describes the executive functions of Cabinet ministers and the organization of government departments. D.P. Gracey explains the evolution, classification and control of the diverse group of government agencies known as Crown corporations.

The final two essays centre on two very significant political and administrative issues. The increasingly complex network of formal and informal administrative relations between the federal government and the provinces is examined. Then, P.K. Kuruvilla assesses the problems and prospects of bilingualism in the federal public service.

3
Identity, Pedagogy and Public Administration: The Canadian Experience*

Kenneth Kernaghan

The impact of external forces on domestic governmental institutions and processes is manifest in British and American influences on public administration in Canada. Indeed, it is customary to explain the evolution of Canadian public administration as an adaptation of selected elements of the British and American administrative systems to the unique political, social, economic and physical environment of Canada. In recent years, a broader range of influences—notably from France and Sweden—has had substantial impact on the discussion of administrative reform in Canada. This change is in part a consequence of the emphasis of the comparative public administration movement on cross-national analysis of public bureaucracies. It is primarily the result, however, of the sheer necessity for all modern governments to seek new structural and procedural devices to cope with the continually accelerating rate of change and their increasing burden of responsibilities. At the same time as this broader spectrum of external influences on domestic analysis of administrative reform has developed, the relative influence of the British administrative model has diminished and the American model has emerged as the predominant external influence on Canadian public administration.

RESEARCH ON CANADIAN PUBLIC ADMINISTRATION

The influence of the United States on the *study* of public administration in Canada has always been, and continues to be, greater than on administrative structures and processes. Political scientists and other scholars in Canada have relied heavily on intellectual ferment in the United States for theoretical developments affecting the study of public administration. Canadian scholars have not demonstrated the imaginative and innovative capacity of such American authors as Downs, Mosher, Redford, Riggs, Simon and Waldo. Although the intellectual exercise of assessing the theoretical and practical consequences of changes in the American bureaucracy may bring vicarious enjoyment to

*Reprinted and updated by permission from Kenneth Kernaghan, "Identity, Pedagogy and Public Administration: The Canadian Experience," *Public Administration (Australia)*, vol. 32, no. 3 (September 1973), pp. 286-296.

Canadian scholars, this dependent status is regrettable in that understanding of Canadian public administration has been retarded. The comparative lack of theoretical writings on Canadian public administration at either the macro- or micro-level inhibits also the full understanding of the Canadian political system which rests in part on knowledge of the role of the bureaucracy in the policy process. The literature on public administration in the United States often strikes a discordant rather than a responsive note in Canada because much of it is inapplicable or irrelevant to Canada's unique political and administrative systems.

The slow development of the study of public administration in Canada and the consequent dearth of research and writing in this field obliged Canadians to rely primarily on American publications for teaching purposes. This problem was partially remedied during the 1960s by the publication of books of readings[1] which have been used as textbooks or as supplements to American or British texts. Moreover, although the research agenda for Canadian public administration is still a very long one, several important gaps in the literature have been filled since 1970.[2]

The major periodical literature is found in two quarterly journals — *Canadian Public Administration*, published since 1958 by the Institute of Public Administration, and *Optimum: A Forum for Management*, published since 1970 by the Bureau of Management Consulting of the Department of Supply and Services. The reports and research studies of royal commissions and task forces[3] are also a rich source of information and analysis on the structures and processes of Canadian public administration. Finally, the Public Service Commission of Canada and the Institute of Public Administration have established the Case Program in Canadian Public Administration which publishes case studies and simulations in public policy and management.

---

[1]J.E. Hodgetts and D.C. Corbett, eds., *Canadian Public Administration*, Toronto, Macmillan, 1960; W.D.K. Kernaghan, ed., *Public Administration in Canada*, Toronto, Methuen, 1968, 1971 and 1977; and W.D.K. Kernaghan, ed., *Bureaucracy in Canadian Government*, Toronto, Methuen, 1969 and 1973.

[2]Volumes in the Canadian Public Administration Series sponsored by the Institute of Public Administration of Canada and published by the McGill-Queen's University Press include Freda Hawkins, *Canada and Immigration: Public Policy and Public Concern*, 1972; J.E. Hodgetts, William McCloskey, Reginald Whitaker and V. Seymour Wilson, *Biography of an Institution: The Civil Service Commission, 1908-1967*, 1972; Kenneth Bryden, *Old Age Pensions and Policy-Making in Canada*, 1974; J.E. Hodgetts and O.P. Dwivedi, *Provincial Governments as Employers*, 1974; and John W. Langford, *Transport in Transition: The Reorganization of the Federal Transport Portfolio*, 1976. An especially notable work is J.E. Hodgetts, *The Canadian Public Service: A Physiology of Government, 1867-1970*, Toronto, University of Toronto Press, 1973.

[3]See for example Canada, *Royal Commission on Government Organization* (Glassco Commission), Ottawa, Queen's Printer, 1962-63, 5 volumes; *Royal Commission on Bilingualism and Biculturalism*, espec. Book 3A — *The Federal Administration*, Ottawa, Queen's Printer, 1969; and *To Know and Be Known: Report of the Task Force on Government Information Services*, Ottawa, Queen's Printer, 1969.

PATTERNS OF ORGANIZATION

The so-called crisis of identity facing public administration is primarily the consequence of two distinct and largely countervailing developments. The first is the historical evolution of public administration under the parentage of *political science*. The second is the continuously expanding dimensions of the study and practice of public administration and the increasingly *inter-disciplinary* approach to its study and teaching. The critical issue bearing upon the status of public administration is whether it should properly be considered a subdiscipline of political science or simply a part of the broader field of administration in general.

The opposing positions on the appropriate theoretical base for the organization of studies in public administration have been succinctly stated by Professors William Robson in Britain and Lynton Caldwell in the United States. Robson asserted that:

> the tendency for public administration to break away from the parent discipline must ultimately weaken both political science as a whole and the study of public administration. It will weaken political science by removing the part of it which brings the teacher into closest relationship with the practical business of government. It will weaken the study of public administration by divorcing it from political theory and the principles of government which underlie political and administrative institutions.[4]

More recently, however, Caldwell argued that:

> the greatest promise for study of public administration in the universities will be in association with the growth of an integrative, organizing, generic concept of administration. From the nucleus of general administrative studies, it may be possible to interrelate more meaningfully the study of administration to the various disciplines and professions. In the modern world, no clear line separates administration in government from the administrative processes of the total society. The organization of administrative studies in the university must ultimately correspond to this reality.[5]

Both approaches are persuasive when viewed from different theoretical perspectives and in different national settings.

PUBLIC ADMINISTRATION AS ADMINISTRATION

Those who view public administration as a generic process contend that the study of administration may be most fruitfully pursued by dividing

---

[4]William Robson, *The University Teaching of Social Sciences: Political Science*, UNESCO, 1954, p. 47.
[5]Lynton Caldwell, "Public Administration and the Universities: a Half Century of Development," *Public Administration Review*, vol. 25, March, 1965, p. 60.

the general field into public, business, hospital, educational, police, or other types of administration. To proponents of this view, the similarities between these various forms of administration are greater than their differences. This belief has led to the establishment of "professional" schools or faculties of administrative studies.

It appears also that a growing number of scholars are convinced that intellectual developments are moving inexorably in the direction of a rigorous *discipline* of administrative studies. This new discipline will be interdisciplinary and integrative in its subject content and teaching approach. Its program will be characterized by a flowing together for mutual enrichment of the present "academic" and "professional" streams in administrative studies. Discussion of the distinctive nature of "public" administration will be founded on a solid base of knowledge about the concepts and techniques of administration generally. All students, regardless of the type of administration in which they are primarily interested, e.g. public, business, educational, will normally be required to take a group of "core subjects" in administration. The "core subjects" will include organizational behaviour, accounting, micro-economics, macro-economics and quantitative methods. Specilization in a particular type or problem of administration will be founded on this base of common knowledge.

Canadian universities have established faculties or schools of public administration which grant distinct degrees in public administration and provide specialized training for public service careers.[6] At both the graduate and undergraduate levels, the programs offered are integrative and interdisciplinary but vary in content and purpose. Some are "professional" in orientation; others stress the "academic" approach. Some organize their programs around the concept of public policy; others simply offer courses on various aspects of public policy. In several universities, mid-career programs for administrative practitioners are an integral part of the course of study.

Clearly, a number of alternative structural arrangements for the teaching of public administration are possible — and available. The programs lead to one- or two-year M.A. degrees, to B.A. degrees with Honours in public administration, to B.A. degrees in Administration with some subject emphasis on "public" administration and to special certificates in public administration. One of the most difficult problems of designing public administration programs at the undergraduate level is reconciling the desire for a high degree of specialization with the widely expressed need for a liberal education.

---

[6]For elaboration on these programs, see G. Bruce Doern, "The Teaching of Public Administration in Canadian Universities," in Kenneth Kernaghan, ed., *Executive Manpower in the Public Service: Make or Buy,* Toronto, Institute of Public Administration of Canada, 1975, pp. 80-102.

A different kind of education is required for teachers and scholars than for aspiring and practising public servants. A teacher of public administration holding a Ph.D. degree will likely continue to receive a substantial portion of his education in political science supplemented by courses in economics, sociology, psychology and research methods, and by some practical experience in the civil service. The graduate training of civil servants, however, may best be carried out in a school or faculty organized and staffed specifically for this purpose. Given the existing high demand for public employees at all levels of Canadian government during the next decade, there is an easily demonstrable need for both kinds of programs.

PUBLIC ADMINISTRATION AS POLITICAL SCIENCE

The emergence of alternative patterns of organization for the teaching of public administration has weakened the already tenuous links between public administration and political science. As these organizational bonds become more fragile, it is important to evaluate the pedagogical and intellectual implications of treating public administration as a sub-field of political science.

The political scientist teaching public administration, whether at the graduate or undergraduate level, is often suspect in the eyes of both his academic colleagues and practising administrators. To his colleagues, he is too practically oriented in teaching and too policy oriented in research. To practitioners, he is too academically oriented and of little assistance in resolving policy issues. He has been aptly described as "the academic's practical man and the public administrator's academic."[7]

The ignorance of many political scientists about the content and purpose of the study of public administration is unfortunate. If public administration is to live comfortably as a subdiscipline of political science, even for teaching purposes, it is essential that those political scientists *not* teaching public administration try to learn something about the field. It is a continuing source of amazement and dismay that some political scientists teaching the government and politics of particular nation-states make little or no reference to administrative structures or to the role of bureaucrats in the political system.

The major approaches to the study of the broad range of subjects in public administration may be classed as managerial, political and socio-psychological. The "politics" of public administration forms the core of most introductory courses in the field (i.e., focus on the interaction in a political system between administrators and other participants, both

---

[7]Dwight Waldo, "Public Administration," *The Journal of Politics*, vol. 30, no. 2, May, 1968, p. 445.

governmental and non-governmental, concerned with the determination of government objectives). The content of the "traditional" course supplements this "political" approach with examination of managerial functions whereas more recent emphasis in course design is on organization theory. The truly imaginative and knowledgeable teacher strives to utilize the contributions of all three approaches.

Despite difficulties associated with the teaching of public administration in political science departments, there are sound theoretical grounds for continuing this teaching arrangement. Knowledge of the administrative structures of government and of the political and legal environment in which the public administrator works is essential to understanding of the political system. In addition, the bureaucracy plays a central role on the output side of the political system through its active involvement in the making, enforcement and adjudication of laws and regulations. Less evident, but extremely significant, intellectual bonds between public administration and political science lie in their shared concern for inquiry into such key theoretical concepts as responsibility, authority and the public interest. Political theorists who fail to explore the meaning of these themes in the particular milieu of public administration omit a perspective essential to adequate analysis.[8] All these factors attest to the status of public administration as an integral part of the study of political science.

The most productive approach for political scientists may be to treat public administration as a *subdiscipline* both on the basis of existing organizational patterns and of theoretical links between public administration and political science. It seems probable also that theoretical developments in *public* administration are more likely to issue from the research efforts of political scientists than other disciplinary representatives. Political scientists may resolve the identity crisis, at least to their own satisfaction, by ceasing to agonize over the vast scope of public administration and by seeking agreement on achievements made toward a general theory of public administration.

CONCLUSIONS

Despite these organizational, pedagogical and theoretical problems, the future of public administrative studies in contemporary democratic states will be an exciting and challenging one. Civil servants participate actively in policy formulation and execution; government responsibilities in old and new policy fields grow steadily; and societal and technological

---

[8]Glendon Schubert, for example, has acknowledged the valuable contributions of senior federal administrators in the United States in reformulating his thinking "about some aspects of the subject" of public-interest theory. *The Public Interest*, Glencoe, Illinois, The Free Press, 1960, p. ix.

change is increasingly turbulent and rapid. These developments will ensure a high demand for administrative practitioners, for teachers of public administration and for research to support and explain their activities. The future emphasis in education for public administration will be increasingly on the training of public officials for various levels of government. This trend will be accompanied by the continuing establishment of public administration programs, whether "academically" or "professionally" oriented, on an interdisciplinary basis. Whatever success schools or faculties of public administration enjoy in promoting a professional education through more practically-oriented teaching, a large number of universities will continue to offer graduate and undergraduate programs in public administration along traditional academic lines.

That even these "traditional" programs will be more interdisciplinary in course content and interdepartmental in organization has significant implications for relations between public administration and political science. The interdepartmental programs will include courses taught by faculty members attached to the established academic departments of Political Science, Economics, Sociology, Psychology and others. Through the development of interdepartmental co-operation in public administration studies at both the graduate and undergraduate levels, students may benefit from a greater choice of courses in public administration within a coherent program. The scope of public administration is now so broad and its subject matter so heterogeneous that it cannot realistically be considered *solely* as a subdiscipline of political science. It is clear that appropriate settings for education in public administration exist outside the structural framework of political science departments and that a variety of organizational patterns has evolved. Each of these forms of organization serves a different, but still important, purpose. Moreover, a diversity of arrangements for public administration studies in Canada is essential to take account of the fact that many university courses in public administration are still taught within political science departments.

4

Challenge and Response: A Retrospective View of the Public Service of Canada*

J. E. Hodgetts

John Donne's comment that "no man is an island" applies with equal relevance to organizations created by man to serve his needs. Thus, the central proposition I hope to demonstrate by this excursion into the past is that our public service has been shaped to the environment in which it has had to operate and that changes in the environment bring about alterations in the public service.

When the Founding Fathers met one hundred years ago they were seeking to grapple with the forces of change then confronting them. The result was a constitutional document that has proven surprisingly durable over the ensuing years. But constitutions are notably rigid, and it has been largely within the public services—local, provincial and federal—that we find the main evidences of adaptation to changing conditions and emergent social needs which have provided the necessary flexibility. I see no evidence for claiming that this administrative adaptation has followed any iron laws of administrative growth. We are here concerned with a most complex set of interacting forces in which the organization acted upon, i.e., the public service, is far from passive. While the public service bears the marks of environmental factors that press upon it, society also bears the imprint of the activities and enhanced authority of public servants.

In considering the environmental pressures that have set the goals and moulded the shape of the public service over our first century, we find that some have remained relatively unchanged. These we may describe as the constants or "the givens" with which the public service must live. They include the pervasive impact of our geographical setting, the constitutional framework, the legal base of administration and the political system. The elements of the environment subject to the greatest change and requiring the greatest flexibility of response from the public service have been economic, technological, cultural and philosophical factors. I should like to show briefly how each of these has contributed to the public service we know today.

The powerful persuasion of geography has been noted by Sir Ernest Barker in his examination of the growth of European public services. The

*Reprinted by permission from J.E. Hodgetts, "Challenge and Response: A Retrospective View of the Public Service of Canada," *Canadian Public Administration*, vol. 7, no. 4 (December 1964) pp. 409-421.

large Egyptian bureaucracy, for example, he attributed to the Nile and the costly irrigation works required to harness it. England's insular position, on the other hand, delayed the emergence of the large centralized bureaucracies which grew up on the Continent largely to service the needs of standing armies. In Canada, for the better part of its first half century, geography dictated the major goals which the public service was to pursue. The Department of the Interior, the giant amongst early federal departments, was described as late as 1936 as "the barometer of Western conditions". The so called barometric departments were those concerned with opening up the west, encouraging its population and settlement and providing the water or rail transportation to serve as the linkage for these activities.

Not only did geography dictate the goals, it also imposed the conditions which governed the way in which the tasks of public servants had to be performed. If administrative apoplexy was to be avoided at the centre, public servants had to be widely dispersed: police and protective services, agents for immigration, for colonization and Indian affairs, fisheries overseers, customs collectors, surveyors and construction teams on railways and canals, spread often in isolated places across a continental domain.

New means of communication have alleviated the problems of communication and administration in remote outposts. But the harsh facts of our geography still exact a high price for preserving a union based on an artificial East-West axis against the counterpull of the geographically more natural North-South axis.

Thus, from the outset, geography forced Canada to adapt its services to dispersed operations. The subsequent expansion of welfare and regulatory activities necessitated the continuation of dispersed or area administration, governed now less by the limitations on our means of communications but more by the need to preserve a face-to-face relationship with individual citizens seeking benefits and services. Consequently a physical decentralization of the work force, which took root as a logical response to the challenge of administering across a continent, continues in being as a vital necessity to provide the flexible response to the contemporary state's positive welfare and regulatory functions. Decentralization is now as much dictated by the need to preserve democratic responsiveness of the administrative machine as it is a natural outcome of the original geographic challenge.

It is passing strange that this, perhaps the most obvious feature of our public service, has received so little formal analysis. It is one of a number of areas that warrant fuller discussion and study.

The second constant feature of the environment is the constitutional framework which was evolved one hundred years ago. It is no reflection on the Founding Fathers to claim that a division of labour between provinces and dominion made one hundred years ago is bound to become outmoded. Formal constitutional amendment has been infrequent and judicial interpretation has not always been in conformity with rapid changes in social philosophy, new needs, or revolutionary transformations in technology. Flexibility has been provided by the development of what the Rowell-Sirois Commission called "administrative expedients." These have ranged from the sporadic assembling of a diplomatic conference between dominion and provincial leaders, ministerial or official conferences for more limited purposes—often in conjunction with national interest groups (as happened, for example, in the case of labour and agriculture),—formal agreements rather like treaties, joint advisory committees, the use of federal officers to perform provincial tasks (and vice versa), and the employment of federal funds to finance provincial programs.

At the outset, most of these expedients were not developed because potential conflict was restrained by the limited undertakings of public organizations at all levels. Beginning with fisheries and then moving into labour and industrial relations, on to health and welfare and the regulation of interprovincial trade, the respective jurisdictions began to touch, then overlap: inevitably friction was generated. The limitations on and unevenness of provincial revenues required action on a broader front. Thus, throughout the years, one can see the administrative response of the federal public service gathering momentum in distinct stages. First, it began to act as a centralized data collecting source; from statistics it went on to research; research results required dissemination and so we move to extensive publication (and some would say public relations); next came conditional grants that required "policing" by federal officials; ultimately certain programs came to be operated by the federal government.

Two factors contribute to the perpetuation and even the continued expansion of the federal public service in such areas. First, there is the natural reluctance to dismantle an organization by giving up these programs. The historic rationale has been that the provincial services were less than adequate for the task involved — an estimate that today bears hard critical examination. The other factor has been the inability of the tax-poor provinces to carry the burden of these new services. Once again, I would offer this entire area as a rewarding subject for fresh examination: we need full scale studies of provincial public services to begin with and of the administrative interrelations that have developed between provincial and federal public departments. Here, we must content ourselves with noting that the cumulative results of these developments have induced the federal government to assume fact-gathering, research, promotional and grant dispensing responsibilities that are quite different in kind from the more directly program-oriented, operational jobs undertaken by the provinces. At the same time, these activities have introduced in unprecedented numbers new types of professional, scientific and technical personnel into the public service whose problems of adaptation to the traditional hierarchical organization has received far less study than they deserve.

The third fixed element of the environment is the legal foundation for public administration. At Confederation, the tension between executive and legislature built up during the previous period of colonial rule inclined the Canadian Parliament to adopt a more assertive attitude than the British Parliament towards the public service. The British North America Act bears signs of this attitude in the oft-invoked phrase tied to the few sections concerning the disposition of the public service "until the Parliament of Canada [or the provincial legislature] otherwise provides". The fact is that the Parliament of Canada has "otherwise provided" in much more detail than has ever been the case in the United Kingdom, the most outstanding testimonial being the Civil Service Act of 1868, which had its precursors in pre-Confederation times and continues to this day with its counterpart in every province. No such act, significantly, has ever been passed in Britain.

This is not the place to thread my way through a most complex maze. That it *is* a maze, I know, for in a personal effort to explore the legal foundations of public administration I found to my surprise that there were few available guides in this lonely enterprise. I do not propose to inflict the details of my explorations on you but I can at least state the problem and its implications for the public service.

The essential difficulty derives from the union of executive and legislative functions which we have inherited from Britain. That union creates what I might call a legal ambivalence from which it is hard to say whether the public service is directed by sovereign parliament or by the executive. Put in another way, the question is: are public servants employees of parliament or employees of the executive, standing in the place of the Crown?

That this is not an academic question can be readily demonstrated by indicating the problem of identifying the centres of authority for handling the organization and management of the public service. Parliament clearly must authorize the creation of a department, but the executive determines when the department shall begin to function. Moreover, since a new department involves a money bill and only the executive can initiate such a bill, one must assume that even the major organizational units are dictated by the executive, with rather automatic ratification by parliament. For more detailed re-organization, parliament has in effect devolved authority on the executive through the *Public Services Rearrangement and Transfer of Duties Act*. A glance at the organic acts for each department shows that parliament has made no effort to bind the executive's hands by stipulating a detailed organizational breakdown. Equally, the day-to-day organization-and-methods work has been left by parliament entirely to the discretion of departments or to other management bodies.

In the field of management, the dichotomy is much more evident and perplexing. First, there is the question, previously noted, of the apparently dual allegiance of the public servant. For all practical purposes, including appointment, classification, promotion, pay scales, and tenure, the civil servant appears to be a servant of the executive (which in practical terms might be logically extended to read a servant of the party in power). In the performance of his functions, he is responsible through the hierarchy to his minister. Yet many members of parliament, stressing the term "public" in public servant, claim to occupy the role of employer. When at the same time they claim the Public Service Commission as their specially selected agency to perform this function on their behalf, further problems arise. Indeed the Public Service Commission is perhaps the chief victim of this legal dualism, on the one hand being regarded as the peculiar instrument of parliament in its role of employer but on the other often sharing management functions with executive agencies, such as Treasury Board, which parliament in its indecision has divided between them.

This commentary on the legal basis of administration could be prolonged but I have perhaps said enough to support the conclusion that because the legal ambivalence of our system has not been confronted head on we have grown into a confused system of divided management responsibilities that is cumbersome to work and difficult to live with.

The fourth and final fixed feature of the environment is our political system or, more accurately, the conventions that have grown up around that system. The three elements of this system that have left the deepest imprints on the public service are the conventions surrounding cabinet-making, the doctrine of ministerial responsibility and, that handmaiden of the party system, patronage.

The well-known convention that cabinets must be so constructed as to represent significant regional, provincial, religious and ethnic groupings in a pluralistic community needs no elaboration. Its implications for the public service, though obvious, have scarcely ever been noted. Even in 1867 a cabinet of fourteen members was needed to meet all the claims for weighted representation. Critics at the time asked how it was that in the United States as compared to Canada "forty million instead of four were ably governed by an administration of seven members instead of fourteen". But the necessity of securing a representative cabinet overrode any objections. On the other hand, if the American model did not commend itself, neither did the British system of making a distinction between the cabinet and the much larger Ministry. The Canadian convention in short was and continues to be that all Ministers should be in the cabinet.

The rejection of both the American and British models had these consequences: (1) for nearly half a century we were overstocked with departments and the slow accretion of government duties could readily be absorbed within a relatively static group of portfolios; (2) but, when the duties of the state began to mount at an accelerated pace, we were left little room to manoeuvre. If more departments were created to embrace the new tasks and if all ministerial heads by convention had to be in the cabinet, that body would soon reach an unmanageable size. The alternative was to create a variety of non-departmental entities to undertake the newer tasks. The generous provision of departmental portfolios and their extremely elastic walls enabled us to absorb a great deal of this expansion and necessitated surprisingly few additions to the original departmental roster. But it has meant that some departments have come to embrace a variety of ill-assorted functions simply as a means of housing what otherwise might become administrative orphans. The consequent problems of co-ordination through the cabinet and other centralized agencies have been acute.

The practical restrictions on the number of departmental portfolios also account in part for the profusion and variety of non-departmental entities. The effort to seat them comfortably within the traditional framework of ministerial responsibility has led to an incoherent "second" public service that represents a piecemeal, haphazard response to the growing burden of state activities, even as it confuses the legislator and general citizen.

Indeed, the doctrine of ministerial responsibility is the second feature of the political setting whose implications for the public service need brief elaboration. The principle not only establishes a bridge across which most of the traffic between parliament and the public service is routed but, applied collectively to the cabinet, it ensures a unity of purpose and a coordination of direction at the top. Parliament benefits by being able to home in on one identifiable target; the public servant benefits because he does not have to debate publicly any challenge of his political overlords. His anonymity preserves the constitutional fiction of his political non-commitment and thus ensures his permanency in office whenever there is a change in the governing political party.

The benefits of the doctrine are obvious and desirable but a literal application in today's enlarged public service poses an impossible burden on the Minister. This was recognized on the administrative side at the very beginning by giving the Minister a permanent Deputy and on the legislative side, but much more recently, by giving him a Parliamentary Secretary. But the fact remains that there have been constant pressures that force the Minister into a "managing" rather than a "directing" role, thereby compelling Ministers in both their individual and collective capacities, to concern themselves with too much detail, at the expense of general coordinating and policy-making functions. The convention that the cabinet provides regional representation makes sense only if most matters are brought before cabinet. Thus, in contrast to England where statutes generally confer authority on individual Ministers, in Canada they more commonly confer powers on the Governor-in-Council, i.e., Ministers in their collective capacity. If to this we add the historic reliance on patronage, we can see why Ministers have been unable to extricate themselves from direct involvement in the details of management. Sir George Murray's succinct epitaph (written in 1912) accurately described a predicament that certainly existed until 1939. "Ministers," he concluded, "both have too much to do and try to do too much."

The significance of patronage, the third element of the political system to be examined here, is that the measures taken to eradicate it have left an enduring mark on the public service. A formal self-denying ordinance is necessary, at some time or another, if patronage is to be eliminated. In Britain, this was done by executive decree but in Canada, as has been noted, by statute, authorizing a Civil Service Commission to institute a rigorous regimen of controls. Over time the desired result was achieved of preventing the unfit from gaining admission to the public service; but for many years this negative approach dominated to the exclusion of more positive measures required to attract the best candidates available. The Civil Service Commission was given additional and comprehensive authority over most of the personnel management field. Thus the orientation toward control, generated by its primary function as patronage eliminator, tended (so to speak) to rub off on to the other management responsibilities that demanded a more positive, service-minded approach.

A somewhat parallel development occurred in the field of expenditure control in an effort to prevent speculation and patronage. When the Glassco Commission came to examine this situation, it found that departmental managers had been caught in the pincers of centralized agencies and have had to operate in that atmosphere of distrust which had been responsible in the first place for the imposition of such controls. It was the thesis of the Glassco Commission that, while the system had been a legitimate and logical response to the evils of patronage and dishonesty, the departments were, in the vernacular, "big boys now" and should be put more on their own mettle. The readjustments required to meet this thesis will make heavier calls on the initiative and ability of departmental managers and will require centralized agencies to think less in terms of negative control and more in positive terms of guidance, service and setting standards for the departments.

I may remind you at this stage that I distinguished at the beginning between the constant and variable elements of the environment that have helped mould our public service. Having touched on the constants, let me now turn to the variables, beginning with the economic setting.

Economic historians have familiarized us with the importance of staple products to Canada's economic growth and well-being. The characteristic features of staples such as fish, fur, timber, minerals, wheat and pulpwood is that they are all extractive enterprises, based on the exploitation of a great wealth in natural resources requiring bulk transportation and access to markets abroad. Neither the exploitation, transportation or marketing of these staples has taken place within an Adam Smith type of economy. Government has been heavily committed from the outset to mapping out and making inventory of these resources; it has been deeply engaged as regulator, constructor and operator of transport systems by water, rail and air; it moved early into promotional activities — the first trade commissioner dates back to the 1880's as does the first agricultural research station, and only slightly later do we find such services as forecasting facilities. Governments have engineered the formation of economic interest groups such as the livestock producers and the pulpwood producers — presumably the better to deal with them. Today the major concern of at least one third of our federal departments is still with problems associated with the production, conservation, and transportation of and the trade in our main staple products.

This clear cut identification of the departments with staple products is only one example — though a most persistent one — of how the unique features of the Canadian economy have shaped the public service. As government has more and more been drawn into an operating and regulatory role, we find that the new responsibilities have largely devolved on non-departmental agencies. A point has now been reached where the number of people employed in these sectors of the public service is nearly as large as the number employed in the departmental system proper. It is not surprising that, in devising non-departmental forms, governments have looked to the private industrial or commercial concerns for their models. We are still struggling to find a solution to the problems of grafting the consequent collection of heterogeneous administrative entities on to the conventional departmental system with its tradition of ministerial responsibility. We are also still seeking for ways to bridge the gap between the personnel in the public service proper and in the other portion excluded from it, to the end that there may be truly *one* public service. In short, the mixed economy, with its avoidance of outright governmental monopoly and its favoring of a system of economic parallelism in transport, communication and finance, has produced a corresponding organizational "mix" in the public service itself.

Nor does the impact of the world of private economic organization end here. It finds expression in a pervasive assumption that only a "businessman's approach" to the public service can produce efficiency. We find early expression of this philosophy in the attempt to levy appropriate charges for the services that governments provide specific groups of beneficiaries. And, in the report of the Glassco Commission, dozens of such services have been identified, accompanied by evidence that some pay their way, others are given free, some make a profit, others lose money. The Royal Commission's reminder that we need to set this part of our administrative house in order is merely a reiteration of the old plea to inject sound business principles into public administration. The Commission's recommendation that many of these services might well be contracted out to private concerns is not so much a free enterpriser's special pleading but a legitimate concern to help public organizations keep their attention focussed on their main job, subject to as few peripheral distractions as possible.

The major impact of the businessman's approach is to be found in the contemporary reliance on private management consultant firms that are refinements on the early school of efficiency experts nourished at the beginning of this century by Taylor and his followers. We owe to this school the detailed classification plans which were inaugurated after World War I in the civil service. The modern consultant is in the main an offshoot of the accountant, though his advice now ranges from financial and accounting practices through paperwork and systems analyses to feasibility studies on computers. His main customer is government and one of his most lasting marks will be found in the reports of the Glassco Commission. We find here the accountant's concern for identifying "real" costs; the businessman's concern for relating revenues from services to the costs of providing them; the need to import the new techniques of systems analysis that have proven effective in private business. In brief, there is the assumption that the differences between private and public organization are not so substantial that practices proven successful in the private realm cannot be applied with equal effectiveness to the public organization. This is an assumption that in my view must constantly be tempered by the other environmental factors I have been discussing and to which private organizations need pay much less attention.

Turning from the economic setting to the impact of changing technology on the public service, we find a two-edged situation. In the broadest sense, changing techniques affect the substance of administrative activity — they alter the things that have to be done by administrators, by inducing the state either itself to sponsor the development of the techniques or else to grapple with the social and other problems posed by their widespread adoption. In the narrower sense, new techniques influence administrative procedures. We live in an age of gadgetry and public servants are no more immune to the charm of applying gadgets to their daily labours than are others in private organizations.

The Canadian public service has grown up during a century in which there have been more technological innovations than in all of man's past history. It was born in the steamboat and railway age, witnessed the emergence of telegraph and telephone, saw the origin and full onslaught of the internal combustion engine and, while still adjusting to these developments, has had to make its peace with the air age, the electronics revolution, the atom, and now outer space.

The incredible fertility of man, the innovating engineer and scientist, has left man, the social scientist, staggering for breath. The steamboat and railway brought the state into the centre of activity as owner, maintenance man and operator or regulator. The automobile age has left its most indelible imprint on provincial and local public services, as they have had to grapple with highway construction, traffic regulations, and all the social and economic problems of urban concentration that have sprung up in the wake of the automobile.

Jurisdiction over the air for transportation and communication purposes was settled in favour of the federal government in 1932 and the stage was set for a fresh crop of agencies and further adaptation of the public service to meet the challenges. From virtual monopolies of national services, designed to pioneer in these new fields, the state has gradually permitted the private sector to emerge as a full partner. Similarly, in responding to the nuclear revolution, the state has harnessed the conventional component by regulatory action but has assumed, itself, nearly the full burden of research and development. With the largest research resources and establishments in the country, the federal government's relationship with universities and the increasing importance of science in government now raise problems that we are only beginning to assess, let alone solve.

One should also observe that many technological changes have affected the means of communication and transportation. These have required such substantial capital investment that the state has had to become an active participant as developer and owner. The consequent fostering of an interdependent economy brought new regulatory problems, most of which had to be met on a national front. World-wide application of these techniques has shrunk the world and produced further problems of international trade and communication that also fall naturally on the shoulders of the federal government.

Apart from these broad repercussions of technological change, there are also the products which derive from the new technology and affect the procedures of the public service. One of the most important consequences of the age of gadgets is the ease with which paper can now be created and the resulting problems of record keeping, storage, filing and so on. Historically, the mechanics of paper management were characterized unflatteringly but accurately as the "donkey work" in the civil service. (There is more than a shadow of home truth in the classification of the first females in the British public service as "female typewriters".) Yet, as the Glassco Commission has emphasized, the new gadgets and procedures necessitate an upgrading of those concerned with the management of paper if the government is not, like the sorcerer's apprentice, to be drowned in a flood of its own creation. At this point we can confidently coin a neo-Parkinsonian Law: *the quantity of paper will rise to meet the capacity of the machines available for processing it.* It is still difficult to know how the electronics revolution will affect an organization where there is so much routine repetitive work that lends itself to automation. At the least, its wide-scale application will necessitate major re-training programs.

The high costs of the more versatile automatic data processing equipment imply that the new technology may force a reversal of the traditional pattern of dispersed and decentralized operations as work gets concentrated in a few large electronic machine shops. On the other hand, it may well be that centralized processing is quite compatible with — indeed, a genuine encouragement to — more effective decentralization, because the new machines can improve reporting and control techniques. It would be pure speculation to carry this line of inquiry further but, now we are in the throes of numbering the nation, it may not be too unrealistic to visualize our master cards going into the computer and slipping us anything from a birth certificate to an old age pension, a request for payment of back taxes to a passport. At the best we should see improved, though depersonalized, service to the public and the collation of new masses of data from which our social planners in the future should be able to make more confident and accurate predictions.

From this Orwellian world that is less fantastic than it seemed less than a decade ago, let us turn to the cultural setting. Canada is a middle power both in the figurative and literal sense, geographically positioned next door to the United States and still bound by tradition and sentiment to England. At good neighbour rallies, we extol the virtues of our undefended frontier, which on closer inspection is seen to bristle with defences, most of them of the Canadian government's own making. Tariffs and the all-Canadian railway were but the precursors of a host of other expressions of the do-it-yourself philosophy inspired by national pride and a reluctance to be beholden to our more powerful neighbour. The airplane and radio brought government monopolies as chosen instruments of national policy. The Canada Council was a far-too-modest answer to the American foundations; the proposal to re-direct the Canadian advertisers' dollars to Canadian publications and the BBG's prescription of a fifty-five per cent quota of "Canadian content" for broadcasting are all recent evidences of the same spirit.

If a number of the federal government's most important cultural activities have evolved in response to our defensive posture toward United States cultural penetration, it is equally true that the organization of the public service itself bears marks of our constant borrowing. Here, however, we have tended to gyrate between American practice and

British tradition. Our Public Service Employment Act and the Public Service Commission are more American than British in conception, intent and in the powers conferred; so, too, is our classification system. Our attempts to create a cadre of senior administrative officers and the abortive reports of such Royal Commissions as the Murray and Gordon Commissions show much clearer traces of the British pattern. The most recent reports from the Glassco Commission are an interesting amalgam of American management practices and British institutional devices, both adapted to the Canadian setting.

Apart from the significant and continuing pressure from these external cultural influences the Canadian public service has to face a unique indigenous cultural factor — the principle of bilingualism enshrined in the B.N.A. Act. The hyphenated premierships, the double-barrelled ministries and, more particularly, the rotating capitals that characterized the pre-Confederation public service reveal that the bicultural nature of the earlier union gave much blunter expression than we have since given to the concept. For nearly a century the federal public service has shown at times even a deliberate disregard of this cultural fact of life and is now an obvious target for the moderate nationalist as well as the extremist in French-speaking Canada. The problem goes deeper than a mere recognition of two official languages, for it extends to the whole cultural context and will not be easily ameliorated by well-intended gestures on the part of English-speaking groups. The situation is probably most acute at headquarters, particularly at the senior officer level. Working within an essentially unilingual communication system, bilingualism becomes a one-way street where the only person who needs to be bilingual is the French-speaking officer. That he is called upon to make his home in a alien cultural environment only adds to the difficulties. With the rapid industrialization and bureaucratization of the Province of Quebec, the opportunities for advancement in executive ranks are so enhanced that it will probably be increasingly difficult to make the Ottawa service attractive to French-speaking recruits. On the other hand, Canada, as an officially bilingual country, has a potentially important contribution to make in fulfilling obligations to the international community. This fact by itself should be additional incentive to mount a more effective campaign to bring the federal public service into line with the realities of its long and much neglected bicultural tradition.

I close with a brief reference to what might be called the philosophical pressures that have shaped the public service. I am referring here to the familiar transition from a *laissez-faire* to a collectivist philosophy which is a world-wide phenomenon. The repercussions on the public service have been obvious. The new expectations and demands for broader and better services have led to an enormous growth in the number of public servants and an increasing complexity and variety of administrative organizations. It is an expansion shared by all levels of government and by no means confined to the federal public service. The vast expansion in the scale of operations means that more and more attention must be devoted to the auxiliary or housekeeping services that exist simply to look after the "care and feeding" of the public bureaucracy. Problems of internal management, as the Glassco Commission reveals, assume much more significant proportions and older techniques of centralized control prove incapable of coping with the new situations or else, in trying to cope, bring irritation and frustration in their wake. Public services geared to a slower, steadier breathing rhythm find that each day now brings what appears to be a new crisis, until the realization dawns that these are not crises, but part of the speeded-up rhythm of our lives. No organization, let alone any public official, can cope for long with crisis administration unless interested in abnormal psychology and ready to become a patient of the psychatrist. Current preoccupation with planning evidences an effort to meet the new problems of administrative change not on a crisis basis but as part of normal administrative life.

The collectivist philosophy has changed the scale, the pace, the very tone of administration. These are problems of which the working civil servant is aware. The general public probably goes on believing in its old stereotype of the public servant who, like the fountains in Trafalgar Square, "plays from ten until four." And it is the response of the general public that brings me to my final point. The shift from *laissez-faire* to collectivism has been accompanied by an unprecedented shift in the balance of real power, discretion and initiative — away from courts, legislatures and even cabinets to public servants. The shift is inescapable and necessary but the public cannot be blamed for suspecting that the "faceless" men, the establishment, the mandarins or what you will are up to no good, that their rights are being invaded even as they are ostensibly being served by public employees. It is from this sense of unease that the proposals for an Ombudsman, a public defender, emanate.

I have, perforce, had to use the technique of the quick-sketch artist to present this hasty, episodic perspective on our developing public services. I trust that if you stand far enough back the likeness is reasonably accurate in its general outlines and focus, even if many of the details need much more amplification, qualification or clarification.

5
The Executive and the Departmental Structure*

A.M. Willms

THE EXECUTIVE

Cabinet ministers in Canada bear extremely heavy responsibilities both as members of Parliament and as the top executives of government departments. Although the legislative and executive roles of ministers overlap, attention will be focussed here on their executive functions as members of the Cabinet and heads of administrative departments.

The executive tasks of ministers have been well stated by the Glassco Commission:

> ... ministers need not be administrative experts; on the contrary, it is desirable save in the stress of emergencies, that they do not become deeply involved in the administrative process. As members of the Cabinet, their principal obligation is to reflect and give effect to the collective point of view — drawing together the public interests, attitudes and aspirations that find expression in the political process, and, by reconciling these, providing the basis for an essential unity of government in policy and action. As heads of departments, it is the task of ministers to define the ends to be pursued, and to instill their own sense of purpose and of urgency in the permanent officials.[1]

For each government department there is a Cabinet minister who takes full responsibility for its actions and who is credited with its achievements. Each minister is responsible to Parliament for the operation of his department and by convention the act of every public servant in the department is regarded as the act of the minister. The extent to which a minister can in fact be held accountable for the maladministration of his departmental subordinates is not clear. In practice, a minister's survival under such circumstances depends largely on his influence within his party and whether the party feels it can face criticism of its administration without being defeated in Parliament or at the next election.

The Canadian Cabinet tends to be excessively large in membership because the Prime Minister traditionally appoints ministers to meet the demands for representation of provinces and regions and of ethnic, linguistic, and religious groups. Clearly, the Prime Minister must take account of such a crucial political consideration despite possible adverse

---

*A.M. Willms, "Organization in Canadian Government Administration," unpublished manual (Ottawa, Carleton University, 1965). Revised and abridged by the editor.
[1]*Royal Commission on Government Organization*, vol. 5 (Ottawa, Queen's Printer, 1963), p. 33.

effects on the fulfillment of administrative needs. Canada now has twenty-five federal departments and about four times as many agencies. The number and diversity of these administrative units creates a span of control that is far too wide for a Cabinet which has onerous political and constitutional responsibilities. The Glassco Commission, however, recognized the primacy of political factors over administrative interests in organizing the executive structure of government.

> Above all, the organization of government, no less than the policies it pursues, must reflect the order of importance, in the minds of the public, of the problems requiring attention. Unless there is, in rough form, this correlation between the content of ministerial posts and the degree of public concern, government policy and action will almost certainly fail to respond adequately to public wants.[2]

Indeed, new departments or agencies may have to be established to emphasize or point up a new government policy. It may not be sufficient merely to enunciate new functions and allot these to an existing department or agency. To give these government activities prominence in the public mind another administrative unit may have to be created. The establishment of Central Mortgage and Housing Corporation immediately after the war and of the Department of Consumer and Corporate Affairs in 1967 are striking examples of this need. Since it is very difficult to dissolve a governmental unit once it has been set up, the number of units tends to increase.

A good case can be made on administrative-managerial grounds for fewer, more uniform, and necessarily larger administrative units. The following comments pertain specifically to departments although they are generally applicable to government agencies also. The overhead cost for adequate departmental services in small units may be disproportionately large, and the provision of such services as organization and methods or research and development may not be warranted. In addition, the existence of larger departments permits much more coherent government planning. Central control agencies such as the Treasury Board and the Public Service Commission can more readily stay out of planning when the allocation of scarce resources can be thrashed out in a few large departments. For example, if all the labour functions, including unemployment insurance, were centred in one department, the Treasury Board would be less concerned with the proportion of funds that should go to each of the various governmental units in the labour field. Larger departments also provide a wider field of training, development and advancement for capable junior and intermediate staff. The advantages of specialization can best be realized in larger departments, whether in the line functions, the staff functions, or the

---

[2]*Royal Commission on Government Organization*, pp. 41-42.

departmental services. A substantial measure of decentralization is almost inevitable in larger departments and with fewer, but more comprehensive field offices, the government can expect greater effectiveness with smaller overhead costs. Moreover, in a federal state many government activities require consultation and coordination between provincial and federal administrators; fewer and larger departments would make such cooperation easier.

There are, however, persuasive arguments for a large number of smaller departments. Individual ministers and deputy ministers can handle a small department more effectively than a large department. This is not so much a factor of size in manpower or budget as of political sensitivity and diversity of functions. The more sensitive the departmental functions in the political-social-economic atmosphere of the day, the more care must be given to policy decisions and the more skill must be employed in representing the department to the Cabinet, Parliament and the public. The more diverse the functions, the more overall policies must be coordinated by the man who must answer to Parliament for their implementation.

Instead of decreasing the size of any department, perhaps the functions of government could be redistributed so that similar functions would come under one responsibility and the diversity of some of the larger departments would be decreased. Such a reallocation could actually reduce the number of departments.

DEPARTMENTAL STRUCTURE

In general, the structure of departments resembles the normal scalar pyramid of private or corporate enterprise. At the top is the deputy minister who is the administrative head of the department and at the bottom are the numerous employees who actually carry out most of the functions of the department. In between are the various levels of supervision, management and specialization which make up the pyramidal structure. There is some uniformity in the terminology used to describe departmental organization at or near the pyramid's peak. The deputy minister or deputy head is at the pinnacle; below him there are assistant deputy ministers, or in a few instances, associate deputy ministers. Below the assistant deputy minister in the departmental pyramid are the branch heads who are usually called Directors or Directors-General. The branches are often further subdivided into divisions with Directors or Chiefs in charge. The divisions are subdivided in turn into what may be called sections, units, groups, services, staff, offices, or detachments and the head of each may carry any one of a great variety of titles.

The deputy minister often has a staff to assist him in his management of the department and he may also retain direct control of one or several of the branches or of the administrative services. Sometimes the deputy minister has a government agency reporting to him. Thus the Deputy Minister of Agriculture has the Agricultural Stabilization Board and the Board of Grain Commissioners reporting to him. The span of control of a deputy minister may cover anywhere from two or three to twelve or more subordinates. Most departments have only two or three assistant deputy ministers but as the size of the departments increases this number will grow.

The planning and organization of an individual department's internal structure requires a different approach from that which is taken in dividing up the functions of government between departments and agencies. The different approaches reflect the different objectives involved. In the division of the total functions of government among administrative units, the primary aim is to allot functions to a structure that satisfies political and public needs. Although the aim of the internal organization of a department or agency is to carry out the assigned functions as efficiently and effectively as possible, the minister's politicial and constitutional role remains an important determinant of the final structure. An organization plan should

1. Recognize the division of powers between the federal and provincial governments; in sensitive areas of jurisdiction even the appearance of federal overlapping into provincial fields must be avoided unless government policy on the subject is clear.
2. Recognize that the government exists to serve the people; recommendations that are administratively sound must also be acceptable to the segment of the population the agency has been set up to serve. In field organizations, in particular, it is sometimes necessary to modify organization principles to meet such a situation and to provide for local requirements.
3. Recognize that the minister concerned is one member of the Cabinet and that the functions of the agency, including the funds necessary for carrying them out, are often subject to balancing mechanisms within the Cabinet which supersede purely administrative considerations. Recommendations which propose the extension of an agency's functions into areas where other agencies have an interest, for instance, should be made only after the most careful exploration with the agencies concerned.[3]

In planning the department's structure, an initial decision must be made as to whether the parts of the department will be organized according to the criteria of purpose, process, clientele, or area. In the past,

---

[3]Civil Service Commission, *The Analysis of Organization in the Government of Canada* (Ottawa: Queen's Printer, 1964), pp. 13-14.

the factor of purpose (or function) has probably been given too much prominence in the building of branches, divisions and sections of departments. It is unwise to assume that if purpose is used to allocate the job to the department that it can also be used consistently in designing the whole departmental structure. It is often quite undesirable to emphasize the purpose factor within the department because

1.   Design of departmental branches or divisions by purpose often results in too much emphasis in each branch or division on a small part of the department's overall functions; there may be too much concern for the parts and not enough for the final product.
2.   Subdivision by purpose leaves little scope for competition between units which is an effective form of setting work standards and motivating units and employees.
3.   Specialization by purpose can lead to overspecialization with attendant difficulties in effective employee development.

There probably isn't a department or an agency that does not use all four organization factors in one way or another. It is the manager's responsibility to choose the factor or factors applicable and to decide to what extent each is necessary. In this decision consistency appears to have little virtue and the manager may combine the use of several or all of the factors as circumstances dictate.

6
Federal Crown Corporations in Canada*

D.P. Gracey

The primary purpose of this essay is to examine the existing and potential means by which the federal executive[1] may control and direct Crown corporations.[2] As a basis for this analysis, the essay begins with a brief explanation of the rationale for creating Crown corporations, their evolution and their present three-fold classification.

---

*An original article written for this volume.
[1]In this essay, the term "executive" refers to the Cabinet and Cabinet ministers.
[2]Referring to those 56 Crown corporations now listed in the revised Schedules of the Financial Administration Act, including the Company of Young Canadians (CYC), Polysar Limited and the Centennial Commission. The Centennial Commission and the CYC have been wound down and await parliamentary action to be removed from the Schedules. Owing to its sale to the Canada Development Corporation (a mixed enterprise), Polysar is no longer considered to be a Crown corporation and awaits parliamentary action to have its name removed from the Schedules.

The Crown corporation provides a valuable alternative to the traditional government department as an instrument for the achievement of public-policy objectives. A Crown corporation can manage a given function with a higher degree of autonomy from the political process than the departmental form allows. It can also remove the management of a function from bureaucratic controls and allow for the use of personnel and budgetary practices generally associated with the private sector. Furthermore, the Crown corporation set-up permits businessmen to be appointed to the boards of directors, thereby bringing their business expertise to the management of commercial or quasi-commercial activities on behalf of the government. The Crown corporation can also be an effective tool when gaps in the economy cannot be filled by the private sector because it is either inappropriate or impossible for the private sector to become involved. This may be the result of the strategic importance of the industry (i.e. nuclear energy development) or of the industry's lack of attraction to private investors. Finally, the Crown corporation structure establishes an institution that can contract, sue and be sued in its own name as well as borrow and acquire, hold, manage and dispose of property in a less cumbersome manner than a government department.

In view of Canada's relatively long experience with public enterprise, it is surprising that Canadians are not more knowledgeable about the Crown corporation form of government administration.

The first recognizable ancestor of the Crown corporation form is the Board of Works established by Lord Sydenham in 1841 in the United Provinces to construct a canal system. It is notable that because the Board's relationship with government was ambiguous and confusing for the political leaders of the time, it was soon shorn of its corporate status.

Canada's first major venture into public enterprise did not occur until 1919 when the Canadian National Railways (CNR) was established. The decision by the Canadian government to nationalize the financially troubled, but strategically vital, transcontinental railways under one publicly owned corporate entity was based neither on ideology nor any kind of "national vision." Rather, it was a pragmatic step that the government took, somewhat unwillingly, to protect its own investments, those of private shareholders and Canada's credit in foreign capital markets.

It seems that neither the government nor the public was particularly enamoured with the CNR experiment, because the next venture into public enterprise did not occur until 1935 when R.B. Bennett's Conservative government created the Canadian Broadcasting Corporation (CBC).

However, within the fifteen-year interval following the creation of the CBC, there were thirty-three government-owned corporations in existence. In that interval two significant events occurred: during World War II the federal government, in managing the war effort, was forced to resort to management structures other than the traditional departmental form; and C.D. Howe, a Cabinet minister who felt comfortable with business organizations and uncomfortable with government bureaucracy, left behind a long list of government-owned corporations as he moved through various wartime and post-war ministerial portfolios.

By the mid-point of the century, therefore, the publicly owned corporation seemed to have achieved a fairly high level of legitimacy. The problem was that in its haste to establish such corporations, the government had not developed a standard model for creating them, nor had it developed systems by which it could exert effective control, direction and accountability over them.

The executive is the pivotal point in the control and direction of federal Crown corporations by the Government of Canada.[3] Through various constituent acts and general statutes, such as the Financial Administration Act (FAA), Parliament has left to the executive, either expressly or by implication, the preponderance of traditional shareholders' rights and duties with respect to Crown corporations. Parliament has taken to itself the means by which it may exert broad supervision over Crown corporations, including the tabling of annual reports and capital budgets in Parliament, the right to gain information from Crown corporations through the designated minister and the power to call the managements of Crown corporations before Committees of the House. It is, however, the executive — not Parliament — that approves the capital and operating budgets of Crown corporations, hires and dismisses directors, sets the remuneration to be paid to directors, receives the agenda and minutes of directors' meetings, approves corporate by-laws and short-term loans or advances and, in some cases, actually incorporates the Crown corporation.

In 1950, the Cabinet proposed a Bill to Parliament, part of which was designed to provide a uniform method of financial control for Crown corporations and to provide for their annual reporting to Parliament via the tabling of annual reports and capital budgets through the appropriate minister. In general terms the Bill, which was approved by Parliament as the Financial Administration Act (FAA),[4] was intended to lay a foundation for a more uniform and systematic relationship between the executive and Parliament on the one hand and the Crown corporations on the other. Until the promulgation of the FAA, Crown corporations did

---

[3]The general relationships of the federal ministry to Crown corporations and the ways in which the ministry may exercise control over the corporations vary from one corporation to another.

[4]*Revised Statutes of Canada*, 1970, Chapter F-10.

not necessarily report to Parliament. As long as Crown corporations such as Polymer (now Polysar) were able to conduct their affairs so as not to require Parliamentary appropriations or loans to make up deficits, they could avoid Parliamentary scrutiny indefinitely.

The FAA provides the foundation of the financial administration of the Government of Canada. Part VIII of the Act is entirely devoted to the financial control of Crown corporations. And in Section 66 of that Part, the term Crown corporation is defined as a corporation that is ultimately accountable to Parliament (through a minister) for the conduct of its affairs. Section 66 also establishes the three-fold classification of Crown corporations.

The first classification includes what the FAA refers to as "departmental" Crown corporations (e.g., National Museums of Canada, National Research Council). These corporations are always agents of Her Majesty and, theoretically, are responsible for "administrative, supervisory or regulatory services of a government nature." Departmental corporations were to be in essence departments of government over which the Cabinet or the appropriate minister would exert more or less continuous control and direction in much the same way as it would over a department of government. Although the rationale does not hold true for all departmental corporations, it appears in general, that a corporate personality for such organizations was deemed necessary to facilitate the acquisition, holding, management and disposal of property as well as to allow the corporations to sue and be sued in their own names and not as agents of the Crown. In a number of cases the departmental Crown corporations are now integrated within a department, their only distinguishing characteristic being their legal status as corporate entities.

The second group of corporations defined by the FAA are the "agency" Crown corporations (e.g., National Capital Commission, Royal Canadian Mint). These corporations are always agents of Her Majesty and, theoretically, are "responsible for the management of trading or service operations on a quasi-commercial basis, or for the management of procurement, construction or disposal activities...."

The final classification includes those corporations known as "proprietary" Crown corporations. These are the companies which are sometimes referred to as "the commanding heights" of our public enterprise such as Air Canada, Canadian National Railways and Petro-Canada. According to the FAA, proprietary Crown corporations are responsible for the "management of lending or financial operations" or commercial and industrial operations "including the production of or dealing in goods and supplying of services to the public." Proprietary Crown corporations are also expected to be financially self-sustaining like private sector corporations and are therefore "ordinarily required to conduct ... operations without (Parliamentary) appropriations."

All of the federal Crown corporations in legal existence are grouped in one of the three classifications in an annex to the FAA known as the Schedules. The Schedules contain four groupings known as A, B, C and D. Schedule A includes all those organizations which are departments of government and are not Crown corporations. Schedules B, C and D include all the Crown corporations to which Part VIII applies. Schedule B includes all departmental corporations, Schedule C all agency corporations, and Schedule D all proprietary corporations.

Certain other corporations not included in the Schedules of the FAA in any of the above groupings are often described as "unclassified" Crown corporations. Indeed, the most recent edition of the *Public Accounts of Canada* (Volume III) lists four corporations — the Bank of Canada, St. Clair River Broadcasting Ltd.,[5] the Canadian Wheat Board and the National Arts Centre Corporation — as Crown corporations, presumably "unclassified" Crown corporations.

In may cases, however, the term "unclassified" Crown corporation is a misnomer, for there is evidence that the executive and Parliament did not intend such corporations to be brought under the purview of the FAA as Crown corporations.

Having established the definition and three-fold classification of Crown corporations, the FAA went on to establish the pattern of financial control which the government would exert over them. Departmental corporations were to be subject to the general provisions of the FAA found in parts other than Part VIII applying to Crown corporations. In other words, in their financial relationship with the government, departmental corporations were to be treated as ordinary departments of government, unless provisions in their constituent acts dictated otherwise. The focus of Part VIII, therefore, is on the agency and proprietary corporations and the two groups are treated uniformly under Part VIII with two significant exceptions. Agency Crown corporations are required to submit annual capital and operating budgets.[6] (Capital budgets are approved by the Cabinet on the recommendation of the appropriate minister, the Minister of Finance and the President of the Treasury Board.) Proprietary Crown corporations are required to submit only annual capital budgets for approval by the Cabinet on the recommendation of the three ministers. After approval by the Cabinet, capital budgets are tabled in Parliament. Agency corporations are also enjoined to undertake their contractual commitments subject to regulations which may be promulgated by the Cabinet.

---

[5] St. Clair River Broadcasting is a subsidiary of the CBC, incorporated under the Ontario Companies Act to operate CKLW-TV in Windsor, Ontario. The company was established in order to allow for ownership by the CBC in partnership with a private broadcasting company. The company is now wholly owned by the CBC.
[6] FAA, *op. cit.*, Section 70 (1).

The rationale for requiring agency corporations to submit both operating and capital budgets to the executive for approval and to be subject to regulations respecting contracts was that agency corporations were to have much less independence from government than proprietary corporations. It was envisaged by the drafters of the FAA that proprietary corporations were to have as much independence from government as private sector corporations have from the shareholder. Proprietary corporations were to be managed by individuals from the private sector and their management of the corporations was not to be subject to the supervision of the government, except in a general or policy sense through capital budgets. On the other hand, agency corporations were to be subject to both operational and policy supervision through annual operating and capital budgets and through control over contracts.

Given the fact that the FAA was promulgated over two decades ago, how relevant is Part VIII to today's political and administrative climate? Although Part VIII at the time of its presentation was seen to be a "new and experimental section which was very difficult to work out,"[7] its present relevance is a tribute to the original drafters. Few statutes, however, can be in force for twenty years without having some inadequacies or anachronisms develop. A close examination of Part VIII of the FAA and experience with it indicates that some amendments are urgently required, especially with respect to the Schedules, annual budgets and annual reports.

The most apparent anachronisms in the FAA are the Schedules whose listings, in some cases, have only the most tenuous connection with the definitions of Section 66 (3) of the FAA. For example, the St. Lawrence Seaway Authority has an accumulated deficit in the order of $140 million and at its current level of activity must clearly rely on government appropriations. Yet, the Authority is listed as a proprietary Crown corporation "ordinarily required to conduct (its) operations without appropriations."

In the interests of consistency, the Canadian Broadcasting Corporation should probably not be listed as a Crown corporation given the fact that Parliament has dictated that similar organizations, incorporated since the CBC, were not to be Crown corporations. Citing the requirement for independence in the development of the arts, humanities and sciences, the St. Laurent government chose not to list the Canada Council in the Schedules of the Act. Noting that artistic policy is inevitably controversial and indicating that management should be given the "freest possible hand", the Pearson government did not include the National Arts Centre Corporation (NAC) in the Schedules of the Act.

---

[7] *Minutes of the House of Commons Standing Committee on the Public Accounts,* 1951, p. 99.

Yet the CBC, which embodies many of the elements of the mandate of the NAC and pursues many of the same objectives in the field of the arts as the Canada Council, continues its status as a Schedule D Crown corporation and continues to rely on government appropriations for financing.

Departmental corporations which perform granting or advisory functions on behalf of the government, such as the Medical Research Council, National Research Council, Economic Council of Canada and the Science Council, should probably have and be seen to have more independence from the government than departmental Crown corporation status provides. The transfer of such corporations to another Schedule of the FAA, or completely out of the Schedules, to assume a status of independence such as that held by the Canada Council might, therefore, be considered by the government.

Should the Schedules of the Act be revised, the government might wish to take the opportunity to evaluate the roles and mandates of all Crown corporations now listed in the Schedules. Are there some Crown corporations that are largely neutral in the performance of public policy objectives? If so, consideration should be given either to winding down such corporations and having their functions picked up by the private sector, or inviting the private sector to purchase all or a portion of their equity. Are there Crown corporations that now administer functions which could more effectively be administered within a departmental framework? If so, such corporations should be wound down in whole or in part and their functions transferred to a department of government.

Annual budgets submitted by Crown corporations under the FAA have, in large part, not lived up to their potential as instruments of financial control and accountability. With very few exceptions, annual budgets do not impart to the appropriate ministers and the Cabinet the kind or amount of information which would allow them to assess the performance of Crown corporations in achieving either corporate or government objectives. Nor do they allow for the assessment of the impact which approval of a particular annual budget might have on future resource requirements and on the achievement of government or corporate objectives.

In the past there have been sporadic attempts by ministers and departmental officials to have certain Crown corporations produce the requisite material to support a particular budget. In most cases, these attempts have not resolved the issues satisfactorily, and in some cases they have produced severe frustrations on both the government and corporate sides. In most instances this frustration was a consequence of the government using the only tool readily available to it — refusal of budget approval until the requisite supporting documentation was provided. In at least one recent case this procedure resulted in a capital budget being approved by the Cabinet some months after the termination of the fiscal year to which the budget applied.

The government has recently moved to correct this serious problem. The president of the Treasury Board, on behalf of his colleagues in the government, has asked Crown corporations to make substantial adjustments to the form and content of annual capital and operating budgets. Perhaps of more significance, however, each Crown corporation has also been asked to prepare and submit to the government a corporate plan, approved by the board of directors of each company. This plan is to be submitted a few months prior to the submission of the annual budget into the program forecast exercise and entails (1) a comprehensive statement of corporate objectives, priorities and policies as well as economic, financial and social benefits expected from these; and (2) a full explanation of how the proposed financing would affect the achievement of corporate objectives and government objectives as they apply to the corporation.

The plan would be cast in a five-year time horizon and be subject to annual updating. After government approval through the responsible minister, in close consultation with his colleagues, the Minister of Finance and the president of the Treasury Board, the plan would act as the foundation on which the annual budgets would be prepared and submitted for approval through Main Estimates. The government has asked that the quality and integrity of annual budgets be upgraded to equal or exceed the standards required for public offerings of public companies in the private sector.

Through these reforms the government seems to hope to achieve a number of objectives: to use the full potential of annual budgets as instruments of financial and policy control, direction and accountability; to allow ministers, through early submission of corporate plans, to analyze the financing requirements in all of the policy and operating sectors of the federal government; to provide clear objectives against which the performance of the managements of Crown corporations may be objectively assessed; and, through early approval of corporate plans, to allow Crown corporations more lead time in which to adjust their financing and operational plans, prior to the commencement of each fiscal year.

It is important to note that the government has *asked* Crown corporations to submit corporate plans. It has not directed them to do so, for it has no express legal authority under the FAA, or elsewhere, to make a binding directive of this nature. It is evident that Part VIII of the FAA is in need of substantial amendment to give the government the authority to achieve effective financial and policy control over all Crown corporations.

On the whole, the annual reports of Crown corporations have failed as instruments of effective accountability and control in much the same way as have annual budgets. Annual reports are too often prepared for public relations purposes, with a plentiful supply of photographs and attractive colours to catch the eye, but little in the way of detailed information to allow the government or Parliament to assess objectively the performance of Crown corporations. It is to be hoped that the improvements in annual budgets will be reflected in improvements in the quality of annual reports. Annual reports in future could contain a copy of each corporation's corporate plan, with any necessary deletions to protect the commercial secrecy of the corporation and to avoid intrusion by government and Parliament into the internal administration of the corporation. Annual reports might also contain a discussion of the achievement of corporate objectives, measured against the approved corporate plans, and the reasons for any shortcomings. For those corporations over which the government has the power of a binding directive, the annual reports could show the financial losses or gains incurred in pursuit of those objectives, separated from the financial performance of the corporation in pursuing strictly corporate objectives as defined by the board of directors.

The major reason for the lack of consistency in relationships between the government and Crown corporations is the absence of one overriding piece of legislation which would impose at least a 'minimum floor' of consistency for all Crown corporations. In the absence of such a statute, a number of factors contribute to the present degree of inconsistency and become important in defining the relationship between government and Crown corporations.

The methods of incorporation to which the government has resorted (either by articles of incorporation under the Canada Business Corporations Act (CBCA) and its predecessors, or through special individual incorporating Acts of Parliament) have resulted in two distinct relationships. The articles of incorporation companies are, as a rule, more independent of government than are the special act corporations. The relationship of the articles of incorporation companies with the government is defined by the CBCA or by the Canada Corporations Act (CCA)[8] and the designated minister's legal status is that of a trustee shareholder. The incorporating legislation of the special act corporations usually defines a degree and type of control over the company which a shareholder would normally not have under the CBCA or the CCA.

Further inconsistencies become evident when one begins to analyze and compare special incorporating acts. No two incorporating acts define the same relationship between the corporation and the government. For

---

[8]All corporations incorporated under the CCA have a five-year period in which to bring themselves under the CBCA.

example, some constituent acts give to the government the power of a directive over a Crown corporation; most constituent acts do not. The source and type of directive also vary from corporation to corporation. In some cases the directive may come only from the appropriate minister (Atomic Energy Control Board). In others the directive may come only from the Cabinet (Petro-Canada). The directive may be limited to policy (Petro-Canada), or be totally unlimited in scope, applying both to policy and operations (Canadian Commercial Corporation, Royal Canadian Mint). Some consituent acts give to the Cabinet the power to *fix* the salaries of the chairman, chief executive officers and directors. Others, give the Cabinet power to *approve* the salaries proposed by the board of directors. In others the Cabinet has *no* control over the salaries. Pursuant to their respective incorporating acts, some chairmen, presidents and directors serve "during pleasure", meaning that they may be removed at any time by the Cabinet. Others serve "during good behaviour", making them more independent of the government as a result of their more secure tenure.

Because there is inconsistency in the legal relationship, each minister and the management of each corporation are able to develop a relationship in accordance with their own personalities and styles of administration. Superimposed over the legal relationship, therefore, is an informal relationship, defined by the individuals involved, which is just as inconsistent as the legal relationship — if not more so.

A serious problem which besets the government with respect to Crown corporations is the inability of the ministry to issue binding directives to all corporations. Recent experience has illustrated that in many cases the government has need of a method by which it can force a Crown corporation to pursue a certain objective. Obvious examples of such objectives are the government's policies with respect to official languages, austerity policies and regional growth and development. Such power is available to the government over some of the articles of incorporation in the same way as it is available to private sector sole shareholders over private sector companies — through the unanimous shareholders agreement defined by the CBCA.[9] The same type of directive power seems called for with respect to Crown corporations where it does not already exist, either pursuant to the CBCA or the special act of incorporation. Such a power does, however, have the potential for abuse.

To guard against misuse or abuse of the directive power, directives should probably emanate from the Cabinet on the recommendation of the appropriate minister, be in writing and be made public as soon as

---

[9] The Canada Business Corporations Act, *The Canada Gazette*, Part III, Chapter 33, March 24, 1975, Section 140 (2).

possible after promulgation. In order to protect the commercial viability of Crown corporations expected to operate on a commercial basis, (e.g., the proprietary Crown corporations) the directive power should be accompanied by a provision whereby such corporations would be compensated for losses incurred through implementation of a directive. As proposed earlier in this paper, a further check might be to have annual reports reflect the cost of such directives by identifying the assets or liabilities and revenues or expenses involved in the corporation's pursuit of a directive from the government.

One of the problems raised in the report of the Commission of Inquiry into the financial affairs of Air Canada (the Estey Report)[10] was that subsidiaries of Crown corporations may be used in ways detrimental to the government's control over Crown corporations. There is evidence that at least one federal Crown corporation has used a subsidiary to undertake activities indirectly which the parent Crown corporation could not do directly under the company's constituent act. The use of subsidiaries and the type of financial reporting which has, as a rule, occurred can also remove the management of the subsidiary from examination by the government and Parliament.[11] In order to exert adequate control and accountability over subsidiaries, it may be that all Crown corporations should be required by legislation to seek the approval of the government before establishing a subsidiary. In giving its approval the government could ensure that the subsidiary is undertaking an activity which is allowed by the parent's charter and will be instrumental in achieving the government's public policy objectives. Prior approval could also ensure that the financial statements of the subsidiary are fully disclosed in the parent company's annual reports as part of the consolidated or combined financial statements and that the government has access, through the parent, to the financial accounts of each subsidiary, either for internal government purposes or for tabling in Parliament.

The federal government's policy of appointing public servants as directors of Crown corporations is unique to Canada.[12] In some cases the

---

[10]Honourable Willard Z. Estey, *Air Canada Inquiry Report*, (Ottawa: Information Canada, October 1975).

[11]See W.Z. Estey, *ibid.*, Chapter 8. Air Canada and its parent, Canadian National Railways, established a subsidiary of CN to engage in the business of chartering, tour wholesaling, ground reception services and the financing of the total travel package on behalf of Air Canada and CN. Air Canada personnel were appointed to the board and the company came under the general supervision of the president of Air Canada. The Report found that Venturex was established to allow Air Canada to do something indirectly that it could not do directly, that the accounts of Venturex were consolidated in neither the Air Canada accounts nor the CN accounts by the auditors and that it would have been difficult for either Parliament or the executive to be informed of Venturex activities even though the losses of Venturex amounted to over nine million from 1973 to December 31, 1974.

[12]The practice is also fairly widespread at the provincial level in Canada

constituent act of a federal Crown corporation (e.g., the Export Development Corporation) calls for the appointment of public servants to sit as ex-officio directors. In most cases, however, where public servants sit on the boards of Crown corporations, the appointment is not made to satisfy a requirement of the constituent act.

Although a policy has never been enunciated, there seem to be three reasons for the appointment of public servants to the boards of Crown corporations: to bring a special expertise to the deliberations of the boards; to act as a communication link between the boards and ministers (not necessarily the responsible minister); and, finally, to bring a particular departmental or ministerial interest before the board.

One can be reasonably certain that the practice has not been dictated by a desire to economize or by a lack of competent individuals from the private sector to be members of the boards. Indeed, one could be forgiven for thinking that the government was suspicious of its own actions in setting up certain Crown corporations and has circumscribed their independence by appointing public servants to the boards. In the extreme, a board composed of public servants can look and operate as any bureaucratic interdepartmental committee does.

The present situation generally seems to be that a senior public servant wears "two hats" when serving on the board of a Crown corporation. One hat represents the department in which he is employed; the other his directorship. When serving as a director does the senior public servant act in the best interests of the corporation or of his department? Is he to be a watchdog for his department and the government over the affairs of the Crown corporation? Is corporate information made available to him in his capacity as a director to be made available to other officials of his department? To whom is he loyal? The minister to whom he reports or the corporation of which he is a director? Obviously, when the public servant reports to a minister other than the minister to whom the corporation which he serves reports, the ambiguity can have serious implications.

If the public servant sometimes finds his position ambiguous, the chairman of the board, who maintains the corporation's connection with the responsible minister, can be in a position of even greater ambiguity. He may face a board composed in part of one or more senior public servants from the department of the minister to whom he reports on behalf of the corporation. The appointment of public servants to the boards of Crown corporations involved in the management of activities on a commercial or quasi-commercial basis seems also to contradict one of the basic, though admittedly not the sole, *raisons d'être* of the Crown corporation form. (That is to separate the management of an activity from bureaucratic management and to bring individuals experienced in business to the management of such activities through a Crown corporation.)

There are many cases where public servants should be appointed as directors of Crown corporations, for example, when they bring a special expertise to the board. However, the federal government may wish to evaluate the practice and refrain from the appointment of public servants except where such appointments do not mar, or in any way confuse, the lines of communication from the corporation through the chairman to the appropriate minister. When appointed as directors for Crown corporations, public servants should see their role as bringing a special expertise to the corporation — not as being a government watchdog on the internal affairs of the corporation.

When an individual is appointed from the private sector to the board of a Crown corporation, the government, through the appointing minister, should not only ensure that the individual meets reasonable standards of business competence but also should ensure that the individual is aware of government policy objectives and is willing to pursue those policies through the corporation. The federal government might also wish to consider whether or not the directors and officers of all Crown corporations should be brought under the same regime of duties, liabilities and responsibilities that apply to private sector corporations (including a minority of federal Crown corporations) under the CBCA.[13]

The broad duties of directors and officers under the CBCA are set forth in Section 97 (1), where it is stated unequivocally that "directors shall manage the affairs of a corporation," qualified only by the power of the shareholders to issue a unanimous shareholders' agreement. The CBCA also specifies that the directors may delegate their functions except those which involve their specific personal liabilities.[14] The government might also wish to ensure, through whatever powers are available to it, that private sector directors sit on the committees of boards of directors — especially the important committees, such as the executive committees — in the same proportion that public servants sit on the full board of directors.

These reforms assist in another area. Many Crown corporations have followed a practice common in the private sector whereby the chairman of the board also assumes the functions of the chief operating officer (e.g. the president of the corporation). In some cases this practice has given rise to a situation where the individual who acts as both chairman and chief operating officer takes control of all significant corporate powers himself, relegating the board of directors to a minor role. In such cases, the corporation's policies and management run the risk of becoming cast in the image of one man whose directives are not

---

[13]CBCA, *op. cit.* See Sections 113 to 119 and Sections 125, 232 and 234.
[14]*Ibid.,* 117 (3).

necessarily in line with government policy.[15] If the boards of directors of such corporations were to be reformed as suggested above, the boards might reinstate themselves and their prerogatives *vis-à-vis* the chairman and the chief operating officer and act as a balance within the corporation against undue centralization of power.

Crown corporations have been, and doubtless will continue to be, valuable instruments of the federal government in the achievement of public policy objectives. For even with its imperfections the Crown corporation form is a viable and remarkable instrument. However, for the Crown corporation form to continue to be an effective policy tool some significant steps must be taken to ensure its evolution.

This essay proposes that the Government of Canada establish an omnibus Crown Corporations Act which will provide a consistent and systematic foundation for the relationship between the government and Crown corporations as the FAA was designed to supply a consistent and systematic financial relationship. Secondly, the essay proposes that significant amendments and additions be made to the FAA and its Schedules to bring that legislation in line with the exigencies of the present political and administrative climate. Finally, it is suggested that if these reforms are implemented, it will be easier for the government to avoid further intrusion into the management of Crown corporations. The practice of appointing public servants to the boards might, therefore, be reconsidered.

7
Federal-Provincial Administrative Liaison in Canada*

Institute of Intergovernmental Relations

The formal concept of federalism, involving a distinct division of powers and responsibilities, is no longer a workable concept in Canada. Conditions have changed since the constitutional division was first made. The cross-flow of interests between the political units has become

---

[15]On the other hand, it can be argued that a Crown corporation, effectively run by one individual, is much easier for the ministry to control than a corporation managed by a chairman, board of directors and a chief operating officer.

---

*Reprinted and abridged by permission from Institute of Intergovernmental Relations, Queen's University, *Report on Intergovernmental Liaison on Fiscal and Economic Matters,* under the direction of R.M. Burns (Ottawa: Queen's Printer, 1969). Updated and supplemented by the editor.

too rapid and the currents too varied to permit the operation of the rather rigid structure that such dual federalism requires.

The classical form of federalism where each jurisdiction acts within its legally defined limits is strictly a product of the law which created it. Intergovernmental liaison or co-operation, even where formally provided, is a more informal process, dependent on the actions and reactions of varying interests. In this lies its strength through its adaptability, and its weakness where it lacks a firm base in the specific sanctions of the constitution. The task we face is to utilize its adaptability while containing its pragmatism within the limits of the law and the constitution.

THE PRESENT STRUCTURE OF LIAISON

The increasing demands of governmental responsibility have resulted in the rapid growth of intergovernmental involvement. No longer is it practicable, and in fact it rarely has been completely so, for each jurisdiction to attempt to carry out its assigned responsibilities without regard to what others may be doing. Thus we have an extremely complex network of intergovernmental relationships. For its purpose, the structure may be large enough. Unfortunately, taken as a whole, it has grown in response to individual demands rather than developing to meet the total requirements of the situation.

The liaison structure we have in Canada is extremely diverse both in form and effect. It covers a broad area from the top where formal matters of total government policy are dealt with through a spectrum of formal administrative arrangements to the day-to-day contacts, often devoid of formal sanction, which go to make up so much of the stuff of public activity.

A GENERAL DESCRIPTION OF THE MACHINERY

1. Formal Conferences and Committees

The formal machinery of intergovernmental liaison in Canada takes on a wide variety of forms. These are the institutions, organizations, conferences and committees which exist on a more or less continuing basis. An inventory compiled in 1967 contained some one hundred and seventy such bodies and the list has changed and grown considerably since that time.[1] It is possible to identify a number of different classes within this listing.

---

[1] As of June 1970, there were 57 formal committees at the ministerial and deputy ministerial level, 260 multilateral committees and subcommittees involving officials and another 150 bilateral committees of the same type. See Gordon Robertson, "The Changing Role of the Privy Council Office," *Canadian Public Administration,* vol. 14, Winter 1971, p. 497. See Tables I and II at the end of this essay for the frequency of federal-provincial meetings according to category, level of representation and area of government activity during 1975.

(i) Federal-Provincial Committees

These are the standard type of consultative bodies and while they generally have some formal structure they vary substantially in their construction and method of operation. They are composed of ministers and/or officials, both federal and provincial, who come together as official representatives of their governments to discuss matters of mutual interest, ranging from broad policy questions to some of a highly technical and specialized nature. They must be accepted *de facto* as committees of government even though in most cases they lack formal statutory existence, for they operate through the participation of individual governments, each in its own right. These committees are of different types. Some are considered to be continuing bodies for consultation and these generally meet with some regularity and thus tend in many cases to develop an institutional character. Other committees are not given such a formal identity. They come together on an *ad hoc* basis and are not regarded as permanent consultative bodies in the same sense, although their availability for meeting as required is fully recognized. Still others may be referred to in the current jargon as 'task forces.' While they are usually formally constituted by order-in-council or ministerial decree, they have a limited task to perform and a terminable existence. It is intended as a rule that they should disappear after their assigned work is complete. Such operations as the Tax Structure Committee or the Committee on Financial Institutions and Securities Regulation could properly come under this last classification.

The Government of Canada, by virtue of its position, is generally, although not in every case, the central co-ordinating influence and provides the chairman and secretarial services.

(ii) Interprovincial Committees

Strictly, these might be excluded from a survey of federal-provincial liaison machinery, but the extent of federal interest is sufficient in many cases to warrant their inclusion. They are, as a rule, consultative bodies of some formal structure, composed of provincial representatives, ministerial and/or official. They convene for the purpose of considering general matters of inter-provincial interest, for the exchange of information and experience, or for the purpose of developing joint approaches to the central government.

The pervasive influence of the federal interest is such, however, that in a good many cases, while federal representation is officially lacking, the national government participates by having observers present. As a result, while officially interprovincial, these bodies thus may often take on some important elements of a federal-provincial role. The annual conferences of the mines ministers are an example. The provinces assume responsibility for organization and in most cases take turns in acting as hosts.

(iii) Advisory Councils

There are several groups now in existence which are appointed under federal statute or order-in-council to act as advisory bodies to federal ministers. These councils, where there is provincial representation, function as federal-provincial committees to a certain extent. Some of these groups have only official government representation; others are a mixture of officials and representatives of private organizations. A few exist which have no official representation whatsoever, although they may have regional representation and act in an advisory capacity. These do not fit into the scheme of our study of inter-governmental bodies. There are also some such councils or committees which are intended as administrative advisory bodies to federal departments. One also finds on occasion advisory bodies to provincial ministers in fields of special interest, where federal officials act in an advisory capacity. The Dominion Council of Health illustrates this advisory approach at the federal level, as do the Agricultural Co-ordinating Committees in some provinces, at the provincial level.

(iv) Quasi-Independent Associations

There are certain bodies which are made up wholly, or almost so, of ministers and/or civil servants. They are supported largely by public funds but are not federal-provincial committees in the usual sense of the term. They are constituted as associations and function to some extent as professional organizations or special interest groups. While this aspect varies from case to case, their stimulus comes more from within themselves than from the governments, and the participants, at least in theory, function more as association members than as representatives of governments. However, they serve the purpose of bringing together people in a particular field from all governments and they can contribute to a considerable extent to intergovernmental consultation and co-ordination. Examples of such bodies include the Canadian Council of Resource and Environment Ministers, which has its own letters patent and its own staff, the Canadian Association of Administrators of Labour Legislation, and the Association of Canadian Fire Marshals.

(v) Other

In many cases, the groups or conferences to which we have referred in the four previous categories will have sub-committees. Committees at the regional level are also found, composed of federal regional representatives and officials from one or more provinces.

Certain non-government organizations or professional associations may also serve as vehicles for intergovernmental liaison. They have in most cases a substantial number of members who are ministers or officials from across Canada. When members come together to discuss their areas of interest, considerable intergovernmental liaison inevitably is a by-product of the meetings. The Canadian Good Roads Association and the Institute of Public Administration of Canada are examples of this type of liaison operation.

2. Other Formal Provisions

The conferences and committees already noted are by no means the only vehicles for intergovernmental exchange. Many federal departments have regional offices located across the country which frequently have as part of their responsibility the facilitating of communication with provincial offices. Federal-provincial committees are often established at the regional level through these offices. The degree of delegation to regional offices varies widely and this, of course, affects the extent to which consultation can be effective at the local level. There are signs of increasing departmental interest in the approach.

The reciprocal of this situation could be considered as the establishment of provincial offices in Ottawa. Most provinces seem to have considered this approach at one time or another but so far only Alberta, which has had a permanent representative in Ottawa for some years with limited terms of reference, and Quebec which has a press office, have actually taken any action. There seems to be considerable reluctance to establish what many fear would be an additional barrier to communication between the departments of federal and provincial governments with like interests.

3. Informal Processes

Without doubt the most frequently used and often the most effective form of liaison is the informal day-to-day contact which is used in the ordinary course of business by both ministers and administrators. Much of this depends on the degree of development in the intergovernmental relationship and to this extent it can be a product of more formal channels. Conversely, more formal relationships can develop from personal and official contacts at the informal level. Every day there is a multitude of contacts and communications between officials of both levels of government. These may be by telephone, letter or personal visit. Modern means of communication are increasingly becoming more heavily utilized in the process of intergovernmental exchange although there is still room for a great deal more to be done.

The facility with which these communications are carried on between government offices varies widely and depends on such factors as the nature of the work, the experience of the people concerned, and the personal relationships. As a general rule, the longer that officials of both levels of government have been involved with each other in a program area, the more likely it is that there will be good communication between them. In large part this depends on the development of trust, respect and often friendship between key officials. While we have been speaking primarily of relationships at the official level, much of the same can be said of ministerial contacts although here political considerations may provide a deterrent to open communications on some occasions. Another general observation is that the most well-developed informal consultative processes occur in the most specialized or professional areas of activity. Indeed, in many cases communication between governments in a specialized field is often better than communication internally between government departments. It even seems possible that in some of these specialized areas the officials of both levels of government feel more identification with and even loyalty to their field of activity than to their respective governments. The results of this can be seen in development of some of the joint programs.

There is no easy way to measure or evaluate the different forms and processes of intergovernmental liaison. Each may be suitable to its particular area of operation and the circumstances of the times. What is clear is that there is an extensive structure of intergovernmental liaison that has grown over the years. What is perhaps less clear is the extent to which the structure has adapted or is adaptable to the changing needs.

4. Internal Processes

The effectiveness of intergovernmental liaison depends to a substantial extent on how well communication flows *within* governments. Governments use a number of devices to help co-ordinate their relationships with other governments. The use of a departmental division or a separate department for federal-provincial relations to facilitate intergovernmental communication and internal co-ordination is sometimes found.

The internal organization, while strictly speaking not part of the machinery of government liaison itself, is nevertheless an essential ingredient in the effective development and use of any such machinery. One of the biggest obstacles to effective co-ordination of public policies is often the lack of really effective communication within governments themselves.

CENTRAL GOVERNMENT ACTIVITY

1. General Government

Within this group fall the consultations concerned with policy matters at the highest level. The senior body is the Federal-Provincial Conference of the Prime Minister and Premiers which is convened by the Federal Government and is chaired by the Prime Minister. At these conferences the heads of government are generally accompanied by whatever ministers and officials are necessary. They discuss a wide variety of matters of prime importance to all governments.

Federal-Provincial Conferences, or Dominion-Provincial Conferences as they have been called in the past, have a long history. The first was not convened until 1906 and meetings were sporadic until the 1930's. Since that time they have become an increasingly regular feature of the intergovernmental relationship and recently have been meeting regularly at least once a year. Despite their established use in the system, these conferences have never been formally constituted as continuing vehicles of federal-provincial consultation either by the constitution or by other statute.

The (continuing) Constitutional Conference, which first met in February, 1968, is, in effect, the Plenary Conference of Prime Ministers and Premiers, but convened under a special name to carry out a particular task — to review the Constitution and determine what changes might be necessary or desirable. Sub-committees are to be created as required (see below). The specific questions included in the program for the Constitutional Conference and its committees are: official languages, fundamental rights, distribution of powers, reform of institutions linked with federalism, including the Senate and the Supreme Court of Canada, regional disparities, amending procedure and provisional arrangements, and mechanisms of federal-provincial relations.

The Continuing Committee of Officials is a senior sub-committee of officials which reports to the Constitutional Conference and assists the Conference in its work, including the co-ordination of research and staff work connected with the constitutional review. It is understood that all sub-committees of officials which may be formed to study particular aspects of the review will report to this Committee. (If any ministerial sub-committees are formed, these would have to report to the Constitutional Conference.) The Committee is composed of senior civil servants, frequently the Clerk of the Executive Council or his equivalent, from all governments. The first meeting of this Committee took place in May of 1968.

The Secretariat of the Constitutional Conference was established in 1968 to serve the Constitutional Conference, the Continuing Committee, and associated groups. It was replaced in 1973 by *The Canadian Intergovernmental Conference Secretariat* which serves all federal-provincial meetings of First Ministers as well as any other intergovernmental conferences wishing to use the Secretariat's services.

In historical terms, *interprovincial conferences* pre-date the federal-provincial ones, the first having been called by Premier Mercier of Quebec in 1887. They have been repeated at irregular intervals since, the last being the "Confederation of Tomorrow Conference" of November, 1967. This was an interprovincial conference of first Ministers (with federal observers present) which was convened by Ontario in November of 1967 to discuss the state of the Canadian federation and the direction in which it might develop in future. *The Interprovincial Continuing Committee of Premiers* created by the Confederation of Tomorrow Conference, is composed of the first Ministers of four provinces who meet from time to time to consider developments related to the subject matter of the Conference.

The Conference of Provincial Premiers began meeting annually in 1960 to discuss general questions of mutual interest. The Government of Canada does not participate in these meetings although a federal observer has always been invited and one or more federal officials usually attend. The objects of these Premiers' Conferences are a bit vague but for the most part they have confined their activities to those matters where no direct federal interests have been involved. Whether this will continue in the face of a lack of exclusive interprovincial matters of sufficient importance to engage their interests is a matter for speculation. The presence of the federal government provides an essential element in most cases where positive results are required on a national scale.

2. Financial and Economic Matters

While an attempt has been made on several earlier occasions to develop some machinery of liaison in this area, it was not until 1964 that a successful effort was made to develop a means of co-ordinated approach to fiscal and economic problems.

At the plenary conference in Quebec in 1964, proposals were made by the Government of Canada which resulted in much the same group of ministers meeting as two different committees. The first of these, the Tax Structure Committee, was assigned the responsibility of acting as a 'task force' to examine the allocation of the tax resources of governments in Canada in relation to their expenditure responsibilities.

The second group, composed of the ministers responsible for the finance portfolio in the federal and provincial governments, was informally constituted. It was decided that the ministers should meet annually toward the close of the calendar year and just before the formulation of the next budgets to discuss the economic and financial situation in Canada and the various provinces. The intention was that such a discussion should give the ministers guidance for framing their plans for the following year in a way which might be appropriate for the economic circumstances. The hope has been expressed that these meetings will increase in sophistication to the point where substantial harmonization of fiscal and economic policies may be achieved. There are signs that this aim may be realized.

The Federal-Provincial Continuing Committee on Fiscal and Economic Matters has had the longest continuing life of any of the groups which could be said to have a general policy advisory concern as against more specific program activity. It is a committee of senior officials (in the most cases deputies of the finance ministers) representing Canada and the provinces, which was formed in 1956 by the Federal-Provincial Plenary Conference to exchange views and information on fiscal and economic matters and to deal with matters referred to it by agreement of ministers of the governments concerned. Since 1964 it has been concerned in considerable measure with its responsibilities for the staff work in connection with the Tax Structure Committee and the meetings of the finance ministers.

3. Financial Institutions Regulation

This is new area of intergovernmental interest stemming from changes in the financial system of Canada with the growth of "near-banks" and similar type institutions. Ministerial and officials' committees in financial institutions and securities regulations were established in 1967 on a 'task force' basis to define rules and seek co-ordination between governments in this area. The ministerial committee includes generally the finance minister and one other minister from each government.

4. Other Categories

Some committees are concerned with programs which bear directly on economic development (e.g., agriculture, resources, industry, manpower). Others have to be kept in mind because of their important fiscal influences (and, at least indirect, economic effects), such as health and welfare.

The situation varies from field to field. Agriculture has been a shared jurisdiction since Confederation and federal-provincial meetings have taken place over a long period. There are now a wide range of consultations, from general policy discussions at the ministerial level to very specialized consultations at the technical level.

A noteworthy development in 1967 was the formation of an interprovincial council of education ministers. This is a formally constituted organization with a permanent staff and is an example of possible developments in areas of provincial responsibility. The embryo group is said to have played a useful role in helping to iron out some of the federal-provincial disagreements over new manpower training agreements.

The Energy and Resource group includes the Canadian Council of Resource and Environment Ministers. This body is unique in the catalogue of intergovernmental machinery, being a corporate association of ministers. The annual Ministers of Mines Conference is a hybrid organization bringing together provincial ministers and officials, industry representatives, and federal observers. There are a great many groups operating on a regional basis in matters of water resources and there is a variety of bodies in other resource fields.

The Health and Welfare sector has been the centre of federal-provincial consultation for many years and particularly in the post-war period. Interests have been broad, ranging from policy considerations at the ministerial level to very specialized studies (especially in the health field) in numerous technical committees. The advisory council device is used for federal-provincial consultation here. A most notable example of this approach is the Dominion Council of Health which has functioned since 1919.

There are relatively few formal consultative bodies in the categories of Industry and Trade or Public Works-Housing, but there are numerous specialized committees at the official level in the field of statistics. There are also a number of other groups concerned with a variety of matters.

TABLE 1
Frequency of Federal-Provincial Meetings and Conferences According to Level of Representation and Area of Government Activity, 1975

	First Ministerial	Ministerial	DM	ADM	Officials	Total
General Government	—	3	11	—	4	18
Finances	1	3	7	1	6	18
Agriculture	—	8	9	4	2	23
Transportation	—	15	15	14	13	57
Education	—	2	2	—	5	9
Energy and Resources	3	12	27	6	3	51
Environment	—	19	29	20	25	93
Manpower-Labour	—	23	8	2	11	44
Statistics	—	2	1	4	30	37
Welfare	—	4	5	9	4	22
Health	—	2	15	6	15	38
Industry and Trade	2	7	55	43	50	157
Urban Affairs	—	23	9	14	32	78
Justice and Laws	—	13	3	3	3	22
Consumer Affairs	—	7	4	1	3	15
Communications	—	6	1	—	2	9
Native Affairs	—	11	4	12	11	38
Miscellaneous	—	7	18	15	13	53
Total	6	167	223	154	232	782

TABLE 2
**Frequency of Federal-Provincial Meetings and Conferences
According to Category and Level of Representation, 1975**

	Bilateral	Regional	Multilateral	Total
First Ministerial	4	—	2	6
Ministerial	99	10	58	167
Deputy Ministerial	148	12	63	223
Asst. Deputy Ministerial	111	14	29	154
Officials	128	9	95	232
Total	490	45	247	782

8
Bilingualism in the Canadian Federal Public Service*

P.K. Kuruvilla

In 1965, the Royal Commission on Bilingualism and Biculturalism jolted Canadians with its ominous finding that Canada was "passing through the greatest crisis in its history"[1] — a crisis arising primarily from differences of opinion about the appropriate use of French and English in Canadian society. In response to the Commission's subsequent recommendations,[2] the federal Parliament unanimously passed the Official Languages Act[3] in July 1969, declaring English and French the official languages of Canada and guaranteeing them equality of status in all the institutions of the Parliament and the Government of Canada. In June 1973 a Parliamentary Resolution, supported by all political parties, reaffirmed the provisions of the Act and adopted a number of basic principles governing its implementation.

The government's stated objective is to achieve full and equal participation of Anglophones and Francophones in the public service while preserving the merit principle in recruitment and promotion. Responsibility for attaining these ends is shared by the Treasury Board, the Public Service Commission, the Privy Council Office, the Department of the Secretary of State, the Office of the Official Languages

---

*An original article written for this volume.
[1] *A Preliminary Report* (Ottawa: Queen's Printer, 1965), p. 13.
[2] See the 5-volume final *Report* of the Commission (Ottawa: Queen's Printer, 1969), especially Book 3A.
[3] *Statutes of Canada*, 1969, c. 54.

Commissioner, the Bilingual Districts Advisory Board and the individual departments and agencies.[4]

Despite all these efforts, bilingualism in the public service continues to be one of the most controversial public policy issues in Canada. The remainder of this essay will, therefore, examine four major areas of controversy surrounding the policy of bilingualism. These areas are the creation of bilingual districts, the target percentages of bilingual employees, the classification of public service positions into different linguistic categories and the establishment of French language working units, and the cost of bilingualism.

The Official Languages Act provides that areas where the linguistic minority forms at least ten percent of the population must be designated as federal bilingual districts for purposes of bilingual services. Although the government has so far established only one bilingual district (the National Capital Region), it is firmly committed to creating such districts across the country. However, public reaction, especially in English Canada, has been generally unfavourable to the recommendations of the Bilingual Districts Advisory Board with respect to those areas to be designated as bilingual districts.[5]

Some critics of the concept of bilingual districts contend that there is no pressing or universal need for such districts in Canada. The Commissioner of Official Languages has noted that opposition may also be due, in part, to the government's lacklustre information efforts and to distortions of the truth about bilingual districts by vocal groups that are opposed to bilingualism in general. Still other critics, including the Official Languages Commissioner, are concerned about the many practical and administrative obstacles to effective implementation of the concept. The Commissioner argues that (1) it will be extremely difficult to draw the boundaries of the districts so as to satisfy everyone; (2) bilingual districts will be psychologically disastrous to all linguistic groups within them in that the isolated minority language group may develop a ghetto mentality, the third language groups (including native peoples) may view the districts "as a consecration of their imagined 'inferior' status," and the irritation of the local majority language group may be increased; (3) the provinces and municipalities are not yet prepared to match federal bilingual services and the average citizen who does not readily distinguish between jurisdictions may view the federal bilingual districts as tokenism; (4) the gradual strengthening of the cultural infrastructure supporting French-speaking communities out-

---

[4]For an account of the responsibilities of these bodies, see Commissioner of Official Languages, *Second Annual Report, 1971-1972* (Ottawa: Information Canada, 1973), pp. 3-7.
[5]There have been two Advisory Boards. The first, chaired by Roger Duhamel, recommended in 1971 the creation of thirty-seven bilingual districts. The second, chaired by Professor Paul Fox, recently recommended the creation of thirty districts.

side Quebec may reduce the value of bilingual districts. On the basis of these and other arguments, the Commissioner has advocated that the concept of bilingual districts be substantially modified or abandoned altogether.[6]

The government has also established the following targets for the percentage of bilingual employees in the bilingual districts in each occupational category:

Category	Percentage
Executive	60
Administrative and Foreign Service	50
Administrative Support	35
Scientific and Professional	15
Technical	15
Operational	15

Originally, these target percentages were to be met by 1975 but, when this goal proved to be administratively unrealistic, the target date was changed to 1978.

The difficulty in achieving the original targets may be attributed primarily to the problems associated with the language training program in the public service. The Public Service Commission has been steadily expanding its language training facilities and now employs more than one thousand instructors in impressive facilities located not only in the National Capital Region but also in large cities across the country.

One major difficulty in laguage training has always been the absence of strong support from senior officials in certain departments and agencies for bilingualism in general and language training in particular. This lack of support prevents junior officials from taking full advantage of language training because it is the more senior officials who nominate them for these courses. A senior official has explained why some of his colleagues have not enthusiastically supported language training.

> Increased bilingualism (i.e., the ability to use both English and French effectively) in the federal service is a national policy that is widely accepted by federal managers as necessary for Canada's survival. Yet it creates a dilemma for the manager since he and his subordinates are required to take time from their regular duties in order to learn another language. This time must be dedicated to language training without any compensating reduction in workload and without the addition of compensating manpower. The goal of national unity therefore conflicts with a manager's drive for operational productivity. In the absence of clear and consistent guidance as to where day-to-day priorities lie, managers juggle their manpower around to fit in

---

[6]Commissioner of Official Languages, *Second Annual Report, 1971-1972* (Ottawa: Information Canada, 1973), pp. 29-31.

language training. "Being pulled off French" to help meet a pressing deadline is a common phenomenon that results from this ambiguity and conflict of priorities.[7]

More recently, departmental managers have been permitted to bring in temporary replacements for those on language courses. Also, the government has reduced drastically the practice of taking away thousands of public servants periodically for short language courses in favour of offering fewer courses of longer duration. Despite these improvements, the disruptions and delays caused by absences and new personnel remain.

The most serious problem which the language training program has encountered is the public servants' poor rate of progress in learning a second language. By 1975, over sixty thousand public servants had engaged in language training, but less than fifteen thousand had completed their courses successfully and about twelve thousand had dropped out of the language programs altogether.[8]

It is the opinion of influential and informed observers that the success of second language training programs depends heavily on the motivation of the trainees and on the opportunities to use the second language outside the classroom. However, there seems to be little motivation among public servants to master a second language except for career advancement. Even those who genuinely want to learn a second language for its own sake are often discouraged by the pressure of work between training sessions which makes their learning process a difficult one. Similarly, the insufficient opportunities for both language groups to use their newly acquired linguistic ability in the generally unilingual environment of the public service impedes development of a positive attitude toward language training. As a result of these and other weaknesses in the language training system, the Official Languages Commissioner has recently suggested that the federal government would serve better both public servants and taxpayers if it got out of language training and left the job to elementary and secondary schools, which might yield a far richer linguistic harvest.[9]

Another controversial area of the policy on bilingualism has been the government's decision to classify public service positions into four different linguistic categories and to establish unilingual French language work units in certain departments. By November 1974,

---

[7]H.L. Laframboise, "Administrative Reform in the Federal Public Service: Signs of a Saturation Psychosis," *Canadian Public Administration*, vol. 14, no. 3 (Fall, 1971), p. 309. For a detailed examination and critique of the government's language training programs, see Gilles Bibeau, *Report of the Independent Study on the Language Training Programmes of the Public Service of Canada*, 12 vol. (Ottawa, 1976).
[8]See Public Service Commission, *Annual Report*, 1970 to 1975.
[9]*Fifth Annual Report*, pp. 11-12 and 24-27.

language requirements were established for the 281 664 positions in the public service as follows:

Bilingual Positions	53 584 (19% of total)
French Positions	35 566 (13% of total)
English Positions	169 576 (60% of total)
English or French Optional Positions	22 938 (8% of total)[10]

Most of the criticism of this classification system has centred on the first two categories. It has been argued that bilingual positions have been created in a hurry and forced upon the public service without sufficient regard to possible consequences. The Public Service Alliance of Canada, the largest public employee union, contends that the problem of bilingualism in the public service has a geographic dimension and should therefore be tackled on a geographic and selective basis rather than on a service-wide basis. The Alliance has also denounced the government's policy of assigning an increasing number of top positions to French-speaking Canadians because this practice undermines the merit system of recruitment and promotion and compromises the careers of unilingual public servants who have been in the public service for many years. Moreover, the hasty creation of a large number of bilingual positions will necessitate the hiring of many French-speaking Canadians merely because they are French-speaking, without due regard to the need for French in the position or the real merit of the candidate.

The Bibeau Commission, on the basis of its detailed study of language training in the public service, reported that the hasty identification of bilingual positions has resulted in many methodological errors in the preparation of identification criteria. This situation has given rise to the designation of numerous bilingual positions which do not correspond to the real needs of Canadian society and the public service. The Commission therefore recommended an entire reworking of the identification of positions in terms of the language competence they really require.[11]

The creation of unilingual French language units has been equally contentious. A few units were created on an experimental basis in 1971 but their number has increased steadily. In 1974, there were 33 633 employees in these units of whom 11 percent were located in the National Capital Region, 87 percent in the Province of Quebec (excluding Hull) and 2 percent elsewhere in Canada or overseas.[12]

---

[10] *Report on Official Languages in the Public Service,* tabled in the House of Commons on November 21, 1974, by the president of the Treasury Board.
[11] Bibeau, *op. cit.,* vol. 1, pp. 54-59, 226-27.
[12] *Report on Official Languages in the Public Service,* tabled in the House of Commons on November 21, 1974.

In August 1975, the government announced that French language units will be created so that at least 10 percent of each department's supervisory personnel in four of the occupational groups — Executive, Administrative and Foreign Service, Scientific and Professional, and Technical — will be formed into units working in French. This figure will rise to at least 20 percent in the managerial departments such as Finance, the Treasury Board and the Privy Council Office.[13] This policy was adopted partly in response to the recommendation of the Official Languages Commissioner who has promoted the creation of more French language units to increase the representation of French Canadians in the public service.

The public service unions have opposed French language units from their very inception. They have argued first that the units will set back the general cause of bilingualism because whenever there are separate unilingual units, whether English or French, the truly bilingual person will be relegated to the background and obliged to act merely as translator. Secondly, when promotions within the units are determined, the merits of those outside the units will be ignored, and language should not be the most important factor in determining promotions anywhere in the public service. Thirdly, the units will lead to costly duplication of work and increased inefficiency resulting from inevitable slowdowns or breakdowns in communications. Fourthly, the establishment of these units will eventually "ghettoize" the public service — especially its French-speaking membership — and this will reinforce the divisions that already exist.

The final area of controversy over the language policy is its enormous and ever increasing cost. The cost of bilingualism seems already to have exceeded one billion dollars. An important item not included in this calculation is the cost of paying the salaries of thousands of public servants while they attend language courses. The Official Languages Commissioner has estimated that from now on the annual cost of bilingualism might amount to four or five hundred million dollars.[14] Those who criticize the language policy on economic grounds argue that it is unlikely that Canada ever will receive a reasonable return on this huge investment in bilingualism.

It is important to note that many of the criticisms of the language policy are unfair and incomplete in that they show only one side of the linguistic coin. There is much to be said on the other side as well.

In regard to bilingual districts, the Official Languages Commissioner, although he is not favourably disposed to the districts, has noted some of their advantages. First, bilingual districts would provide minority

---

[13]Statement in the House of Commons on August 6, 1975, by the president of the Treasury Board.
[14]*Fifth Annual Report, 1975*, p. 3.

language rights an unmistakable legal underpinning. Secondly, the districts would provide scattered language communities with a sense of security and symbolic recognition that the two official languages share equal status nationally. Thirdly, the districts would help educate local linguistic minority groups about their rights. Fourthly, with the 10 percent criterion for defining eligibility for bilingual services, the districts would eliminate the danger of the standards of "significant demand" and "feasibility" prescribed in the Official Languages Act being applied arbitrarily and inconsistently by local personnel. Fifthly, the districts, with their clearly demarcated boundaries, would help to clarify and confirm the role of the Languages Commissioner to defend the linguistic rights of those adversely affected.[15]

The requirement that the public service must serve the public in both English and French and the target percentages of bilingual employees pose very difficult problems for such governmental bodies as the Public Service Commission and the Treasury Board. These bodies strive to strengthen the bilingual capacity of the public service through large-scale language training programs for employees already in the service. Such measures as refining the methods of selecting trainees, improving teaching techniques, attracting more competent teachers and establishing well-equipped training centres will improve these programs. There are, however, no swift and simple solutions in sight for such serious language training problems as the trainees' lack of motivation, the inability of some trainees to learn a second language and the lukewarm support for language training from some senior officials.

Note should be taken also of the efforts of the Public Service Commission, before it embarked on the present ambitious training program, to enhance the bilingual capacity of the public service. These efforts involved the large-scale transfer of employees with necessary language skills to positions that required them and the recruitment of new employees who were already bilingual. These programs were inadequate, however, to meet the bilingual requirements of the public service within a reasonable period of time, and they affected adversely the career status of many existing employees who were unilingual.

The government is likely to continue its existing language training programs. However, to achieve an adequate bilingual capacity for the public service over the long run, it may be necessary to accept the Languages Commissioner's recommendation for a broad extension of second language teaching in primary and secondary schools across the country.

It is frequently argued that the general emphasis on bilingualism and in particular the classification of positions into linguistic categories has

---

[15]See *Second Annual Report, 1971-1972*, pp. 28-29 and *Fifth Annual Report, 1975*, pp. 16-19.

adversely affected the careers of unilingual employees. The government has taken measures to avoid this situation. The 1973 Parliamentary Resolution and the related Guidelines[16] promised protection of the job security and career prospects of unilingual employees, especially those who have devoted many years of their working lives to government service.

For example, according to the Resolution and Guidelines, a knowledge of both English and French is an important element in the selection of candidates for positions designated as bilingual. But unilingual candidates are permitted to compete on an equal footing with bilingual candidates for bilingual positions, provided that they indicate formally their willingness to become bilingual. If unilingual candidates are successful in such a competition, they are appointed on an interim basis and their appointment becomes permanent if they complete the training and meet the language standard for the position within one year. If the employee is unable to attain the required proficiency, he will be entitled to an appointment, at the rate of pay received during the conditional appointment, to another position for which he is qualified. If no such position is available, he will be appointed to a position which has a salary maximum at least within the range of one annual increment of the salary held when the conditional appointment was made. Then, if a position is still not available, a position will be created for the employee until an established position becomes available. The Resolution and Guidelines also provide important safeguards for unilingual incumbents of bilingual positions and for new entrants to the public service.

Employee unions, however, have received these guarantees with guarded optimism and, despite government assurances, have continued to express concern that the implementation of the provisions of the Resolution and Guidelines might still distort the principles and safeguards set out there.

It is too early to assess definitively the success of the unilingual French language units. In the government's view, however, these units have been very successful in achieving their two officially stated goals: (1) to enhance the recruitment of young unilingual Francophones by offering them the opportunity to work in their mother tongue and (2) to provide Anglophone public servants who have devoted many hours to learning French with an opportunity to solidify their newly acquired skill in an actual work situation. The Official Languages Commissioner has also commended the French language units for the encouragement and practical opportunity they provide for French-speaking Canadians to contribute to their country's public service in their own language.

Finally, it may be argued that the expenditure involved in

---

[16]See the June 1973 Parliamentary Resolution and the Treasury Board *Guidelines on Language Requirements*, June 29, 1973.

implementing the government's language policy is not excessive in view of the goal of national unity which the policy is designed to achieve. Many of those who oppose various parts of the language policy seem to be unmindful of certain historical and political realities of Canadian society and Canadian federalism.

CASE REFERENCES

Canadian Cases in Public Administration
  Dr. Stockfield's Resignation
  The Shared Authority
  B and B or Not
  Fear of Flying
  This Hour Has Seven Days
  The Foot and Mouth Disease Epidemic, 1952

Case Program in Canadian Public Administration
  L'Affaire "Caloil"

BIBLIOGRAPHY

Ashley, C.A. and Smails, R.G.H., *Canadian Crown Corporations*. Toronto, The Macmillan Company of Canada, 1965.

Balls, Herbert R., "Improving Performance of Public Enterprises Through Financial Management." *Canadian Public Administration*, Vol. 13, No. 1, Spring 1970, pp. 100-123.

Bowland, J.G., "Geographical Decentralization in the Canadian Federal Public Service." *Canadian Public Administration*, Vol. 10, No. 3, September 1967, pp. 323-361.

Bridges, The Right Hon. Lord, "The Relationships between Governments and Government-Controlled Corporations." *Canadian Public Administration*, Vol. 7, No. 3, September 1964, pp. 295-308.

Brown-John, C. Lloyd, "Defining Regulatory Agencies for Analytical Purposes." *Canadian Public Administration*, Vol. 19, No. 1, Spring 1976, pp. 140-57.

Bryden, Kenneth, "Executive and Legislature in Ontario: A Case Study on Governmental Reform." *Canadian Public Administration*, Vol. 18, No. 2, Summer 1975, pp. 235-52.

Canada, Royal Commission on Bilingualism and Biculturalism, *Report*. Vol. 3, Ottawa, Queen's Printer, 1967.

Canada, Royal Commission on Government Organization (Glassco Commission) *Report*: Vol. 1, *Management of the Public Service*, reports 1-4; Vol. 2, *Supporting Services for Government*, reports 5-11; Vol. 3, *Supporting Services for Government*, reports 12-13 and *Services for the Public*, reports 14-18; Vol. 4, *Special Areas of Administration*, reports 19-23; Vol. 5, *The Organization of the Government of Canada*. Ottawa, Queen's Printer, 1962-63.

Cloutier, Sylvain, "Senior Public Service Officials in a Bicultural Society." *Canadian Public Administration*, Vol. 11, No. 4, Winter 1968, pp. 395-406.

Cole, Taylor, *The Canadian Bureaucracy, 1939-1947*. Durham, N.C., Duke University Press, 1949.

Cole, Taylor, *The Canadian Bureaucracy and Federalism: 1947-1965*. Denver, Colorado, University of Denver Press, 1966.

Doern, G. Bruce *et al.*, "The Structure and Behaviour of Canadian Regulatory Boards and Commissions: Multidisciplinary Perspectives." *Canadian Public Administration*, Vol. 18, No. 2, Summer 1975, pp. 189-215.

Doern, G. Bruce, "The Teaching of Public Administration in Canadian Universities." In Kenneth Kernaghan, ed., *Executive Manpower in the Public Service: Make or Buy*. Toronto, Institute of Public Administration of Canada, 1975, pp. 80-102.

Fleck, James D., "Restructuring the Ontario Government." *Canadian Public Administration*, Vol. 16, No. 1, Spring 1973, pp. 55-68.

Garant, Patrice, *La fonction publique: canadienne et québecoise*. Québec: Les Presses de l'Université Laval, 1973.

Gélinas, André, "Le cadre général des institutions administratives et la déconcentration territoriale." *Canadian Public Administration*, Vol. 18, No. 2, Summer 1975, pp. 253-68.

Gélinas, André, "Trois modes d'approche à la détermination de l'opportunité de la décentralisation de l'organisation politique principalement en système fédéral." *Canadian Public Administration*, Vol. 9, No. 1, March 1966, pp. 1-26.

Gow, James Iain, ed., *Administration publique québecoise*. Montreal, Librairie Beauchemin, 1970.

Hanson, A.H., *Public Enterprise: A Study of its Organization and Management*. Brussels, International Institute of Administrative Sciences, 1956.

Hicks, Michael, "The Treasury Board of Canada and its Clients: Five Years of Change and Administrative Reform, 1966-71." *Canadian Public Administration*, Vol. 16, No. 2, Summer 1973, pp. 182-205.

Hodgetts, J.E., "The Public Service: Its Past and the Challenge of its Future." *Canadian Public Administration*, Vol. 17, No. 1, Spring 1974, pp 17-25

Hodgetts, J.E. and Corbett, D.C., eds., *Canadian Public Administration*. Toronto, The Macmillan Company of Canada, 1960.

Irvine, A.G., "The Delegation of Authority to Crown Corporations." *Canadian Public Administration*, Vol. 14, No. 4, Winter 1971, pp. 556-79.

Kernaghan, W.D.K., "An Overview of Public Administration in Canada Today." *Canadian Public Administration*, Vol. 11, No. 3, Fall 1968, pp. 291-308.

Kernaghan, W.D.K., ed., *Bureaucracy in Canadian Government*. Toronto, Methuen Publications, 1969.

Kuruvilla, P.K., "Administrative Culture in Canada: Some Perspectives." *Canadian Public Administration*, Vol. 16, No. 2, Summer 1973, pp. 284-297.

Kwavnick, D., "French Canadians and the Civil Service of Canada." *Canadian Public Administration*, Vol. 11, No. 1, Spring 1968, pp. 97-112.

Laframboise, H.L., "Portfolio Structure and a Ministry System: A Model for the Canadian Federal Service." *Optimum*, Vol. 1, No. 1, (1970), pp. 29-46.

Langford, John W., *Transport in Transition: The Reorganization of the Federal Transport Portfolio*. Montreal, McGill-Queen's University Press, 1976.

Paranteau, Roland, "Une nouvelle approche dans la formation des administrateurs publics: l'Ecole nationale d'administration publique." *Canadian Public Administration*, Vol. 15, No. 3, Fall 1972, pp. 465-480.

Phidd, R.W., "The Economic Council of Canada: Its Establishment, Structure and Role in the Canadian Policy-Making System, 1963-74." *Canadian Public Administration*, Vol. 18, No. 3, Fall 1975, pp. 428-73.

Porter, John, *The Vertical Mosaic: An Analysis of Social Class and Power in Canada*. Toronto, University of Toronto Press, 1965, chapter 14.

Pross, A. Paul and Wilson, V. Seymour, "Graduate Education in Canadian Public Administration: Antecedents, Present Trends and Portents," *Canadian Public Administration*, Vol. 19, No. 4, Winter 1976, pp. 515-541.

Schultz, Richard, "Intergovernmental Cooperation, Regulatory Agencies and Transportation Regulation in Canada: The Case of Part III of the National Transportation Act." *Canadian Public Administration*, Vol. 19, No. 2, Summer 1976, pp. 183-207.

Smiley, D.V. "The Structural Problem of Canadian Federalism." *Canadian Public Administration*, Vol. 14, No. 3, Fall 1971, pp. 326-343.

Yeomans, D.R., "Decentralization of Authority." *Canadian Public Administration*, Vol. 12, No. 1, Spring 1969, pp. 9-25.

CHAPTER 3
PROBLEMS OF MANAGEMENT

The essay in Chapter 1, by Gibson demonstrates the importance of effective utilization of human resources in organization and management. A key means of achieving this end is the successful motivation of employees. The motivation factor is central to the discussion in this chapter of closely related functions — leadership, decision making and communications.

Hersey and Blanchard begin this chapter with a review of the contributions to the present theory on motivation by Mayo, McGregor, Homans, Argyris, Herzberg and Likert. The usefulness of insights into employee motivation, however, depends largely on effective leadership. Thus, in the second selection, Felix Nigro outlines the two major approaches to leadership and the types of leadership styles.

The integral link between leadership and decision making is shown in the next essay by Herbert Simon. He explains the several stages of the decision-making process and draws the important distinction between programmed and non-programmed decisions. He then describes the traditional techniques for making these polar types of decisions and the new techniques for programmed decision making associated with operations research.

The motivation of workers, the application of the appropriate leadership style and the making of effective decisions depend in large part on the quality of communications within an organization. Indeed, in Felix Nigro's words, "it is frequently stated that communications and decision making are inseparable." Nigro demonstrates the central role of communications in management through a discussion of the direction of communications flow, measures to improve communications and the implications of an informal communications network.

In the final essay of this chapter, A.W. Johnson treats the important management problem of achieving efficiency in government and business. He follows an explanation of the concepts of "administrative," "policy" and "service" efficiency with an examination of the special difficulties of achieving an "efficiency motivation" in the public service.

9
Motivating Environment*

Paul Hersey and Kenneth H. Blanchard

In 1924 efficiency experts at the Hawthorne, Illinois, plant of the Western Electric Company designed a research program to study the effects of illumination on productivity. At first, nothing about this program seemed exceptional enough to arouse any unusual interest. After all, efficiency experts had long been trying to find the ideal mix of physical conditions, working hours, and working methods which stimulate workers to produce at maximum capacity. Yet, by the time these studies were completed (over a decade later), there was little doubt that the work at Hawthorne would stand the test of time as one of the most exciting and important research projects ever done in an industrial setting. For it was at Western Electric's Hawthorne plant that the Human Relations Movement began to gather momentum, and one of its early advocates, Elton Mayo of the Harvard Graduate School of Business Administration, gained recognition.[1]

ELTON MAYO'S HAWTHORNE STUDIES

In the initial study at Hawthorne, efficiency experts assumed that increases in illumination would result in higher output. Two groups of employees were selected: an *experimental* or *test group* which worked under varying degrees of light, and a *control group* which worked under normal illumination conditions in the plant. As lighting power was increased, the output of the test group went up as anticipated. Unexpectedly, however, the output of the control group went up also — without any increase in light.

Determined to explain these and other surprising test results, the efficiency experts decided to expand their research at Hawthorne. They felt that in addition to technical and physical changes, some of the behavioral considerations should be explored, so Mayo and his associates were called in to help.

Mayo and his team started their experiments with a group of girls

*Reprinted by permission from Paul Hersey and Kenneth H. Blanchard, *Management of Organizational Behaviour*, 2nd ed. (Englewood Cliffs, N.J.: Prentice-Hall, 1972), pp. 43-66.
[1] For detailed descriptions of this research see F.J. Roethlisberger and W.J. Dickson, *Management and the Worker* (Cambridge: Harvard University Press, 1939); T.N. Whitehead, *The Industrial Worker*, 2 vols. (Cambridge: Harvard University Press, 1938); Elton Mayo, *The Human Problems of an Industrial Civilization* (New York: The Macmillan Company, 1933).

who assembled telephone relays, and, like the efficiency experts, the Harvard men uncovered astonishing results. For over a year and a half during this experiment, Mayo's researchers improved the working conditions of the girls by implementing such innovations as scheduled rest periods, company lunches, and shorter work weeks. Baffled by the results, the researchers suddenly decided to take everything away from the girls, returning the working conditions to the exact way they had been at the beginning of the experiment. This radical change was expected to have a tremendous negative psychological impact on the girls and reduce their output. Instead, their output jumped to a new *all-time high*. Why?

The answers to this question were *not* found in the production aspects of the experiment (i.e., changes in plant and physical working conditions), but in the *human* aspects. As a result of the attention lavished upon them by experimenters, the girls were made to feel they were an important part of the company. They no longer viewed themselves as isolated individuals, working together only in the sense that they were physically close to each other. Instead they had become participating members of a congenial, cohesive work group. The relationships that developed elicited feelings of affiliation, competence, and achievement. These needs, which had long gone unsatisfied at work, were now being fulfilled. The girls worked harder and more effectively than they had worked previously.

Realizing that they had uncovered an interesting phenomenon, the Harvard team extended their research by interviewing over twenty thousand employees from every department in the company. Interviews were designed to help researchers find out what the workers thought about their jobs, their working conditions, their supervisors, their company, and anything that bothered them, and how these feelings might be related to their productivity. After several interview sessions, Mayo's group found that a structured question-and-answer-type interview was useless for eliciting the information they wanted. Instead, the workers wanted to talk freely about what *they* thought was important. So the predetermined questions were discarded, and the interviewer allowed the worker to ramble as he chose.

The interviews proved valuable in a number of ways. First of all, they were therapeutic; the workers got an opportunity to get a lot off their chests. Many felt this was the best thing the company had ever done. The result was a wholesale change in attitude. Since many of their suggestions were being implemented, the workers began to feel that management viewed them as important, both as individuals and as a group; they were now participating in the operation and future of the company and not just performing unchallenging, unappreciated tasks.

Second, the implications of the Hawthorne studies signaled the need for management to study and understand relationships among people. In these studies, as well as in the many that followed, the most significant factor affecting organizational productivity was found to be the interpersonal relationships that are developed on the job, not just pay and working conditions. Mayo found that when informal groups identified with management, as they did at Hawthorne through the interview program, productivity rose. The increased productivity seemed to reflect the workers' feelings of competence — a sense of mastery over the job and work environment. Mayo also discovered that when the group felt that their own goals were in opposition to those of management, as often happened in situations where the workers were closely supervised and had no significant control over their job or environment, productivity remained at low levels or was even lowered.

These findings were imporant because they helped answer many of the questions that had puzzled management about why some groups seemed to be high producers while others hovered at a minimal level of output. The findings also encouraged management to involve workers in planning, organizing, and controlling their own work in an effort to secure their positive cooperation.

Mayo saw the development of informal groups as an indictment of an entire society which treated human beings as insensitive machines that were concerned only with economic self-interest. As a result, workers had been taught to look at work merely as an impersonal exchange of money for labor. Work in American industry meant humiliation — the performance of routine, tedious, and oversimplified tasks in an environment over which one had no control. This environment denied satisfaction of esteem and self-actualization needs on the job. Instead only physiological and safety needs were satisfied. The lack of avenues for satisfying other needs led to tension, anxiety, and frustration in workers. Such feelings of helplessness were called "anomie" by Mayo. This condition was characterized by workers feeling unimportant, confused, and unattached — victims of their own environment.

While anomie was a creation of the total society, Mayo felt its most extreme application was found in industrial settings where management held certain negative assumptions about the nature of man. According to Mayo, too many managers assumed that society consisted of a horde or mob of unorganized individuals whose only concern was self-preservation or self-interest. It was assumed that people were primarily dominated by physiological and safety needs, wanting to make as much money as they could for as little work as possible. Thus, management operated and organized work on the basic assumption that workers, on the whole, were a contemptible lot. Mayo called this assumption the

"Rabble Hypothesis." He deplored the authoritarian, task-oriented management practices that it created.

DOUGLAS McGREGOR'S THEORY X AND THEORY Y

The work of Mayo and particularly his exposure of the Rabble Hypothesis may have paved the way for the development of the now classic "Theory X — Theory Y" by Douglas McGregor.[2] According to McGregor, traditional organization with its centralized decision making, superior-subordinate pyramid, and external control of work is based upon assumptions about human nature and human motivation. These assumptions are very similar to the view of man defined by Mayo in the Rabble Hypothesis. Theory X assumes that most people prefer to be directed, are not interested in assuming responsibility, and want safety above all. Accompanying this philosophy is the belief that people are motivated by money, fringe benefits, and the threat of punishment.

Managers who accept Theory X assumptions attempt to structure, control, and closely supervise their employees. These managers feel that external control is clearly appropriate for dealing with unreliable, irresponsible, and immature people.

After describing Theory X, McGregor questioned whether this view of man is correct and if management practices based upon it are appropriate in many situations today: Isn't man in a democratic society, with its increasing level of education and standard of living, capable of more mature behavior? Drawing heavily on Maslow's hierarchy of needs, McGregor concluded that Theory X assumptions about the nature of man are generally inaccurate and that management approaches that develop from these assumptions will often fail to motivate individuals to work toward organizational goals. Management by direction and control may not succeed, according to McGregor, because it is a questionable method for motivating people whose physiological and safety needs are reasonably satisfied and whose social, esteem, and self-actualization needs are becoming predominant.

McGregor felt that management needed practices based on a more accurate understanding of the nature of man and human motivation. As a result of his feeling, McGregor developed an alternate theory of human behavior called Theory Y. This theory assumes that people are *not*, by nature, lazy and unreliable. It postulates that man can be basically self-directed and creative at work if properly motivated. Therefore, it should be an essential task of management to unleash this potential in man. The

---

[2]Douglas McGregor, *The Human Side of Enterprise* (New York: McGraw-Hill Book Company, 1960). See also McGregor, *Leadership and Motivation* (Boston: MIT Press, 1966).

properly motivated worker can achieve his own goals *best* by directing *his own* efforts toward accomplishing organizational goals.

TABLE 1

List of Assumptions About Nature of Man which Underline McGregor's Theory X and Theory Y

Theory X	Theory Y
1. Work is inherently distasteful to most people.	1. Work is as natural as play, if the conditions are favorable.
2. Most people are not ambitious, have little desire for responsibility, and prefer to be directed.	2. Self-control is often indispensable in achieving organizational goals.
3. Most people have little capacity for creativity in solving organizational problems.	3. The capacity for creativity in solving organizational problems is widely distributed in the population.
4. Motivation occurs only at the physiological and safety levels.	4. Motivation occurs at the social, esteem, and self-actualization levels, as well as physiological and security levels.
5. Most people must be closely controlled and often coerced to achieve organizational objectives.	5. People can be self-directed and creative at work if properly motivated.

Managers who accept the Theory Y image of human nature do *not* usually structure, control, or closely supervise the work environment for employees. Instead they attempt to help their employees mature by exposing them to progressively less external control, allowing them to assume more and more self-control. Employees are able to achieve the satisfaction of social, esteem, and self-actualization needs within this kind of environment, often neglected on the job. To the extent that the job does not provide need satisfaction at every level, today's employee will usually look elsewhere for significant need satisfaction. This helps explain some of the current problems management is facing in such areas as turnover and absenteeism. McGregor argues that this does not have to be the case.

Management is interested in work, and McGregor feels that work is as natural and can be as satisfying for people as play. After all, both work and play are physical and mental activities; consequently, there is no inherent difference between work and play. In reality, though, particularly under Theory X management, a distinct difference in need satisfaction is discernible. Whereas play is internally controlled by the individual (he decides what he wants to do), work is externally controlled by others (the worker has no control over his job). Thus, management and its assumptions about the nature of man have built in a difference between work and play that seems unnatural. As a result, people are stifled at work and hence look for excuses to spend more and more time away from the job in order to satisfy their esteem and self-actualization needs (provided they have enough money to satisfy their physiological and safety needs). Because of their conditioning to Theory X types of management, most employees consider work a *necessary evil* rather than a source of personal challenge and satisfaction.

Does work really have to be a necessary evil? No — especially in organizations where cohesive work groups have developed and where the goals parallel organizational goals. In such organizations there is high productivity, and people come to work gladly because work is inherently satisfying.

GEORGE C. HOMANS'S HUMAN GROUP THEORY

Management is often suspicious of strong informal work groups because of their potential power to control the behavior of their members and, as a result, the level of productivity. Where do these groups get their power to control behavior? George C. Homans has developed a model of social systems which may be useful to the practitioner trying to answer this question.[3]

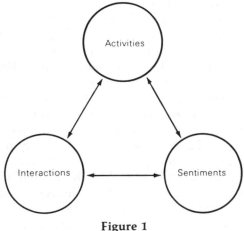

Figure 1
The Mutual Dependence of Activities,
Interactions and Sentiments

There are three elements in a social system. *Activities* are the tasks that people perform. *Interactions* are the behaviors that occur between people in performing these tasks. And *sentiments* are the attitudes that develop between individuals and within groups. Homans argues that while these concepts are separate, they are closely related. In fact, as Figure 1 illustrates, they are mutually dependent upon each other.

---

[3]George C. Homans, *The Human Group* (New York: Harcourt, Brace & World, Inc., 1950).

A change in any of these three elements will produce some change in the other two.

In an organization certain activities, interactions, and sentiments are essential, or required from its members, if it is to survive. In other words, jobs (activities) have to be done that require people to work together (interactions). These jobs must be sufficiently satisfying (sentiments) for people to continue doing them. As people interact on their jobs, they develop sentiments toward each other. As people increase interaction with each other, more positive sentiments will tend to develop toward each other. The more positive the sentiment, the more people will tend to interact with each other. It can become a spiraling process until some equilibrium is reached. As this spiraling process continues, there is a tendency for the group members to become more alike in their activities and sentiments — in what they do and how they feel about things. As this happens, the group tends to develop expectations or norms that specify how people in the group "might" tend to behave under specific circumstances. For example, a group of workers might have a norm that "you should not talk to the boss, or help him, any more than necessary." If the group is cohesive enough, that is, the group is attractive to its members and they are reluctant to leave it, then it will have little trouble in getting members to conform. People who deviate significantly from group norms usually incur sanctions from the group. "The group has at its disposal a variety of penalties, ranging from gentle kidding to harsh ostracism, for pressuring deviant members into line."[4] The group member may react in several ways. He may decide to go ahead and continue to deviate from group norms. If the resulting pressure from his peers becomes too great, he may leave the group.

The influence group pressures can have in achieving conformity in the perceptions and behavior of people is well documented. For example, S.E. Asch conducted a classic experiment in which groups of eight college men were each asked to match the length of a line with one of three unequal lines.[5] Seven members of each group were privately told to give the same incorrect answer. The uninstructed member was the last one asked to give his answer and was thus confronted with the dilemma of either reporting what he saw as being correct or reporting what all the others had said in order to be congruent with the group. Asch reported that "one-third of all the estimates were errors identical with or in the direction of the distorted estimates of the majority."[6] If pressure can

---

[4]Anthony G. Athos and Robert E. Coffey, *Behavior in Organizations: A Multi-dimensional View* (Englewood Cliffs, N.J.: Prentice-Hall, Inc., 1968), p. 101.
[5]S.E. Asch, "Effects of Group Pressure upon the Modification and Distortion of Judgments," in *Groups, Leadership and Men,* ed. Harold Guetzkow (New York: Russell and Russell Publishers, 1963), pp. 177-90. Also in Dorwin Cartwright and Alvin Zander, *Group Dynamics,* 2nd ed. (Evanston, Ill.: Row, Peterson & Company, 1960), pp. 189-200.
[6]*Ibid.*

cause distorted behavior in this kind of exercise, imagine what peer group pressure can induce with more subjective judgments.

It should be reiterated that strong informal work groups do not have to be a detriment to organizations. In fact, as Mayo discovered at Hawthorne, these groups can become powerful driving forces in accomplishing organizational goals if they see their own goals as being satisfied by working for organizational goals.

CHRIS ARGYRIS'S IMMATURITY-MATURITY THEORY

Even though management based on the assumptions of Theory X is perhaps no longer appropriate in the opinion of McGregor and others, it is still widely practiced. Consequently, a large majority of the people today are treated as immature human beings in their working environments. It is this fact that has produced many of our current organizational problems. Chris Argyris, while at Yale University, examined industrial organizations to determine what effect management practices have had on individual behavior and personal growth within the work environment.[7]

According to Argyris, seven changes should take place in the personality of an individual if he is to develop into a mature person over the years.

First, an individual moves from a passive state as an infant to a state of increasing activity as an adult. Second, an individual develops from a state of dependency upon others as an infant to a state of relative independence as an adult. Third, an individual behaves in only a few ways as an infant, but as an adult, he is capable of behaving in many ways. Fourth, an individual has erratic, casual, and shallow interests as an infant but develops deeper and stronger interests as an adult. Fifth, a child's time perspective is very short, involving only the present, but as he matures, his time perspective increases to include the past and the future. Sixth, an individual as an infant is subordinate to everyone, but he moves to equal or superior position with others as an adult. Seventh, as a child, an individual lacks an awareness of a "self," but as an adult, he is not only aware of, but he is able to control "self." Argyris postulates that these changes reside on a continuum and that the "healthy" personality develops along the continuum from "immaturity" to "maturity."

These changes are only general tendencies, but they give some light to the matter of maturity. Norms of the individual's culture and personality inhibit and limit maximum expression and growth of the adult, yet the tendency is to move toward the "maturity" end of the

---

[7]Chris Argyris, *Personality and Organization* (New York: Harper & Row, Publishers, 1957); *Interpersonal Competence and Organizational Effectiveness* (Homewood, Ill.: Dorsey Press, 1962); and *Integrating the Individual and the Organization* (New York: John Wiley & Sons, Inc., 1964).

continuum with age. Argyris would be the first to admit that few, if any, develop to full maturity.

TABLE 2
Immaturity-Maturity Continuum

Immaturity	Maturity
Passive	Active
Dependence	Independence
Behave in a few ways	Capable of behaving in many ways
Erratic shallow interests	Deeper and stronger interests
Short time perspective	Long time perspective (past and future)
Subordinate position	Equal or superordinate position
Lack of awareness of self	Awareness and control over self

In examining the widespread worker apathy and lack of effort in industry, Argyris questions whether these problems are simply the result of individual laziness. He suggests that this is *not* the case. Argyris contends that, in many cases, when people join the work force, they are kept from maturing by the management practices utilized in their organizations. In these organizations, they are given minimal control over their environment and are encouraged to be passive, dependent, and subordinate; therefore, they behave immaturely. The worker in many organizations is expected to act in immature ways rather than as a mature adult.

According to Argyris, keeping people immature is built into the very nature of the formal organization. He argues that because organizations are usually created to achieve goals or objectives that can best be met collectively, the formal organization is often the architect's conception of how these objectives may be achieved. In this sense the individual is fitted to the job. The design comes first. This design is based upon four concepts of scientific management: task specialization, chain of command, unity of direction, and span of control. Management tries to increase and enhance organizational and administrative efficiency and productivity by making workers "interchangeable parts."

Basic to these concepts is that power and authority should rest in the hands of a few at the top of the organization, and thus those at the lower end of the chain of command are strictly controlled by their superiors or the system itself. Task specialization often results in the oversimplification of the job so that it becomes repetitive, routine, and unchallenging. This implies directive, task-oriented leadership where decisions about the work are made by the superior, with the workers only carrying out those decisions. This type of leadership evokes managerial controls such as budgets, some incentive systems, time and motion studies, and standard operating procedures which can restrict the initiative and creativity of workers.

Argyris feels that these concepts of formal organization lead to assumptions about human nature that are incompatible with the proper development of maturity in human personality. He sees a definite incongruity between the needs of a mature personality and the formal organizations as they now exist. Since he implies that the classical theory of management (based on Theory X' assumptions) usually prevails, management creates childlike roles for workers that frustrate natural development.

An example of how work is often designed at this extremely low level was dramatically illustrated by the successful use of mentally retarded workers in such jobs. Argyris cites two instances, one in a knitting mill and the other in a radio manufacturing corporation in which mentally retarded people were successfully employed on unskilled jobs. In both cases, the managers praised these workers for their excellent performance. In fact, a manager in the radio corporation reported:

> The girls proved to be exceptionally well-behaved, particularly obedient, and strictly honest and trustworthy. They carried out work required of them to such a degree of efficiency that *we were surprised they were classed as subnormals for their age.* Their attendance was good, and their behavior was, if anything, certainly better than that of any other employee of the same age.[8]

Disturbed by what he finds in many organizations, Argyris, as did McGregor, challenges management to provide a work climate in which everyone has a chance to grow and mature as an individual, as a member of a group by satisfying his own needs, while working for the success of the organization. Implicit here is the belief that man can be basically self-directed and creative at work if properly motivated, and, therefore, management based on the assumption of Theory Y will be more profitable for the individual and the organization.

More and more companies are starting to listen to the challenge that Agryris is directing at management. For example, the president of a large company asked Argyris to show him how to better motivate his workers. Together they went into one of his production plants where a product similar to a radio was being assembled. There were twelve girls involved in assembling the product, each doing a small segment of the job as designed by an industrial engineer. The group also had a foreman, an inspector, and a packer.

Argyris proposed a one-year experiment during which each of the girls would assemble the total product in a manner of her own choice. At the same time they would inspect, sign their name to the product, pack it, and handle any correspondence involving complaints about it. The girls were assured that they would receive no cut in pay if production dropped but would receive more pay if production increased.

---

[8]N. Breman, *The Making of a Moron* (New York: Sheed & Ward, 1953).

Once the experiment began, production dropped 70 percent during the first month. By the end of six weeks it was even worse. The girls were upset, morale was down. This continued until the eighth week, when production started to rise. By the end of the fifteenth week production was higher than it had ever been before. And this was without an inspector, a packer, or an industrial engineer. More important than increased productivity, costs due to errors and waste decreased 94 percent; letters of complaint dropped 96 percent.

Experiments like this are being duplicated in numerous other situations.[9] It is being found over and over again that broadening individual responsibility is beneficial to both the workers and the company. Giving people the opportunity to grow and mature on the job helps them satisfy more than just physiological and safety needs, which, in turn, motivates then and allows them to use more of their potential in accomplishing organizational goals. While all workers do *not* want to accept more responsibility or deal with the added problems responsibility inevitably brings, Argyris contends that the number of employees whose motivation can be improved by increasing and upgrading their responsibility is much larger than most managers would suspect.

FREDERICK HERZBERG'S MOTIVATION-HYGIENE THEORY

As people mature, we have noted that needs such as esteem and self-actualization seem to become more important. One of the most interesting series of studies that concentrates heavily on these areas was directed by Frederick Herzberg of Case-Western Reserve University.[10] Out of these studies has developed a theory of work motivation which has broad implications for management and its efforts toward effective utilization of human resources.

Herzberg, in developing his motivation-hygiene theory, seemed to sense that scholars like McGregor and Argyris were touching on something important. Knowledge about the nature of man, his motives and needs, could be invaluable to organizations and individuals.

> To industry, the payoff for a study of job attitudes would be increased productivity, decreased absenteeism, and smoother working relations. To the individual, an understanding of the forces that lead to improved morale would bring greater happiness and greater self-realization.[11]

Herzberg set out to collect data on job attitudes from which

---

[9]For other examples of successful interventions, see Argyris, *Intervention Theory and Method: A Behavioral Science View* (Reading, Mass.: Addison-Wesley Publishing Company, 1970).
[10]Frederick Herzberg, Bernard Mausner, and Barbara Synderman, *The Motivation to Work* (New York: John Wiley & Sons, Inc., 1959); and Herzberg, *Work and the Nature of Man* (New York: World Publishing Co., 1966).
[11]Herzberg, Mausner, and Snyderman, *The Motivation to Work*, p. ix.

assumptions about human behavior could be made. The motivation-hygiene theory resulted from the analysis of an initial study by Herzberg and his colleagues at the Psychological Service of Pittsburgh. This study involved extensive interviews with some two hundred engineers and accountants from eleven industries in the Pittsburgh area. In the interviews, they were asked about what kinds of things on their job made them unhappy or dissatisfied and what things made them happy or satisfied.

In analyzing the data from these interviews, Herzberg concluded that man has two different categories of needs which are essentially independent of each other and affect behavior in different ways. He found that when people felt dissatisfied with their jobs, they were concerned about the environment in which they were working. On the other hand, when people felt good about their jobs, this had to do with the work itself. Herzberg called the first category of needs *hygiene factors* because they describe man's environment and serve the primary function of preventing job dissatisfaction. He called the second category of needs *motivators* since they seemed to be effective in motivating people to superior performance.

Hygiene Factors

Company policies and administration, supervision, working conditions, interpersonal relations, money, status, and security may be thought of as hygiene factors. These are not an intrinsic part of a job, but they are related to the conditions under which a job is performed. Herzberg relates his use of the word "hygiene" to its medical meaning (preventative and environmental). Hygiene factors produce no growth in worker output capacity; they only prevent losses in worker performance due to work restriction.

Motivators

Satisfying factors that involve feelings of achievement, professional growth, and recognition that one can experience in a job that offers challenge and scope are referred to as motivators. Herzberg used this term because these factors seem capable of having a positive effect on job satisfaction often resulting in an increase in one's total output capacity.

In recent years motivation-hygiene research has been extended well beyond scientists and accountants to include every level of an organization from top management all the way down to hourly employees. For example, in an extensive study of Texas Instruments, Scott Meyers concluded that Herzberg's motivation-hygiene theory "is easily translatable to supervisory action at all levels of responsibility. It is a framework on which supervisors can evaluate and put into perspective the constant barrage of 'helpful hints' to which they are subjected, and hence serves to increase their feelings of competence, self-confidence, and autonomy."[12]

TABLE 3
Motivation and Hygiene Factors

Hygiene Factors Environment	Motivators The Job Itself
Policies and administration	Achievement
Supervision	Recognition for accomplishment
Working conditions	Challenging work
Interpersonal relations	Increased responsibility
Money, status, security	Growth and development

Herzberg's framework seems compatible with Maslow's hierarchy of needs. Maslow refers to needs or motives, while Herzberg seems to deal with the goals or incentives that tend to satisfy these needs. Examples can be cited. Money and benefits tend to satisfy needs at the physiological and security levels; interpersonal relations and supervision are examples of hygiene factors that tend to satisfy social needs, while increased responsibility, challenging work, and growth and development are motivators that tend to satisfy needs at the esteem and self-actualization levels.

Figure 2 shows the relationship between these two frameworks.

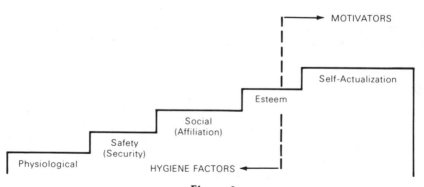

Figure 2
The Relationships Between the Motivation-Hygiene
Theory and Maslow's Hierarchy of Needs

---

[12]Scott M. Meyers, "Who Are Your Motivated Workers," in David R. Hampton, *Behavioral Concepts in Management* (Belmont, Calif.: Dickenson Publishing Co., Inc., 1968), p. 64. Originally published in *Harvard Business Review*, January-February 1964, pp. 73-88.

We feel that the physiological, safety, social, and part of the esteem needs are all hygiene factors. The esteem needs are divided because there are some distinct differences between status per se and recognition. Status tends to be a function of the position one occupies. One may have gained this position through family ties or social pressures, and thus this position is not a reflection of personal achievement or earned recognition. Recognition is gained through competence and achievement. It is earned and granted by others. Consequently, status is classified with physiological, safety, and social needs as a hygiene factor, while recognition is classified with self-actualization as a motivator.

Perhaps an example will further differentiate between hygiene factors and motivators. This might help explain the reason for classifying needs as Herzberg has done as well as in a hierarchical arrangement.

Let us assume that a man is highly motivated and is working at 90 percent of capacity. He has a good working relationship with his supervisor, is well satisfied with his pay and working conditions, and is part of a congenial work group. Suppose his supervisor is suddenly transferred and replaced by a person he is unable to work with, or he finds out that someone whose work he feels is inferior to his own is receiving more pay. How do these factors affect a man's behavior? Since we know performance or productivity depends on both ability and motivation, these unsatisfied hygiene needs (supervision and money) may lead to restriction of output. In some cases this is intentional, while in others the individual may not be consciously aware that he is holding back. In either case, though, productivity will be lowered as illustrated in Figure 3.

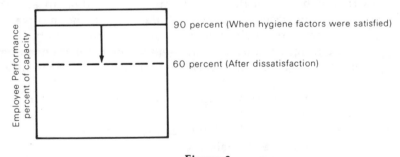

90 percent (When hygiene factors were satisfied)

60 percent (After dissatisfaction)

Employee Performance percent of capacity

Figure 3
Effect of Dissatisfying Hygienes

In this illustration, even if his former supervisor returns and his salary is readjusted well above his expectations, his productivity will probably increase only to its orginal level.

Conversely, let us take the same person and assume that

dissatisfaction has not occurred; he is working at 90 percent capacity. Suppose he is given an opportunity to mature and satisfy his motivational needs in an environment where he is free to exercise some initiative and creativity, to make decisions, to handle problems, and to take responsibility. What effect will this situation have on this individual? If he is able to successfully fulfill his supervisor's expectations in performing these new responsibilities, he may still work at 90 percent capacity, but as a person he may have matured and grown in his ability and may be capable now of more productivity, as illustrated in Figure 4.

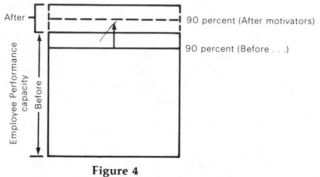

Figure 4
Effect of Satisfying Motivators

Hygiene needs, when satisfied, tend to eliminate dissatisfaction and work restriction but do little to motivate an individual to superior performance or increased capacity. Satisfaction of the motivators, however, will permit an individual to grow and develop in a mature way, often implementing an increase in ability. Herzberg encourages management to design into the work environment an opportunity to satisfy the motivators.

Prior to Herzberg's work, many other behavioral scientists were concerned with worker motivation. For several years there was an emphasis on what was termed "job enlargement." This was purported to be an answer to the overspecialization that had characterized many industrial organizations. The assumption was that a worker could gain more satisfaction at work if his job was enlarged, that is, if the number of operations in which he engaged was increased.

Herzberg makes some astute observations about this trend. He claims that doing a snippet of this and a snippet of that does not necessarily result in motivation. Washing dishes, then silverware, and then pots and pans does no more to satisfy and provide an opportunity to grow than washing only dishes. What we really need to do with work,

Herzberg suggests, is to *enrich* the job. By job enrichment is meant the deliberate upgrading of responsibility, scope, and challenge in work.

RENSIS LIKERT'S MANAGEMENT SYSTEMS

Most managers, if asked what they would do if they suddenly lost half of their plant, equipment, or capital resources, are quick to answer. Insurance or borrowing are often avenues open to refurbish plant, equipment, or capital. Yet when these same managers are asked what they would do if they suddenly lost half of their human resources — managers, supervisors, and hourly employees — they are at a loss for words. There is no insurance against outflows of human resources. Recruiting, training, and developing large numbers of new personnel into a working team takes years. In a competitive environment this is almost an impossible task. Organizations are only beginning to realize that their most important assets are human resources and that the managing of these resources is one of their most crucial tasks.

Rensis Likert and his colleagues of the Institute for Social Research at the University of Michigan emphasized the need to consider both human resources and capital resources as assets requiring proper management.[13] As a result of behavioral research studies of numerous organizations, Likert implemented organizational change programs in various industrial settings. It appears these programs were intended to help organizations move from Theory X to Theory Y assumptions, from fostering immature behavior to encouraging and developing mature behavior, from emphasizing only hygiene factors to recognizing and helping workers to satisfy the motivators.

Likert in his studies found that the prevailing management styles of organization can be depicted on a continuum from System 1 through System 4. These systems might be described as follows.

System 1

Management is seen as having no confidence or trust in subordinates, since they are seldom involved in any aspect of the decision-making process. The bulk of the decisions and the goal setting of the organization are made at the top and issued down the chain of command. Subordinates are forced to work with fear, threats, punishment, and occasional rewards and need satisfaction at the physiological and safety levels. The little superior-subordinate interaction that does take place is usually with fear and mistrust. While the control process is highly concentrated in top management, an informal organization generally develops which opposes the goals of the formal organization.

[13]Rensis Likert, *The Human Organization* (New York: McGraw-Hill Book Company 1967); see also Likert, *New Patterns of Management* (New York: McGraw-Hill Book Company, 1961).

System 2

Management is seen as having condescending confidence and trust in subordinates, such as master has toward servant. While the bulk of the decisions and goal setting of the organization are made at the top, many decisions are made within a prescribed framework at lower levels. Rewards and some actual or potential punishment are used to motivate workers. Any superior-subordinate interaction takes place with some condescension by superiors and fear and caution by subordinates. While the control process is still concentrated in top management, some is delegated to middle and lower levels. An informal organization usually develops, but it does not always resist formal organizational goals.

System 3

Management is seen as having substantial but not complete confidence and trust in subordinates. While broad policy and general decisions are kept at the top, subordinates are permitted to make more specific decisions at lower levels. Communication flows both up and down the hierarchy. Rewards, occasional punishment, and some involvement are used to motivate workers. There is a moderate amount of superior-subordinate interaction, often with a fair amount of confidence and trust. Significant aspects of the control process are delegated downward with a feeling of responsibility at both higher and lower levels. An informal organization may develop, but it may either support or partially resist goals of the organization.

System 4

Management is seen as having complete confidence and trust in subordinates. Decision making is widely dispersed throughout the organization, although well integrated. Communication flows not only up and down the hierarchy but among peers. Workers are motivated by participation and involvement in developing economic rewards, setting goals, improving methods, and appraising progress toward goals. There is extensive, friendly superior-subordinate interaction with a high degree of confidence and trust. There is widespread responsibility for the control process, with the lower units fully involved. The informal and formal organizations are often one and the same. Thus, all social forces support efforts to achieve stated organizational goals.[14]

In summary, System 1 is a task-oriented, highly structured authoritarian management style, while System 4 is a realtionships-oriented management style based on teamwork, mutual trust, and confidence. Systems 2 and 3 are intermediate stages between two extremes which approximate closely Theory X and Theory Y assumptions.

---

[14]Descriptions adapted from Likert, *The Human Organization*, pp. 4-10.

To expedite the analysis of a company's present behavior, Likert's group developed an instrument which enables members to rate their organization in terms of its management system. This instrument is designed to gather data about a number of operating characteristics of an organization. These characteristics include leadership, motivation, communication, decision making, interaction and influence, goal setting, and the control process used by the organization.

In testing this instrument, Likert asked hundreds of managers from many different organizations to indicate where the *most* productive department, division, or organization they have known would fall between System 1 and System 4. Then these same managers were asked to repeat this process and indicate the position of the *least* productive department, division, or organization they have known. While the ratings of the most and the least productive departments varied among managers, almost without exception each manager rated the high-producing unit closer to System 4 than the low-producing department. In summary, Likert has found that the closer the management style of an organization approaches System 4, the more likely it is to have a continuous record of high productivity. Similarly, the closer this style reflects System 1, the more likely it is to have a sustained record of low productivity.

Likert has also used this instrument not only to measure what an individual believes are the present characteristics of his organization but also to find out what he would like these characteristics to be. Data generated from this use of the instrument with managers of well-known companies have indicated a large discrepancy between the management system they feel their company is now using and the management system they feel would be most appropriate. System 4 is seen as being most appropriate, but few see their companies presently utilizing this approach. These implications have led to attempts by some organizations to adapt their management system to more closely approximate System 4. Changes of this kind are not easy. They involve a massive reeducation of all concerned from the top management to the hourly workers.

SUMMARY AND CONCLUSIONS

We have tried through the material presented to examine what is known today about understanding and motivating employees. The attempt has been to review theoretical literature, empirical research, and case examples with the intention of integrating these sources into frameworks which may be useful to managers for analyzing and understanding behavior. Analyzing and understanding are necessary, but the real value of the application of the behavioral sciences will be their usefulness in directing, changing, and controlling behavior.

10
Leadership*

Felix A. Nigro

Frequently the complaint is heard that an organization "lacks leader-ship." What is meant is that action of some sort should have been taken, but no one assumed the initiative in trying to get others to see the need for action, and thus nothing was accomplished. In other cases, the criticism is that the organization does not have "good leadership." Decisions are made and action taken, but those responsible for persuading others to accept their ideas led them in the wrong direction. These statements reveal both the *nature* and the importance of leadership. The essence of leadership is influencing the actions of others. Where the attempt to exercise such influence is not even made, there is a default of leadership. Where the attempt is made and others are persuaded to agree to certain action but the anticipated results do not materialize, the consequences may be serious for the organization.

APPROACHES TO LEADERSHIP

The Trait Approach

Not too long ago even learned, as distinguished from popular, discussions of leadership had a certain mystic quality. The leader was conceived of as someone blessed with certain qualities which made it relatively easy for him to bend others to his will. Nobody was really sure of the exact complement of leader personality traits, but it was generally assumed that many of these characteristics were inherited. Today most social scientists are convinced that the trait approach to leadership is fallacious, because those conducting research on the qualities of leaders have been unable to agree on what those qualities are. In 1940, one scholar compiled a long list of traits which were identified in one or more studies as distinguishing characteristics of leaders as opposed to nonleaders. Only about five percent of these traits, however, were common to four or more of the studies. Such a low percentage of agreement could hardly substantiate the claim that leaders basically have the same personality characteristics. Examination of the research conducted since 1940 has shown the same lack of consistency in the findings on leadership qualities.[1] Cartwright and Zander summarize the present state of knowledge as follows:

*Reprinted by permission from F.A. Nigro, *Modern Public Administration* (New York: Harper & Row, 1965), pp. 252-280.
[1]Dorwin Cartwright and Alvin Zander (eds.), *Group Dynamics, Research and Theory,* 2nd ed., Harper & Row, New York, 1960, p. 490.

On the whole, investigators in this field are coming to the conclusion that, while certain minimal abilities are required of all leaders, these are also widely distributed among non-leaders as well. Furthermore, the traits of the leader which are necessary and effective in one group or situation may be quite different from those of another leader in a different setting. This conclusion, if adequately substantiated, would imply that the selection of leaders must consider a man's suitability for the type of functions he is to perform in a given situation and it would raise questions about the desirability of formal arrangements which maintain the responsibilities of leadership in the same person regardless of the changing task of the group and the changing requirements upon leaders.[2]

The Situation Approach

Accordingly, most writers now support this situational approach, although actually it is not new. Long before the term "situational approach" came into usage, Mary Parker Follett was calling attention to the emergence in American life of "leadership by function." In the late 1920s, this wise lady, whose writings are classics in management literature, gave several lectures on leadership.[3] In these lectures, she noted that in scientifically managed organizations three types of leadership could be distinguished: the leadership of position, of personality, and of function. There was nothing new about the first two, because they represented the accepted views on leadership. The man holding a position which gave him formal authority over others obviously could make himself a leader. If he had a forceful personality, he could do this much more easily. This kind of individual combined the leadership of position with that of personality.

Something was absent, however, in such a conception of leadership. It failed to take into account the possibility that some persons, in fact quite a few in modern specialized organizations, exercised leadership because of their expert knowledge. The organization depended on them to give sound technical advice to their superiors. In many situations these experts actually did the "leading", because others were influenced by their judgments. Miss Follett stressed that "we have people giving what are practically orders to those of higher rank. The balance of stores clerk, as he is called in some places, will tell the man in charge of purchasing when to act. The dispatch clerk can give 'orders' even to the superintendent. The leadership of function is inherent in the job and as such is respected by the president of the plant." She noted that "the man possessing the knowledge demanded by a certain situation tends in the

[2] Ibid., p. 491. See also Robert G. Wall and Hugh Hawkins, "Requisites of Effective Leadership", Personnel, Vol. 39, No. 3, May-June 1962, pp. 21-28.
[3] See Mary Parker Follett, "Some Discrepancies in Leadership Theory and Practice", in Henry C. Metcalfe and L. Urwick (eds.), Dynamic Administration, Harper & Row, New York, 1940, pp. 270-294. See also in this same collection of her papers the essay, "Leader and Expert", pp. 247-269.

best managed businesses, and other things being equal, to become the leader at that moment."[4]

A distinction must be made between *formal* and *effective* authority. Formal authority is the basis for what Miss Follett called leadership of position. Sometimes someone in a position of formal authority is unable to persuade others to accept his ideas. He lacks effective authority. The explanation for this may very well be that he does not possess "the knowledge demanded by the situation." In any event not all effective authority is concentrated in the hands of a few persons at the top of the organization. Subordinates frequently exercise effective authority because they "know best" about a particular operation.

It should be made clear that Miss Follett did not consider that the leadership of function and the leadership of personality could not be combined in the same person. Nor did she deny that personality played a very large part in leadership. She did believe, however, that leadership of function was becoming more important than leadership of personality. She felt that the success of an organization depended a good deal on its being "sufficiently flexible to allow the leadership of function to operate fully — to allow the men with the knowledge and the technique to control the situation."[5] Miss Follett makes an interesting point about Joan of Arc. This great woman possessed leadership of personality because of the "ardor of her conviction and power to make others share that conviction." Yet it is also related that "no trained artillery captain could excel Joan of Arc in the placement of guns."[6]

What are some of the other factors which affect the requirements for leadership, apart from expertise in a particular subject matter field? A change in the nature of the situation which confronts the group may call for a different kind of leader. The pilot in a bomber crew may be an excellent leader while the plane is in flight, but prove a very poor one if it crashes "and the crew is faced with the task of surviving or finding its way to safety."[7] The qualities needed to keep the crew working together efficiently in the air are not necessarily the same as those required when the men are afoot in a desperate situation for which advance planning was not possible. Similarly, the kind of activity influences the leadership requirements. The competent head of a public agency might be unsuited for a leadership role in a church group, yet a minor employee in the same public agency might be admirably equipped to lead the church group. Within the church, one person might be excellent for work with preschool children, another for youth activities, and so on. Thus, the characteristics of the followers obviously constitute an important

---

[4]*Ibid.*, p. 277.
[5]*Ibid.*, p. 278.
[6]*Ibid.*, p. 172.
[7]Cartwright and Zander, *op. cit.*, p. 495.

variable in the situation. It takes one kind of person to lead a labor gang, another to direct professional activities. Within the professional ranks, supervisors lacking certain formal qualifications deemed essential by the subordinates, will prove ineffectual; a dean without the Ph.D. will not command the respect of many of the university professors. If the leadership assignment requires conciliation of various groups, the individual's personal background can eliminate him from consideration, as in an international agency, where the person's nationality might make him unacceptable to one or more parties to a dispute. These are only a few of the ways in which the situation can vary, thus altering the requirements for leadership. Readers of this essay will probably be able to supply other examples.

LEADERSHIP STYLE

Usually three types of leadership styles or patterns are identified: authoritarian, democratic, and laissez-faire. Because democracy is so important a value to Americans, it will disturb some people that democracy may not be feasible with some work groups and in some work situations. Therefore, it is advisable to make clear at once in any discussion of leadership style that, as Golembiewski states, "the research literature does not consistently support any one leadership style."[8] On the other hand, while Pfiffner and Sherwood also recognize this to be so, their analysis is that "most of the research has seemed to support the desirability of moving toward the democratic type."[9] At this point, it seems wise to refer to some of these research studies.

Research Findings on Leadership

One of the most famous of these experiments was conducted with a group of ten-year-old boys at the University of Iowa in the late 1930s.[10] Four adult leaders were "trained to proficiency" in the three different leadership styles, authoritarian, democratic, and laissez-faire. The specific leadership behavior under each style is shown in Table 1. Each of these adult leaders was assigned to direct the activities of a boys' club consisting of five boys who met after school to engage in hobby activities. The boys in each of the four groups were roughly similar in terms of

[8]Robert T. Golembiewski, "Three Styles of Leadership and Their Uses", *Personnel*, Vol. 38, No. 4, July-August 1961, p. 35. See also Erwin S. Stanton, "Which Approach to Management — Democratic, Authoritarian or ...?", *Personnel Administration*, Vol. 25, No. 2, March-April 1962, pp. 44-47.

[9]John M. Pfiffner and Frank P. Sherwood, *Administrative Organization*, Prentice-Hall, Englewood Cliffs, New Jersey, 1960, p. 364.

[10]The description of these experiments which follows is from Ralph White and Ronald Lippitt, "Leader Behavior and Member Reaction in Three 'Social Climates'" in Cartwright and Zander, *op. cit.*, pp. 527-553.

TABLE I
Characteristics of the Three Treatment Variables[11]

Authoritarian	Democratic	Laissez-faire
1. All determination of policy by the leader	1. All policies a matter of group discussion and decision, encouraged and assisted by the leader	1. Complete freedom for group or individual decision, with a minimum of leader participation
2. Techniques and activity steps directed by the authority, one at a time, so that future steps were always uncertain to a large degree	2. Activity perspective gained during discussion period. General steps to group goal sketched, and when technical advice was needed two or more alternative procedures from which choice could be made	2. Various materials supplied by the leader, who made it clear that he would supply information when asked. He took no other part in work discussion
3. The leader usually dictated the particular work task and work companion of each member	3. The members were free to work with whomever they chose, and the division of tasks was left up to the group	3. Complete nonparticipation of the leader
4. The dominator tended to be "personal" in his praise and criticism of the work of each member; remained aloof from active group participation except when demonstrating	4. The leader was "objective" or "fact-minded" in his praise and criticism, and tried to be a regular group member in spirit without doing too much of the work	4. Infrequent spontaneous comments on member activities unless questioned, and no attempt to appraise or regulate the course of events

social and economic background and mental, physical, and personality characteristics. The adult leaders were shifted every six weeks from one club to another, and every time they switched to a new group they changed to a different leadership style. All the boys' clubs met in the same places and carried out the same activities under the same conditions. During these meetings, observers were present to study the boys' behavior in detail. The boys themselves were later interviewed to determine their reaction to each leadership style. Home visits were also made to the parents to discover what the impact of each leadership pattern had been on the boys' conduct at home.

The basic findings were as follows:

---

[11]From Ralph White and Ronald Lippitt, "Leader Behavior and Member Reaction in Three 'Social Climates'" in D. Cartwright and A. Zander (eds.), *Group Dynamics, Research and Theory,* Harper & Row, New York, 1960, p. 528.

1. Under laissez-faire supervision, the boys proved less efficient. Furthermore, they did not like the club activities as much as when they were treated democratically. They did less work and poorer work than when under democratic supervision. The complete freedom they had under laissez-faire conditions led them to play more than when under either democratic or authoritarian supervision.

2. If efficiency is evaluated both in terms of work production and social satisfactions, democracy was clearly superior to both laissez-faire and autocracy. The boys worked as efficiently under authoritarian as they did under democratic supervision, but they enjoyed themselves more under democracy.

3. There was a significant difference in the boys' behavior when a democratic, as contrasted with a dictatorial, adult leader temporarily left the room. The boys in democracy kept right on working, but those under iron rule "stopped working as if glad to be relieved of a task which they 'had' to do." Work production went down precipitously during leader-out periods under autocracy whereas the decline was only slight under democracy.

4. The boys showed more originality and creative thinking under democracy than under either laissez-faire or autocracy, for "there was a larger amount of creative thinking about the work in progress than in autocracy, and it was more sustained and practical than in laissez-faire."[12]

5. Autocracy can create much hostility and aggression, including aggression against scapegoats. "Dominating ascendance," meaning imperious treatment of one boy by another, illustrated by such language as "shut up," took place much more often in the autocratically managed groups. Real hostility between the boys and aggressive demands for attention were also more characteristic of the autocratic groups. Destruction of work materials and property was not unusual when the meetings of the autocratic groups ended, but it did not take place at all in the democratic groups.

As to scapegoat behavior, it was evidenced in the autocratic, but not in the democratic groups. Held down by the adult leader when he was playing the authoritarian role, the boys vented their spleen on some innocent member of the group. They took out on him their accumulated resentments against the adult leader. They could not openly defy the leader, so they directed their "aggressions" against other club members who had done nothing to them.

Upon return to democratic or laissez-faire treatment after autocracy, the boys sometimes released their "bottled-up tensions." The change to relative freedom after repressive control resulted in their breaking loose and engaging in much aggressive behavior, with the

---

[12]*Ibid.*, p. 541.

democratic adult leader now the scapegoat. The boys appeared to say to themselves, "Aha! *Now* I can do what I've been wanting to do in this club![13] After a couple of days, however, the "thrill of new-found freedom" wore off and the boys again exhibited the "spontaneous interest" characteristic of democracy.

6. There was more group-mindedness and friendliness in democracy. The pronoun "we" was used much more often in the democratic than in the autocratic groups. The kinds of remarks made by the boys in the democratic groups indicated the existence of greater group cohesion than under autocracy. "Friendly playfulness" was more pronounced, and there was a greater readiness to share group property.

A number of studies made with adult workers have also shown that democratic supervision produces better results. Frequently cited are those of the Institute for Social Research of the University of Michigan. The major finding was that work output was directly correlated with the amount of freedom the supervisor gave the worker. A comparison was made between the production achieved by groups of clerical workers functioning under "close" or "general" supervision. Close supervision meant that the supervisor "watched" the subordinates and checked constantly on how they were carrying out their tasks. Under general supervision, the supervisor put the workers on their own and employed an honor system. It was found that production was highest in work units headed by supervisors who practiced general supervision. Furthermore, the high supervisors, in terms of production, in most cases themselves received general, rather than close, direction from their own superiors. Finally, the high supervisors were generally content to leave the detailed performance of the work to their subordinates, and to concentrate on their supervisory responsibilities. In this respect. they were "people-oriented." The low supervisors tended to neglect their supervisory responsibilities and to spend too much time actually trying to do a share of the production job themselves. Accordingly, they were considered to be "work-oriented."[14]

Later studies at Michigan and elsewhere, however, showed that employee-centered behavior by the supervisor did not necessarily result in increased production. They showed that "all kinds of combinations may occur — high morale and low production, low morale and low production, high morale and high production — which indicates the lack of any fixed and clear-cut relationship."[15] For this reason, Golembiewski argues that it is a mistake to try to answer the question, "Which kind of

---

[13]*Ibid.*, p. 545.
[14]Daniel Katz, Nathan Maccoby, and Nancy C. Morse, *Productivity, Supervision, and Morale in an Office Situation,* Survey Research Center, Institute for Social Research, Ann Arbor, Michigan, 1950.
[15]Pfiffner and Sherwood, *op. cit.*, p. 415.

leadership should we use?" The really pertinent question he feels is, "Which kind of leadership *when?*"[16]

Selecting the Appropriate Leadership Style

Robert Tannenbaum and Warren H. Schmidt take up this problem in a most stimulating essay.[17] Their analysis is particularly valuable because they organize it around the central question of decision making. Figure 1 reproduces a continuum which they have prepared showing the range of possible leadership behavior available to the manager. They explain each of the "behavior points" shown on the bottom line of the continuum as follows:

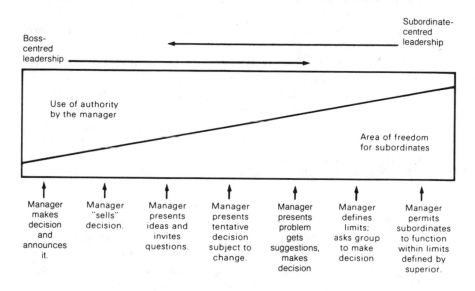

Figure 2
Continuum of Leadership Behavior.

1. *The manager makes the decision and announces it.* Here the executive gives his subordinates no opportunity to participate directly in the decision-making process. He decides what the problem is, determines the possible courses of action, selects one of them, and then tells the subordinates to carry it out. In making his decision, he

---

[16]Golembiewski, *op. cit.*, p. 35.
[17]Robert Tannenbaum and Warren H. Schmidt, "How to Choose a Leadership Pattern", *Harvard Business Review*, Vol. 36, No. 2, March-April 1958, pp. 95-101.
[18]From Robert Tannenbaum and Warren H. Schmidt, "How to Choose a Leadership Pattern", *Harvard Business Review*, Vol. 36, No. 2, March-April 1958, p. 96.

may or may not take into account how the employees will react to it. He may or may not use coercion in getting them to do as he says.

2. *The Manager "sells" his decision.* There is no difference between this and 1., except that the manager does try to persuade the subordinates to accept the decision. He recognizes that some employees may not like the decision and may try to resist it, so he is careful to make clear what they will gain by accepting it. Note that the area of authority exercised by the manager remains large.

3. *The manager presents his ideas and invites questions.* The difference between this and 2. is that the manager gives the subordinates the opportunity to explore with him the implications of the decision. Instead of simply explaining why they should accept it, he invites them to ask questions, and he takes the time to go into some detail about "his thinking and his intentions." At this point on the continuum, the "area of freedom for subordinates" begins to look significant.

4. *The manager presents a tentative decision subject to change.* Here for the first time, the subordinates are allowed to have some influence on the decision. The executive retains responsibility for identifying the problem and developing a proposed solution, but only on a tentative basis. Before making a final decision, he asks the subordinates to give their frank reactions, but he also makes clear that he is retaining the right to decide the question as he sees fit.

5. *The manager presents the problem, gets suggestions, and then makes his decision.* In 1. through 4. above, the manager in every case makes the decision himself, although in 4. it is a tentative one. In 5., he asks the subordinates for their opinions before he makes any decision, final or tentative. He respects their knowledge of operating problems and knows that they may be able to suggest solutions that would not occur to him. After evaluating their ideas, as well as his own, he "selects the solution that he regards as most promising."

6. *The manager defines the limits and requests the group to make a decision.* Here the manager delegates to the subordinates the authority to make a certain decision. He states exactly what the problem is and makes clear the restriction on what the employees can decide. As a hypothetical example, the manager tells the subordinates that a new parking lot will be built for the use of the employees. A ceiling figure of $100 000 for the construction costs has been fixed. So long as this figure is not exceeded, the group can decide to build whatever kind of lot it wants, an underground one or a surface one with multilevel facilities. The management may not like the employees' decision but will accept it within the financial limit.

7. *The manager permits the group to make decisions within prescribed limits.* The difference between 6. and 7. is that in 7. a general grant of decision-making power is made, not limited to any one problem. The

example given is of teams of managers or engineers whose responsibility is not only to identify problems but also to decide what to do about them. The only limits on what the group can do are those specified by the official to whom the team leader reports. This leader may or may not himself participate in the making of the decision. If he does, he has no more authority than any other team member. He commits himself in advance to support whatever decision the group makes.[19]

Under 6 and 7, the subordinates' "area of freedom" widens greatly. The question remains, however, as to which of the leadership behaviors shown on the continuum is appropriate at a particular time. Tannenbaum and Schmidt identify three sets of factors which bear upon this question:

Forces in the manager
Forces in the subordinates
Forces in the situation.[20]

Forces in the Manager

By "forces in the manager" Tannenbaum and Schmidt mean his own preferences, based on his past history and experiences. Is he the type who strongly believes that people should participate in decisions which affect them as individuals? Or is he someone who has long been convinced that the supervisor must stoically assume the burden of making the decisions himself because he is paid to do so? How much confidence does he have in other people in general and in his present subordinates in particular? Some managers are so constituted that they become uneasy if there appears to be an element of risk and uncertainty in the operations they supervise. This kind of executive is better off if he frankly acknowledges to himself that he is not the person to make delegations of authority as broad as those shown on behavior points 6. and 7. of the continuum.

Forces in the Subordinates

"Forces in the subordinates" refers to the expectations of the employees as to how the supervisor should behave in his relations with them. It also means the personality requirements of each individual in the group as these bear upon the question of the kind of direction he responds to best. The executive can allow greater freedom to subordinates under the following conditions:

1. The subordinates have relatively high needs for independence.
2. They *want* to assume responsibility, rather than to avoid it.
3. They have a "relatively high tolerance for ambiguity," meaning they would rather receive broad instructions than be tied down by clear-cut instructions.

---

[19]*Ibid.*, p. 97.
[20]*Ibid.*, p. 98.

4. They are interested in the problem and believe that it is important.
5. They understand the goals of the organization and identify with them.
6. They have the necessary knowledge and experience to be able to deal with the problem.
7. They are accustomed to sharing in decisionmaking. This is what they expect and are prepared for, rather than being denied such a role.[21]

If these conditions do not exist, there may be no alternative to running "a one-man show." Depending on his assessment of these factors, the executive may on one occasion decide to make the decisions himself, on another to let the subordinates participate. If the manager has the respect of the subordinates, they will understand why in the one case he brings them in and in the other he does not.

Forces in the Situation

"Forces in the situation" refers to the "critical environmental pressures" which surround the manager, stemming from "the organization, the work group, the nature of the problem, and the pressures of time."[22]

As to the organization, it has values and traditions which condition the manager's behavior. Someone newly appointed from the outside "quickly discovers that certain kinds of behavior are approved while others are not." There is a great compulsion for him to select that kind of behavior on the continuum which conforms to his superiors' concepts of how he should conduct himself. Sometimes this is referred to as the "management climate" in the agency; in other words, the lower ranking executives tend to imitate the behavior of the higher ones. The latter are a very important part of the "situation."

Other organizational factors influencing the extent of employee participation are: the size of the organization units; their geographical distribution; and whether or not information about work plans must be kept confidential. In a very large and dispersed organization, it may be impossible to have as much employee participation as the management would like. If the activity is one involving the national security, work plans and other information obviously cannot be communicated as freely to the employees.

"Group effectiveness" is another consideration. Before he gives a problem to the work group to solve, the manager must be convinced that it is equal to the task. Has the group functioned effectively in the past? Does it seem confident of its ability to cope with this kind of assignment?

The "nature of the problem" also sets limits on the extent to which the manager can safely delegate. Perhaps the problem is one with which

---

[21]*Ibid.*, p. 99.
[22]*Ibid.*, p. 100.

the work group is not familiar, so he must handle it himself. There is no virtue in asking any one subordinate or a group of workers to take on responsibilities they are not ready to assume. Yet the executive wants to be sure that he is making full use of the special knowledge and abilities of his staff. Tannenbaum and Schmidt suggest that the manager should ask himself, "Have I heard the ideas of everyone who has the necessary knowledge to make a significant contribution to the solution of this problem?" If he asks this question and answers it honestly, he is more likely to select the most appropriate leadership pattern.

"Pressure of time," meaning the need to act quickly, may force the manager to make the decision himself, without consulting with his subordinates. Leisurely consideration of every problem is not possible in the swift-moving environment of government. The manager does not by any means have full control of his time schedule; his own supervisors set deadlines for him. Unforeseen situations arise which make it necessary for him to make the best decision possible in a very short period of time. Under such circumstances, all he can do is consult with as many subordinates as possible, assuming that he even has time to do this.

The great value of the preceding analysis is that it makes clear the different considerations which should influence the decision as to leadership style. If the "boss-centered" type is used on occasion, this does not mean that the managers in question must be tyrants at heart. Of course, some may have such tendencies, evidenced by their use of "boss-centered" leadership even when it is not necessary. The point is that the manager should use the leadership pattern which is called for by the particular situation.

11
The Executive as Decision Maker*

Herbert A. Simon

What part does decision making play in managing? I shall find it convenient to take mild liberties with the English language by using "decision making" as though it were synonymous with "managing."

What is our mental image of a decision maker? Is he a brooding man on horseback who suddenly rouses himself from thought and issues an order to a subordinate' Is he a happy-go-lucky fellow, a coin poised his thumbnail, ready to risk his action on the toss? Is he an alert, gray-haired businessman, sitting at the board of directors' table with his

*Reprinted by permission from Herbert A. Simon, *The Shape of Automation* (New York: Harper & Row, 1965).

associates, caught at the moment of saying "aye" or "nay"? Is he a bespectacled gentleman. bent over a docket of papers, his pen hovering over the line marked (X)?

All of these images have a significant point in common. In them, the decision maker is a man at the moment of choice, ready to plant his foot on one or another of the routes that lead from the crossroads. All the images falsify decision by focusing on its final moment. All of them ignore the whole lengthy, complex process of alerting, exploring, and analyzing that precedes that final moment.

INTELLIGENCE, DESIGN AND CHOICE IN DECISION MAKING

In treating decision making as synonymous with managing, I shall be referring not merely to the final act of choice among alternatives, but rather to the whole process of decision. Decision making comprises three principal phases: finding occasions for making a decision; finding possible courses of action; and choosing among courses of action. These three activities account for quite different fractions of the time budgets of executives. The fractions vary greatly from one organization level to another and from one executive to another, but we can make some generalizations about them even from casual observation. Executives spend a large fraction of their time surveying the economic, technical political, and social environment to identify new conditions that call for new actions. They probably spend an even larger fraction of their time, individually or with their associates, seeking to invent, design, and develop possible courses of action for handling situations where a decision is needed. They spend a small fraction of their time in choosing among alternative actions already developed to meet an identified problem and already analyzed for their consequences. The three fractions, added together, account for most of what executives do.[1]

The first phase of the decision-making process — searching the environment for conditions calling for decision — I shall call *intelligence* activity (borrowing the military meaning of intelligence). The second phase — inventing, developing, and analyzing possible courses of action — I shall call *design* activity. The third phase — selecting a particular course of action from those available — I shall call *choice* activity.

Let me illustrate these three phases of decision. In the past five years, many companies have reorganized their accounting and other data processing activities in order to make use of large electronic computers. How has this come about? Computers first became available commercial-

---

[1]The way in which these activities take shape within an organization is described in some detail in James G. March and Herbert A. Simon, *Organizations*, Wiley, New York, 1958, Chaps. 6 and 7.

ly in the early 1950s. Although, in some vague and general sense, company managements were aware that computers existed, few managements had investigated their possible applications with any thoroughness before about 1955. For most companies, the use of computers required no decision before that time because it hadn't been placed on the agenda.[2]

The intelligence activity preceding the introduction of computers tended to come about in one of two ways. Some companies — for example, in the aircraft and atomic energy industries — were burdened with enormously complex computations for engineering design. Because efficiency in computations was a constant problem, and because the design departments were staffed with engineers who could understand, at least in general, the technology of computers, awareness of computers and their potentialities came early to these companies. After computers were already in extensive use for design calculations, businesses with a large number-processing load — insurance companies, accounting departments in large firms, banks — discovered these new devices and began to consider seriously their introduction.

Once it was recognized that computers might have a place in modern business, a major design task had to be carried out in each company before they could be introduced. It is now a commonplace that payrolls can be prepared by computers. Programs in both the general and computer senses for doing this are relatively easy to design in any given situation.[3] To develop the first computer programs for preparing payroll, however, was a major research and development project. Few companies having carried their investigations of computers to the point where they had definite plans for their use failed to install them. Commitment to the new course of action took place gradually as the intelligence and design phases of the decision were going on. The final choice was, in many instances, almost *pro forma*.

Generally speaking, intelligence activity precedes design, and design activity preceeds choice. The cycle of phases is, however, far more complex than this sequence suggests. Each phase in making a particular decision is itself a complex decision-making process. The design phase, for example, may call for new intelligence activities; problems at any given level generate subproblems that, in turn, have their intelligence, design, and choice phases, and so on. There are wheels within wheels within wheels. Nevertheless, the three large phases are often clearly discernible as the organizational decision process unfolds. They are

---

[2]Richard M. Cyert, Herbert A. Simon, and Donald B. Trow, "Observation of a Business Decision", *Journal of Business*, Vol. 29, 1956, pp. 237-248.
[3]For a good discussion on the use of the computer for such purposes, see Robert H. Gregory and Richard L. Van Horn, *Automatic Data-Processing Systems*, Wadsworth, San Francisco, 1960.

closely related to the stages in problem solving first described by John Dewey:

> What is the problem?
> What are the alternatives?
> Which alternative is best?[4]

It may be objected that I have ignored the task of carrying out decisions. I shall merely observe by the way that seeing that decisions are executed is again decision-making activity. A broad policy decision creates a new condition for the organization's executives that calls for the design and choice of a course of action for executing the policy. Executing policy. then, is indistinguishable from making more detailed policy. For this reason, I shall feel justified in taking my pattern for decision making as a paradigm for most executive activity.

Developing Decision-Making Skills

It is an obvious step from the premise that managing is decision making to the conclusion that the important skills for an executive are decision-making skills. It is generally believed that good decision makers, like good athletes, are born, not made. The belief is about as true in the one case as it is in the other.

That human beings come into the world endowed unequally with biological potential for athletic prowess is undeniable. They also come endowed unequally with intelligence, cheerfulness, and many other characteristics and potentialities. To a limited extent, we can measure some aspects of that endowment — height, weight, perhaps intelligence. Whenever we make such measurements and compare them with adult performance, we obtain significant, but low, correlations. A man who is not a natural athlete is unlikely to run the four-minute mile; but many men who are natural athletes have never come close to that goal. A man who is not "naturally" intelligent is unlikely to star in science; but many intelligent scientists are not stars.

A good athlete is born when a man with some natural endowment, by dint of practice, learning, and experience develops that natural endowment into a mature skill. A good executive is born when a man with some natural endowment (intelligence and some capacity for interacting with his fellow men) by dint of practice, learning, and experience develops his endowment into a mature skill. The skills involved in intelligence, design, and choosing activities are as learnable and trainable as the skills involved in driving, recovering, and putting a

---

[4]John Dewey, How We Think, Heath, New York, 1910, Ch. 8.

golf ball. I hope to indicate some of the things a modern executive needs to learn about decision making.

Executive Responsibility for Organizational Decision Making

The executive's job involves not only making decisions, himself, but also seeing that the organization, or part of an organization, that he directs makes decisions effectively. The vast bulk of the decision-making activity for which he is responsible is not his personal activity, but the activity of his subordinates.

Nowadays, with the advent of computers, we can think of information as something almost tangible; strings of symbols which, like strips of steel or plastic ribbons, can be processed — changed from one form to another. We can think of white-collar organizations as factories for processing information. The executive is the factory manager, with all the usual responsibilities for maintaining the factory operation, getting it back into operation when it breaks down, and proposing and carrying through improvements in its design.

There is no reason to expect that a man who has acquired a fairly high level of personal skill in decision-making activity will have a correspondingly high skill in designing efficient decision-making systems. To imagine that there is such a connection is like supposing that a man who is a good weight lifter can therefore design cranes. The skills of designing and maintaining the modern decision-making systems we call organizations are less intuitive skills. Hence, they are even more susceptible to training than the skills of personal decision making.

Programmed and Nonprogrammed Decisions

In discussing how executives now make decisions, and how they will make them in the future, let us distinguish two polar types of decisions. I shall call them *programmed decisions* and *nonprogrammed decisions*, respectively. Having christened them, I hasten to add that they are not really distinct types, but a whole continuum, with highly programmed decisions at one end of that continuum and highly unprogrammed decisions at the other end. We can find decisions of all shades of gray along the continuum, and I use the terms programmed and nonprogrammed simply as labels for the black and white of the range.[5]

Decisions are programmed to the extent that they are repetitive and routine, to the extent that a definite procedure has been worked out for handling them so that they don't have to be treated *de novo* each time they

---

[5]See March and Simon, *op. cit.*, pp. 139-142 and 177-180 for further discussion of these types of decisions. The labels used there are slightly different.

occur. The obvious reason why programmed decisions tend to be repetitive, and vice versa, is that if a particular problem recurs often enough, a routine procedure will usually be worked out for solving it. Numerous examples of programmed decisions in organizations will occur to you: pricing ordinary customers' orders; determining salary payments to employees who have been ill; reordering office supplies.

Decisions are nonprogrammed to the extent that they are novel, unstructured, and consequential. There is no cut-and-dried method for handling the problem because it hasn't arisen before, or because its precise nature and structure are elusive or complex, or because it is so important that it deserves a custom-tailored treatment. General Eisenhower's D-Day decision is a good example of a nonprogrammed decision. Remember, we are considering not merely the final act of ordering the attack, but the whole complex of intelligence and design activities that preceded it. Many of the components of the decisions were programmed — by standard techniques for military planning — but before these components could be designed they had to be provided with a broader framework of military and political policy.

I have borrowed the term program from the computer trade, and intend it in the sense in which it is used there. A *program* is a detailed prescription or strategy that governs the sequence of responses of a system to a complex task environment. Most of the programs that govern organizational response are not as detailed or as precise as computer programs. However, they all have the same intent: to permit an adaptive response of the system to the situation.

In what sense, then, can we say that the response of a system to a situation is nonprogrammed? Surely something determines the response. That something, that collection of rules of procedure, is by definition a program. By nonprogrammed I mean a response where the system has no specific procedures to deal with situations like the one at hand, but must fall back on whatever *general* capacity it has for intelligent, adaptive, problem-oriented action. In addition to his specific skills and specific knowledge, man has some general problem-solving capacities. Given almost any kind of situation, no matter how novel or perplexing, he can begin to reason about it in terms of ends and means.

This general problem-solving equipment is not always effective. Men often fail to solve problems, or they reach unsatisfactory solutions. But man is seldom completely helpless in a new situation. He possesses general problem-solving equipment which, however inefficient, fills some of the gaps in his special problem-solving skills. And organizations, as collections of men, have some of this same general adaptive capacity.

The cost of using general-purpose programs to solve problems is usually high. It is advantageous to reserve these programs for situations that are truly novel, where no alternative programs are available. If any particular class of situations recurs often enough, a special-purpose program can be developed which gives better solutions and gives them more cheaply than the general problem-solving apparatus.

My reason for distinguishing between programmed and nonprogrammed decisions is that different techniques are used for handling the programmed and the nonprogrammed aspects of our decision making. The distinction, then, will be a convenient one for classifying these techniques. I shall use it for that purpose, hoping that the reader will remind himself from time to time that the world is mostly gray with only a few spots of pure black or white.

Table 1 below will provide a map of the territory I propose to cover. In the northern half of the map are some techniques related to programmed decision making, in the southern half, some techniques related to nonprogrammed decision making. In the western half of the map I placed the classical techniques used in decision making — the kit of tools that has been used by executives and organizations from the time of the earliest recorded history up to the present generation. In the eastern half of the map I placed the new techniques of decision making — tools that have been forged largely since World War II, and that are only now coming into extensive use in management in this country. I shall proceed across the map from west to east, and from north to south, taking up, in order, the north-west and the south-west quadrants, the north-east quadrant, and the south-east quadrant.

I can warn you now to what conclusion this joureny is going to lead. We are in the midst of a major revolution in the art or science — whichever you prefer to call it — of management and organization. I shall try to describe the nature of this revolution and to discuss its implications.

TRADITIONAL DECISION-MAKING METHODS

Let us examine the western half of our map of decision-making techniques. This half represents methods that have been widely understood and applied in human organizations at least from the time of the building of the pyramids. In painting with a broad brush, I may convey the impression that there was no progress in organizational matters during the course of three millennia. I do not believe this to be true, and I do not intend to imply it. But the progress that was made did not enlarge the repertory of basic mechanisms to which I shall refer.

We shall consider, in turn, techniques for making programmed decisions and techniques for making nonprogrammed decisions.

Traditional Techniques for Programmed Decisions

"Man," says William James, "is born with a tendency to do more things than he has ready-made arrangements for in his nerve centers. Most of

TABLE I
Traditional and Modern Techniques of Decision Making

Types of Decisions	Decision-Making Techniques	
	Traditional	Modern
Programmed: Routine, repetitive decisions Organization develops specific processes for handling them	1. Habit 2. Clerical routine: Standard operating procedures 3. Organizational structure: Common expectations A system of subgoals Well-defined informational channels	1. Operations Research: Mathematical analysis Models Computer simulation 2. Electronic data processing
Nonprogrammed: One-shot, ill-structured novel, policy decisions Handled by general problem-solving processes	1. Judgment, intuition, and creativity 2. Rules of thumb 3. Selection and training of executives	Heuristic problem-solving technique applied to: (a) training human decision makers (b) constructing heuristic computer programs

the performances of other animals are automatic. But in him the number of them is so enormous, that most of them must be the fruit of painful study. If practice did not make perfect, nor habit economize the expense of nervous and muscular energy, he would therefore be in a sorry plight."[6]

Habit is the most general, the most pervasive, of all techniques for making programmed decisions. The collective memories of organization members are vast encyclopedias of factual knowledge, habitual skills, and operating procedures. The large costs associated with bringing new members into organizations are principally costs of providing the new members, through formal training and experience, with the repertoire of skills and other habits they need in their jobs. Partly, the organization provides these habits; partly, it acquires them by selecting new employees who have already learned them in the educational and training institutions that society maintains.

Closely related to habits are standard operating procedures. The only difference between habits and standard operating procedures is that the former have become internalized — recorded in the central nervous system — while the latter begin as formal, written, recorded programs. Standard operating procedures provide a means for indoctrinating new members into the habitual patterns of organizational behavior, a means for reminding old members of patterns that any one member uses so infrequently that they never become completely habitual, and a means for bringing habitual patterns out into the open where they can be examined, modified, and improved.

Organization structure, over and above standard operating procedures, is itself a partial specification of decision-making programs. The organization structure establishes a common set of presuppositions and expectations as to which members of the organization are responsible for which classes of decisions; it establishes a structure of subgoals to serve as criteria of choice in various parts of the organization; and it establishes intelligence responsibilities in particular organization units for scrutinizing specific parts of the organization's environment and for communicating events requiring attention to appropriate decision points.

In the past, the improvement of programmed decision making in organizations has focused largely upon these techniques: upon improving the knowledge, skills, and habits of individual employees by means of training programs and planned tours of duty; upon developing better standard operating procedures and securing adherence to them; and upon modifying the structure of the organization itself, the division of labor, the subgoal structure, the allocation of responsibilities.

---

[6]William James, *The Principles of Psychology*, Henry Holt, New York, 1890 or Dover, New York, 1950, Vol. 1, p. 113.

Mankind has possessed for many centuries an impressive collection of techniques for developing and maintaining predictable programmed responses in an organization to those problems posed by its environment that are relatively repetitive and well-structured. The history of the development of these techniques has never been written — much of it is undoubtedly buried in prehistory — but one can point to particular periods of innovation. The scientific management movement, and particularly the development of standard methods for performing repetitive work, is one of the most recent of these.

Traditional Techniques for Nonprogrammed Decisions

When we turn to the area of nonprogrammed decisions, we have much less to point to in the way of specific, describable techniques. When we ask how executives in organizations make nonprogrammed decisions, we are generally told that they "exercise judgment," and that this judgment depends, in some undefined way, upon experience, insight, and intuition. If the decision we are inquiring about was a particularly difficult one, or one that yielded especially impressive results, we may be told that creativity was required.

There is a scene in *Le Malade Imaginaire* in which the physician is asked why opium puts people to sleep. "Because it possesses a dormitive faculty," he replied triumphantly. To name a phenomenon is not to explain it. Saying that nonprogrammed decisions are made by exercising judgment *names* that phenomenon but does not explain it. It doesn't help the man who lacks judgment (i.e., who doesn't make decisions well) to acquire it.

Making programmed decisions depends on relatively simple psychological processes that are somewhat understood, at least at the practical level. These include habit, memory, simple manipulations of things and symbols. Making nonprogrammed decisions depends on psychological processes that, until recently, have not been understood at all. Because we have not understood them, our theories about nonprogrammed decision making have been rather empty and our practical advice only moderately helpful.

One thing we have known about nonprogrammed decision making is that it can be improved somewhat by training in orderly thinking. In addition to the very specific habits one can acquire for doing very special things, one can acquire the habit — when confronted with a vague and difficult situation — of asking, "What is the problem?" We can even construct rather generalized operating procedures for decision making. The military "estimate of the situation" — a checklist of things to consider in analyzing a military decision problem — is an example of such an operating procedure.

There is nothing wrong with such aids to decision making except that they don't go nearly far enough. They graduate the decision maker from nursery school to kindergarten, perhaps, but they don't carry his education much further.

How then do executives discharge their responsibilities for seeing that decision making in their organizations, nonprogrammed as well as programmed, is of high quality? Let me propose an analogy. If you have a job to do, and you don't have the time or the skill to design and produce just the right tool to do it, you look around among the tools you have or can get at the hardware store and select the best one you can find. We haven't known very much about how to improve human decision-making skills, but we observe that some people have these skills much better developed than others. Hence, we rely on selection as our principal technique for improving complex decision-making skills in organizations.

Even our selection techniques are not nearly as adequate as we should like. To some limited extent we have found out how to assess human qualities by formal testing. In the main, however, we select a good decision maker for an organizational position by looking for a man who has done a pretty good job of decision making in some other organizational position that is almost equally taxing. This is a simple-minded approach to the problem, but it is the only moderately successful one that we know.

We supplement our selection techniques with two kinds of training: the professional training in basic principles that generally precedes entrance into organizational life, and the training through experience and planned job rotation that the organization itself can provide. Man is a learning animal. If he is subjected to a sequence of problem situations of progressively greater difficulty and of difficulty appropriate to the level of skill he has attained, he will usually show an increasing capacity to handle the problems well. For problems of a nonprogrammed sort neither he nor we know from whence the improvement comes. The processes of learning have been as mysterious as the processes of problem solving. But improvement there is. We are thus able, in a crude way, to use training and planned experience as a means for improving nonprogrammed decision making in organizations.

Appropriate design of the organization structure is important for nonprogrammed, as it is for programmed, decision making. An important principle of organization design that has emerged over the years has been called facetiously "Gresham's Law of Planning." It states that programmed activity tends to drive out nonprogrammed activity. If an executive has a job that involves a mixture of programmed and nonprogrammed decision-making responsibilities, the former will come to be emphasized at the expense of the latter. The organizational implication of Gresham's Law is that special provision must be made for nonprogrammed decision making by creating specific organizational responsibilities and organizational units to take care of it. The various kinds of staff units that are so characteristic of large-scale modern organizations are mostly units specialized in particular aspects of the more complex nonprogrammed decision-making tasks. Market research units and research departments, to cite some examples, specialize in the intelligence phase of decision making; planning departments and product development departments specialize in the design phase. The creation of organizational units to carry on these activities allocates brain-power to nonprogrammed thought, and provides some minimal assurance that such thought will occur in the organization.

In summary, we have not had, in the past, adequate knowledge of the processes that are involved in decision making in complex situations. Human thinking, problem solving, and learning have been mysterious processes which we have labeled but not explained. Lacking an understanding of these processes, we have had to resort to gross techniques for improving nonprogrammed decision making; selection of men who have demonstrated their capacity for it; further development of their powers through professional training and planned experience; protection of nonprogrammed activity from the pressure of repetitive activity by establishing specialized organizational units to carry it on. We cannot say that these traditional techniques have failed — decisions do get made daily in organizations. Neither can we say that we might not do very much better in the future as our knowledge of the decision-making process grows.

NEW TECHNIQUES FOR PROGRAMMED DECISION MAKING

World War II brought large numbers of scientists trained in the use of mathematical tools into contact for the first time with operational and managerial problems. Designers of military aircraft could not plan aircraft armament without making assumptions about the formations in which the planes would be flown and the strategy of their commitment to action. Mathematical economists responsible for material allocation had to come to grips with complex logistics systems. The need for solving these problems, coupled with the tools of quantitative analysis that the scientists and econometricians brought with them, have produced some new approaches to management decision making that are of fundamental importance.[7]

---

[7]See Table I, eastern half.

Operations Research

Many people — notably some of the pioneer operations researchers themselves — have tried to define operations research. The net result is usually to identify it with scientific method or straight thinking applied to management problems, and to imply that it is something that can be done only by natural scientists. Definitions of this kind, unintentionally imperialistic, raise the hackles of those identified with the earlier phrase "scientific management," who had thought that clear, scientific thinking is what they had always been doing. Except in matter of degree (e.g., the operations researchers tend to use rather high-powered mathematics), it is not clear that operations research embodies any philosophy different from that of scientific management. Charles Babbage and Frederick Taylor will have to be made, retroactively, charter members of the operations research societies.

A more understandable and defensible definition of operations research is a sociological one. Operations research is a movement that, emerging out of the military needs of World War II, has brought the decision-making problems of management within the range of interests of large numbers of natural scientists and, particularly, of mathematicians and statisticians.[8] The operations researchers soon joined forces with mathematical economists who had come into the same area — to the mutual benefit of both groups. And by now there has been widespread fraternization between these exponents of the "new" scientific management and men trained in the earlier traditions of scientific management and industrial engineering. No meaningful line can be drawn any more to demarcate operations research from scientific management or scientific management from management science.[9]

Along with some mathematical tools, which I shall discuss presently, operations research brought into management decision making a point of view called the systems approach. The systems approach is no easier to define than operations research for it is a set of attitudes and a frame of mind rather than a definite and explicit theory. At its vaguest, it means looking at the whole problem — again, hardly a novel idea, and not always a very helpful one. Somewhat more concretely, it means designing the components of a system and making individual decisions

[8]Some standard works on operations research by leading members of the group are C. West Churchman, Russell L. Ackoff, and E. Leonard Arnoff, *Introduction to Operations Research*, Wiley, New York, 1957; and Philip M. Morse and George E. Kimball, *Methods of Operations Research*, Wiley, New York, 1951. The Operations Research Society of America publishes the journal *Operations Research*.

[9]The term "management science" was the trademark invented by the quantitatively oriented social scientists, primarily econometricians, who entered this area and who initially distinguished themselves from the operations researchers. The Institute of Management Sciences was organized in 1954. Its journal is the quarterly *Management Science*.

within it in the light of the implication of these decisions for the system as a whole.[10] We now know a *little* about how this might be done:

1. Economic analysis has something to say about rational behavior in complex systems of interacting elements, and particularly about the conditions under which the choices that are optimal for subsystems will or will not be optimal for a system as a whole. Economic analysis also has a great deal to say about the price system as a possible mechanism for decentralizing decision making.[11]

2. Mathematical techniques have been developed and adapted by engineers and economists for analyzing the dynamic behavior of complex systems. Under the labels of servo-mechanism theory and cybernetics, such techniques underwent rapid development at about the time of World War II. They have considerable usefulness in the design of dynamic systems.[12]

Systems design is such a modish, if not faddish, word at the moment that I don't want to exaggerate the amount of well-understood technique that stands behind it. Nevertheless, it is fair to say that we can approach the design and analysis of large dynamic systems today with a good deal more sophistication than we could ten years ago.

The Mathematical Tools

Operations research progressed from the talking to the action stage by finding tools with which to solve concrete managerial problems. Among the tools, some of them relatively new, some of them already known to statisticians, mathematicians, or economists were linear programming, dynamic programming, game theory, and probability theory. Behind each of these formidable terms lies a mathematical model for a range of management problems. Linear programming, for example, can be used to provide a mathematical model for the operations of a gasoline refinery, or a commercial cattle-feed manufacturing operation. Dynamic programming can be used as a model for many inventory and production planning situations. Game theory models have been used to represent marketing problems. Probability models have been used in a wide variety of contexts — they have been, perhaps, the most versatile of all.

Whatever the specific mathematical tool, the general recipe for using it in management decision making is something like this:[13]

---

[10]See Churchman *et al, op. cit.,* pp. 109-111.
[11]See Tjalling C. Koopmans (ed)., *Activity Analaysis of Production and Allocation,* Wiley, New York, 1951.
[12]The word cybernetics was first used by Norbert Wiener in *Cybernetics,* Wiley, New York, 1948, p. 19. A good exposition of these techniques may be found in Arnold Tustin, *The Mechanism of Economic Systems,* Harvard University Press, Cambridge, Massachusetts, 1953.
[13]See Churchman *et al, op. cit.,* Ch. V.

1.   Construct a *mathematical model* that satisfies the conditions of the tool to be used and which, at the same time, mirrors the important factors in the management situation to be analyzed.
2.   Define the *criterion function*, the measure that is to be used for comparing the relative merits of various possible courses of action.
3.   Obtain *empirical estimates* of the numerical parameters in the model that specify the particular, concrete situation to which it is to be applied.
4.   Carry through the mathematical process of finding the course of action which, for the specified parameter values, maximizes the criterion function.

In any decision-making situation where we apply this recipe successfully, we have, in fact, constructed a *program* for the organization's decisions. We have either annexed some decisions that had been judgmental to the area of programmed decision making,[14] or we have replaced a rule-of-thumb program with a more sophisticated program that guarantees us optimal decisions — optimal, that is, within the framework of the mathematical model.

But certain conditions must be satisfied in order to apply this recipe to a class of decision problems. First, it must be possible to define mathematical variables that represent the important aspects of the situation. In particular, a quantitative criterion function must be defined. If the problem area is so hopelessly qualitative that it cannot be described even approximately in terms of such variables, the approach fails. Second, the model will call for certain parameters of its structure to be estimated before it can be applied in a particular situation. Hence, it is necessary that there be ways of making actual numerical estimates of these parameters — of sufficient accuracy for the practical task at hand. Third, the specification of the model must fit the mathematical tools to be used. If certain kinds of nonlinearities are absolutely crucial to an accurate description of the situation, linear programming simply won't work — it is a tool adapted to mathematical systems that are, in a certain sense, linear. Fourth, the problem must be small enough that the calculations can be carried out in reasonable time and at a reasonable cost.

Some relatively simple management problems — for example, many problems of factory scheduling — turn out to be far too large for even such a powerful tool as linear programming. It is easy for the operations research enthusiast to underestimate the stringency of these conditions. This leads to an ailment that might be called mathematician's aphasia. The victim abstracts the original problem until the mathematical intractabilities have been removed (and all semblance to reality lost),

---

[14]Thus, operations research, in addition to providing techniques for programmed decisions, also expands their boundaries.

solves the new simplified problem, and then pretends that this was the problem he wanted to solve all along. He expects the manager to be so dazzled by the beauty of the mathematical results that he will not remember that his practical operating problem has not been handled.

It is just as easy for the traditionalist to overestimate the stringency of the conditions. For the operations research approach to work, nothing has to be exact — it just has to be close enough to give better results than could be obtained by common sense without the mathematics. Furthermore, it is dangerous to assume that something is essentially qualitative and not reducible to mathematical form until an applied mathematician has had a try at it. For example, I have often been told that "you can't place a dollar value on a lost order from inventory runout." But why, the answer goes, can't you estimate the penalty cost of taking emergency action to *avoid* losing the order — shipping, for example, by air express? Thus, many things that seem intangible can be reduced, for management decision-making purposes, to dollars and cents.

But we need not spin out these generalities. Mathematical techniques are now being applied in a large number of situations. In many of these situations, when mathematical techniques were first proposed there was much head shaking and muttering about judgment. The area of application is large. It is growing. But there is no indication that it will cover the whole of management decision.

Enter the Computer

It was an historical accident with large consequences that the same war which spawned operations research saw also the birth of the modern digital computer as a practical device.[15] The computer was conceived as a device for exploring by numerical analysis the properties of mathematical systems too large or too complex to be treated by known analytic methods. The systems of differential equations that were arising in aerodynamics, meteorology, and the design of nuclear reactors were obvious candidates for this treatment. It was soon realized that even larger problems were generated by the linear programming and dynamic programming models of management decision problems. Whatever the conceptual power of the mathematical models that have been used in operations research, their actual use in practical schemes for decision making hinged on the fortuitous arrival on the scene of the computer.

While computers were initially conceived as devices for doing arithmetic on problems that had first been cast in a mathematical form having known solution procedures, it gradually became clear that there were other ways of using them. If a model or simulation of a situation

---

[15]A general book on the history of the development of computers and on their use by management is John A. Postley, *Computers and People*, McGraw-Hill, New York, 1960.

could be programmed for a computer, the behavior of the system could then be studied simply by having the computer imitate it and without solving, in the traditional sense, the mathematical equations themselves. In putting it this way, I make simulation sound like a simpler and more powerful technique than it really is. In general, we would need to simulate the behavior of the system not under a single set of conditions but over a whole range of conditions. Having simulated it, we would need some procedure for evaluating the results — for deciding whether the system behavior was satisfactory or not. Finally, before we could simulate the behavior, we would have to estimate accurately enough the structure of the system — simulation techniques do not at all reduce the burden of providing numerical estimates.

In spite of these limitations and difficulties, simulation has enabled an airline to determine how many reserve aircraft it should keep on hand, has been used to study highway congestion, has led to improvement in inventory control procedures for a huge warehousing operation, and has accomplished many other difficult tasks.

Of course, the bread-and-butter applications of computers to business decision making have had little to do with either mathematical models or simulation. They have had to do with automating a whole host of routine and repetitive data-processing activities that had for many years been highly programmed but not nearly so completely automated. Through this development, large-scale data processing is becoming a factory operation, an operation that exceeds in degree of automation all but a very few manufacturing processes.

The Revolution in Programmed Decision Making

The revolution in programmed decision making has by no means reached its limits, but we can now see its shape. The rapidity of change stems partly from the fact that there has been not a single innovation but several related innovations, all of which contribute to it.

1. The electronic computer is bringing about, with unexpected speed, a high level of automation in the routine, programmed decision making and data processing that were formerly the province of clerks.
2. The area of programmed decision making is being rapidly extended as we find ways to apply the tools of operations research to types of decisions that have up to now been regarded as judgmental — particularly, but not exclusively, middle-management decisions in the area of manufacturing and warehousing.
3. The computer has extended the capability of the mathematical techniques to problems far too large to be handled by less automatic computing devices, and has further extended the range of

programmable decisions by contributing the new technique of simulation.

4. Companies are just beginning to discover ways of bringing together the first two of these developments: of combining the mathematical techniques for making decisions about aggressive middle-management variables with the data-processing techniques for implementing these decisions in detail at clerical levels.

Out of the combination of these four developments there is emerging the new picture of the data-processing factory for manufacturing, in a highly mechanized way, the organization's programmed decisions — just as the physical processing factory manufactures its products in a manner that becomes increasingly mechanized. The automated factory of the future will operate on the basis of programmed decisions produced in the automated office beside it.

12
Communications*

Felix A. Nigro

Communications has been defined as "that process whereby one person makes his ideas and feelings known to another."[1] However, experience has shown time and time again that more is required than the desire to communicate. One must be able to adjust to situations and personalities. Any organization relies on at least a fair degree of harmonious interaction among its employees in order to achieve its objectives, and, wherever there is friction, there will be a block at that point in the communications network. Yet, even when people enjoy good working relations, successful communication is not easy. Also needed is the ability to make one's thoughts entirely clear to the other person, and for this to be possible, the individual's own thinking must be absolutely clear. Vague instructions reflect cloudy thinking; "If an executive cannot shape up in his own mind a clear concept of policies, objectives, programs, and organization structure, and cannot produce a clear picture in the minds of others, he is seriously handicapped."[2]

*Slightly abridged by permission from Felix A. Nigro, *Modern Public Administration* (New York: Harper & Row, 1965), pp. 188-207.
[1]Lawrence A. Appley, *Management in Action,* American Management Association, New York, 1956, p. 182.
[2]*Ibid.,* p. 186.

Decisions must be explained properly to those who are to put them into effect. The individual may know exactly what he wants to say but is unable to express himself clearly. Yet, if a sound decision is communicated poorly, the desired results will not be obtained. Decisions themselves are based on communications received from different sources, and subordinates present their recommendations, both written and oral. In written communications, the individual may use the wrong words or employ expressions that cloud his real meaning, and similar confusion results from lack of clarity in oral communications. Sometimes, too, a cause of the difficulty is failure on the part of one or both of the communicators to listen properly. All of these aspects are vital in the decision-making process discussed previously, and for this reason, it is frequently stated that communications and decision making are inseparable.

Further power in the organization is measured by the respect commanded by an official's communications. Since communication is basically interaction, study of the communications pattern in an organization will reveal the role of each of the participants.

> Let us suppose that a man is foreman in a factory, and that we are watching him at work. What do we see and hear? We watch him, perhaps, overseeing a battery of punch presses, going from one man to another as they tend the machines, answering their questions and showing them, if they have made mistakes, where they have gone wrong. We see him also at his desk making out records. That is, we see that he has a certain kind of job, that he carries on certain activities. We see also that he deals with certain men in the plant and not with others. He goes to certain men and talks to them; others come to his desk and talk to him. He gets his orders from a boss and passes on the orders to members of his own department. That is, he communicates or, as we shall say ... interacts with certain persons and not with others, and this communication from person to person often takes place in a certain order — for instance, from the boss to the foreman and then from the foreman to the workers — so that we can say ... that the foreman occupies a position in a chain of communications.[3]

TYPES OF COMMUNICATIONS

From the standpoint of the direction in which communications flow, three types can be distinguished: (1) downward; (2) upward; and (3) lateral. Let us discuss each of these in turn.

Downward Communication

Downward communication refers to the directives and other messages which originate with the officials at the top of the organization and are

---

[3]George C. Homans, *The Human Group*, Harcourt, Brace, and World, New York, 1950, pp. 11-12.

transmitted down through the hierarchy — through the intervening levels of supervision — until they reach the lowest-ranking worker in the chain. The traditional approach to administration concentrated on this kind of communication and pretty much ignored the other two. It was assumed that the management was in a position to make decisions which were in the best interests of the workers. Once made, these decisions could be "dropped in the chute," so to speak, and be expected to slide smoothly down the hierarchy. If any hitch developed in the implementation of the decisions at any point in this downward chain, it was attributed to the shortcomings of the workers concerned. Furthermore, top management held the ultimate authority, so it could invoke means to force compliance with its instructions.

The Hawthorne experiments showed that downward communication was not so simple. Management could not make decisions which would be accepted at lower levels without first encouraging upward communication, that is the transmission of information and opinions by the workers up the same hierarchy, in other words, travelling the reverse route. In large organizations, downward communication is difficult enough to begin with, because orders must descend through numerous intermediate levels before the point of execution is reached. Misunderstandings can easily occur when instructions pass through so many people. If little upward communication exists, the difficulties are multiplied, because the orders themselves are apt to be unrealistic and to meet with worker resistance.

Upward Communication

Many years have passed since the Hawthorne experiments, but few organizations have been able to develop really effective systems of upward communication — that is, messages that are passed from the lower levels of the hierarchy up to the management. Earl Planty and William Machaver identify a number of barriers to upward communication:

1. Physical distance or inaccessibility
2. Dilution or distortion at each level
3. The attitude of the supervisor
4. The inferior status of the subordinate
5. Tradition.[4]

Workers separated by great distances from the source of authority at the top of the organization have difficulty in communicating upward.

---

[4]See Earl Planty and William Machaver, "Upward Communications: A Project in Executive Development," *Personnel*, Vol. 28, No. 4, January 1952, pp. 304-317.

A field worker, for example, may have relatively infrequent contact with the head of the field office. The latter in turn may have only limited opportunity to see, and therefore to express his ideas fully to his superiors at headquarters. The same is true even when all the workers are located in the same area. The larger the organization, the greater the number of links in the supervisory chain, and the principle of "following channels" requires that no link in this chain be bypassed; everyone must deal through his immediate chief. It is not surprising, then, that few messages that are voluntarily initiated by the lowest worker ever travel upward until they finally reach the desk of the top executive. Reports required by the top management must traverse this route, but they do not have the spontaneity that really should characterize the system of upward communication.

As information is passed up the hierarchy, it is subject to a filtering process at each level. Some of this is deliberate; a good deal is unconscious. The picture of operations as described by a subordinate may not square with the superior's conception of the situation, particularly when the subordinate reports that some things are not going well at all. "Problems" are disturbing, and a typically human reaction is to refuse to believe that they exist or are as serious as they are painted to be. (Good news ascends the hierarchy much more easily than bad news.) The tendency is to "edit" the reports to present a brighter picture. An agency head can sometimes appear to be unbelievably blind as to what is really going on in his agency; yet based on the reports he gets everything *is* fine: these reports simply do not present him with all the facts. Consequently, the upwards reporting system is often of very limited value in locating trouble spots in the agency's operations.

The executive represents to the subordinate someone who wields power and could damage the subordinate's prospects for advancement. This creates a communications block, for the subordinate is wary even though the superior may urge him to be frank. Subordinates who, for one reason or another, feel secure in their positions tend to express themselves the most frankly to their superiors. The subordinate is handicapped at the outset of any upward communication, because he is not free to break in on the superior and intrude on his time. If the chief has something on his mind, he can, at any time, ask the subordinate to see him as soon as possible. In a sense, he controls their time; they in no sense control his. They must, rather, petition an audience with him. There are usually several who want to see the chief at the same time, and he is very busy, as it is, satisfying the other demands on his time.

Upward communication is in a very important sense "unnatural." It is like rowing upstream, against the current. Downward communication has the great force of tradition behind it. There is nothing at all unusual about communications originating at the top of the hierarchy and being routed downward. By contrast, upward communication is unconventional. In most organizations, it is not established procedure for the employees spontaneously to direct upward any large numbers of communications. The employee who attempts to do so may even take a risk. Further, the management that genuinely wants to encourage upward communication will have difficulty because the upward route will generally have been used so rarely in the past that the employees will remain reluctant to use it.

Management can embark on a program to stimulate upward communication. The management should not expect such communication to be spontaneous with the employees, nor is it enough simply to tell the workers that upward communication is desirable. Most of the employees will require clear evidence that the management really is interested in their opinions. Since an important change is being made in the worker's accustomed role, he understandably needs help and encouragement in making the shift from mere cog to full participant in the aims of the organization. Some workers may be so used to playing an insignificant role that they have become quite indifferent to the future of the organization. Thus, the management must change the whole outlook of these workers if it is to succeed in getting them to participate in any system of upward communication.

Superior officers should follow a consistent policy of listening to their subordinates. This may involve adapting to a willingness to face bad news. The mangement should encourage its supervisors to do this, and the example set by the agency head in this respect will normally have a great influence on the other executives. If he encourages communications from below, and accepts even negative reports, his key assistants are likely to do the same with their subordinates.

The most unfriendly atmosphere for upward communication is one in which the management seems to isolate itself, keeping information to itself and considering many matters "confidential" and not to be revealed outside the inner circle. A management which practices such limited downward communication automatically inhibits upward communication, and, in effect, builds a wall between itself and the rest of the organization. For subordinates to initiate upward communication in such an atmosphere would be almost tantamount to defiance. Fortunately, such an attitude by the management is now considered old fashioned and tends to be the exception rather than the rule.

The supervisor should exercise care in selecting his "communicators" — that is, those who provide him with information — and make sure that these communicators are not merely "reflectors" of what he is predisposed to seeing. Some executives make a point of surrounding themselves with at least one or two "no" men in a conscious effort to avoid the "conspiracy of smoothness". For example, Attorney-General Robert Kennedy acted as a "communicator" in his brother's Cabinet.

Some newspaper reports indicated that as the President's brother the Attorney-General was able to be far more blunt with the Chief Executive than any other member of the administration, and this bluntness may explain why the late President depended so much on his younger brother.

The superior officer should also strive to correct those of his personal habits which prevent the subordinate from speaking to him freely. Again, the superior must first be aware of these mannerisms, and humans are typically blind when it comes to personal failings. Yet some self-prompting is possible once the supervisor has become aware of these tendencies and has really decided to encourage the subordinate. It should be pointed out here that superior officers frequently feel a compulsion to demonstrate their superiority to their subordinates. With some, this is a protective device; if they *appear* to know more than their subordinates, they can feel they are living up to their official roles in the organization. Other supervisors are vain and would in any case treat their subordinates with condescension. While the supervisor must never forget his responsibilities as a superior officer, his position hardly means that he is always better apprized of all the facts than is the subordinate. Once the supervisor recognizes that his subordinates are likely to possess information that he does not, he is much more apt to encourage subordinates to communicate with him freely.

Another common mistake is for the superior to state his own position before he listens to the subordinate, rather than inviting the subordinate to give his opinions on the particular problem. There may be no intention on the part of the superior to force his views on the subordinate, but the latter is quickly placed in a difficult position: he must agree with the boss. Few people will want to challenge the chief so openly. Encouraging one's subordinates to express their views holds another advantage. Some workers prefer to leave all decisions to someone else in order to avoid the responsibility. Such an attitude generally serves to impair the calibre of the individual's work, which ultimately reflects on the supervisor, as well as adds to his load of decision making. If, however, the supervisor encourages free expression of ideas from his subordinates, he is likely to lead this sort of individual to develop his capacity for greater responsibility. The supervisor will never succeed in this if he merely asks his subordinates for reactions to his own ideas.

Where it is indicated and feasible, the superior officer should *use* the information given to him by his subordinates. Nothing is more destructive of free expression — and of upward communication — than the chief's failure to act upon the ideas and problems reported to him. The subordinates are led to believe that they are wasting their time, and may even wish that the superior had not gone through the formality of listening. The purpose of communication is to achieve organizational objectives. Action at some point is essential if subordinates are to continue to feel motivated in contributing to these objectives by communicating significant information to their superiors.

Lateral Communication

Lateral communication is that which takes place among workers of the same level in the hierarchy, or among individuals of different levels who are not in a superior-subordinate relationship. Lateral relationships will frequently go from one agency to another, and are not restricted to intra-agency relationships. We use the term *lateral* instead of *horizontal* in order to be able to include *all* across-the-organization contacts.

Traditional organization theory is based on the organization chart and the system of *scalar* authority it depicts. The scalar principle means that the different positions of authority are shown in descending order of importance. The limitations of the chart give the clue to the inadequacies of traditional theory, as is so well revealed in the following statement:

> The relation between the scheme of activities and the scheme of interaction in an organization is usually represented by the familiar organization chart, which shows the organization divided into departments and subdepartments, the various officers and subofficers occupying boxes, connected by lines to show which persons are subordinates to what other ones. Every such chart is too neat; it tells what the channels of interaction ought to be but not always what they are. The pyramid-type chart is particularly misleading because it shows only the interaction between superiors and subordinates, the kind of interaction that we shall call, following Barnard, *scalar.* It does not show the interaction that goes on between two or more persons at about the same level of the organization, for instance, between two department heads....
> This kind of interaction we shall call lateral interaction, though we must remember that there are borderline cases where the distinction between scalar and lateral interaction disappears. The conventional organization chart represents the scalar but not the lateral interaction. *If it were not for the unhappy association with predatory spiders, the facts would be much better represented by a web, the top leader at the center, spokes radiating from him, and concentric circles linking the spokes. Interaction takes place along the concentric circles as well as along the spokes.*[5]

Lateral communication is of great importance in assuring coordination of organizational objectives. The members of the organization should work together as a cohesive unit, but, if they are to do so, they must communicate their plans and intentions to one another clearly. Traditional organization theory has emphasized coordination through command; that is, through the downward communications of the

---

[5]Homans, *op. cit.*, pp. 104-105. Italics ours.

superior. As Thompson explains: "each person's behavior is considered to be determined by the commands of his superior. If every superior is able to give integrated, rationally consistent commands, the organization will automatically be a coordinated system of behavior."[6] The fallacy in this reasoning is that the superior officer is not in a position to give subordinates these "integrated, rationally consistent commands."[7] The subordinates are likely to know the details of operations in their bailiwicks better than he can be expected to know them. Thompson continues:

> Specialization has long outrun human ability to coordinate in this fashion. Not only is the person in the command position increasingly dependent upon subordinates for the interpretation of incoming data and the initiation of activities, but interdependencies far beyond command jurisdictions have developed. Consequently, most coordination is programmed, built into routines.[8]

The concept of coordination by command is basically authoritarian in nature: The way to get the subordinates to work together is to order them to do so; if they fail to obey, punitive corrective measures should be taken. Overlooked is the fact that there are serious limits to the coordination which can be imposed on the employees from above. Such coordination tends to be nominal, simply because it is forced on the worker, and, at best, he only grudgingly complies. Real teamplay is characterized by spontaneity. The individual wants to cooperate because he derives *personal* satisfaction from functioning as a member of the team.

In modern organizations, decision making is not monopolized by just a few top people. Management depends on the specialized skills and knowledge of its subordinates and modern administrations recognize this. Today, they invite workers to participate in the decision-making process. Logically, this requires the encouragement of both upward and lateral communication. The wise superior finds it advantageous to encourage his subordinates, not only to express their ideas to him freely, but also to settle as many problems as possible among themselves. If they are to cooperate in this manner, they must obviously be in close contact with one another.

Obstacles

Just as in the case of upward communication, the lateral pattern of interaction presents its difficulties. In some respects, effective lateral communication is even more difficult to achieve. In upward communication, the subordinate must adjust to only one person — his immediate

---

[6]Victor A. Thompson, *Modern Organization*, Knopf, New York, 1961, p. 181.
[7]*Ibid.*
[8]*Ibid.*, p. 183.

supervisor. In lateral communication, workers must deal with several coworkers. and any one department head must try to work together harmoniously with all other department heads; he must also develop effective working relationships with department heads and other officials of outside agencies.

The very division of an organization into specialized parts creates barriers to lateral communication and coordination. Specialists typically develop strong loyalties, not to the organization as a whole, but to their own areas of interest. The tendency is for them to regard members of other specialized groups as threats to their own positions in the organization. The members of each specialized group think its function is the most important in the agency. Furthermore, specialized professions have their peculiar frames of reference and technical language. The members of each can communicate among themselves effectively, but they frequently have difficulty grasping the point of view of outsiders.

Horizontal cliques also provide the clue to much of the difficulty in lateral communications. Besides the frictions between specialists, there are rivalries and consequent tensions between the different organization units. Departments compete with other departments for bigger appropriations and more prominent roles in the total government program. Similarly, within any one department, the bureaus and other subdivisions fight for special status. The rival organization units eye one another with suspicion and sometimes with considerable hostility. Instead of freely exchanging information on operating plans, they may try to keep one another in the dark. Deviousness, instead of open discussion of mutual problems, may characterize the conversations between their respective personnel. The principal officials in each department may play their cards close to their chests, always afraid of being out-maneuvered by the other party.

The very complexity of modern organization also creates difficulties, just as it does in the case of downward and upward communications. The more persons an official must consult, both within and outside the agency, the more complicated the process of lateral communication becomes. Often he is uncertain as to whom he should consult, because the lines of responsibility within the agency are not that clearly defined. If he must check with another agency, his problem becomes even more difficult, for he may be unfamiliar with the work assignments of the officials in that agency. Valuable time is lost before he can identify the particular individual with whom he should deal. Furthermore, both in intra- and interagency contacts, physical separation may delay and impede communications, as is illustrated in communications between widely separated field offices. Merely looking at the organization chart of a large public agency will give some idea of the complexities of lateral communication. Although the interaction between the numerous departments, divisions, and organization units is not shown on the chart, the very number of these horizontally placed units suggests the intricate pattern of interrelationships necessary for efficient operation. Naturally, the red tape increases as documents and other communications are directed laterally from points inside and outside the agency.

A further difficulty arises from the fact that the person initiating a lateral communication usually cannot exert the same pressure as can a supervisor on his own subordinates. In dealing with coequals, representatives of other agencies, or even the subordinates of others, the official must usually rely on persuasion. This may mean far more delay in lateral than in downward communication, where the traditional flow of authority does give the communication at least some ring of urgency.

Improving Lateral Communication
The first step in developing efficient communications is to build a sound organization structure and to make clear everybody's responsibilties. As to achieving coordination, George F. Grant stresses what he calls "unity by agency objective."[9] By this he means that employees at all levels will work together better if the leaders of the agency clearly explain the importance of the agency program and of their own particular contributions to it. Many different techniques can be employed in this effort, but obviously a very superior quality of leadership is required if the employees throughout the agency are to be induced to work together as a team. Furthermore, there may be important limits to the degree to which any individual may be expected to identify with the organization with which he works. Thompson writes:

> Although some individuals undoubtedly give considerable loyalty to their bread-and-butter organization, it is only one loyalty among many. If the organization becomes the only object of one's loyalty, then the organization becomes a totalitarian state. Most people probably give their first or primary loyalty to their primary groups — the family, the informal work group, etc. The sharing of values and reality perceptions throughout the larger organization is, therefore, an illusion.[10]

One need not wholly agree with Thompson, but there must be some realization of the limitations to employee identification with organizational goals. Yet professional ties improve communication in grant-in-aid and other intergovernmental programs. Individuals within the same profession can get along well, despite the fact that they are of different governmental levels, due to their professional loyalties.

Apart from vocational specialization, there is another important way in which the members of modern organizations are specialized; they

[9]George F. Gant, "Unity and Specialization in Administration," in Felix A. Nigro (ed.), *Public Administration, Readings and Documents*, Holt, Rinehart and Winston, New York, 1951, pp. 126-135.
[10]Thompson, *op. cit.*, p. 185.

are "socially specialized," that is, they have become specialized in working with one another. In efforts to improve lateral communication, it must be recognized that it takes a good deal of time before individuals can become specialized in this way:

> We understand people easily through our experience with them, which teaches us their special use of words, the meaning of intonation and gestures, whether they are matter of fact or emotional, given to exaggeration or understatement, are reticent or voluble, and many other subtle characteristics of communication. Without the confidence that accompanies this kind of understanding, reticence, hesitation, indecision, delay, error, and panic ensue.
>
> "Know your people" is nearly as important as "know your language" in the communication upon which organized effort depends. The difficulty of communication on matters of concrete action between individuals who have not known each other is a matter of common experience, but its importance with respect to organization seems to be forgotten because the organizations we know have, in fact, developed usually through long periods. At a given time nearly everyone has habitual relations with most of those with whom he needs to communicate regularly.[11]

The agency head naturally wants his subordinates to cooperate and to pull together; yet it takes a real effort to get even the heads of organization units to work together properly. Above all, the agency head must be aware of the probable existence of at least some sensitive relationships between them. With this awareness, he is in a much better position to induce coordinated efforts. The staff conference is frequently mentioned as a valuable tool for achieving coordination, yet the experienced executive knows that some of his subordinates may come to these meetings determined to conceal their real thoughts and plans from the others. He will also be well aware that some of the positions taken may be reactions to certain individuals and their personalities, rather than to the objective situation. Subordinate A may react negatively to suggestions made by subordinate B simply because it is B who makes them. If C were to make them, his reaction might be different. Thus if the executive is to be successful in improving lateral communication, he must first be effective in improving the interpersonal relationships among his subordinates. Unless he understands his role in this way, the kinds of communications he evokes from them will likely consist of mere words unsupported by any real desire to cooperate. Surface appearances of harmony may be maintained during the conference — polite words may be exchanged — but, as a coordinating device, the meeting will have been a failure. Obviously, there are limits to what the executive can do to promote better personal relationships between his subordinates. It is a certainty, however, that he will have very little success unless he is first

---

11Chester I. Barnard, "Education for Executives," in Robert Dubin (ed.), *Human Relations in Administration*, Prentice-Hall, Englewood Cliffs, N.J., 1961, p. 20.

able to interpret accurately the feelings behind the communications they initiate, both when in a staff conference or when conferring with him individually.[12]

INFORMAL COMMUNICATIONS

The formal communications network will always be supplemented by an informal one. If clearances are difficult to obtain through the formal channels, contact can be made informally with a friend who can expedite things. The "grapevine" can damage the organization by carrying ugly gossip and false information, but it also can play a constructive role. Valuable information that an individual will normally not be willing to communicate through the official channels is often transmitted to superior officers very rapidly through the grapevine. For instance, John Jones may be unhappy about a certain condition in his office, but he is not inclined to "jump" channels and complain to the management. He expresses himself freely to his friends, one or more of whom may have an "in" with the top officials in the agency. They informally communicate John Jones's dissatisfactions, whereupon management can look into a situation of which it had not been aware. Thus, the friendship ties characteristic of the informal organization remove some of the communication blocks in upward communication. They perform the same function in facilitating lateral and even downward communication: the superior officer may want to give a subordinate personal advice, but he feels that his official capacity does not permit it. He talks freely to another employee who is in a position to pass the advice on to the person concerned. Obviously, considerable skill must be developed in utilizing these informal channels if the desired results are to be obtained. The dangers are great, because information which is fed into the gossip mill can easily be distorted and do more harm than good.

Eugene Walton observes that the "organization's informal communications network begins to hum whenever the formal channels are silent or ambiguous on subjects of importance to its members."[13] This indicates that the management stands to profit from knowing what kind of information is being transmitted through the grapevine. Walton has investigated the means by which employees learn of significant organization developments. In cases where the employees have heard about these developments mostly through the grapevine, there is a clear indication that the official channels were not functioning as efficiently as

---

[12]An excellent treatment of this problem is Warren H. Schmidt and Robert Tannenbaum, "The Management of Differences," in Tannenbaum, Weschler, and Masarik (eds.), *Leadership and Organization: A Behavioral Science Approach,* McGraw-Hill, New York, 1961, pp. 101-118.
[13]Eugene Walton, "How Efficient is the Grapevine?" *Personnel,* Vol. 38, No. 2, March-April, 1961, p. 45.

they should have been. Of course, no matter how good the formal system of communications, the grapevine will still exist, but it should not have to do the job of advising employees of management policies. This is the responsibility of the formal organization.

In closing this chapter, the following words of Herbert A. Simon are very much to the point:

> No step in the administrative process is more generally ignored, or more poorly performed, than the task of communicating decisions. All too often, plans are "ordered" into effect without any consideration of the manner in which they can be brought to influence the behavior of the individual members of the group. Procedural manuals are promulgated without follow-up to determine whether the contents of the manuals are used by the individuals to guide their decisions. Organization plans are drawn on paper, although the members of the organization are ignorant of the plan that purports to describe their relationship.[14]

13
Efficiency in Government and Business*

A.W. Johnson

The Royal Commission on Government Organization — the Glassco Commission — aroused an unusual interest in efficiency in government. For some, its reports — frequently unread — confirmed a long-standing suspicion that governments always have been, and always will be, inefficient. For others the Commission's reports held out a new hope that business-like methods can and will be introduced into government. For still others the reports revealed once again a profound misunderstanding on the part of businessmen as to the processes of parliamentary government, and confirmed once more the need for continuing organization and methods studies within government. For a few — the management consultants — the reports and the public interest which they aroused created a sort of happy hunting ground where new commissions and new studies could be proposed with confidence — all of them requiring the specialized skills of the management consultant.

However heterogeneous the responses to the Glassco Commission's work, anyone who is interested in perfecting the processes of

---

[14]Herbert A. Simon, *Administrative Behavior*, Macmillan, New York, 1957, p. 108.

*Reprinted and slightly abridged by permission from A.W. Johnson, "Efficiency in Government and Business," *Canadian Public Administration*, vol. 6, no. 3 (September 1963), pp. 245-260.

government will welcome warmly this new-found interest in government administration.

Having said this, I find myself wanting to sound a note of caution about the premises which seem to underlie the discussions of the Glassco reports, and indeed the reports themselves.

First, there seems to me to be abroad an assumption that "everyone knows what efficiency means." It is simply a matter of good organization, of effective management practices, of streamlined procedures, and the like. But is this all that there is to efficient government, to effective government? Are there not other dimensions to "efficiency" which are equally important to, if not more important than, the purely administrative or management aspect?

Second, the proposition seems to have been accepted, without too much critical scrutiny, that the methods by which efficiency is achieved in business are equally applicable in government — or very nearly so. There is a science of administration, in other words, which can be employed with equal effectiveness in business or in government. But is it true that the "efficiency techniques" of business are entirely applicable in government — or at least in all phases of government? Can efficiency in the public services be achieved simply by perfecting the "horizontal" processes — organization, financial management, personnel management, and the like? Or are there large areas of public administration where new "efficiency techniques" must be evolved, or the conventional ones substantially adapted if the unique program problems of the public services are to be evaluated effectively?

Third, I find myself wondering, if governments are less efficient than they might and should be — and surely all of us will acknowledge that they are — why is this so? Is it enough to say that organization is defective, or that procedual practices are deficient, and they should be remedied? Or should we stop to consider whether there is in the civil service a sufficient "efficiency motivation" — a motivation upon which we can build so as to ensure a *continuing* concern for effective operation? Or must we reconcile ourselves to the need for periodic royal commissions which will shake up the public services on these occasions, only to be followed by intervals of decline and decay? This sometimes seems to be the assumption which underlies the public discussions of the Glassco reports.

These are the questions which I want to consider. Please notice that I am not pretending to analyze the Glassco Commission reports, nor to analyze the analyses that have been made of them. Instead, what I am trying to do is to question whether we really have thought through what we mean by efficiency in government, whether we really know the methods by which it can be achieved, and whether we have considered carefully enough the source of efficiency motives in government — if any.

WHAT IS EFFICIENCY?

My first question is what do we mean when we talk of efficiency? The conventional notion is clear enough: it simply means reducing administrative expenses, eliminating waste and extravagance, and speeding up service to the public. This is what I am inclined to call "administrative efficiency."

The notion of "administrative efficiency" first was developed, as we all know, in private business — specifically, in manufacturing enterprises. Its pioneers — Henri Fayol and Frederick W. Taylor — were seeking to increase productivity, to maximize production, and they sought to do so by improving work arrangements. Given the production of a certain commodity, given sometimes the present technology, how could an enterprise best divide and order the processes of manufacture in order to maximize output and minimize inputs? The techniques they used are well known: product simplification and standardization, production planning and control, proper division of work, the use of management improvement techniques, staff training and the development of happy staff relations, performance analysis and control, and the rest.

I do not want to elaborate on these techniques of "administrative efficiency" right now — that will come later. My present purpose is to point out the premises upon which "administrative efficiency" is based: this kind of efficiency takes for granted the policy decisions which created the manufacturing enterprise in the first place. "Administrative efficiency" *assumes* that the right product is being produced; it *assumes* that the market for the product exists or can be developed; it *assumes* that the plant is properly located; and frequently it *assumes* that the technology of production being used is the appropriate technology.

But notice that if the wrong policy decisions had been made in the first place — if the plant were poorly located or the market were insufficient — not all the administrative efficiency in the world would compensate for these errors in decision-making. There is, in short, another kind of efficiency which is of a higher order than "administrative efficiency," and that is "policy efficiency" — the making of the right policy decisions.

In manufacturing enterprise the components of "policy efficiency" — though it is not called that — are well known. Economic studies precede a decision to manufacture a new product — studies both of the potential market for the product, and of the manufacturing processes which will have to be developed. Feasibility studies determine the economics of the enterprise — studies which forecast the sales revenues and all of the costs of production: capital, labour, raw materials, transportation, and so on. Plant location studies compare the economics of alternative plant locations, given the differentials between the wage costs, transportation costs, and power costs of different areas. Financial analysis determines how much of the capital can be interest-bearing and how much must be equity capital in order that costs might be minimized, while at the same time retaining control in the hands of the sponsors of the enterprise. "Policy efficiency," in short, is what the economists call proper resource allocation.

The same distinction between administrative efficiency" and "policy efficiency" can be made in government. "Administrative efficiency" — what the Glassco Commission concerned itself with primarily — consists of good organization, efficient procedures, effective financial control, proper inventory control, appropriate paperwork and systems management, and the rest. "Policy efficiency," on the other hand, is a matter of making the right policy decisions, of selecting the appropriate programs in order to achieve the government's objectives.

Let me give a few examples. If a highway is properly located, given the trends in population distribution, travel patterns and the rest, the taxpayers will be saved enormous sums of money in their travel costs. If welfare programs are constructed so as to return people to the active labour force, the social aid bill which the taxpayers bear will be significantly reduced. If treatment programs in mental hospitals are calculated to return patients to the community the number of mental institutions required will be controlled. If education programs produce the kind of trained labour force which the economy requires, the numbers of unemployed will be reduced. On a more sophisticated level still, if a proper balance is achieved between monetary policy, fiscal policy and trade policy, the rate of growth of the economy will be increased, and the cost to the community of unemployment will be reduced.

Here once again, the economies of "policy efficiency" greatly outweigh the savings which can be achieved by "administrative efficiency." One bad policy decision — for example, the construction of an uneconomic railway or road — will cost the taxpayer more than can possibly be saved by better control over the purchase of underwear for the armed forces.

It is important, in other words, not to be misled when we talk about efficiency. "Administrative efficiency" unquestionably is important, but let no one think that it is the only kind of efficiency, or even that it is the most important kind.

Now let me build into this framework a third kind of efficiency — "service efficiency." This is an obscure phrase, I know, but it is the only one I can think of to describe "effectiveness" as opposed to "efficiency."

All of us are familar, I am sure, with the conflict which sometimes exists between administrative economies on the one hand, and the provision of better service to the public on the other. Let me give some examples. It is almost always possible to achieve economies of scale through the centralization of services, such as health and welfare. But the effect of doing so is to make the services less accessible to the public. It is always possible to enforce safety programs more efficiently by giving the safety inspectors more power, or by making the regulations more explicit; but the effect is to subject the citizen to requirements that are sometimes impractical, if not downright hostile to his freedom of action. It is frequently possible to streamline financial processes by reducing some of the controls over departmental spending, but to do so may be to reduce parliamentary control over the government and the civil service.

I acknowledge that I have collected under this heading of "service efficiency" a heterogeneous group of public service objectives, including service to the public, responsiveness to public opinion, and the preservation of parliamentary control. But my point, I hope, is clear: efficiency in government must be measured not in economic terms alone. Equally, indeed more important, it must be measured in terms of the effectiveness with which it provides public services within the context of constitutional government. Public services must be readily and equally accessible to all citizens. They must be close enough to the citizen, in fact, that he can exert an influence upon them — adapting them to the needs of the community as the needs of the community change. The regulatory functions of the state must be discharged not for the sole purpose of protecting people and their property, but also with the purpose of preserving to the maximum extent possible the rights of the citizens being regulated. All public services must be provided and financed in such a way that the cabinet remains in control of the bureaucracy and that parliament remains in control of both. The prime measure of efficiency in government, I am arguing, is whether the government provides the public services the public wants and where it wants them, and whether the public services provided and the public servants who provide them remain firmly in the control of the public's representatives.

Let me make one more point about "service efficiency." In business this kind of efficiency is less distinguishable from "policy efficiency" and "administrative efficiency" than it is in government. If an enterprise fails to provide what the public wants, or fails to respond to shifts in consumer tastes, an economic penalty sooner or later must be paid. Sales will decline. So "service efficiency" in business is looked upon in economic terms. In government, however, the penalty for inefficiency in service is a political or a constitutional one: the government is defeated or constitutional processes are eroded, or both. And only a fairly perceptive observer will see the relationship — perhaps I should say the conflict — between "administrative efficiency" and "service efficiency."

My first observation, then, is this: it is a mistake to judge efficiency only in administrative terms. It would be possible to have the slickest and the most streamlined government in the world, and yet to have public policies which resulted in a gross misallocation of resources, or public services which were quite incompatible with the objectives of constitutional democracy. I am not suggesting by any means that we should ignore administrative efficiency: quite the contrary, it is one of our primary goals. But I do suggest that as public servants we have a responsibility to look to the broader kinds of efficiency as well — "policy efficiency" and "service efficiency" — if we are to serve the public well.

EFFICIENCY METHODS

If I have identified correctly the several kinds of efficiency in government, the next question is whether we know how to achieve them. It is usually assumed — I suspect that the Glassco Commission assumed — that the methods by which business achieves efficiency are equally applicable in government. This may be so. But if, on the other hand, a different approach is required in government, or a substantial adaptation of business methods is needed, we will be misled if we simply try to transplant into the public service the "efficiency techniques" of private business. At best we will have done an incomplete job.

It is in the field of "administrative efficiency," of course, that the approach of private business is best known. The goal, as we all know, is to maximize output and to minimize expense. This means that each factor of production — labour, equipment, and so on — must be identified, and its contribution to production — its productivity — must be measured. If the productivity of a given factor, labour for example, can be increased, then the cost per unit of production will be reduced. If on the other hand, the productivity of a given factor of production has reached its limit, management may seek to substitute a cheaper production factor — equipment in place of labour, for example.

The key to this approach is measurability: you must be able to measure the inputs — man-hours, equipment hours and so on — and you must be able to measure the outputs — units of commodity produced. Having done this it becomes possible to establish a "standard" as to the quantity of inputs required in order to produce a given unit of output. The standard may be the average of previous levels of productivity, or it may be a target level established through controlled production experiments. In either event these standards are applied to the manufacturing process, and the various factors of production are expected to perform at the target levels.

There are, of course, techniques for raising productivity to the standards which have been set, or for raising the standards themselves. These include greater specialization in the manufacturing processes, production planning and control, improvements in organization and coordination, the simplification of work processes through work study and measurement, staff training and so on.

These techniques were developed specifically for manufacturing operations, but they have been adapted to office operations. This has been possible wherever inputs and outputs have both been found to be measurable. Production planning and control takes the form of planning and controlling paper operations and paper flows. Work simplification takes the form of analyzing what is "added" at each stage of the office procedure, and of eliminating steps which are found to be unnecessary. Staff training and development and space layout studies both are applied much as they are in manufacturing operations. And office equipment — notably, today, data-processing equipment — is substituted for labour where it is found to be a cheaper "input" than are clerical man-hours.

These techniques have been found to be applicable in many office operations, but by no means in all. Wherever the output is diffuse, or does not lend itself to precise measurement, it is unlikely that these conventional efficiency techniques can be used. This is true not only in the production of office services but in the production of other services as well — legal, medical and personal services, to name a few. The point to be noted is that business itself has found it difficult, sometimes impossible, to apply the efficiency techniques of commodity-producing industries to industries which produce services. And this is nearly always where the output does not lend itself to precise measurement. We should no more expect to be able to apply the "efficiency techniques" of commodity-producing industries to government than we are able to apply them to other service industries. Some government services, such as large-scale paperwork operations, road building, the production and sale of electric power, and sewer and water systems, lend themselves to these "efficiency techniques." But a great many do not.

Consider some of the services which governments provide: public health nursing, primary and secondary schools, agricultural extension, social work services, and psychiatric research, to name a few. In each case the work inputs are measurable enough: staff time, differentiated between different classes of workers, materials used, equipment employed, travel expenses, telephone expenses, and so on.

But the output of these employees — the ultimate output — is extremely difficult to measure. This is partly because it is inherently difficult to identify and to measure, and partly because the results become apparent only several years after the services have been rendered. Here are some examples. The results of the child health clinics conducted by public health nurses become apparent only in the morbidity and mortality statistics of the future. The results of the education given in primary and secondary schools are felt only when the children involved have become active members of the labour force — and then it is difficult to compare what is with what might have been had the schooling not been given. The agricultural education given farmers by "Ag Reps" becomes evident years later in higher and more stable crop production, but even then it is difficult to establish a clear casual relationship. The effect of social workers' efforts may never be known statistically; all we know is that certain families or young people or offenders have become active and productive members of the community. The relationship between psychiatric research and more effective treatment of the mentally ill becomes known, and even measurable statistically, but the lag between the cause and the effect is very substantial indeed.

Obviously we cannot expect to measure real output at the time the service is given and sometimes we may never be able to do so (though I think we should try much harder than we do). All we can hope to do is to measure the units of service given — and even here the exercise is sometimes futile (for example in primary and secondary education). But it *is* possible in some branches of government to measure the units of service that are provided — the number of clinics held by the public health nurse or the number of farm equipment demonstrations given by the agricultural representative — and where this is possible the conventional "efficiency techniques" may be adapted to the needs of the public service.

My point, then, is this: the methods used by business to achieve "administrative efficiency" may be used directly by governments only in a few areas of public service. If we are to develop "efficiency techniques" for the rest of the service we must adapt and innovate to a very considerable extent.

"POLICY EFFICIENCY"

The same holds true of "policy efficiency." Business administration schools have developed a considerable body of knowledge as to how manufacturing enterprises can achieve "policy efficiency" — they teach market analysis, plant location analysis, alternative forms of industry organization, including horizontal and vertical integration, the strategy of competition and so on. But none of this is useful to us in the public service.

What *is* useful, however, are the underlying methods being used by businessmen. What I am talking about now — or trying to — is the use of scientific method, of rational planning. There is, of course, a lot of guesswork in the policy decisions of boards of directors, but the forward-looking firm seeks to reduce the guesswork to a minimum. The elements in decision-making are analyzed and measured statistically wherever possible: market trends, changes in consumer tastes, whether involuntary or induced, trends in costs, trends in technology, the behaviour of competitors, and so on. And alternative courses for achieving a given objective are examined before a decision is made. To take a simple example, the productive capacity of an industry is expanded only after markets have been analyzed, after alternative plant locations have been examined, after alternative methods of production have been explored, and so on.

There are areas of government where the same analytical processes can easily be employed. Road location by departments of highways is a good example: public servants study traffic patterns and road-use trends, and then, using the benefit-cost analysis approach, determine the optimum location and design of a highway. This sort of approach is quite common in the engineering phases of government work — though I suspect that the public is quite unaware of the use of these planning techniques.

It is more difficult to apply such planning techniques in the area of social policies, though some advances have been made. It is in this area, however, where there is the greatest room for innovation and adaptation.

Let me give you some examples. Governments have assumed responsibility for the community's costs of hospitalization and, to a substantial extent, for the costs of nursing home care for the aged and the disabled. Having done so, they inevitably confront demands for enlarged facilities, as hospital utilization rises and as the population of the aged and disabled increases. Two courses are open to the government. One is to meet the demand, locating the facilities as rationally as possible, using population studies as a guide. The other is to determine whether alternative forms of care are possible or preferable. Are there disabilities for which preventive or even earlier treatment would reduce the incidence of institutionalization? Is it possible to embark upon rehabilitation programs which would reduce the length of stay in institutions, thus increasing the "turnover" in public institutions, to put it crudely? Is it possible to provide home-care services which would be less costly than institutionalization?

In other words, the objective is to care for the sick and the disabled, and the problem is not necessarily one of providing more capital facilities. The economic and social costs might be lower if alternative methods of prevention, treatment and rehabilitation, were adopted.

To make policy decisions such as these — and all of us could give many more examples — is to achieve efficiency in government of the highest order. But to do so requires a highly imaginative and a very skillful public service — to say nothing of the cabinets and parliaments involved. Clearly "policy efficiency" in government is not a matter simply of adopting the techniques of business "policy efficiency": we in government must evolve our own techniques. Moreover, we will have saved pennies and lost dollars for the taxpayer if we preoccupy ourselves solely with "administrative efficiency."

EFFICIENCY INCENTIVES

My first two points, then, are these: efficiency in public administration has more dimensions than just one, and it will not be achieved simply by adopting the conventional "efficiency techniques." Public servants must concern themselves with all three kinds of efficiency — "policy," "administrative," and "service" — and they must do more than merely copy the "efficiency techniques" of business. They must adapt them and develop new ones.

My third question now comes into focus: are there in the public service sufficient incentives to efficiency? Is there the "will" to find the "way" to efficiency in government? The most melancholy part of public attitudes about the public service, is the assumption that there are not. We who are civil servants are, of course, inclined to dispute this, occasionally by rather pontifical pronouncements about our dedication to public service, and about our personal motivations — which we conceive to be of the highest order.

Now, I am not disputing these motivations, nor am I deriding them. They are most important. But I think the public would be relieved if they could see something more substantial, something less personal, perhaps even something less "chancy" than individual dedication.

The question that occurs to all of us, I'm sure, is why the efficiency motivation of business is so readily accepted as being sufficient, and how it really operates. I am referring, of course, to the profit motive. Can we assume with confidence that the profit motive operates automatically in industry? If so, how is it made effective — how is it "institutionalized"? If we had the answers to these questions we might have some clues as to where to look in the civil service for equivalent or alternative efficiency motivations.

It is probably fair to say that the profit motive in business influences primarily the owners of an enterprise, and top management staff whose effectiveness is judged largely by the profit and loss statement. And undoubtedly this motivation has a very real influence in the quest by these people for "policy efficiency."

But "administrative efficiency" cannot be achieved by top management alone: in the final analysis it can be only the product of the efforts of employees who are far removed from the direct benefits of greater productivity. It is the middle management people, the foremen and supervisors, indeed the workmen themselves, who must be relied upon to introduce new procedures and methods, to improve space layout, to speed up work flows, and so on. Yet these people rarely, if ever, see a profit and loss statement, and a good many of them would be unable to interpret one if they did see it. Moreover, even if they were able to read financial statements it would be most difficult for them to discern a clear and direct relationship between "administrative efficiency," higher productivity, and greater personal rewards. The effects of collective bargaining are more likely to be perceptible, even to foremen and supervisors.

What top management must do, then, is somehow to communicate at least to middle-management levels a "drive for efficiency." In some enterprises this is attempted by profit-sharing schemes. If this device were very common in private business, one might conclude that top management had in this way been able to make the profit motive operate among superintendents, supervisors, and foremen. The efficiency motivation even at these levels would then be the profit motive. But unless I am mistaken, it is a fact that profit sharing schemes are not that common in large-scale business enterprises.

What then is the "efficiency motivation"? How does top management instill in a large corporation the desire for efficiency — a desire which may flow from the profit motive but which is capable of existing by itself? I have the impression that what happens in a well-run corporation is that a sort of "efficiency value" is developed, and that this comes to be subscribed to by an important number of middle-management employees. The whole structure of rewards and penalties is designed to promote the efficient worker and the effective supervisor; and middle management people know that their success will be measured by the productivity of their departments. So efficiency, of and by itself, becomes the objective of the successful superintendent or foreman.

It would be idyllic to believe that this condition is produced with ease, or that it is common in all large-scale enterprises. In point of fact, businessmen themselves are not prepared to rely upon this approach alone. In addition to relating their system of rewards and penalties to employee-productivity — to the extent that their union contracts permit — business managers employ special teams whose job it is constantly to seek out improvements in organization and procedures. Work flow analysis, the examination of production processes, and all of the techniques of business engineering are used by these units to try to cut expenses and increase productivity. In smaller enterprises the services of management consultants may be used for the same end. To the extent that the "efficiency value" has been accepted by middle management people they will welcome the work of the systems analysts; to the extent that it hasn't the "time and motion boys" will be resented.

This oversimplification of the institutionalization of an "efficiency motivation" in private corporations is not meant to exalt business efficiency. Anyone who has had any experience in or association with corporate enterprise knows that there is room for improvement in business administration as well as in public administration. But my point is this: it is not a perception of the relationship between "administrative efficiency" and profits which drives middle management people or efficiency experts; it is the desire to prove their own ability to increase productivity. This is not to say that this "drive" has no relationship to the profit motive; it is merely to say that it can motivate people who are not themselves impelled by a desire for higher profits.

This being so, it seems to me reasonable to suppose that the same kind of efficiency motivation can exist in the public service, provided there is a will on the part of governments and senior public servants to create and to develop it. Since governments are not impelled by a profit motive, the question is whether there are other impulses, that will cause them to instill in the public service an "efficiency value."

I suggest that there are. First, it is well known that inefficiency in government, whether manifested by indolent civil servants, or obstructive red-tape, or sheer incompetence, is quick to engage public criticism. And nothing can be more damaging, politically, to governments. Even if the public were docile, or immune to inefficiency in public administration, you can be sure that parliamentary oppositions would do their best to make people aware of the deficiencies of government bureaucracy. Certainly it has been my experience that ministers of the Crown react rather quickly to the complaints of citizens or of the opposition that they have encountered slothfulness, or rudeness, or inefficiency on the part of the public service. It is the ministers and their parliamentary supporters, after all, who pay the penalty for public dissatisfaction — just as it is the shareholders and the managers who are the losers when profits decline.

There is another reason, too, that ministers and senior public servants are impelled to take an interest in efficiency. All of us have learned that it isn't easy to enlarge our appropriations for the purpose of improving or expanding the programs for which we are responsible. Treasury boards and finance committees are notoriously difficult in these matters. But if we can demonstrate economies in some part of our department, the men on the treasury benches are more favourably disposed to an increase in the allotment for another part of the department. Moreover, the competition for funds is keen enough when budgets are being formulated that treasury board officials will often be told when departments feel that others are being profligate in their spending.

There is, in short, a constant competition for scarce resources in government — just as there is in the private sector of the economy — and finance officials like officials of operating departments are keenly aware of this fact. It has been my experience that this, in combination with the concern to avert public criticism, operates effectively to create in senior civil servants a real concern for efficiency.

I have said nothing about the "service motivation" which operates in government. It is all too easy to sound pompous or righteous in doing so. But I nevertheless believe it to be true that the great majority of cabinet ministers and senior civil servants are in the public service because of a concern that government should meet the social and economic needs of the community. And because of this motivation they are just as concerned about efficiency in public administration as businessmen are about efficiency in business administration. The question is whether they succeed in communicating their concern to the middle management levels of the civil service.

The techniques that senior public servants use to instill a concern for efficiency in their division heads and supervisors are the same that private management employ. First, promotion through the higher ranks of the civil service is based, so far as I can discern, upon demonstrated ability. This, like the system of rewards used in private business tends to focus the attention of middle management people upon efficiency and effectiveness. What is often misleading, I think, is the fact that efficiency assumes different forms in the public service; the result is that it is not readily recognizable to people who are accustomed to the patterns of efficiency in business.

Second, governments, like businesses, have established special agencies for the purpose of ensuring that departments do in fact organize their work effectively. Shortly after the second World War, Organization and Methods units were established in the Government of Canada and the Government of Saskatchewan, and since then Organization and Methods units, and the use of management consultants, have proliferated in federal departments, in provincial governments, and in municipal governments. These agencies operate in much the same manner as do their counterparts in industry.

SPECIAL PROBLEMS IN PUBLIC ADMINISTRATION

I am arguing, in short, that the methods by which an "efficiency motivation" is institutionalized in the civil service are not too dissimilar from those used in private business. Having said this, I think it is fair to observe that there are special problems which must be overcome in government.

First, some governments, notably the Government of Canada, are such large organizations, and are so scattered geographically, that extra efforts are required to make the "efficiency motivation" operative. In a sense large governments should be compared with a national railway system rather than with a compact and homogeneous industrial enterprise.

Second, departmentalization in government is fundamentally different than it is in business. Each agency of the public service tends to operate a group of programs which are differentiated clearly from those of other agencies, with the result that a single approach to efficiency becomes impossible. Moreover, because of the principle of individual ministerial responsibility, it is more difficult to impose a central or unified approach to the management of the differentiated affairs of the several departments. The result is that it is possible to find some departments that are operated more efficiently than others. And it is not always easy for the cabinet to impose "efficiency requirements" on the weaker departments; certainly not as easy as it is for the management of a private business to do with respect to recalcitrant divisions of a relatively monolithic corporate enterprise.

Third, there is more frequently in government a conflict between "service efficiency" and "administrative efficiency." I was alluding to this when I spoke of the principle of individual ministerial responsibility. Greater "administrative efficiency" is sometimes possible, but only at the cost of diluting or modifying the arrangements of constitutional government. A cabinet is not a monolithic structure, any more than Canada is a homogeneous nation. And if individual ministers, like distinctive cultures in our nation, display a highly individual approach to the management of their affairs, it is not an easy matter, nor is it always proper, to impose a single or a unified approach. Similarly, a prime measure of success in government is whether parliamentary control is preserved and maintained. There is no doubt in my mind that financial processes in government could be streamlined if parliament's annual appropriation control were abandoned. But "service efficiency" — the preservation of parliamentary control — must take precedence.

Special difficulties are encountered also in achieving "policy efficiency." It seems to me reasonable to suppose that some government programs become obsolete during the passage of time, and that superior policies could be evolved for achieving the same ends. But the plain truth is, or so it seems to me, that there are strong, built-in pressures from the electorate to retain almost any public program which you might care to mention. Equally, new policies undoubtedly are adopted which are not the most efficient way of achieving a goal — indeed the goal itself may be questionable. I'm sure, for example, that most of us could select as illustrations some of Canada's tax laws; measures which are incredibly difficult to administer, but the results of which seem not to justify the effort involved. Yet each of these was built into the tax laws to meet the pressures of some part of the electorate.

It is not for me, as a civil servant, to identify more specifically than this alleged examples of "policy inefficiency." I content myself with the assertion that such inefficiencies, if they do exist, are the product largely of the political process in Canada. And if in fact we are getting the kind of government which we vote for, it is simply a contradiction in terms to suggest that these policy aberrations are in fact inefficiency. They may be inefficient ways of achieving an objective, or the objective itself may be inefficient in economic terms. But as long as the policies involved are the product of democratic processes they are legitimate in themselves — they are the product of "service efficiency".

CASE REFERENCES

Canadian Cases in Public Administration
    Dr. Stockfield's Resignation
    The Shared Authority
    Dr. Aphid's Accident
    The Frustrated Purchasing Agent
    The Vague Purchasing Assignment
    The Successful Leader
    This Hour Has Seven Days
    The Foot and Mouth Disease Epidemic, 1952

BIBLIOGRAPHY

Argyris, Chris, *Personality and Organization*. New York, Harper & Row Publishers, 1957.

Blake, R.R. and Mouton, J.S., *The Managerial Grid*. Houston, Texas, Gulf Publishing Company, 1964.

Davis, Keith, *Human Relations At Work*. New York, McGraw-Hill Book Company, 1962.

Dubin, R., ed., *Human Relations in Administration*. Englewood Cliffs, N.J., Prentice-Hall, 1961.

Dubin, R. *et al.*, *Leadership and Productivity*. San Francisco, Chandler Publishing Company, 1965.

Gellerman, Saul W., *Management by Motivation*. New York, American Management Association, 1968.

Gellerman, Saul W., *The Management of Human Relations*. New York, Holt, Rinehart & Winston, 1966.

Gore, William J., *Administrative Decision-Making: A Heuristic Model*. New York, John Wiley & Sons, 1964.

Gore, William J., and Dyson, J.W., eds., he Making of Decisions: A Reader in Administrative Behaviour. New York, Free Press of Glencoe, 1964.

Harmon, Michael M., "Social Equity and Organizational Man: Motivation and Organizational Democracy." *Public Administration Review*, Vol. 34, No. 1, January-February 1974, pp. 11-18.

Herzberg, Frederick, Mausner, B. and Snyderman, B., *The Motivation to Work*. New York, John Wiley and Sons, 1959.

Kirkhart, Larry and Gardner, Neely, eds., "Symposium: Organization Development." *Public Administration Review*, Vol. 34, No. 2, March-April 1974, pp. 97-140.

Lindblom, Charles, "The Science of Muddling Through." *Public Administration Review*, Vol. 19, No. 1, 1959, pp. 79-88.

Mailick, Sidney, *Concepts and Issues in Administrative Behavior*. Englewood Cliffs, N.J., Prentice-Hall, 1962.

McGregor, D.M., *The Human Side of Enterprise*. New York, McGraw-Hill Book Company, 1960.

Percival, Nora, ed., *Communication Within the Organization*. New York, American Management Association, 1967.

Redfield, Charles E., *Communication in Management*. Chicago, The University of Chicago Press, 1969.

Selznick, Philip, *Leadership in Administration: A Sociological Interpretation*. New York, Row, Peterson, 1957.

Tannenbaum, Robert *et al.*, *Leadership and Organization*. New York, McGraw-Hill Book Company, 1961.

Tead, Ordway, *The Art of Leadership*. New York, McGraw-Hill, 1935.

Wilensky, Harold L., *Organizational Intelligence, Knowledge, and Policy in Government and Industry*. New York, Basic Books, 1967.

Wilson, H.T., "Rationality and Decision in Administrative Science." *Canadian Journal of Political Science*, Vol. 6, No. 2, June 1973, pp. 271-94.

CHAPTER 4
PLANNING AND FINANCE

The essays in this chapter extend our discussion of management with an analysis of the functions of planning and financing. On every list of management functions, planning usually stands first for two reasons: logically, it precedes all other action and, practically speaking it is the function which is most involved with every other function.

The first three essays focus on new approaches designed to improve planning, organizational performance, resource allocation and program evaluation. Walter Baker explains the philosophy and utility of Management by Objectives (MBO). An excerpt from a Treasury Board publication describes the purposes, administrative implications and anticipated benefits of the Planning Programming and Budgeting System (PPBS). Henning Frederiksen analyzes the Operational Performance Measurement System (OPMS) which was designed to improve program evaluation for more effective implementation of MBO and PPBS.

Herbert Balls then summarizes the major elements of financial administration and control. The final essay in this chapter focuses on the critical role of the Auditor General in the control of government expenditure.

14
Management by Objectives*

Walter Baker

As a philosphy, management by objectives involves a belief in participative management and incorporates the central tenets of Douglas McGregor's "Theory Y," that "the motivation, the potential for development, the capacity for assuming responsibility, the readiness to direct behavior towards organizational goals are all present in people . . ." and that the essential task of management is "to arrange organizational conditions and methods of operation so that people can achieve their own goals *best* by directing *their own* efforts toward organizational objectives."[1]

Unless a manager is committed to a considerable degree of involvement in decision-making by his subordinates, he will experience great difficulty operating within a framework of management by objectives. It demands a style of management that contrasts sharply with that of the authoritarian "boss," benevolent or otherwise, and equally sharply with the charismatic leader of strong, dominant personality who may obtain apparently excellent results while breaking all normal bureaucratic rules and, in the process, leaving subordinates operating in highly ambiguous surroundings and considerably dependent on his personal strengths for organizational progress.

One central facet of management by objectives as a philosophy and style of management, then, is a belief in democratic, participative, cooperative management. A second is a commitment to purposive, planned, "rational" management, in which different managerial levels combine their best efforts, both in setting goals and in working purposefully towards them.

To many public administrators, therefore, management by objectives is not something new, radical or addition to their current beliefs about what constitutes effective management. Yet many who believe themselves fully sympathetic to the philosphy and style of management outlined above do not make an operational commitment to stating clearly their purposes or objectives. When Luther Gulick declared that ". . . a clear statement of purpose universally understood is the outstanding guarantee of effective administration" he anticipated the major point of

---

*Reprinted and abridged by permission from Walter Baker, "Management by Objectives: A Philosophy and Style of Management for the Public Sector?" *Canadian Public Administration,* vol. 12, no. 3 (Fall 1969), pp. 427-443.
[1]Douglas McGregor, "The Human Side of Enterprise," in Warren G. Bennis and Edgar H. Schein, eds., *Leadership and Motivation: Essays of Douglas McGregor,* Cambridge, Mass., MIT Press, 1966, p. 15.

departure for proponents of management by objectives. While the proposition that clarity of objectives is an essential prerequisite to an efficient use of resources is probably acceptable to the vast majority of practising managers, it is reasonably certain that many do not seek this clarification in a systematic way from year to year.

MANAGEMENT BY OBJECTIVES AS A SET OF TECHNIQUES

As an interrelated set of techniques, management by objectives incorporates a process containing several distinct stages.

I *The clarification of overall purposes by top management,* preferably in consultation with lower echelons of management.

Practitioners begin with a recognition that what is sought is a mosaic of complementary objectives, set in conjunction with each other at all managerial levels of the organization from top management down to, say, first-line supervisor. The first stage in developing this mosaic is for top management to review what, in the business sector, tends to be known as the "master strategy" of the organization, its main formal reason for existing. This review of overall objectives is particularly important in modern society where a rapidly changing environment can cause such objectives to lose their relevance and hence threaten the organization's viability.

II *Analysis by top management of the results expected of those reporting directly to them,* if overall objectives are to be met.

Assuming that the proper review has taken place and that it is concluded that overall objectives are still meaningful or, alternatively, that they have been adjusted to new environmental needs, the vital problem of translating them into day-to-day action remains. This process of translating overall goals into a dynamic action system embraces, of course, the management process in its entirety. In modern organizations, the management system which carries out this process is increasing in complexity and in larger organizations many people are normally involved, in complicated interrelationships, in seeking to meet the overall objectives of the oganization. If order and system are to be achieved among a potentially chaotic jumble of individuals, each engaged in discrete activities that might otherwise be meaningful only to him, then proponents of management by objectives suggest that a first imperative is that at every managerial level in the organization each manager must be clear concerning *the results expected of him* and hence his unit, and also concerning how these results will contribute to the total result desired if the organization's overall objectives are to be met.

As a system and set of procedures, management by objectives is *results oriented,* therefore. Whereas many managers, in seeking to obtain maximum performance from their subordinates, focus upon the activities in which they are engaged, their personality characteristics, their background and their skills, to the practitioner of management by objectives these are all secondary to the results' orientation. It is acknowledged, however, that in achieving results certain activities will be carried out, utilizing certain skills, and that a particular background and personality configuration may aid or retard performance.

The focus upon results does permit, nevertheless, the widest possible range of activities, personalities, skills and background in achieving them. The perennial question concerning what personality configuration produces the strongest manager appears in management by objectives to become relatively inconsequential. What is really important is whether, once objectives are identified, a man can make the maximum use of available resources, working against recognized constraints, to achieve the results logically required if short and long term objectives are to be met. This stands in the starkest contrast with charismatic leadership, where personality characteristics are dominant.

III *Top management and immediate subordinates meet,* hopefully to reach a meeting of the minds on overall objectives and expected results for the organization as a whole, preliminary to having each immediate subordinate indicate the role he expects to play during the coming year in helping to achieve these objectives. At this stage, job responsibilities are clarified and acceptable performance criteria established and mutually agreed upon. Such criteria allow for "expected" and "outstanding" levels of performance.

An important expectation in management by objectives is that superior and subordinate managers will give serious attention to the respective roles of each in seeking to achieve desired results, and that they will have the opportunity to meet and clarify, in detail, these expectations. Three categories of objectives are used for discussion purposes: *(a) routine:* those concerned with meeting every day normal expectations of the position; *(b) problem-solving:* those concerned with identifying and taking steps to remove problems that have interfered in the past with optimal performance; and *(c) innovative:* those concerned with creative and innovative activity that will lead to results beyond those anticipated from routine or problem-solving activity. In other words, in setting realistic objectives every manager's job is broken down into these three aspects—day-to-day routine management, elimination of existing problem areas and the search for improvement through creative, innovative activity.

There is a further refinement in setting individual objectives. Each participant in the process is expected to define his objectives with four key words in mind: *concreteness, attainability, desirability, measurability.* Taking each of these in turn, objectives are expected to be spelled out in such a way that they depart from the realm of the general and, dealing in concrete realities, become clearly understandable—*concrete.* They are expected to be realistic, given the constraints under which management must operate—*attainable*. They are expected to be worth pursuing—*desirable*—and this means particularly in light of competing priorities for available resources, as an objective can appear eminently desirable for itself and yet when measured against competing claims on resources will appear far less worth pursuing. Finally, and of central importance, objectives are to be stated in such a way that there are acceptable indices for measuring progress towards the achievement of these objectives—*measurable*.

At this third stage, therefore, superior and subordinate managers reach agreement on job responsibilities and objectives (routine, problem-solving and creative). They are expected also to reach agreement on priority ratings for objectives in both the short term and the long term. This agreement on priorities is extremely important. Many managers perform superlatively in one particular area of responsibility to the neglect of other important areas and often, therefore, to the detriment of overall objectives. Finally, in setting objectives, agreement is reached concerning "expected" and "outstanding" levels of performance.

Once verbal agreement is reached on objectives, a written memorandum is prepared covering the verbal agreement. This is carefully filed away and becomes a basis for future performance review.

It is expected that each subordinate will then program to meet his objectives and will feel free to consult regularly with his superior should organizational obstacles interfere with optimal performance in his particular role or should there be other ways, generally, in which the superior can assist the subordinate in meeting his goals. Aside from this, it is anticipated that the subordinate will be given a large measure of freedom, working with existing constraints, in working out the means of achieving budgeted results.

IV *This process is repeated throughout the organization to cover all managerial personnel.* As a result there will appear a clear statement in writing of objectives for each level in the organization, the product of careful consultation and subsequent agreement between superiors and subordinates on each reporting level.

V *Top management then reviews the statements of objectives for overall consistency* to make certain that, when the process is finally complete, the budgeted results cover the results expected by top management.

VI The final stage of a system of management by objectives is *performance review*, which occurs at the end of the period for which the objectives were originally set (usually one year). In theory, what happens at this particular point is that a manager and his immediate subordinates meet and review the year's performance against objectives. Because objectives have been concretely stated in measurable terms and because there has been an atmosphere of collaboration and cooperation throughout the year, it is anticipated that at this performance review, there will be very little that will surprise either the manager or his immediate subordinate; they have kept in touch and have made necessary adjustments throughout the year and simply meet for a general appraisal of performance as a basis for a still more realistic statement of objectives for the coming year.

The position taken to this point has been that of the proponent of management by objectives. From such a perspective, management by objectives clearly has relevance to modern management. Yet its great strength may also be its great weakness. The commitment to participative management and to objective rationality with the maximum use of scientific methods in management may not be universally feasible or even desirable. There are dangers, pitfalls and alternatives to management by objectives with which those considering adopting the approach should become familiar.

DANGERS, PITFALLS, ALTERNATIVES

I *The lack of concreteness and concomitant difficulties of implementation.* While the statement of philosophy and style of management does strike a strongly responsive chord in many managers, serious problems arise in adapting actual management practices to a results orientation.

Dr. F.D. Barrett, an experienced Canadian consultant in the field of management by objectives, in working with an organization only newly acquainted with the concept, takes great care to keep expectations at a modest level during the first year of implementation and suggests that only at the end of three years of quite rigorous application will the benefits occur near their optimum level. He insists from the outset on emphasizing the difficulties of implementation, while at the same time making the case for the worthwhileness of the effort involved. If the essence of the management by objectives philosophy and style can be communicated to top management and they agree that it is suited to their particular organizations, and if, further, the initial difficulties of implementation are understood fully and top management is prepared to allocate the necessary resources to overcoming them, then this first problem area concerning management by objectives is no longer compelling.

II *The attainability of management by objectives* is also open to question.

Many of us who have been in administrative positions will question whether administrators invariably can state clearly in advance of action where it is they want to go and what it is they expect to achieve. Those who have worked in organizations which they helped to found know how often, in fact, objectives are clarified as day-to-day decisions are made. Faced with operating choices, we discover, in ways we could not have known beforehand, where our preferences really do lie and only after sufficient exploratory action has occurred are we in a position to state with any clarity, for others to comprehend, where it is we have been and intend in future to go.

III *Desirability*. The arguments of Herbert Simon[2] and Charles Lindblom[3] raise doubts concerning the feasibility of a "rational-comprehensive" approach to setting managerial objectives. Lindblom goes beyond Simon, raising doubts concerning its desirability, even were it attainable, in pointing out how much easier it can be to garner enthusiastic support for a course of action if the underlying objectives of the supporters are not brought into the open for critical analysis.

Organizations are by definition the structured attempt by human beings to work beyond the limits of individual performance. Through combining in rational effort, it is hoped that objectives can be achieved that might otherwise be beyond the competence of the individuals involved. Yet every manager is aware of the very real constraints that work against the application of rationality within organizations. If organizations are attempts at rational behaviour, they are, nevertheless, still human groupings and the "politics" of internal organization can bear considerably on decision-making.

IV *Measurability*. At issue is the question of whether evidence is available that management by objectives does in fact work, that organizations which have adopted it have achieved measurable gains against whatever standards are acceptable over the results achieved in their pre-management by objectives period and, if such gains have been achieved, that they can be traced directly to management by objectives.

In support of management by objectives, one can compile an impressive list of organizations which have used it in its various forms over a considerable period of time and appear to have judged it worthwhile. Nevertheless, there is very little in the literature of management by objectives to indicate that it has been subjected to rigorous, analytical study. As Tosi and Carroll suggest, "For the most part, 'management by objectives' has been implemented on the basis of its apparent theoretical practicability and advantages. There has been only limited research examining its effects."[4]

V *Limited relevance*. There is adequate reason to believe that management by objectives cannot be universally applied, its relevance being limited to certain organizational situations.

In the first place, it assumes the acceptance of a particular philosophy and an ability to manage in a certain style. Yet many now in managerial positions are not attuned to either the philosophy or the style. Moreover, for a variety of reasons it may not be possible or feasible to bring them to accept the philosophy and adopt the management style. Even where a philosophical commitment exists, the demand on skills in interpersonal

[2]Herbert A. Simon, *Administrative Behaviour*, 2nd ed., Glencoe, The Free Press, 1957.
[3]Charles E. Lindblom, "The Science of Muddling Through," *Public Administration Reivew*, Vol. 19, No. 2, Spring, 1959, pp. 79-88.
[4]H.L. Tosi and S.J. Carroll, *Managerial Reaction to Manpower by Objectives*, Academy of Management, December 1968, p. 416.

relations is quite high. Where such skills are weak, developing them is itself a formidable task. The costs in trying to apply management by objectives universally therefore could be simply too great.

CONCLUSIONS

Despite the legitimate objections that can be raised against management by objectives, once the dangers and pitfalls have been noted and the possibility of its limited applicability considered, there can be no question that the focus on objectives is a salutary one. Those involved in managing know how seductive day to day detail is and how fatally easy it is to misallocate resources because goals are unclear. Because experience does indicate that a purposeful regular review of objectives is not as widespread is it might be, this makes the plea for a more systematic, results oriented approach to managing ever more compelling.

A second conclusion is that the recognition of at least a three-fold split in the setting of objectives—routine, problem-solving and innovative—is also very useful. If it is relatively easy to ignore objectives under the pressure of day-to-day business, it is still easier to keep busy on routine matters to the neglect of more demanding problem-solving and innovative activities and creative endeavour. Useful, too, is the insistence upon establishing priorities among objectives, and upon balanced performance throughout the year. The stage of cross-checking and integrating sub-objectives is also worth noting, for its possible contribution to coordination, to ease of communications and to the general broadening of horizons.

Management by objectives, further, appears highly beneficial in achieving meaningful decentralization. When those involved have agreed upon objectives and have worked out satisfactory indicators for measuring performance, it is possible to go the next step and for the superior to delegate freely concerning means. The commitment of budgeted results and measurement indices to writing provides the control framework sufficient to allow considerable latitude in seeking these results.

Finally, management by objectives appears to have a very real part to play in the review of performance, developing executive potential, recognizing executive potential and finding a base for just remuneration.

15
Planning-Programming-Budgeting System in Canada*

Treasury Board

The Treasury Board has taken steps over the past few years to introduce a planning-programming-budgeting approach to resource allocation. One respect in which a PPB System is greatly different from traditional forms of government budgeting is in its concentration on the results or output and benefits as opposed to just a consideration of the resources required. Intensive study is made of feasible alternative ways of attaining defined objectives with a view to determining the approach which is most likely to achieve the greatest benefit for a given cost or, conversely, the approach by which a given objective will be achieved at minimum cost.

In a PPB System, analysis is expected only to promote better decisions since analysis is likely to bring forward a greater range of alternative courses of action for consideration by management and to make more apparent the probable effects of each course of action. The manager remains responsible for the making of decisions. In addition, there are usually considerations bearing on the decisions which it is not possible to include in the analysis. While the analyst will endeavour to ensure that considerations of this kind are brought to the manager's attention, the weight to be given them in deciding on a course of action is a matter for managerial judgment.

The adoption of an analytic approach to government decision-making of the kind that underlies planning-programming-budgeting is probably inevitable in a complex society. The minimum needs of shelter, sustenance, internal order and the like having been met, there are innumerable possible ways of improving the quality of life and not all the ways can be pursued at one time because of limited resources. Choices have to be made as to what should be done in the full realization that the choosing to do some things means that resources will be unavailable to do other things. The complexity of the considerations having a bearing on these choices invites the application of all that modern techniques of analysis and of gathering and processing information have to offer.

It is of the utmost importance that it be understood that the competition for resources extends to *all* the programs of government, even those in which the application of quantitative analysis is most difficult. In these latter instances, the analysis may have to be of a more qualitative kind, concentrating, for instance, on the clarification of

---

*Reprinted and slightly abridged by permission from Treasury Board, *Planning Programming Budgeting Guide* (Ottawa: Queen's Printer, 1969), pp. 4-15.

objectives and a reasoned exploration of alternatives, on attributing numerical values to such factors as may be measurable, and treating factors that defy numerical expression by at least ranking them according to their importance in assessing the alternatives under review.

THE PPB PROCESS AND ITS OBJECTIVES

The concepts common to all planning-programming-budgeting systems are these:

(a)   the setting of specific objectives;
(b)   the systematic analysis to clarify objectives and to assess alternative ways of meeting them;
(c)   the framing of budgetary proposals in terms of programs directed toward the achievement of the objectives;
(d)   the projection of the costs of these programs a number of years in the future;
(e)   the formulation of plans of achievement year by year for each program; and
(f)   an information system for each program to supply data for the monitoring of achievement of program goals and to supply data for the reassessment of the program objectives and the appropriateness of the program itself.

The elements of the Canadian government PPB System have been developed in harmony with the above general concepts and within the context of total resource allocation. By the latter phrase is meant that there is an explicit recognition that the total resources are limited in terms of the individual and collective demands of departments and that there has to be a setting of priorities by the government itself in the light of which departments can plan and budget.

A Framework for Decision Making

Program budgeting is primarily concerned with resource allocation within the department. However, in the final analysis, the resources to be allocated are those of the government as a whole — not the one million or two million dollars with which an individual department may be concerned, but the whole ten billion dollars of revenues and borrowings that the government is currently spending. The Treasury Board is adopting PPB as a means to assist in *total* resource allocation. It is important then for departments to have an understanding of the whole framework into which their respective programs will fit.

The Treasury Board has adopted a functional classification of government expenditures which recognizes that government activity falls into a number of main areas or functions: — General Government

Services, Foreign Affairs, Defence, Transportation and Communications, Economic Development, Health and Welfare, Education Assistance, Culture and Recreation, and Internal Overhead Expenses. The expenditures involved in Fiscal Transfer Payments to the provinces and in Public Debt are set aside under two special functions. This system has three tiers at the governmental level, function, sub-function and functional program and, to the extent that individual departmental programs fall wholly within one functional program, they form a fourth tier. The individual activities which make up departmental programs should each fall entirely within a functional program and thus make up the fifth tier.[1]

Ideally there could exist a complete framework for resource allocation, one which begins at the level of the function where only the broad, intuitive, and in the truest sense "political", decisions can and must be made, and which extends down through the various levels of the hierarchy, with cost-benefit analysis exerting a progressively greater influence on resource allocation as the decisions to be taken fall within ever narrowing terms of reference. At each level there would be clearly specified needs to be met, identifiable results or outputs that could meet the needs, and measureable benefits that could be demonstrated.

Such an ideal state is, of course, not easy to achieve. At the higher levels of decision, it is not possible to rely to any great extent on cost-benefit analysis, in deciding for instance how much should be spent on defence as against social measures. And even after a decision is taken to spend a certain amount on health and welfare, the subsequent decisions as to what should be allocated to health and the other sub-functions are only comparatively easier.

Despite the difficulties, however, there must be at least an implicit functional allocation. A case could be made for higher levels of expenditure in almost every area in which the government operates. For example, the defence of Canada could take all the revenues of the federal government if there were no other demands. The arts, the sciences and education could absorb many more hundreds of millions of dollars. Certain areas of the country contain pockets of poverty that only

---

[1]An illustration of the three levels of this functional classification — functions, sub-functions and functional program — is shown below for the functions of "General Government Services" and "Foreign Affairs".
GENERAL GOVERNMENT SERVICES —
Legislation and Administration: Legislative; Executive; Collection of Taxes and Duties; National Capital Region; other Legislation and Administration.
Protection of Persons and Property: Justice; Correctional Services; Police Protection; Consumer Services; other Protection or Persons and Property.
FOREIGN AFFAIRS —
External Relations: Diplomatic Relations; Contributions to International Organizations.
Assistance To Developing Countries: Other Foreign Affairs.

massive investments can relieve. The ever-growing concentration of the population into cities invites increasing attention to clogged transportation facilities, polluted air and water, and sub-standard housing.

The Setting of Priorities

It is axiomatic that if next year's resources are to be higher by a certain amount than this year's, expenditures for all purposes taken together can rise by no more than the same amount. And it is intuitively obvious that it would be more beneficial for the increase to be distributed unevenly among functions according to the exigencies of the period under review. In other words, expenditures should increase at a faster rate than average for some functional programs, should remain stable in others, and should actually be reduced in still others to free funds for higher priority purposes. Consequently, not only should departmental programs be viewed as competing with one another for a share of the total resources; each program should be viewed as competing with one another for a share of the total resources; each program should be viewed as competing with all other programs belonging to the same or other departments.

A major element of the PPB System will therefore involve seeking the government's guidance as to priorities to be served in allocating resources. This guidance will be sought in the light of forecasts by the Department of Finance as to the magnitude of the funds likely to be available for the next few years according to specific assumptions as to the rate of growth in the economy, tax rates, and the appropriate level of borrowing for budgetary and non-bugetary expenditures — subject of course to any overriding considerations as to the fiscal stance necessary to correct any imbalance in the economy.

The recommendations as to priorities will be based on analysis made of information drawn from various sources, and in particular from departmental Program Forecast Submissions, since these are expected to develop in the quality of their content until they provide by far the best single picture of the needs of the country in federal areas of responsibility.

Expenditure guidelines reflecting the scale of priorities established by Cabinet will be communicated to deputy heads as soon as possible in the period during which departments prepare their Program Forecast Submissions. In those functional areas where the guidelines tend to be more restrictive, they should not be interpreted in any sense as ceilings that may not be breached. The Treasury Board Secretariat does not have and cannot have a sufficiently intimate knowledge of the inescapable commitments that departments must meet or the benefits a more current analysis may show are expected to result from new programs or from the expansion of existing programs. But in cases where the guidelines suggest restricted expansion or contraction in program size, the departments concerned have the advantages of an early notice that their arguments will have to be more than usually convincing and of an opportunity to reassess their own priorities and to consider internal priorities among activities.

At the same time, in those functional areas for which the guidelines suggest expansion will be favoured, no automatic acceptance by the Treasury Board of any particular budget level should be expected. Firstly, there are in many cases two or more departments responsible for operations in any one functional area and the distribution of resources among the departments concerned will depend on the relative benefits forecast. Secondly, even for those functional areas the guidelines might favour, the available new resources will certainly be inadequate to permit the realization of all plans, however meritorious.

Internal Departmental Priorities

A third element in the PPB System is an insistence that departments investigate and make explicit in their Program Forecast Submissions the scale of priorities they recommend for each program in the next fiscal year. That is, departments are requested to show what they consider most urgent or beneficial to be done within each activity and as between activities in the same program. The Treasury Board will take these priorities into account in reaching a balance between resources and demands upon these resources.

This consideration of internal priorities is expected to extend to recommending the elimination of existing activities whose continuance appears to provide a benefit insufficient to justify the funds required or whose elimination would release funds for relatively more beneficial purposes.

Support Programs and Activities

Some programs and activities of the government exist to provide service to other programs and activities and in fact some entire agencies exist for this purpose alone. Some of the literature on planning, programming and budgeting argues the thesis that only those operations providing a direct service to the public should be recognized as elements of program-activity structures, that the costs of support operations should be distributed to those programs providing a direct service and, as it were, the support operations should not appear in the budget.

The federal government PPB System is *not* being developed in accordance with this thesis. Support operations, either those of entirely common service agencies or those which are found in departments or agencies having other operations providing a direct service to the public, may at this time be accepted as programs or activities and as such may appear in the budget in the usual way. Future experience may indeed indicate that support operations should disappear from the budget but at this time the advantages of that approach do not appear to outweigh the difficulties. The foregoing discussion is of course not intended in any way to prejudice any decisions about the merits of charging for common services; this might still be done whether or not the operations providing the common service are treated as programs and activities.

16
Operational Performance Measurement Systems*

Henning Frederiksen

PLANNING PROGRAMMING BUDGETING SYSTEMS (PPBS) AND MANAGEMENT BY OBJECTIVES (MBO)

PPBS and MBO were gradually introduced into the Canadian government in the latter part of the 1960s. PPBS has had a profound effect on the approach by government departments and agencies to planning and budgeting. From the predominantly incremental budgeting in terms of expenditure categories (salaries, travel, postage, rent, repairs), which prevailed prior to 1965, there has been a significant shift in emphasis to planning and budgeting in the context of defined (or re-defined) departmental objectives and sub-objectives, and of programs and activities designed to meet these objectives — structured in a manner to facilitate planning and subsequent evaluation of achievement.

Whereas PPBS was intended to function at the program and activity levels of departmental operations, MBO aimed at the establishment of clearly defined and measurable goals and at the development and execution of work plans designed to achieve these goals. MBO addressed itself to the individual manager and his staff at any level in the management heirarchy of a departmental program providing the manager with a systematic approach to "responsibility centre" planning. Such planning was to be based on a range of short-term goals which, if realized in the course of the fiscal year, would theoretically contribute in the aggregate to the achievement of program objectives. MBO, in its application, further emphasized the dimension of manager-subordinate

*Reprinted and substantially abridged by permission from Henning Frederiksen, "Is Operational Performance in Government Measurable?" *Optimum,* vol. 6, no. 4 (1975), pp. 23-30.

dialogue in the process of goal determination, monitoring and re-negotiation, with the resulting improvement in management-staff relations through greater participation by subordinates in the planning and control of organizational performance.

Both of the two managerial evaluation approaches described briefly in the foregoing have at least the following aspects in common:

— they are results-oriented — the emphasis is on achievement of planned objectives and goals;

— they are cost conscious — goals must be established to fit within the budgetary constraints of available, scarce resources;

— their success depends to a considerable extent on the creation and provision of quantitative output data which can be used in a consistent manner to relate benefits to costs and to develop reliable performance indices.

In Canada, despite their considerable influence on the government's approaches to planning and budgeting at different management levels, PPBS and MBO have both suffered in their implementation from lack of appropriate data needed to quantify program outputs and organizational performance. Consequently, their full potential has not yet been realized.

OPERATIONAL PERFORMANCE MEASUREMENT SYSTEMS (OPMS) — GENERAL METHODOLOGY

As it became increasingly apparent that "the development of measures of program effectiveness and operational performance was critical to ensuring that PPBS did not become merely a slightly improved vehicle for classifying expenditures,"[1] the Planning Branch of the Treasury Board Secretariat in 1971-72 set out to develop a conceptual framework for program evaluation which has become known as "Operational Performance Measurement Systems" (OPMS).

Recognizing that the ultimate objective of the federal government—to improve (or, at least, to preserve) the well-being of Canadians—is extremely difficult to express in meaningful quatitative terms, the proposed system framework uses the proxy approach to program evaluation.

A "proxy" is an approximation or, rather, a substitute for the elusive measure of the ultimate fulfillment of a program objective, and is used where (intellectually *not* literally, speaking) there is no tangible indication of the ultimate fulfillment of a program objective. For example, the Fitness and Amateur Sport Program has developed a project entitled

---

[1]D.G. Hartle, Operational performance measurement in the federal government, *Optimum,* vol. 3, no. 4, 1972, p. 5.

"Participaction," aimed at influencing the lifestyle of Canadians. Whereas changes in lifestyle cannot easily be measured, "audience" size and number of exposures become proxies. The ultimate result is not known, but the steps believed valid to achieve the result are measurable. Proxies are estimated at various points of program visibility, called "proxy levels," by attempting to quantify and interrelate program inputs (level I), operational outputs (level II), program outputs (level III), and program effects (level IV). By definition, the quantitative relationships between the foregoing proxy levels are designed to provide measures, or, at least, indices of the following components to government program performance:

—Operational Efficiency $$\frac{\text{Operational Outputs}}{\text{Program Inputs}}$$

—Operational Effectiveness $$\frac{\text{Program Outputs}}{\text{Operational Outputs}}$$

—Program Efficiency $$\frac{\text{Program Outputs}}{\text{Program Inputs}}$$

—Program Effectiveness $$\frac{\text{Program Effects}}{\text{Program Outputs}}$$

—Program Cost-Effectiveness $$\frac{\text{Program Effects}}{\text{Program Inputs}}$$

To facilitate an understanding of the above concepts, a "Glossary of OPMS Terms" is given in Appendix A.[2]

In the context of the OPMS framework, a program is viewed as consisting of "a series of operational processes that convert primary inputs into the desired program effects. These processes form a hierarchy of means and ends in which, at subsequent stages of the process, intermediate ends in turn become the means for another process."[3] An illustration of this means-end hierarchy is provided in Figure 1.

Since the operational efficiency index is calculated by relating program inputs (resource costs) to operational outputs (goods and services produced, e.g., number of family allowance cheques issued), an analogy can be drawn with certain types of cost accounting systems used in manufacturing operations. In fact, the operational efficiency ratio in OPMS is precisely the inverse of the unit cost of production in the industrial operation. But whereas the most useful forms of cost accounting are based on engineering standards developed from time-and-motion studies or similar work measurement techniques, which permit the budgeting and control of actual cost by reference to

---

[2]From Treasury Board, "Operational Performance Measurement", vol. 1, A Managerial Overview, January 1974, pp. 24-26.
[3]Ibid., p. 7.

Figure 1
The Means/End Hierarchy

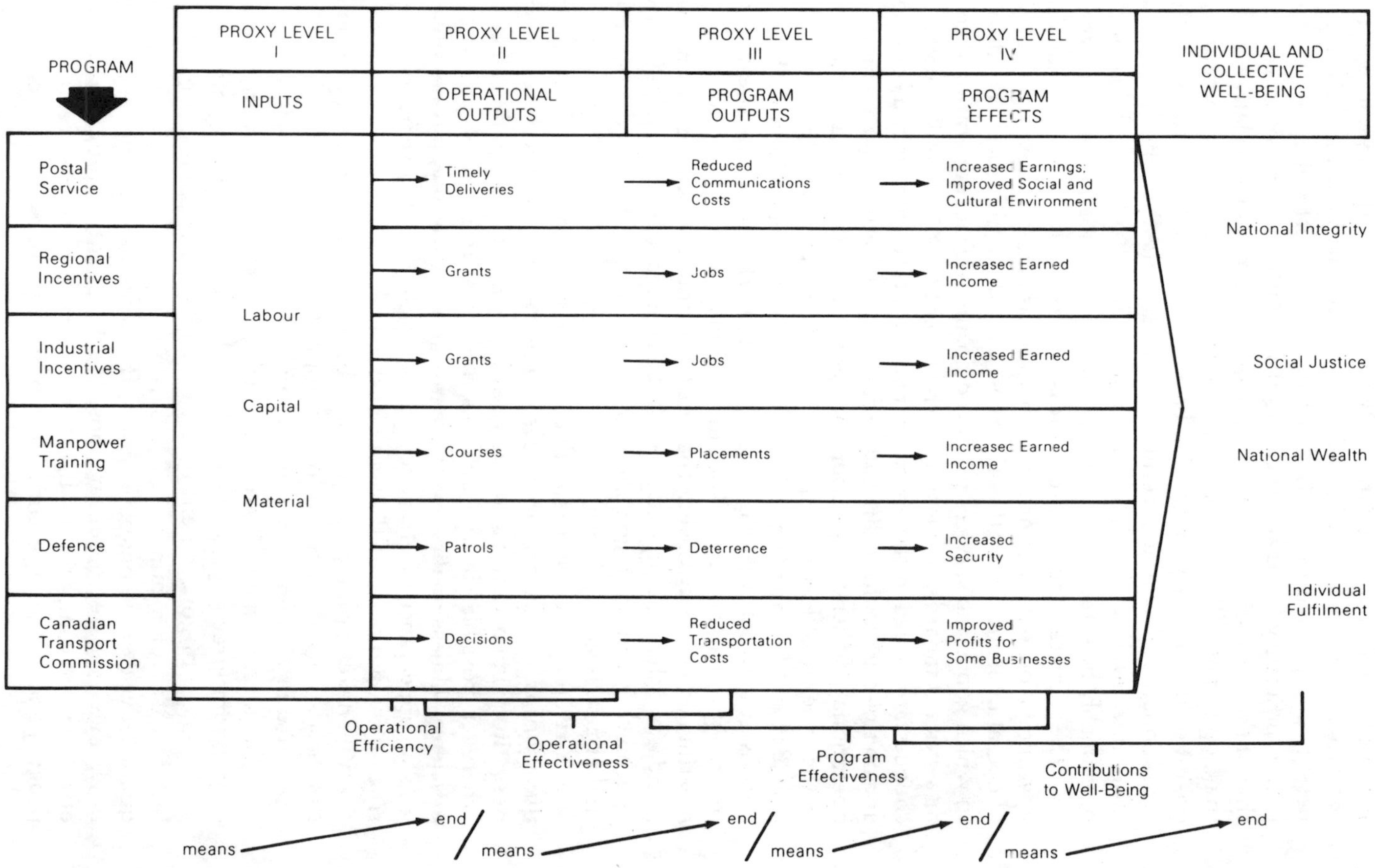

PROGRAM	PROXY LEVEL I / INPUTS	PROXY LEVEL II / OPERATIONAL OUTPUTS	PROXY LEVEL III / PROGRAM OUTPUTS	PROXY LEVEL IV / PROGRAM EFFECTS	INDIVIDUAL AND COLLECTIVE WELL-BEING
Postal Service		Timely Deliveries	Reduced Communications Costs	Increased Earnings; Improved Social and Cultural Environment	National Integrity
Regional Incentives	Labour	Grants	Jobs	Increased Earned Income	Social Justice
Industrial Incentives	Capital	Grants	Jobs	Increased Earned Income	National Wealth
Manpower Training	Material	Courses	Placements	Increased Earned Income	Individual Fulfilment
Defence		Patrols	Deterrence	Increased Security	
Canadian Transport Commission		Decisions	Reduced Transportation Costs	Improved Profits for Some Businesses	

Operational Efficiency — Operational Effectiveness — Program Effectiveness — Contributions to Well-Being

means / end / means / end / means / end / means / end

predetermined cost standards, OPMS uses, as the initial point of reference, the indices calculated to have prevailed during a given base period. Irrespective of the level of operational efficiency in the base period, efficiency levels achieved in subsequent years are compared with that of the base period. In other words, OPMS measures relative, rather than optimum efficiency. On the other hand, if "improvements" in operational efficiency over the base period are seen to be rather sensational, and where careful analysis reveals that the base period efficiency level is completely untypical, new base period levels can presumably be established by using the experience of subsequent years.

The Operational Effectiveness index, calculated by dividing operational outputs into program outputs, is aimed at measuring utility of operational outputs (rather than cost). Without monitoring the degree to which goods and services produced do, in fact, meet operational goals or service standards, (for example, the extent to which family allowance cheques are issued in the appropriate amounts, to the persons entitled, and on time), it would be difficult to determine whether improvements in operational efficiency—cost per cheque issued—had been accomplished at the expense of lowering the levels of service or reducing the benefits provided to the Canadian public. The concept of operational effectiveness is somewhat analogous to that of marketability in the private sector—no matter how efficient the production department is in meeting, or even surpassing the most demanding engineering and cost standards—the entire operation must be deemed to have been ineffective in achieving corporate goals, unless the manufactured products can be sold at a satisfactory profit.

A related aspect is the *quality* of operational outputs. Because the quality of internal work processes influences the operational effectiveness, it is important to identify and segregate the quality factors, wherever possible, in the analysis and measurement of operational efficiency. Unless quality levels are monitored carefully, it is possible to give an appearance of efficiency gains which in reality represent mere trade-offs on quality of the work performed.

Whenever program outputs can be quantified, program efficiency can be expressed in terms of appropriate unit costs, or as a ratio calculated by dividing program outputs by program inputs.

The measurement of program effectiveness requires quantification of program effects (proxy level IV) — the impact of a program on the achievement of government objectives. This is the highest proxy level, but in cases of a number of government programs, the search for quantitative expressions of program effects has yielded little results until now. Even where it appears possible to quantify program impact, effectiveness comparisons using program effects are restricted to programs producing the same kinds of effects, for example, increases in personal incomes. Moreover, care must be taken to give appropriate consideration to possible negative effects upon other programs. It is understood that program evaluation at proxy level IV is largely non-existent.

Before OPMS can be developed and implemented in a given program area, it is essential to secure and retain strong management commitment. OPMS must be seen by all levels of management, from the top down, as a useful planning and control tool, and when the system is in place, it must be the manager's own creation, not that of a systems analyst. The Treasury Board Planning Branch has recommended the following basic procedures in developing the system:[4]

— Identification of measurable operations and their outputs, both program and operational;
— Identification of output attributes (specifications of output quality — errors as a percentage of transactions, number of complaints as a percentage of transactions, time to process an application, a requisition, etc.);
— Identification of input resources — man-years utilized in the production of each output in a selected period and calculation of a "unit cost" for each output in that period;
— Validation of the specification of outputs and allocation of inputs by preparing efficiency indexes for prior years, if data are available, and determining how squarely these sit with the level of efficiency as perceived by management;
— Development of reporting formats including consideration of content, design and frequency of reporting.

The initial procedural emphasis is placed on the identification of MBO system ingredients. The reason for stressing MBO at the beginning is that consideration of the MBO systems framework conditions the manager to think about his operations in results or output terms. Some OPMS experts argue that an MBO system, or the creation of an MBO "climate", is a prerequisite to the successful implementation of an OPMS. There is, at least, growing evidence that prior management exposure to MBO concepts greatly facilitates the establishment of useful output definitions.

A clear identification of the *type of work process* is also essential at the outset, because it will determine the choice of systems approach most likely to yield the best results. It is generally recognized that OPMS in its basic form is primarily suited to repetitive, "assembly-line" types of processes which produce relatively homogeneous outputs — plant inspections, X-ray examinations. These kinds of outputs are easily

---

[4]*Ibid.*, p. 17.

quantifiable, and identification of the inputs required to produce them presents few problems.

A very considerable segment of government activities, however, produces either a series of heterogeneous operational outputs, or a set of intermediate (indirect) outputs which defy quantification. Examples occur frequently in activities such as planning, management and administrative services, research and advisory functions. In these cases it becomes necessary to develop and apply different performance measurement techniques such as Project Control, Activity Analysis, or "Performance Acceptable When".

Potential Benefits

As stated previously, OPMS output data are important to achieving a fuller realization of the potential of PPBS and MBO; in other words, OPMS, if it is implemented on a wider basis in the federal government, should improve the process of allocation of scarce resources, as well as facilitate the assessment of managerial efficiency and effectiveness.

Appropriate operational statistics are useful in the establishment of objectives at the program and activity levels, and of operational goals at the organizational unit (responsibility centre) level. Without objectives and goals expressed in quantitative terms, both long-range and short-term planning remain rather subjective and slightly nebulous, evaluation of alternative plans and courses of action is difficult, and subsequent monitoring of operational results lacks relevance. In consequence, it becomes difficult to pinpoint managerial accountability because precise reference points are absent from the plan.

Moreover, in the absence of output data the preparation of operational budgets can become largely perfunctorq, since funds are allocated on the basis of historic spending patterns and qualitative assessments of future resource needs, rather than being based on clearly defined and well quantified objectives and goals. As a result, reports on the stewardship of funds entrusted to managers frequently concentrate on explanations of the reasons why funds have been overunder expended, that is, they tend to become input-oriented. Little or no reference is made to the impact of deficits and surpluses upon the achievement of planned objectives and goals because of the lack of a clear correlation between the operational plan and the budget.

Finally, where no operational statistics are available, improvements in efficiency and effectiveness cannot easily be built into operational plans and budgets; neither can such improvements be identified in the evaluation of operational performance.

It is hoped that OPMS will be implemented in the majority of government departments and agencies to ensure better resource allocation, provide keener planning and budgeting tools, and assist in the control of managerial efficiency and effectiveness.

Current Limitations

If OPMS was capable of *total* implementation in the operational and administrative areas of government activity, it would cover only $9 billion, or 28 per cent of the federal government's budget for 1975-76. Some $23 billion of budgetary expenditures for statutory payments (for example, Family Allowances, Health Care), grants and contributions, retirement of public debt, and capital expansion would not appear to be amenable to OPMS application. Since complete coverage will probably not be achieved in the operational and administrative areas, one might estimate conservatively that $5 billion, or 15 per cent of the total federal budget (in 1975 terms) might be exposed to OPMS techniques.

Of 32 federal departments surveyed in June 1975, 11 (1/3) use OPMS, and another 16 appear to be potential users. The eleven departments use OPMS output data in support of their annual requests to Treasury Board for additional resources (Program Forecast Submission). As a result, Treasury Board has been able to make more rational and objective decisions concerning the justification for new funds and man-years put forward by these departments. Conversely, the departments have found themselves in a stronger bargaining position *vis-à-vis* the Treasury Board.

From a department's viewpoint, OPMS is a two-edged sword in resource negotiations with Treasury Board: the program manager may find it easier to defend his requests for funds and may encounter a more receptive Treasury Board Secretariat, but at the same time he is expected to commit himself to accomplishing certain improvements in operational efficiency, in return for the allocation of additional resources. Occasionally the net effect has been an overall *reduction*, rather than an increase, in funding and man-year levels!

The predominant use of the OPMS *efficiency index* in the process of bargaining for additional funds and man-years can be extremely dangerous unless due consideration is given to operational effectiveness. Depending on the personal strength of the program manager and his ability to refute arguments by the Treasury Board Secretariat for further improvement in his operational efficiency levels, it is conceivable that the never-ending drive for greater efficiency may gradually deprive a program manager of essential resources to maintain his program at an appropriate level of effectiveness. The result may be an erosion of the quality and level of service provided by the program to the people of Canada.

Another unfortunate aspect of the OPMS concept is the use of the base period approach instead of insisting on the objective determination, wherever possible, of performance standards, against which actual results can be measured. The use of the base period as a "standard" gives an undue advantage to the manager with the "fat" budget, but penalizes, relatively speaking, the manager who is already performing at the highest levels of efficiency, since he is assessed, in the absence of objective and realistic standards, on an equal footing with the inefficient manager — both are required to build efficiency improvement into their projections of new year resource requirements.

Apart from these conceptual concerns and apart from technical problems not treated here, one might consider the more general problem created by the lack of a really strong incentive for a program manager to economize and effect savings through improved efficiency. Seemingly, the most visible marks of the successful bureaucrat are the size and the rate of growth of his organization and, hence, of his budget, a notion which encourages empire-building and spending. Moreover, because of the parliamentary system of expenditure control, and particularly the fund lapsing provisions of the Financial Administration Act, reinvestment or reallocation of funds saved can only be effected to a very limited extent within a given fiscal year. Consequently, the manager knows that economies realized by him through increased efficiency could mar his success image, since his budgets in future years will be reduced. Thus he may regard himself as being penalized by reason of his higher level of managerial efficiency, notwithstanding the possibility of personal financial rewards which may accrue to him by virtue of the Performance Pay system. On the other hand, there are undoubtedly a significant number of extremely dedicated managers within the federal public service who, despite apparent penalties and lack of real incentives, derive a great amount of personal satisfaction from achieving improvements in efficiency and from meeting the highest standards of excellence in their managerial performance.

On balance, and in conclusion, it appears that OPMS, given its limitations, has achieved a partial success in program areas where it fits. Many observers have asked the question: considering the probability that OPMS may never cover more than 15 per cent of the total federal budget, is the administrative cost of this massive systems exercise really warranted? Well, if it is assumed that a 10 per cent over-all improvement in efficiency can be accomplished through the application of OPMS and related techniques, potential savings in government expenditures of $500 million per annum (in 1975-76 budgetary terms) could be realized. Here, then, is the real acid test of the success or failure of OPMS in the federal government! The final answer to our question, therefore, lies somewhere in the future, but may possibly never be known because of the inherent difficulty in isolating the causal relationship between a system and its effects.

Appendix A — Glossary of OPMS Terms

ACTIVITIES. Alternative or complementary means of achieving an objective or set of objectives of a program.

BASE PERIOD. A period of time, e.g., a year, quarter or month, selected as a base for comparing the performance during other time periods.

EFFECTIVENESS. The extent to which an objective or goal is achieved.

EFFICIENCY. The ratio of output to related input.

OPERATION. A work process occurring within a responsibility centre and producing a single type of output.

OPERATIONAL OUTPUT. Goods and services produced by work processes within a program for the purpose of generating program output.

OPERATIONAL PERFORMANCE. A general term which refers to the planning, control and execution of one or more work processes the result of which can be evaluated in terms of operational efficiency and operational effectiveness.

PROGRAM. A group of related departmental activities designed to achieve specific objectives authorized by Parliament. (See Activities)

PROGRAM COST-EFFECTIVENESS. The relationship of program effects to total program inputs.

PROGRAM OUTPUT. Goods and services produced for the purpose of achieving some socio-economic effect.

RESPONSIBILITY CENTRE. An organizational unit in which the manager has been delegated authority to manage financial resources, including responsibility for determining financial requirements, controlling costs in relation to operational accomplishment, and exercising spending authority to approve charges against his budget.

17
Financial Administration in Canada*

H.R. Balls

The financial affairs of the Government of Canada are administered and controlled under the basic principles that no tax shall be imposed and no money spent without the authority of Parliament and that expenditures shall be made only for the purposes authorized by Parliament. The most important constitutional provisions relating to Parliament's control of finances are contained in the British North America (BNA) Act which provides that all federal taxing and appropriating measures must originate in the House of Commons. The government is responsible for introducing all money bills. Financial control is exercised through a budgetary system based on the principle that all the financial needs of the government for each fiscal year should be considered at one time so that both the current and prospective conditions of the public treasury may be clearly evident.

ESTIMATES AND APPROPRIATIONS

Co-ordination of the estimates process is carried out by Treasury Board. The Secretariat to this Board is a separate department of government, its Minister having the designation of President of the Treasury Board. In addition to the President, the Board consists of the Minister of Finance and four other Privy Councillors. Under the Financial Administration Act, the Board may act for the Privy Council in all matters relating to financial management (including estimates, expenditures, financial commitments, establishments, revenues and accounts), personnel management and general administrative policy in the Public Service.

Under present practice departments submit forecasts of their requirements about 12 months before the beginning of a new fiscal year. Forecasts of what they will require in each of the coming three years to maintain the current levels of service in each program are termed "A Budgets". At the same time departments submit forecasts of requirements for new activities or expansion in existing activities — "B Budgets". These proposals are reviewed by Treasury Board in the light of expenditure guidelines approved by the Cabinet which express the government's priorities. The Treasury Board Secretariat prepares recommendations for the budgetary and non-budgetary allocations to each program for Cabinet review. In August of the year preceding the

*Reprinted by permission from H.R. Balls, "Financial Administration in Canada," in *Canada Year Book, 1975* (Ottawa: Information Canada, 1976).

fiscal year, departments are advised of the allocations approved by Cabinet. Departments then develop detailed estimates of their resource requirements for the new year against these approved allocations. These estimates are submitted at the end of October. Following review by Treasury Board and approval by Cabinet they are tabled in Parliament in February.

Main estimates and supplementary estimates are referred to committees of the House of Commons. The timing of such referrals, the timing of committee reports and all other matters having to do with the business of supply in the House of Commons are regulated by the Standing Orders of the House (October 1969). The relevant provisions are briefly summarized here. Section 58 of the Standing Orders establishes three supply periods ending, respectively, not later than December 10, March 26 and June 30. The first supplementary estimates for a year are usually dealt with in the December 10 period and the final supplementary estimates in the March 26 period. In addition, interim supply (consisting of 3/12ths for all items in estimates and extra 12ths for some items) is dealt with in the March 26 period. In the June 30 period, the House is asked to provide full supply. The Standing Orders call for the referral of the new year main estimates to standing committees of the House by March 1 of the then expiring fiscal year and they must report back to the House not later than May 31 in the then current fiscal year. Supplementary estimates are referred immediately after they are tabled, usually to the Miscellaneous Estimates Committee of the House, and dates by which reports must be made to the House are stipulated. In each supply period a number of days are allotted to the business of supply. Opposition motions have precedence over all government supply motions on allotted days and opportunities to put forward motions of non-confidence in the government are provided. On the last allotted day in each period, at 15 minutes before the ordinary time of adjournment the Speaker interrupts the proceedings then in progress and puts every question necessary to dispose of any business relating to supply. No debate takes place after the Speaker has acted in this way and the Appropriation Acts then before the House must be voted on. These Appropriation Acts authorize payments out of the Consolidated Revenue Fund of the amounts included in the estimates, whether main or supplementary, subject to the conditions stated in them.

In addition to the expenditure items included in the annual Appropriation Acts, there are a number of items, such as interest on the public debt and family allowances, authorized under other statutes. Although it is not necessary for Parliament to approve these items annually, they are included in the main estimates for purposes of information. Statutory provision also exists for the expenditure of public money in emergencies where no parliamentary appropriation is available. Under the Financial Administration Act, the Governor in

Council, on the report of the President of the Treasury Board that there is no appropriation for the expenditure and on the report of the appropriate Minister that the expenditure is urgently required, may order a special warrant issued authorizing disbursement of the amount required. Such warrants may be issued only when Parliament is not in session and every warrant must be published in the *Canada Gazette* within 30 days of issue and reported to Parliament within 15 days of assembly. The Fire Losses Replacement Account Act also provides for emergency expenditures for the urgent repair or replacement of property destroyed or damaged by fire, where there is not sufficient money available in the appropriation for the service suffering loss. Such amounts must be charged subsequently to an appropriation or included in the estimates for the department or agency concerned and refunded to the Fire Losses Replacement Account.

In addition, disbursements are made for purposes not reflected in the budgetary accounts but recorded in the government's statement of assets and liabilities, such as loans to and investments in Crown corporations, loans to international organizations and to national, provincial and municipal governments, and loans to veterans. There are also disbursements in connection with deposit and trust accounts and annuity, insurance and pension accounts which the government holds or administers, including the old age security fund and the Canada Pension Plan fund which are operated as separate entities. These disbursements are excluded from the calculation of the annual budgetary surplus or deficit.

THE BUDGET

The Minister of Finance usually presents his annual budget speech in the House of Commons some time after the main estimates have been introduced. The budget speech reviews the state of the national economy and the financial operations of the government for the previous fiscal year and gives a forecast of the probable financial requirements for the year ahead, taking into account the main estimates and making allowances for supplementary estimates. At the close of his address, the Minister tables the formal notices of ways and means motions for any changes in the existing tax rates or rules and customs tariff which, in accordance with parliamentary procedure, must precede the introduction of any money bills. These resolutions give notice of the amendments which the government intends to ask Parliament to make in the taxation statutes. However if a change is proposed in a commodity tax, such as a sales tax or excise duty on a particular item, it is usually made effective immediately; the legislation, when passed, is made retroactive to the date of the speech.

The budget speech is delivered in support of a motion that the House go into committee; debate on this motion may take up six sitting days, but once it is passed the way is clear for consideration of the budget resolutions. When these have been approved by the committee, a report to this effect is made to the House, and the tax bills are introduced and dealt with in the same manner as all other government financial legislation.

REVENUES AND EXPENDITURES

Administrative procedures governing revenues and expenditures are, for the most part, contained in the Financial Administration Act.

With respect to revenues, the basic requirement is that all public money shall be paid into the Consolidated Revenue Fund, which is defined as the aggregate of all public money on deposit to the credit of the Receiver General. The Minister of Supply and Services is the Receiver General for Canada. Treasury Board has prescribed detailed regulations governing the receipt and deposit of such money. The Bank of Canada and the chartered banks are the custodians of public money. Balances are apportioned among the various chartered banks according to a percentage allocation established by agreement among all the banks and communicated to the Department of Finance by the Canadian Bankers' Association. The daily operating account is maintained with the Bank of Canada and the division of funds between it and the chartered banks takes into account the immediate cash requirements of the government and consideration of monetary policy. The Minister of Finance may purchase and hold securities of, or guaranteed by, Canada and pay for them out of the Consolidated Revenue Fund or may sell such securities and pay the proceeds into the Fund. Thus, if cash balances in the Fund exceed immediate requirements they may be invested in interest-earning assets. In addition, the Minister of Finance has established a purchase fund to assist in the orderly retirement of the public debt.

Treasury Board exercises central control over the budgets of departments and over financial administrative matters generally. Although the most important part of this control function is exercised during the annual consideration of departmental long-range plans and of the estimates, the Board has the right to maintain continuous control over certain types of expenditure to ensure that activities and commitments for the future are held within approved policies, that departments follow uniform, efficient and economical practices, and that the government is informed of and approves any major development of policy or significant transaction that might give rise to public or parliamentary criticism.

To ensure enforcement of the decisions of Parliament, the government and Ministers regarding expenditures, the Financial Administration Act provides that no payment shall be made out of the

Consolidated Revenue Fund without the authority of Parliament and no charge shall be made against an appropriation except on the requisition of the appropriate Minister or a person authorized by him in writing. These requisitions, which must meet certain standards prescribed by Treasury Board regulation, are presented to the Receiver General, who makes the payment.

At the beginning of each fiscal year, or whenever Treasury Board may direct, each department, unless otherwise directed by the Board, submits a division into allotments of each vote included in its estimates. Once approved these allotments cannot be varied or amended without the consent of the Board; expenditures charged to appropriations are limited to such allotments. To avoid over-expenditures within a fiscal year, commitments due to be paid within the year for which Parliament has provided or has been asked to provide appropriations are recorded and controlled by the departments concerned. Commitments made under contract that will fall due in succeeding years are recorded since the government must be prepared in the future to ask Parliament for appropriations to cover them. Any unexpended amounts in the annual appropriations lapse at the end of the year for which they are granted, but for 30 days subsequent to March 31 payments may be made and charged to the previous year's appropriations for work performed, goods received or services rendered prior to the end of that fiscal year.

Under the Financial Administration Act, every payment against an appropriation is made by the Receiver General by cheque or other instrument. After presentation for payment, the cheques or instruments are cleared daily by the chartered banks through the Bank of Canada to the Cheque Redemption Control Division of the Receiver General; the banks are then reimbursed through a cheque drawn on the Receiver General's account with the Bank of Canada.

PUBLIC DEBT

In addition to collecting and disbursing public money for budgetary and non-budgetary purposes, the government receives and pays out substantial sums in connection with its public debt operations. The Minister of Finance is authorized to borrow money by the issue and sale of securities at whatever rate of interest and under whatever terms and conditions the Governor in Council approves. Although new borrowings require specific authority of Parliament, the Financial Administration Act authorizes the Governor in Council to approve borrowings as required to redeem maturing or called securities. To ensure that the Consolidated Revenue Fund will be sufficient to meet lawfully authorized disbursements, he may also approve the temporary borrowing of such sums as are necessary for periods not exceeding six months. The Bank of Canada acts as the fiscal agent of the government in the management of the public debt.

ACCOUNTS AND FINANCIAL STATEMENTS

Under the Financial Administration Act, Treasury Board may prescribe the manner and form in which the accounts of Canada and the accounts of individual departments shall be kept. Annually, on or before December 31 or, if Parliament is not then sitting, within any of the first 15 days after Parliament resumes, the *Public accounts,* prepared by the Receiver General, are laid before the House of Commons by the Minister of Finance. The *Public accounts* contain a survey of the financial transactions of the fiscal year ended the previous March 31 and statements of revenues and expenditures and of assets and direct and contingent liabilities, together with other accounts and information required to show the financial transactions and financial position of Canada or which are required by law to be reported in the *Public accounts.* The statement of assets and liabilities included in the *Public accounts* is designed to disclose the amount of the net debt, which is determined by offsetting against the gross liabilities only those assets regarded as readily realizable or interest- or revenue-producing. Fixed capital assets, such as government buildings and public works, are charged to budgetary expenditures at the time of acquisition or construction and are shown on the statement of assets and liabilities at a nominal value of $1. Monthly financial statements are also published in the *Canada Gazette.*

THE AUDITOR GENERAL

The government's accounts are subject to an independent examination by the Auditor General who is an officer of Parliament. With respect to expenditures, this examination is a post-audit to report whether the accounts have been properly kept, the money spent for the purposes for which it was appropriated by Parliament and the expenditures made as authorized; any audit before payment is the responsibility of the requisitioning department or agency. With respect to revenues, the Auditor General must ascertain that all public money is fully accounted for and that the rules and procedures applied ensure an effective check on the assessment, collection and proper allocation of the revenue. With respect to public property, he must satisfy himself that essential records are maintained and that the rules and procedures applied are sufficient to safeguard and control it. The Auditor General reports the results of his examination to Parliament, calling attention to any case which he considers should be brought to the notice of the House. He also reports to Ministers, the Treasury Board or the government any matter which in his opinion calls for attention so that remedial action may be taken promptly. It is the usual practice to refer the *Public accounts* and the *Auditor General's report* to the House of Commons Standing Committee on Public Accounts, which may review them and report the findings and recommendations to the House of Commons.

18
The Auditor General*

Independent Review Committee

The Auditor General of Canada holds a unique position within the federal government structure. The responsibilities of his Office are defined in the Financial Administration Act[1] in terms of the examinations he should make and how he should report. He is required to make such examinations as he considers necessary to ascertain whether in his opinion the accounting for and controls over monies, expenditure and public property are satisfactory and whether "money has been expended for the purpose for which it was appropriated by Parliament". In addition, he must make such examinations as he considers necessary to "certify" the major financial statements of Canada (the statement of assets and liabilities and the statement of expenditures and revenues). Finally, the Auditor General is required to report annually to the House of Commons on the results of these examinations and is directed to call attention to certain specific kinds of cases which he has observed and to any other case that he considers should be brought to the notice of the House of Commons.

IMPACT OF CHANGE IN CANADA

There have been major developments in Canada's Government during the past few decades, and these developments have affected the administration's accountability to Parliament in a variety of areas, including financial matters.

Probably the most important development that has occurred in recent years has been the growth of the Government itself. Between 1959/60 and 1973/74, total federal budgetary spending, including transfer payments to the provinces, rose from $5.7 billion to $20 billion, an annual growth rate of 9.4%. A proportion of this increase is due to inflation; but adjusting for the inflationary factor, the rate of growth is still in the order of 6.3% per annum over the fifteen-year period.

Another important development has been a change in the relationship between the Government and the people. While the public has come to rely increasingly on government in such areas as social security and regulation of the economy, at the same time it seems to have become distrustful of the bureaucracies that have been born out of these

---

*Reprinted and abridged by permission from *Report of the Independent Review Committee on the Office of the Auditor General of Canada* (Ottawa: Information Canada, 1975), pp. 1-77.
[1]Canada, *Revised Statutes*, 1970, Chapter F-10 as amended.

new dimensions of activity. The public sometimes seems alienated and unwilling to accept governmental actions as uncritically as in earlier decades. Many citizens do not feel they know enough about the Government and are attracted by the concept of an independent officer in Ottawa who can tell them "what is really going on". Rightly or wrongly, the Auditor General is widely seen as an important channel for telling the citizen the "inside story". There is a widespread public belief that the Auditor General should be a guardian of the public interest in preventing waste in whatever form it manifests itself. Although it may be simplistic to believe that waste is always obvious and unambiguous, there seems little doubt that, whenever the Auditor General has uncovered waste or inefficiency, the public wants to know about it. Moreover, many believe that even if the Auditor General exposes only a few examples of waste, maladministration or inefficiency, this will have a general salutary effect on ministers and on all members of the public service.

The widening scope of government responsibilities and growth in expenditures has had a major impact on financial matters within the Government itself. In the decades prior to 1960, the principal stress in expenditure management was on regularity. The whole system was oriented toward detailed and careful examination of each transaction, and the process was highly centralized. Accountants and financial administrators were not generally encouraged to be concerned with the reasons for expenditures, for others made those decisions. Their task was mainly to provide a service and to ensure that the financial machinery of their department operated in the approved manner. Specifically, this involved ensuring that travel dollars were spent on travel, that funds for salaries were used for salaries, and so forth. In this context, it was only natural that the Auditor General should concern himself with the mere regularity of public expenditures.

In the 1960s, however, largely in response to the recommendations of the Royal Commission on Government Organization (which, in view of the growth of government, was highly critical of these cumbersome financial techniques), a new approach to expenditure management was adopted. This approach involved two major changes.

One of these was the adoption of PPBS — a planning, programming and budgeting system — which in effect represented an attempt to establish a whole new philosophy of control. Instead of being preoccupied with the detailed regularity of each dollar spent, departments, and their financial managers in particular, were encouraged to devote more time to examining expenditures in the light of the purposes they were designed to serve. In developing requests for future funding, departments were supposed to examine critically their current spending programs, to evaluate the effectiveness of past expenditures and to analyze the comparative cost and effectiveness of alternative methods for achieving objectives. Interest was promoted in cost-benefit analysis and other quantitative techniques designed to promote superior evaluation of expenditure proposals.

The adoption of the form of PPBS used in Canada was not without its difficulties. There are some who believe its potential has never been fully realized, although conceding it has had positive, though limited, effects on planning and budgeting in the administration. Others maintain that the system was simply overrated and that, despite all the effort, little of value has been achieved. For purposes of this discussion, the principal point to note is that old techniques of detailed control were found to be inefficient and PPBS represented a major effort to respond to this problem.

Concurrently with PPBS, a second major change was adopted: the substantial decentralization of financial control. The old central Office of the Comptroller of the Treasury, through which all payments had to be issued, was abolished. Instead, systems for financial control were to be established in each department of the Government, and the Treasury Board role evolved from one of detailed control to one of broad expenditure management. In the process, and in line with the philosophy of program management on which PPBS was founded, departments acquired greatly increased flexibility in the administration of their financial affairs. They were permitted to move funds around within a program without specific and prior Board approval, provided they believed that in doing so they could operate with greater economy, efficiency or effectiveness. No longer was it rigidly required that a dollar allocated to travel be spent on travel. These changes reflected a recognition that in a multi-billion dollar budget it was less important to ensure that every financial *t* was crossed and *i* dotted than it was to know whether funds were being spent in a manner that would ensure the achievement of the purposes for which they were made available.

REPORTING TO THE HOUSE OF COMMONS

The Auditor General is required to report to the House of Commons annually, on or before December 31, on his examination of the accounts for the fiscal year ended the previous March 31. While his report may deal with the work of his Office and various other matters, its main body consists of comments on specific items that have come to his attention as a result of his examinations. It is recognized that its ultimate audience is the people of Canada; and through the communications media, the highlights of his report receive wide publicity. While it does provide the public with a small window on the inner workings of government, the prime purpose of the report is to provide an essential link in Parliament's control of the public purse strings. It is part of the accountability process, and it is in this context that it is considered.

The content of the report is dictated by Section 61(1) of the Financial Administration Act, which requires that the Auditor General report on the results of his examination. It then specifies six types of cases to which he should call attention, concluding with the much discussed phrase "and any other case that he considers should be brought to the notice of the House of Commons".

These specific reporting requirements of the Act deal with only some of the matters on which the Auditor General might be expected to report. The requirements as to what he should examine (Section 58) are much broader in their scope. The assurances and information the House of Commons requires from the Auditor General are discussed below under three headings: the correctness of the accounts; the systems of control; and value for money.

The Correctness of the Accounts

The administration reports on its accountability for funds received and expended through the Public Accounts, which are tabled each year in the House of Commons, usually in September. It is important for Parliament to know that these accounts do provide a proper reporting by the administration. From earliest times, one of the major responsibilities of the Auditor General has been to give this assurance; and in recent years, he has done so mainly by reporting instances where the accounts are incorrect.

This need to reassure the House as to the correctness of the accounts does not imply that the Auditor General should be responsible for checking every figure appearing in the voluminous Public Accounts of Canada. Were he to do so, he would require a staff of thousands. Instead, he should be able to satisfy himself that the basic information is correct by making appropriate reviews and tests of transactions. In particular, he needs to ensure that revenues are properly accounted for and that expenditures are being properly charged. To accomplish this, after he has satisfied himself as to their effectiveness, he will rely on the systems of control and, to a very considerable extent, on the work of the internal auditors within the departments and agencies.

Appropriation Accounts

Each year, after a review of the Estimates, Parliament votes money for various specific purposes through an appropriation act, and this provides the authority for the administration to establish appropriation accounts against which expenditures may be made. Later in the year, two or three supplementary bills are usually passed, based on supplementary estimates, to take care of additional programs or to supplement previous appropriations that have proven to be inadequate. One of the responsibilities of the Auditor General is to assure Parliament that the expenditures actually made are limited to the amounts and purposes for which money was voted. This was the original purpose in creating the office of the Auditor General, and it will continue to be a necessary control under our present system of parliamentary democracy unless Parliament is prepared to lose control of the public purse.

Today, the effectiveness of this control is diminished by the manner in which Parliament appropriates funds. The actualities of the budgetary process differ considerably from the theoretical model one might envisage to provide for parliamentary control of expenditures or from the practice of earlier years, which provided for more detailed control.

In the first place, the annual votes now provide the authorization for only about half the total budgetary expenditures. The other half has already been authorized by other legislation enacted during the current or previous years, which granted a continuing authority to make payments from year to year for specific purposes. The payments of family allowances and unconditional grants to the provinces, for example, are authorized by separate legislation and are not subject to annual votes. The actual or estimated amounts of such statutory payments of a budgetary nature do, however, appear in the Estimates each year, and the amounts actually spent are included in the Public Accounts. But the responsibility of the Auditor General for examining such payments is necessarily limited to seeing that they are within the terms of the legislation and are properly accounted for. In many cases, there is no total dollar limit that cannot be exceeded, as there is on each annual vote.

Second, some of the individual votes included in the appropriation acts are for very substantial amounts (some are in the hundreds of millions of dollars). While an attempt is made to limit them to specific programs, the scope of the programs is frequently very broad indeed and in some cases pertinent detail is lacking. In the main Appropriation Act in 1973, there were only 229 separate votes, covering appropriations totalling more than $10 billion, the average vote being almost $45 million. The responsibility that can be placed on the Auditor General so far as regularity is concerned must be viewed in the light of this fact.

Finally, the wording of many of the votes is highly technical and frequently very lengthy, because it incorporates the statutory authority for entering into certain contracts and for making some payments. In addition, certain appropriations authorize the transfer of monies from one vote to another, all of which is meticulously accounted for in the Public Accounts.

The Systems of Control

Reporting on Control Systems

In addition to wanting assurance that the accounts are correct and that expenditures have been made only as authorized, Parliament needs to be assured that the administration has developed systems of control that will ensure that revenues are being collected as they should be and that public property is being controlled and safeguarded. (The phrase *public property* is defined by the Financial Administration Act as meaning all property other than money, so that it embraces not only land, buildings and equipment, but also loans, investments, accounts receivable and inventories. Some of these are recorded as assets under the present accounting practices of the Government, but many are not.) The Auditor General has been charged with examining these systems of control but has no specific reporting responsibilities in this connection. His annual report, however, usually contains many comments on the subject.

Parliament's primary concern is to ensure that the administration is collecting the monies that it should and is safeguarding the assets for which it is responsible, whether or not the accounting system employed recognizes such assets in the annual financial statements. It should therefore know whether accounting systems are faulty, if proper financial controls have not been implemented, or if controls that have been established have broken down, just as it should know if money has been improperly expended. This has always been of concern to Parliament, but under today's conditions it is absolutely essential to ensure effective control of the public purse. Given the hundreds of thousands of government employees and millions of government transactions, it would be prohibitively expensive to perform detailed audit checks. In the absence of such checks, effective control over public funds is dependent on good financial control systems and the effective management of such systems. With the growth in the use of computers, the development of effective control systems, far beyond what could previously be achieved, is practicable. But Parliament will always need the Auditor General's assurance that there are no major shortcomings or breakdowns in this area.

Value for Money

The Auditor General has an additional, special responsibility with respect to government spending—one that has, in a sense, evolved from and goes beyond the audit of mere regularity. Essentially, his task is to determine whether value has been received for the money the Government has spent.

Value for money, as a concept, is complex and poses problems of judgement for the person making its evaluation. It encompasses three interrelated components: whether the money is expended *economically* and *efficiently* and whether the program on which it is expended is *effective* in meeting its objectives. The first two components, economy and efficiency, are susceptible to reasonably objective definition and measurement, and there should be no discrepancy between a policy approved by Parliament and the carrying out of this policy by the administration in an economic and efficient manner.

The Auditor General has for some years now been interested in assessing value for money in terms of economy and efficiency, though not always under that designation; most frequently he has identified and reported on so-called non-productive payments. His selection of items to report on in this category has usually been based on a judgement as to the economic and efficient use of funds for a specified purpose.

The right of the Auditor General to report on this aspect of government expenditures has been challenged, even in recent years. For example, it has been suggested that the intent of the present legislation is to restrict him to reporting on regularity alone, without regard to whether the money was spent economically or efficiently. This narrow interpretation seems inconsistent with our understanding of Parliament's intention when it appropriates funds for a particular purpose. In making such an appropriation, it surely imposes a trust on the administration not only to use the funds for the specified purposes but, as a trustee, to spend the money prudently—that is, with a view to economy and efficiency. In other words, the administration is expected to ensure that value for money will be obtained.[2]

RELATIONSHIPS OF THE AUDITOR GENERAL WITH THE PUBLIC SERVICE

Department and Agencies

The real influence of the Auditor General derives from his power to expose problems he unearths, thereby creating a strong incentive for the administration to correct the situation. His critical focus is not likely to endear him to the officials who are subject to his scrutiny, and in many cases it may be those same officials who will have to correct the situations referred to in his report. Thus, his relations with the public service will inevitably be complex and delicate, and his success in effecting change will often depend upon how well he and his staff have been able to

---

[2]Editor's Note: The Auditor General Act, introduced in Parliament as Bill C-20 in early November 1976, incorporated many of the recommendations of the *Report of the Independent Review Committee* from which this essay has been taken. One of the most important provisions of the Bill is that the Auditor General may report on whether "money has been expended without due regard to economy or efficiency," that is, whether the government has received "value for money."

develop and maintain their working contacts while the audit is being performed and his report is being compiled. If, in developing criticisms of departments, the Audit Office staff are able to create an atmosphere of frank interchange whereby problems are recognized as such by all concerned, rectification is likely to come about relatively quickly and painlessly.

The nature of the relationships that the Auditor General should enjoy with the public service has been aptly described by the Canadian Institute of Chartered Accountants as "cordial but not cosy." He must be cognizant of, and in some measure sympathetic to, the complex problems and constraints with which officials must wrestle in their daily work. At the same time, he must preserve his capacity to report objectively when the situation requires it.

Treasury Board Secretariat

Questions have sometimes arisen concerning the degree to which the Treasury Board Secretariat should be involved in the development of comments for the Auditor General's report. As the staff agency of the Treasury Board, the Secretariat has a broad responsibility for ensuring that departmental programs are soundly managed and financial procedures properly maintained. The Secretariat and the Auditor General are thus natural allies in the effort to eliminate waste and maladministration. Ideally, their relationship would reflect this.

Where breakdowns occur in existing systems in a department or agency, where there is a failure to implement proper accounting systems and controls, or where wasteful expenditures are made, it is important that corrective action be undertaken immediately. On finding an unsatisfactory condition, the Auditor General's first responsibility is to notify those immediately responsible; if appropriate and timely action cannot be taken at that level, he should report the matter to the deputy minister or the department of the head of the agency concerned. He should also, however, have authority to report the situation to the Treasury Board Secretariat, which has the major coordinating responsibility for financial administration. In any case, it should be up to him to determine whom he will apprise of his findings and how he will do so.

Though the Auditor General and the Secretariat may not always agree, it is apparent that through generally harmonious relations he can have far more influence for change upon the government system than he can if he attempts to exert pressure exclusively through his reports to the House of Commons and through his appearances before the Standing Committee on Public Accounts. Conversely, the Secretariat itself, faced with a recalcitrant department unwilling to subject itself to the rigorous discipline of management and budgeting techniques, may welcome an initiative by the Auditor General in surfacing for public debate an issue with which the internal workings of the administration have been unable to cope.

The Standing Committee on Public Accounts

The Auditor General's report is directed to the House of Commons; once tabled by the Minister of Finance, it is by tradition referred to the Standing Committee on Public Accounts. There is no provision for automatic referral, although for the past few years it has been referred the same day it was tabled. Detailed consideration of the report by the Committee ensues, and witnesses are called. Typically, the Auditor General or members of his staff are in attendance at Committee meetings. At various stages in its deliberations, the Committee formulates its own recommendations, which are then presented in formal reports to the House of Commons. These reports are received by the House but are not ordinarily approved or debated.

Early in 1974, the Secretary of the Treasury Board took unprecedented action by submitting to the Committee a detailed response to matters raised in the Auditor General's 1973 report. This important innovation should become a tradition, for it can help the Committee in its deliberations by providing a clear record of the action that the administration has taken or intends to take on the matters raised.

The impact of the Auditor General's reports can depend to a great extent on how they are treated by the Standing Committee on Public Accounts. In particular, the procedures for handling them should be efficient and should contribute to their effective consideration. At present, there are several possibilities for delay between the time a report leaves the hands of the Auditor General and the commencement of its study by the Committee. The Standing Orders of the House of Commons could be changed to provide that the report be automatically referred to the committee and, if the Committee has not been organized, that it be organized without delay.

ACCOUNTABILITY FOR ADMINISTRATION

As the Standing Committee on Public Accounts begins consideration of the Auditor General's report, it is sometimes open to question whether in seeking to resolve a problem it should turn to ministers or to officials, to the Treasury Board or to departments. When government expenditures and the range of governmental concerns were smaller than they are today, it was presumably possible for a minister to be in relatively close touch with the operations of his department, Today, a Cabinet minister is subject to many and various demands. He must be a spokesman for Cabinet, a constituency representative, an active Member of Parliament, a formulator of departmental policy, a participant in Cabinet (and Cabinet committee meetings) and a voice for regional or other special interests at the national level. Often, he must be absent from Ottawa in order to meet some of these responsibilities.

If the minister effectively carries out all of these tasks, there is little time available for detailed supervision of his department; but Canada's system of government requires that a minister be responsible for all aspects of departmental activities and be prepared to deal with them in the House. Thus, he sometimes finds himself required to answer for trivial problems of administration of which it is quite unreasonable to expect him to be aware and for which he cannot realistically be held responsible.

At the same time, the accountability of the public service for administrative efficiency is unclear. If the principal responsibility for sound administration rests with the deputy minister, and the responsible minister cannot reasonably be expected to supervise him adequately in this regard, how can Parliament (and the public) have any assurance that due regard is being paid to efficiency and good management?

In Britain, an attempt has been made to overcome this difficulty by designating specific senior officials in departments as *accounting officers*. In brief, the substance of the accounting officer concept is as follows. The Treasury appoints an accounting officer for every vote, who is held responsible to Parliament and answerable to the Committee of Public Accounts for the formal regularity and propriety of all the expenditures out of his assigned vote, and for the efficient and economical administration of the organization that he leads. The accounting officer is normally the permanent secretary (deputy minister) of a department and, as such, he is also responsible to the department's minister. The accounting officer concept helps to establish a distinction between accountability for overall policy (for which the minister retains responsibility to Parliament) and accountability for sound administration (for which the accounting officer, to some extent through the Treasury, is responsible to the Committee of Public Accounts).

Although the accounting officer concept as it is implemented in Britain may not be the perfect solution to the problem of establishing clear accountability for administrative matters in the Canadian public service, it may be capable of modification or development to this end. Alternatively some other method of achieving this may evolve. Either development, leading to a more precise definition in government relationships of the distinction between matters of policy and those of management, would assist in correcting situations referred to in the Auditor General's report, since it would help to indicate where responsibility for taking corrective action resides, depending on the nature of the issue and where the basis of the problem exists. Consideration should be given to the means whereby the locus of accountability for sound administration and financial management can be clearly identified in the Canadian Government.

CASE REFERENCES

Canadian Cases in Public Administration
   Mr. Smith's Expense Accounts
   The Renfrew Group

Case Program in Canadian Public Administration
   The Elusive IPB System

BIBLIOGRAPHY

Baker, Walter, "Administrative Reform in the Federal Public Service: The First Faltering Steps." *Canadian Public Administration*, Vol. 16, No. 3, Fall 1973, pp. 381-98.

Baker, Walter, "Management by Objectives: A Philosophy and Style of Management for the Public Sector." *Canadian Public Administration*, Vol. 12, No. 3, Autumn 1969, pp. 427-443.

Balls, Herbert R., "Common Services in Government." *Canadian Public Administration*, Vol 17, No. 2, Summer 1974, pp. 226-241.

Balls, H.R., "Planning, Programming and Budgeting in Canada." *Public Administration (U.K.)*, Vol. 48, Autumn 1970, pp. 289-306.

Bird, Richard M., *The Growth of Government Spending in Canda*. Toronto, Canadian Tax Foundation, 1970.

Canada, *Report of the Auditor General*. Ottawa, Queen's Printer, annual.

Canada, Treasury Board, *Planning Programming Budgeting Guide*. Ottawa, Queen's Printer, 1969.

Cutt, James, "The Program Budgeting Approach to Public Expenditure: A Conceptual Review." *Canadian Public Administration*, Vol. 13, No. 4, Winter 1970.

Denham, Ross A., "The Canadian Auditors General — What is their Role? *Canadian Public Administration*, Vol. 17, No. 2, Summer 1974, pp. 259-73.

Doern, G. Bruce, "The Budgetary Process and the Policy Role of the Federal Bureaucracy." In G. Bruce Doern and Peter Aucoin, eds., *Structures of Policy-Making in Canada*. Toronto, Macmillan, 1971, pp 39-78.

Fenno, Richard, F., Jr., *The Public Purse*. Boston, Little, Brown & Company, 1966.

Golembiewski, R.T., ed., *Public Budgeting and Finance, Readings in Theory and Practice*. Itasca, Ill., F.E. Peacock Publishers, 1968.

Hartle, D.G., "Techniques and Processes of Administration." *Canadian Public Administration*, Vol. 19, No. 2, Spring 1976, pp. 21-33.

Hodgson, J.S., "Management by Objectives." *Canadian Public Administration*, Vol. 16, No. 3, Fall 1973, pp. 422-31.

Laframboise, H.L., "Administrative Reform in the Federal Public Service: Signs of a Saturation Psychosis." *Canadian Public Administration*, Vol. 14, No. 3, Fall 1971, pp. 303-25.

Lyden, Fremont J. and Miller, E.G., eds., *Planning-Programming-Budgeting: A Systems Approach to Management*. 2nd ed. Chicago, Markham Publishing Company, 1972.

Newland, Chester A., ed., "Forum on Management by Objectives in the Federal Government." *The Bureaucrat*, Vol. 2, No. 4, Winter 1973, pp. 351-426.

Novick, D., ed., *Program Budgeting*. Cambridge, Mass., Harvard University Press, 1965.

Padgett, Edward R., "Programming-Planning-Budgeting: Some Reflections Upon the American Experience with PPBS." *International Review of Administrative Sciences*, Vol. 37, No. 3, 1971, pp. 353-62.

"Planning-Programming-Budgeting System: A Symposium." *Public Administration Review*. Vol. 26, No. 4, December 1966, pp. 243-310.

"Planning-Programming-Budgeting System Reexamined: Development, Analysis, and Criticism: A Symposium." *Public Administration Review*, Vol. 29, No. 2, March-April 1969, pp. 111-202.

Shonfield, Andrew, *Modern Capitalism: The Changing Balance of Public and Private Power*. New York and London, Oxford University Press, 1965.

Strick, J.C., "Recent Developments in Canadian Financial Administration." *Public Administration (U.K.)*, Vol. 48, Spring 1970, pp. 69-85.

Ward, N., *The Public Purse: A Study in Canadian Democracy*. Toronto, University of Toronto Press, 1962.

White, W.L. and Strick, J.C., *Policy, Politics and the Treasury Board in Canadian Government*. Don Mills, Science Research Associates (Canada) Limited, 1970.

Wildavsky, Aaron, *The Politics of the Budgetary Process*. Boston, Little, Brown & Company, 1964.

Wildavsky, Aaron, "Political Implications of Budgetary Reform." *Public Administration Review*, Vol. 21, Autumn 1961, pp. 183-190.

CHAPTER 5

PUBLIC PERSONNEL ADMINISTRATION IN CANADA

This chapter on personnel completes our analysis of the basic functions of management. The theory and practice of public personnel administration has developed with striking rapidity during the past few decades. In government departments and agencies, the clerical function of preparing staff requisitions and documenting personnel data has given way to the senior staff function of advising on human relations and to sophisticated techniques of personnel management.

In the first essay R.H. Dowdell explains the personnel function in management, the organization of personnel administration in the federal government and important features of public personnel administration in the Canadian provinces. Then, Kenneth Kernaghan examines major issues in management development for public servants at all levels of Canadian government.

One public personnel activity that has expanded and changed beyond all recognition during the past decade is collective bargaining. The final essay in this chapter by P.K. Kuruvilla describes the evolution of employer-employee relations in the federal public service and analyzes the controversy surrounding the content and administration of the Public Service Staff Relations Act.

19
Public Personnel Administration*

R.H. Dowdell

I. THE PERSONNEL FUNCTION IN MANAGEMENT

The management of an organization is the body of executive and supervisory personnel responsible for defining its objectives, framing its policies and directing the activities of its work force. Management's resources include time, material and people (money may be considered either as a resource in itself or the ability to acquire resources). These resources must be efficiently and effectively employed if management is to achieve its objectives.

Because they behave according to the laws of physics and chemistry, management's material resources possess qualities which are either known or immediately discoverable and their behaviour is predictable. Such is not the case with people. Despite the recent discoveries in the behavioural sciences, much remains unknown about the qualities of *homo sapien*, and his behaviour cannot be so reliably predicted in the work situation or anywhere else. In a sense, the human resources of an organization are not "resources" at all, for all organized social activity is maintained to meet human needs and purposes, and the organization's employees are, in some measure, part of the reason for its existence.

A number of developments have made the task of "people management" in organizations progressively more complicated.

1. The business enterprise or government department of the nineteenth century characteristically employed a few score or at most a few hundred people. The owner-manager, or the minister, hired many of his staff personally and knew a good deal about their backgrounds and personal idiosyncracies. The predominant feature of modern organizations is their large scale. Federal government departments are classed as small if they employ less than 2 000 to 3 000 people. Thirty-six percent of the civilian public service (exclusive of federally owned corporate enterprises) is employed in three departments: Post Office (59 000), National Defence (38 000) and National Revenue (22 000). Six other departments each employ in the 10 000 to 20 000 range and account for another 25 percent. For most employees, whether in the private or public sector, personal relationships are limited to a small fragment of the enterprise. They are separated by many layers of hierarchy from top management, which comes to depend on rules and procedures instead of face-to-face contact in daily activity. The quality of large organizations that Weber described as "rationalism" results in decisions which are

*The editor extends appreciation to Mr. Dowdell for his work in updating this selection.

based on policies and regulations rather than on personal knowledge and the recognition of individual needs. There are now more than 326 000 people at work in the federal public service. Their wages and salaries total more than $4 billion annually.[1] Every year these figures increase, with a regularity that has become a major source of social and political concern. How can the public be certain that all of these people are really needed, and are working with optimum effectiveness? These questions derive from the large scale of government employment, and are addressed to some of the biggest problems in modern public personnel management.

2. In the last 50 years, scientists and managers have systematically studied people at work. Frederick W. Taylor and Frank B. Gilbreth — the founders of "scientific management" — proved that the attention given to improving the way a man works pays off handsomely in productivity. But their belief in piece-rate incentives was based on the wrong assumptions about why people work, and the kinds of satisfactions they derive from it. Motivating forces of a quite a different sort came to light in the studies of group influence and communication techniques at the Hawthorne, Illinois, works of the Western Electric Company. The "Hawthorne studies" set the tone for the "human relations" school, pioneered by F.J. Roethlisberger and Elton Mayo. More recently, men like Rensis Likert, Douglas McGregor, Abram Maslow and Frederick Herzberg — to mention only a few — have done what the physical scientist did in connection with material resources: investigated the characteristics of people so that they can be employed more effectively and in a way that makes work a more meaningful human experience.

TABLE I

Total Federal Government Employment and Payroll, December 1975

	Number of Employees*	Payroll* (× $1000)
Ministries of state and government departments	297316	956846
Departmental corporations	51683	43322
Administrative, regulatory and special funds	12888	43681
General government — Total	326580	1,052210*
Government enterprises	132046	501494
Total	458626	1,553704
Monthly average, October-December	—	517901

* Excludes armed forces personnel.
* Figures shown are for the October-December quarter, 1975.
* Excludes overtime and retroactive payments.

[1]See Table I.

3. Knowledge in itself would do little to improve the management of people at work were it not for a change in the attitudes of the community at large. Since early in this century, society has expressed an increasing concern for human welfare, including the treatment accorded by employers. The law gives employees powerful leverage in pursuit of their own interests by recognizing their right to form associations and by requiring management to negotiate wages and working conditions with them. A management that is harsh, neglectful or indifferent may eventually find itself in violation of other laws on safe working conditions, minimum wages, and employment benefits. In addition, the community can apply economic or political sanctions to an employer who is considered to be guilty of unfair management practices.

4. The typical working man of the 1970's is more highly educated than his father was, and he has a more acute sense of social awareness. In addition to bargaining about wages and working conditions, he is beginning to demand, through his union, a voice in other aspects of management. Productive technology and plant location, for example, have widespread effects on the community, and labour has frequently challenged management's traditional right to make unilateral decisions in these and other matters. So strong is this trend that little credence can be given any longer to the concept of "sacred management prerogatives". The history of labour-management relations makes it clear that yesterday's management prerogatives are circumscribed in today's union contract, and those that management regards as inviolate now may be on the bargaining tables tomorrow.

5. Continuing high levels of economic activity have made labour scarce and expensive. Fringe benefits, transferable pension rights and guaranteed annual wages add up to a substantial management investment in each employee, whether he continues to be productively employed or not. Increasingly complex technology demands skills which cannot be produced entirely through pre-employment education and management is consequently faced with high costs of training after the worker gets on the job. Frequent changes in technology would mean even higher training costs if management did not build on the skilled and experienced staff it already has.

> When a new computer installation is staffed with retrained employees we have found it to have a far greater chance of success than one staffed by new hires. Aside from the obvious morale advantages the reason for this is really quite simple. It is usually easier to train someone in computer techniques than it is to teach a man your business.[2]

It is generally accepted in the private sector that competitive success

---

[2]M.J. Rausco, "Training Implications of Automated Personnel Systems", *Office Administration*, October 1967.

depends more on the quality of people employed by an organization than on technological innovation. The latter will provide at best a temporary advantage which is likely to be overcome by competitors whereas a more competent work force, in particular a creative and capable management group, will be a continuing source of innovation.

Personnel Management and Personnel Administration

Personnel management is that part of management activity which concentrates on making effective use of people in achieving the organization's objectives. For the above reasons personnel management now requires the application of knowledge and skills which supervisors cannot be expected to acquire in addition to mastering the technical side of their jobs. Many aspects of management have become the concern of specialists — finance, law and public relations — and personnel management is no exception. "Personnel administration" is the term applied to the activities of specialists who assist management in the exercise of its personnel functions. These activities can be subsumed under three headings.

Advice. Personnel administrators counsel management on the development and application of personnel policies, and the resolution of problems. They do this in the light of legal requirements imposed by the community and the knowledge about the way people function at work. In this latter respect, their role is analogous to that of the engineer in the physical sciences — they form the link between research and application.

Service. Certain personnel activities which require specialized knowledge and skill are often carried out by personnel administrators as a service to or on behalf of management. The employment office, for example, conducts selective recruitment and tests candidates for basic qualifications, thereby relieving supervisors of the need to interview all but a few candidates to fill a position. Analysts write job descriptions for use in manpower planning, recruitment and training, and they identify and describe factors of significance in the job which are used in establishing wage and salary levels for individual positions.

Control. There are two kinds of control. One involves telling a person what he can or cannot do, and applying sanctions to enforce compliance. The other has come into prominence as a result of developments in cybernetics, and involves monitoring or feedback. This second form of control is the function by which an organization derives information from its own activities, analyzes it, and determines the need for changes. The personnel administrator has a control function in this sense. He informs management, for example, about the number and kind of grievances or accidents that are occurring, the incidents of illnesses among individuals or groups of people, and the frequency and causes of labour turnover (particularly resignations and dismissals). And he advises management on changes in policy and practices which will bring about improvements.

The proper relationship of personnel administration to management is summed up by describing the personnel officer's work as a staff function. He directs no one but his own subordinates. He advises members of management on policies and practices required for effective personnel management, and he assists them in dealing with specific problems. He may provide services for them, such as the employment office and the central administration of benefit programs. He can and should act as the senior executive's spokesman in dealing with lower levels of management, and as his eyes and ears in ensuring that the approved policies are carried out. This role requires that he be a person of considerable influence. But he must nevertheless respect the right of managers at lower levels to disagree with him and go to the senior executive for a decision. They are not going over his head, for he does not stand between them and the head of the organization. Should he attempt to do so, his influence will be short-lived, for he will have destroyed relationships without which he cannot do his job.

The Influence of the Political Environment

Despite broad and growing similarities, personnel mangement in the public service is different in many ways from its counterpart in the private sector. One of the principal differences can be identified at the highest level in government organization. In the public service, the concept of management must include the political heads of departments — i.e. the ministers of the Crown. It is commonly thought that the deputy minister — the senior appointed official under the minister — is the top management official in the department, but reference to any of the Acts of Parliament establishing government departments will dispel this notion. For example, Section 2(2) of the Government Organization Act (1969) reads as follows:

> The Minister of Fisheries and Forestry holds office during pleasure and has the management and direction of the Department of Fisheries and Forestry.

If the Minister is a manager, he is also a politician. Indeed, perhaps first and foremost a politician, for he will not remain a minister for long unless he can get elected to Parliament, be re-elected whenever the occasion demands, and exercise considerable political skill in executing his portion of the government's program.

In a commercial enterprise, the product or service must be produced at a profit. In the long run, there must be prospects of a reasonable rate of return on investment to bring the business into being and ensure its continued existence. The profit criterion is at once an important motive underlying plans, policies and decisions, and a yardstick against which their effectiveness can be assessed. Personnel directors in the private sector are in general agreement that one of their chief objectives is to contribute to their firms' profitability.

The pervasive characteristic of the public service is political rather than commercial. The administrator in the public service implements public policies and programs which have been shaped by political forces. His superiors are politicians — leaders of a political party or coalition which obtained, if not a majority, at least the largest number of seats in the House of Commons because it convinced the electorate it had the best program and was best qualified to carry it out. These elected executives will tend to do the things likely to ensure their re-election and to avoid doing things which jeopardize it. The public service is subject to their direction and accountable to them. They in turn are accountable to Parliament for the conduct of the public service and not the least of the senior public servant's concerns is to avoid embarrassing his minister. Thus the political criterion is to the public service what the profit criterion is to industry — the thread which runs through the decision-making process, and the standard against which these decisions must ultimately be weighed. That is not to say that every action must be calculated for the political advantage of the party in power any more than every action in business must be calculated to maximize profit. Short-run disadvantages must sometimes be borne and there are many actions whose political consequences are too remote to affect decisions significantly. But in the long-run top management of the public service must on balance redound to the credit of the party in power and in the short-run, actions which may produce adverse political consequences must be avoided as much as possible.

If these considerations are true of management generally in the public service, they are equally true of personnel management in particular. In a commercial organization, personnel policies and actions are evaluated by the profit criterion. The political criterion, however, is a nebulous thing at best and less susceptible to objective estimates. It is more likely to be applied by evaluating the sum of immediate consequences arising out of policies and actions. There is a temptation to regard each personnel action as an opportunity to secure a return of political advantage and to avoid those which are politically dangerous. For example, before the reform of the Canadian public service it was generally accepted that the party in power would use its power of appointment to secure or reward political support and the opponents of reform argued that a government must be able to depend on the loyalty of those who administer its policies.

Whatever may be said in theory for personnel practices based on short- or long-term political advantages, the results were generally unfortunate. Although political appointees were sometimes people of great ability (Mackenzie King got his start in the public service as a patronage appointee), it was generally true that their qualifications for the job in question were a secondary consideration and frequently even minimum standards of ability were disregarded altogether. Security of tenure was uncertain and few political appointees tended to regard the public service as a career. The inevitable result was a low standard of competence and a poor quality of service to the public. At a time when government activity was highly circumscribed by today's standards, this situation could be tolerated. However, as the activities of the government began to expand, it became more and more necessary to employ people with the highest possible level of technical and administrative ability. To achieve this, methods of appointment and conditions of employment had to be changed.

The Merit Principle and Merit Systems

The merit principle which has replaced the patronage system as one of the cornerstones of personnel policy in the public service is an attempt to abandon political considerations altogether in managing the human resources of the public service. The significance of this policy may not be readily appreciated. To take politics out of public personnel management is to run counter to the very nature of the public service as an organization established to pursue political objectives. However necessary such a course may be, it generates stresses which are comparable to the psychological effects of repression. The political character of the public service which is denied outward expression in personnel management is nonetheless at the root of many of its problems, and accounts for many of its inconsistencies and shortcomings. One of the criteria by which public personnel management must be judged is its ability to cope with this dualism in its own character.

The merit principle is really two interrelated principles:

1. Canadian citizens should have a reasonable opportunity to be considered for employment in the public service.
2. Selections must be based exclusively on merit, or fitness to do the job.

These principles are among the most important goals of policy in public personnel management. The merit system is the mechanism in use at any given time by which these goals are achieved. The merit principle has become, and should remain, a relatively stable part of our public ethic, although like all ethical tenets it may suffer somewhat in practice. A merit system is an administrative device which can and should be adapted to changing circumstances.

II. THE ORGANIZATION OF PUBLIC PERSONNEL ADMINISTRATION

The relationships involved in the development and implementation of personnel policy in the Canadian public service have been compared to a triangle, comprising the Treasury Board, the departments and the Public Service Commission. The first two are part of the management structure whereas the third is not. Yet the Commission has had a prominent — indeed until recently the pre-eminent — role in this three-way partnership. How this came about and how the Commission's role has waxed and waned relative to that of management is one of the key elements in the evolution of public personnel policy.

Canada inherited from its colonial antecedents a tradition under which offices in the civil government went to supporters of the party in power. Under the patronage system a change of government was usually followed by the dismissal of partisans of the opposition. Additional posts were created where necessary to provide for the faithful. Appointments were made with more regard for political loyalty than competence. Levels of salary which did not attract the able remained unchanged for more than a generation. The tenure of more than one position and sub-contracting a position at a lower rate of pay were commonplace.

The Civil Service Commission: Agent of Reform

Despite these conditions, the first attempts at reform were feeble. A Civil Service Commission responsible directly to Parliament was established in 1908, but its jurisdiction and the system of competitive examination which it inaugurated applied only to positions in Ottawa. During World War I, continued political mismanagement brought the service to a state of near-chaos.

The reforms introduced by the Union Government in 1917 were a drastic remedy for the serious conditions. In one sweep, virtually all the authority of management in personnel administration was stripped away and vested in the Civil Service Commission. The Commission's authority was exclusive in all matters regarding recruitment, selection, promotion, transfer, and the classification of positions. The organization of departments was subject to its scrutiny, even though final approval remained the prerogative of the Governor-in-Council. Pay scales could be changed only in accordance with the Commission's recommendations. Even disciplinary actions such as suspension and demotion were subject to its veto.

Despite the frequent creation of exempt classes and agencies, the personnel system instituted under the Civil Service Act of 1918 continued substantially intact, if not unquestioned, for nearly 50 years. But by the mid-1950's, centralized personnel administration began to break down under its own weight. Cumbersome staffing procedures could not respond quickly enough to secure scarce talent in a continually tight employment market. The system of across-the-board salary increases was a sluggish, undifferentiated, and often inaccurate attempt to maintain a competitive position in the labour market, and to retain staff in the face of attractive opportunities in the prosperous private sector. An increasingly professionalized management *cadre* in departments fretted under the restrictions imposed on them.

Modernizing the Civil Service
In 1958, the Commission published a report entitled *Personnel Administration in the Public Service*[3] in response to a request from the Prime Minister for an enquiry into its own role in the machinery of government. The report recommended a return to the unified service of 1918 by extending the jurisdiction of a modernized Civil Service Act to most of the civilian service. No change was proposed in the basic concepts of the merit principle or the competitive system of selection, but there were many changes designed to streamline their administration. The Commission would retain its exclusive authority in staffing, but be permitted to delegate it to departments. Classification would remain with the Commission, but its role in matters of organization and establishment control would be on a purely consultative basis. It should continue to initiate recommendations on salary and other conditions of employment, but only after presiding over management-staff consultations as a neutral third party. This proposal was made in lieu of any form of collective bargaining for which the civil service was not considered to be ready at that time.

The Commission's report of 1958 was the first step in a process of change whose pace and scope has continued to grow and which shows no sign of slackening. Though many of its recommendations were ignored, the report was the basis for a new Civil Service Act in 1961. This Act did much to modernize procedures, but it did not extend the Commission's jurisdiction to excluded portions of the public service.

The Civil Service Act of 1961 had scarcely been proclaimed in force when other changes of a broader and more profound character were precipitated. The Royal Commission on Government Organization, which had been appointed in 1959, began to publish its recommendations in 1962. The basic theme of the Glassco Report is summed up in these excerpts:

> Above all, departments should, within clearly defined terms of reference, be fully accountable for the organization and execution of their programmes, and enjoy powers commensurate with their accountability. They must be subject to controls designed to protect those general interests of government which transcend departmental interests. But every department should be free of external controls which have no such broad purpose.[4]

These proposals for re-allocation of authority and responsibility in

---

[3] Civil Service Commission, *Personnel Administration in the Public Service,* Queen's Printer, Ottawa, 1958.
[4] The Royal Commission on Government Organization, *Report,* Vol. 1, Queen's Printer, Ottawa, 1962, p. 51.

the field of manpower management are designed to secure effective use of human resources in the public service. They do so by placing responsibility and the necessary degree of authority to discharge it in the hands of the government's operating management, the only place where the necessary links can be forged between people and programmes, between performance and objectives.[5]

Under these basic principles, the Glassco Report took serious exception to much of the Commission's operating role in personnel administration and to the authority vested in this non-management agency to control many important personnel functions. Conceding that the public service, unlike the private employer, is open to the pressure of improper influence on appointments, the Report recommended that "the Commission should continue to certify all initial appointments to the service, to ensure that selection has been made in accordance with proper standards".[6] But recruitment and selection should be a management responsibility. A common recruiting service provided by the Commission would facilitate an orderly approach to the labour market in many classes, especially those at intermediate and junior levels, but it should be the responsibility of the Treasury Board to determine the extent of that service. Departments should be authorized to recruit their own personnel above a salary of about $5 200, and to make promotions and transfers within guidelines established by the Treasury Board.

These recommendations oversimplified a number of complex problems. How, for example, could the Commission certify to the propriety of a selection in which it had no part? A central recruitment service might be desirable for occupations common to many parts of the public service, but departments which are the sole employer in an occupation (e.g. veterinarians, letter carriers and air traffic controllers) are in a better position to meet their own staffing needs. Many such classes had salaries below $5 200, and would come within the Commission's jurisdiction. No arbitrary salary level could adequately define the jurisdiction of the departments and the central recruiting agency.

When civil service personnel legislation was next amended, it was the rearrangement of authorities required to implement collective bargaining more than the Glassco recommendations which influenced the measures that were passed. In 1966, Parliament passed three pieces of legislation which were proclaimed in force in March, 1967:

1. the Public Service Employment Act (replacing the Civil Service Act)
2. amendments to the Financial Administration Act
3. the Public Service Staff Relations Act.

All three had a bearing on the future role of the Commission. The first

---

[5]Ibid., p. 300.
[6]Ibid., p. 321.

established a Public Service Commission to regulate staffing in the portion of the public service over which the former Civil Service Commission had jurisdiction. In addition, prevailing rate employees and ships' crews, previously exempt, were brought under the Act and provision was made to extend it by Order-in-Council to other parts of the service. The amendments to the Financial Administration Act transferred responsibility for position classification to the Treasury Board. The Public Service Staff Relations Act included terms which made the new Public Service Staff Relations Board responsible for pay research and for hearing grievances on disciplinary matters which were previously the subject of appeals to the Commission.

Service or Control?

The legislative changes of 1967 brought about much of what Glassco had recommended regarding the role of the Commission. Only staffing remains as a statutory responsibility. Its training and management consulting services could as readily be provided to departments by the Treasury Board and it is by no means certain that they will not eventually be transferred there. The Commission's appelate function is limited to matters arising out of the administration of the merit system in promotions and transfers, and to cases in which an employee's release from the service is recommended for incompetence or inability to perform his duties. Pay rates and other conditions of employment previously recommended by the Commission are for the most part contained in collective agreements negotiated by bargaining agents for the various occupational groups. Three entire occupational groups (Senior Executive, Personnel Administration, and Organization and Methods) are excluded from bargaining, along with a number of positions in other occupational groups, because of their close identification with management; for these groups and positions, pay rates and conditions of employment are established unilaterally by the Treasury Board, which has generally tended to follow the patterns established in collective agreements.

Despite these changes, the Public Service Commission is not the service agency advocated by Glassco. By law it retains exclusive jurisdiction in the recruitment, selection, promotion and transfer of employees in agencies which are subject to the Public Service Employment Act. Although it may delegate its authority, it retains final responsibility and the power to prescribe policies, standards and procedures. It can revoke appointments which it deems to have been improperly made and it can withdraw delegated authority if departments do not properly exercise it. In short, the Commission provides a staffing service, but not one which departments have any choice about using. It does so in order that it may control staffing in the public service. Control is the objective — service is only the means.

The Alternative to Control

If the Commission remains mainly a control agency, it is because other methods have not been used to ensure that improper pressures do not influence staffing. Yet other methods are available. In financial administration, reform was accomplished without removing management's operating authority. The Auditor General, like the Public Service Commission, is responsible directly to Parliament and hence is outside the management structure in the public service. Unlike the Commission, however, he has no authority except to determine, after the fact, whether funds have been spent in accordance with the authority voted by Parliament and whether adequate measures have been taken to account for revenues and to safeguard public property. His only means of exerting influence are his annual report to Parliament and the day-to-day consultations between his staff and departmental officers. Nevertheless, these influences have proven to be very powerful indeed.

In the United States, many state public service commissions have a watchdog function similar to the Auditor General's. Authority in all personnel matters is vested in management. The Commission has access to records and the authority to conduct hearings, and is required to report to the legislature on the administration of the merit system. Sometimes it is also required to review personnel regulations before they are enacted and to hear appeals from employees against alleged improper recruitment and selection. In these circumstances the Commission can remain independent, non-political and above all influential, without displacing management in some of its most important functions.

This alternative to the present division of authority between management and the Public Service Commission has never been seriously considered in Canada. Personnel administration is still organized as though political patronage were the main obstacle to efficiency in the public service — as indeed it was before the reform of 1918. Today, the major problem in personnel management is the effective utilization of a work force that numbers over 200 000 employees and continues to increase by about three per cent each year. The continuing division of authority between the Commission and the Treasury Board makes manpower management more difficult and less effective despite the best efforts and intentions of the parties involved. It is time to ask whether the price exacted for present methods of protection against patronage is too high.

Central Management: The Treasury Board

The federal Cabinet has a number of committees through which it seeks to expedite the conduct of government business. The most important of these is the Treasury Board. The Board was established in 1867 and for many years it was concerned exclusively with financial management, reviewing departmental statements of income and expenditures, and estimates of future spending. For most of its existence it had little to do with personnel management directly, even during the period of reform which was inaugurated by the Civil Service Act of 1918.

During the depression of the 1930's an acutely cost-conscious government gave the Board the power to restrict the increase of, and if necessary to abolish, permanent civil service positions, to curtail promotions and to reduce salaries. These controls were carried over into World War II, and new ones were introduced — among them a virtual freeze on the reclassification of positions. Restrictions on the creation of permanent positions were continued and many civil servants spent the better part of their career as "temporaries", denied pension rights and certain other benefits of permanent employment. During the war many new government agencies were established under legislation which exempted them from the personnel regime of the Civil Service Act. The Board stepped in to prescribe working conditions and salary schedules for many such agencies and gradually was drawn into broader questions of personnel regulation.

By the end of the war, the Board had firmly established a major role in public personnel management. But it was preoccupied with the financial implications of decisions on personnel matters and sought to keep costs to a minimum by retaining decision-making authority in a myriad of trivial administrative matters. Trapped by its own devices into dealing with literally hundreds of departmental recommendations each week, the Board and its staff had little time to devote to planning, to review of policy, or establishing criteria for effective management in the public service.

The Glassco Royal Commission on Government Organization made the Treasury Board one of the chief targets for criticism in its initial Report. The board was criticized for excessive concern with administrative details, for a narrow emphasis on financial control and for failing to exert leadership in the management of the public service. Among the Commission's most important recommendations was the separation of the Board from the Department of Finance and the creation of a separate Cabinet post — President of the Treasury Board. The Report also recommended an organization structure for the Board's staff to include, under a Secretary of deputy minister rank, three divisions dealing with the review of government programs, personnel policy and management improvement.

In 1963 all federal political parties committed themselves to support a form of collective bargaining in the public service. When the Public Service Staff Relations Act was passed in 1967, the Treasury Board became the employer for most of the public service. In keeping with its new responsibility for negotiating and implementing collective agreements, the Board was also given the responsibility for position classification in the service — a function previously administered by the Public Service Commission.

The Board is now clearly identified as the central management agency in the public service. The Personnel Policy Branch, headed by a Deputy Secretary, was completely reorganized in 1966 as part of the reconstitution recommended by Glassco. In keeping with the policy of disengagement from detail, it has made substantial progress in developing policy guidelines within which decision-making authority is being delegated to departments. Most important of all, it has assumed an effective management role in areas of personnel policy which, until recently, were largely ignored or left by default to the Public Service Commission: notably, training policy, manpower planning, and staff development.

Personnel Administration in the Departments

The removal of most of the responsibility in personnel matters from management obviated a role for personnel specialists in departments for many years. Deputy ministers had little authority in personnel management and accordingly accepted little responsibility for it. Their departments were small enough during the 1920's and 1930's that they could take an active personal role in many appointments, promotions and classification matters. The personnel specialist's role developed around the clerical activities in payroll, leave and attendance left behind when accounting services were centralized under the Comptroller of the Treasury in 1931.

During World War II many thousands of temporary employees had to be recruited under conditions of an acute labour shortage and had to be trained in duties which reflected new functions of government. Departments found it necessary to assign senior people to carry out the recruitment, organization and training of this greatly expanded work force. In 1946 the Royal Commission on Administrative Classification in the Public Service, under the chairmanship of Walter Gordon, criticized the generally rudimentary machinery for the administration of departmental personnel matters and recommended "the appointment in every department of an experienced and properly qualified personnel officer with adequate rank and power" as the means of promoting general efficiency, improving staff management and affording relief to deputy ministers.[7] In implementing this recommendation, many departments turned to the Civil Service Commission as the only source of staff with sufficiently expert knowledge in personnel matters. The

[7]The Royal Commission on Administrative Classification in the Public Service, *Report,* King's Printer, Ottawa, 1946.

greater part of the departmental personnel officer's responsibilities at that time involved liaison with the central agencies, particularly the Civil Service Commission and it was therefore highly desirable to obtain someone who knew the inner workings of these organizations.

Until the early 1960's there was no concensus in the public service as to what the role of the departmental personnel officer should be or how the personnel unit should be organized, either internally or in relation to other elements of the departmental hierarchy. Many personnel divisions were several levels removed from top management and exerted little influence. Standards of selection for personnel officers were low and training was inadequate. If departments were to do a better job of personnel management, even within the limited authority they then had, they had to have the assistance of personnel specialists who were better qualified and more appropriately organized.

Studies by the Public Service Commission, the Treasury Board, the Glassco Royal Commission and a number of private consultants have been unanimous in recommending that deputy ministers should have direct access to professional advice in the management of their two major resources — finance and personnel. As a result, personnel administration in most departments has been reorganized. Intervening levels in the organization have been removed and the director of personnel administration now reports directly to the deputy minister. In the two largest departments — National Defence and Post Office — he has the rank of assistant deputy minister.

Internal Organization of Personnel Units

Former patterns of organization of the departmental personnel function showed variations which could not be justified by the uniqueness of each department and were caused by a failure to achieve a common understanding of the importance and scope of the functions. Furthermore, these patterns of organization failed to provide solutions to problems which limited the effectiveness of personnel administration:

1. Excessive preoccupation with day-to-day matters of detail, to the detriment of research, planning, and policy formulation as the basis for a competent advisory role.

2. A tendency for line managers to feel that personnel management will and should be looked after by the specialists — a condition caused by over-centralization and a failure to provide competent personnel advice to all levels of management.

3. Stunted development of important areas of personnel administration, such as health, safety, staff relations and employee communications.

The organization of most personnel divisions now follows a pattern developed by the former Chairman of the Public Service Commission, J.J. Carson, previously the head of the Glassco task force study of personnel management. The Carson Model is based on an important premise —

that almost all day-to-day personnel administration be conducted by officers responsible to their branch directors or field unit heads. The central personnel unit in the department should be responsible for the functional guidance of these officers whose role would be to advise line officers closest to the problems. In this way the central unit would be free to concentrate on the development and evaluation of policy, while line officers would have advice more directly available to them in the fulfillment of their responsibilities for personnel management (see Figure I).

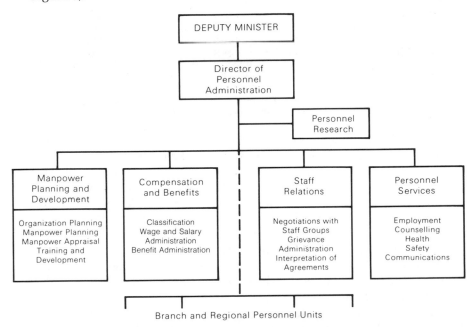

Figure 1
A Model Organization Plan for Departmental Personnel Units

III. PERSONNEL ADMINISTRATION IN THE PROVINCES

Taken together, the ten provincial governments in Canada employ a larger civilian work force than the federal government. More significantly, their rate of growth has been sharply higher in recent years.[8] Between 1959 and 1971, federal employment increased by 18.9 percent, while the provincial services grew by 80.9 percent (and municipal services by 141.7 percent).[9]

---

[8]For a more complete treatment of this subject, see J.E. Hodgetts and O.P. Dwidevi, *Provincial Governments as Employers*, McGill-Queen's University Press, Montreal, 1974.
[9]*Ibid*, p. 7.

TABLE II
Provincial Government Employment March, 1976*

	General Services	Government Enterprises
Newfoundland	13794	2877
Prince Edward Island	4325	274
Nova Scotia	17592	6141
New Brunswick	25316	3415
Quebec	84073	25717
Ontario	105728	33442
Manitoba	14758	11742
Saskatchewan	16632	9009
Alberta	44466	15562
British Columbia	39498	22461
Total	366182	130640

*Source: Statistics Canada, *Provincial Government Employment, January-March, 1976;* British Columbia, *Public Service Commission Annual Report, 1975-76.*

The reform of personnel administration in the provinces came later than it did at the federal level, followed different lines of development and, with some exceptions, has generally not achieved as much. All of the provinces have established a Civil or Public Service Commission, thereby pre-empting a title that is widely identified with merit-oriented personnel administration. Some have gone further and conferred upon the Commission certain of the trappings of independence from the government in the manner of their federal counterparts. Others have been content to use the title, while making the agency directly responsible to the political executive in the manner of any other department of government.

The Commission's independence, whether real or imaginary, poses the same problem at the provincial as at the federal level. An agency independent of government cannot be assigned or presumed to exercise functions in support of the government's personnel management responsibilities. If the Commission is to be truly independent, or even if the appearance of independence is to be preserved, the Commission can function, at best, as a staffing agency and possibly as a training service as well. Other personnel functions will develop in or gravitate toward an agency that is clearly identified as having the government as management. Thus, in provinces which have an independent Commission — New Brunswick and Manitoba — the secretariat of the Treasury Board or the management committee of the Cabinet is responsible for classification and pay administration, labour relations, and manpower development. However, the consequences of the prevalent division of personnel functions within the federal service are mitigated by the fact that neither tradition nor law confers upon the Commission the authority of its federal counterpart.

In the other provinces, the Commission could be as appropriately called the Personnel Department of the public service. In most cases, the multi-member format is retained but, with the exception of British Columbia, only the chairman is a full-time member. Alberta retains the title Public Service Commissioner for a single office of deputy minister rank, but the organization he heads is called the Personnel Administration Office. The chairman or commissioner has deputy minister rank in all provinces. His appointment is made by Cabinet and he is accountable to a Minister in the same manner as any other deputy minister. Saskatchewan dropped the last vestige of independence in 1972 by deleting the chairman's six-year tenure in favour of "appointment at the pleasure of Her Majesty."

In these provinces, the Commission performs all of the functions of a central personnel agency. The Treasury Board or Cabinet management committee secretariat, if there is one, or the Finance Department staff, if there is not, has a role in personnel policy that emphasizes budgetary implications. In this organizational context, the Commission is able to function as a clearly identifiable management agency. As such it normally acts as the employer representative in collective bargaining in addition to fulfilling its responsibilities in job evaluation, training and manpower development, and staffing. Centrally located in the machinery of government, the Commission also provides advisory and administrative services for portions of the public service that are not subject to the Public Service Act or its equivalent. Thus, it is possible for the Commission to exert a strong influence on personnel management in the provincial public sector.

Unfortunately, this arrangement of responsibilities has inherent conflicts which tend to limit the potential influence of the Commission. The basic problem is the juxtaposition of the regulatory and the advisory service functions.

Like the federal Commission, provincial Commissions were established first and foremost as control agencies, and their primary *raison d'être* is still to control the key functions of staffing and job classification. The departments perceive them as control agencies and, therefore, are not likely to approach a Commission for purely advisory or consultative services. Even in matters which ultimately depend on a Commission decision, there is a tendency for the departments to reach their own decisions without advance consultation or advice about the accomplishment of an objective within the regulatory framework, and then cajole or pressure the Commission into acquiescing. If the Commission agrees, it often rubber-stamps; if it disagrees — even in a small proportion of cases — it strengthens an already negative image. In either case, its influence is diminished. A truly independent agency might withstand this kind of pressure, but one that is government directed cannot do so indefinitely.

These conflicts in the role of the Public Service Commission have led one province after another to abandon the integrated personnel function in favour of the federal model. As this essay is being revised (September 1976), British Columbia is in the process of transferring collective bargaining and job classification to a newly created central agency. Saskatchewan's Commission Chairman, appointed in March 1976, is a former senior analyst in the Province's Budget Bureau; Alberta's government has had the Commission's role under review, and the fact that the Public Service Commissioner's position has been vacant for nearly a year suggests that the issues are contentious and will remain so. Quebec has divided its personnel functions into three parts rather than two: a Public Service Commission which is essentially a staffing agency; a Civil Service Department which, among other things, is responsible for staff relations and job classification; and a Treasury Board staff which supervises both with a watchful eye on the budget. Manitoba and New Brunswick have been limited to staffing activities for some time. Newfoundland is in the process of reorganizing and modernizing its public service, and the assignment of responsibilities is not yet clear. Nova Scotia and Prince Edward Island retain a unified personnel function and seem to have escaped, for the moment at least, the changes that have occurred in other provinces.

With appropriate legislative changes, a reduction of the Commission's role could have enabled it to concentrate more effectively on administering a better protected and more comprehensive merit system. Unfortunately these changes were not made. Legislation governing personnel administration in most provinces provides only a rudimentary merit system at best, and leaves a large portion of the public service free of any constraints on the appointment process. None of the provinces requires that the best qualified candidate be appointed. All but Saskatchewan limit the Commission's role to determining that a candidate is basically qualified for appointment. Departments may choose from among any qualified candidates referred to them, and thus they decide on "merit" according to their own criteria. Saskatchewan limits this choice only slightly by requiring the Commission to certify the best three candidates, but the deputy minister can reject any or all of these and request the certification of more.

In all of the provinces, the Commission's mandate — and thus the merit system — applies only in a carefully circumscribed portion of the public service. For the most part, blue-collar workers are not covered, thereby permitting whatever extent of patronage past practice and current political requirements have sanctioned. All provinces make full, if not consistent, use of legislative provisions which give newly established government agencies substantial autonomy in making appointments. Where these measures are not sufficient to limit the inconvenience of a centrally administered merit system, public service legislation usually provides some form of escape clause. Few of these are as generous as Saskatchewan's, where the Public Service Act allows the government to remove any position from the "classified" service and make an appointment to it by order-in-council.

Limitations on the application of the merit system are not markedly different in provinces which have an "independent" Public Service Commission than they are in provinces where the Commission is unmistakably a management agency. It has to be concluded, then, that realization of the merit concept depends less on legislative and institutional arrangements than on traditions, attitudes, and public tolerance.

20
Management Development for Canada's Public Services*

Kenneth Kernaghan

The subject of management development in our government services is not generally perceived as a major public policy issue. It is not a topic that has aroused much controversy in our public forums or private salons. However, the calibre of human resources at the senior echelons of our public services is crucial to the effective and responsible development and implementation of public policies. Discussions of public policy issues are frequently based on the questionable assumption that the appropriate number and quality of government employees will be available to develop solutions and put policy decisions into effect. The federal Cabinet acknowledged the importance of the manpower issue when in 1969 it identified public service personnel management as a matter of high priority. The Cabinet's concern was expressed as follows:

> Without greatly improved executive personnel and public service management, the government will not be able to elaborate policies and implement programs in a speedy, imaginative and progressive manner, much less gain the confidence and participation of the public service and of the public in a modern, efficient and socially sensitive government administration.

*Reprinted and abridged by permission from Kenneth Kernaghan, "Management Development for Canada's Public Services: Report of the Rapporteur," in Kenneth Kernaghan, ed., *Executive Manpower in the Public Service: Make or Buy* (Toronto, Institute of Public Administration of Canada, 1975), pp. 1-18.

Thus the issue of management development intertwines with all major public policy questions. The examination of management development in this essay is divided into the following three sections:

I.   Definitions
II.   The Identification of Needs
III. Make and/or Buy?

I. DEFINITIONS

As a basis for discussion, it is important to define such central terms as executive, manager, management development, public sector management and manpower planning.

The word manager denotes a clearer and more useful administrative role than the word executive. At the municipal level, the word executive is not commonly used to describe senior administrators. At the federal and provincial levels, the term executive designates or connotes a distinct category or group of senior administrators with diverse skills and responsibilities.

Thus, the term executive is too broad in one sense and too narrow in another. It includes some individuals whose primary responsibilities are not managerial and it refers to the most senior group of administrators, thereby excluding a large number of officials discharging important management functions at lower levels of government service.

The managerial cadre can usually be separated from the larger executive cadre which is composed of a heterogeneous group of senior officials, many of whose major responsibilities lie in the sphere of policy advice or policy coordination rather than of management. Admittedly, most executives perform some management functions but there are executives who fulfill primarily management functions and who can appropriately be described as senior managers. Also, the management role is performed by officials extending vertically from the first-line supervisor to the executive or senior manager. It is therefore essential to identify and prepare managers at lower levels for ascendancy to senior positions.

Moreover, it is necessary to keep in mind the variety of knowledge and skills required of the senior manager at different levels of government. It is equally important to remember that post-secondary institutions are engaged in the education of persons who enter government service considerably below the executive level.

A second problem of definition arises from various usages of the terms management development, management training and management education. Governments and community colleges usually describe their efforts to improve the management knowledge, skills and attitudes of public employees as management training and development programs whereas universities customarily use the term management education. In some government jurisdictions, development is viewed as a part of the general training effort; in others, development refers to efforts to enhance the employee's capacity to take on greater responsibilities whereas training refers to efforts to improve the employee's skills so that he may perform his existing duties more effectively.

This diverse usage of the same words constitutes a significant obstacle to effective communication among those involved in management training and education. My reading of the literature in this area suggests that it is useful and proper to view management development as a process which aims to improve managerial performance by increasing knowledge, developing skills, moulding values and broadening perspectives. Thus, the process of management development subsumes both training and education, and includes on-the-job experience as well.

Although the words training and education are often used interchangeably, an important distinction may be made between them. Management training is practical in its objective and content; it is designed to develop skills which are directly relevant to the employee's existing job; and most of this training is conducted within the government services, although the resources of external education and training institutions may be utilized. Management education is less practical in its orientation; it seeks to prepare individuals, whether they are existing or aspiring public employees, for a future position in the career government service, usually at the middle to senior levels of the services; and most of this education is now provided by the universities but is also provided by governments and by other educational institutions (e.g. community colleges and educational consultants).

Thus the key components of the process of management development in the public sector are:

1.   formal classroom training, primarily within the government services.
2.   formal classroom education, primarily within the universities.
3.   on-the-job training and experience.

It is important for subsequent discussion to keep in mind that only governments can provide the third component.

The term public sector management tends to be used more frequently by practitioners than the term public administration. The increasing usage of the former term by university teachers of public administration indicates that they are prepared to admit they are engaged in "management" education. This usage also connotes an approach that is more practical and professional than theoretical and academic. While the terms are often used synonymously, it is clear that public administration is a broader, more inclusive term than public sector management.

The concept of manpower planning is closely related to management development. Manpower planning in the public sector is the process through which a government strives to ensure (1) that it has the appropriate number and quality of human resources to carry out its responsibilities now and in the future and (2) that opportunities are provided for individual employees to pursue and realize personal career ambitions. Manpower planning requires the integration of a government's need for human resources of a particular quality with individual needs and aspirations. The essential components of a manpower plan are (1) a staffing and recruiting policy, (2) a training and development policy and (3), in some government jurisdictions, a language policy. The focus in this essay is on the second component, namely training and development policy.

II. THE IDENTIFICATION OF NEEDS

There are two major dimensions to needs identification in relation to management development in the government services. These are:

1. the determination of the knowledge, skills and attributes required to fill present and projected management positions and
2. the determination of the number of persons with the appropriate qualifications required to fill the gap between the existing supply of and the anticipated demand for human resources.

These two dimensions are examined below under the headings of management profiles and manpower needs.

Management Profiles

A management profile refers here to a descriptive statement of the knowledge, skills, experience and personal characteristics required for management positions at a specific level and location in the administrative hierarchy now and in the foreseeable future. No single management profile can be applied to all management positions. There is need for a number of management profiles which set out the educational, experiential and personal qualifications required of those who now hold or will hold management positions at various levels of the administrative pyramid and at all levels of Canadian government. This is a formidable challenge indeed! The profiles must provide a picture of existing as well as projected management positions and are therefore difficult to formulate in precise terms. Profiles, however, are a valuable tool because they inform manpower planners of the types of people to be recruited, trained and educated to fill particular positions.

Until recently, little effort was made to develop profiles of occupational groups — much less of the large number of government employees who are managers but who are spread throughout a variety of occupational groups. Most of the work completed or under way in this area is a result of federal initiatives. For example, the federal government has developed an executive profile for its own jurisdiction[1] and the federal Ministry of State for Urban Affairs is sponsoring studies in several large municipalities to identify the need for managers.

Public service managers, like managers in any large organization, require a common core of knowledge and skills related to the performance of management functions. They also require special knowledge, skills and values related specifically to government employment. Based on these premises, management training and education for government service should include:

1. a *management* core consisting of such components as organization theory, administrative behaviour, finance, personnel, economic analysis and quantitative methods and
2. a *public management* core consisting of such components as policy analysis, the political, economic and social environment of public sector management, public law and public service ethics.

Once an existing or prospective public manager has acquired these two sets of core capacities, he may further his public sector management education by specializing in substantive policy areas (e.g. urban policy, social policy, intergovernmental relations) or in management areas related specifically to the public sector (e.g. planning, budgeting, personnel, industrial relations).

Some public servants contend that management education for public service can be obtained in schools of business as well as in schools of public administration or public management and that individuals educated in management can adapt to the public service environment. Others believe that business schools provide a perspective, philosophy and knowledge base that is not as appropriate to public sector employment as that transmitted in schools of public administration. They assert further that the development of a "public service ethic", which, interpreted broadly, entails dedication to the public's interest, is central to public service management and thus to public service education and training.

There is much debate among teachers and practitioners of public administration as to whether management is, or can be, a profession and whether a primary purpose of management development is the creation of a group or class of professional managers. Discussion of this issue is

---

[1]For an account of this work and a prediction of the probable future makeup of the executive profile, see Walter Baker, "Executive Manpower Requirements of the Canadian Public Services in the 1980's," in Kenneth Kernaghan, ed., *Executive Manpower in the Public Service: Make or Buy*, Toronto, Institute of Public Administration of Canada, 1975, pp. 39-62. See also John J. Carson and William McCloskey, "Manpower and Educational Planning in the Canadian Federal Public Service," *Optimum*, vol. 5, no. 3 (1974), pp. 14-21.

complicated by confusion as to whether the debate is about the profession of management or the profession of public management and by the absence of a consistent definition of the word profession.

Views on the possibility and desirability of management as a profession range from missionary zeal to abhorrence. Advocates contend that professional managers already exist, that there is a management role which requires the performance of common functions in all large organizations and that, therefore, there is a core of management knowledge and skills which forms the basis of a profession. Opponents raise the spectre of a powerful class of managerial technicians who share the same knowledge and skills base and the same value system and whose management capacity enables them to move from one organization to another regardless of environmental differences. There is some concern that elected officials cannot have sufficient influence on the shape of society if they depend on advice from apolitical — even amoral — technocrats. Some opposition to professional management is also based on the belief that courses offering the common core of management knowledge and skills confer literacy in the field of management, not professional status.

If we adopt the very liberal definition of profession, namely "(1) a reasonably clear-cut occupational field, (2) which ordinarily requires higher education at least through the bachelor's level, and (3) which offers a lifetime career to its members,"[2] then a profession of public management already exists and includes a very large number of people. Under this definition, public management would not, however, constitute a profession in the same sense as such fields as medicine and law which meet stricter criteria for professional status. A typical list of such criteria states that a profession:

1. involves activities essentially intellectual
2. commands a body of specialized knowledge
3. requires extended professional preparation
4. demands continuous in-service growth
5. affords a life career and permanent membership
6. sets up its own standards
7. exalts service above personal gain
8. has a strong, closely knit professional organization.[3]

Those who support the fact or the potential of public management as a profession are impatient with others who insist that the field meet all or most of these criteria. There is, however, little point in claiming to be a

---

[2]Frederick C. Mosher, *Democracy and the Public Service*, New York, Oxford University Press, 1968, p. 106.
[3]National Education Association, *The Yardstick of a Profession*, Washington, D.C., National Education Association, 1948, p. 8.

professional if your own colleagues, much less those members of well-established professions, do not acknowledge this status. Neither university teachers nor administrative practitioners recognize a formal set of standard educational requirements for admission to a profession of public management. It is true that there is increasing agreement among university teachers on a body of specialized knowledge and skills which should be acquired for the Master's degree in public administration. However, only a small proportion of existing public service managers have acquired these formal educational prerequisites. Most have acquired equivalent qualifications through practical experience and are therefore entitled to an equal opportunity to enter the ranks of professional management. It is no easy task to specify with any precision the necessary qualifications for acceptance as a professional public service manager since managers come to their posts from a variety of directions and with a variety of backgrounds.

Despite these considerations, public servants at the senior levels of their respective governments view the practice of management as a profession and consider themselves to be professionals. Moreover, in the United States, the practice of public administration is commonly referred to as a profession and many — indeed most — university programs in public administration are described as professional programs. Developments in Canada appear to support the view that public management or public administration is moving closer to a profession in that there is substantial agreement on a common body of knowledge essential for public managers; pre-entry and continuing education are more widely available in universities and colleges; opportunities for in-service training and education are expanding; and there is much emphasis on public service as a career. Several central criteria for professional status still remain to be fulfilled, however. Whether these requirements will eventually be met depends largely on the extent to which teachers, scholars and practitioners cooperate in the pursuit of professional public management. A significant indicator of our proximity to this professional status will be the ability of governments and universities to develop senior public service managers with the increasingly sophisticated qualifications specified by management profiles.

Manpower Needs

The success of the search for the best and the brightest public service managers will be greatly enhanced by the availability of accurate and up-to-date management profiles. It is clearly important to know what kinds of managers are needed at what levels and by what date before it is possible to specify with any precision the requirements for management training and education.

We have seen, however, that the preparation of management

profiles is at a very rudimentary stage in most governmental jurisdictions. Thus, much staffing and management development is based on impressionistic evidence of manpower needs. Few governments have made a systematic effort to identify their existing and future needs for public service managers and to devise programs to train and educate persons to fill these needs. There are, however, a number of obstacles to designing and implementing a rational, comprehensive approach to management development.

In the first place, many elected representatives and senior government employees are unaware of the dimensions of the problem and of the pressing need for action. It is understandable that elected representatives are not sensitive to the need for management development. Politicians are not anxious to allocate resources to training and education programs for public employees because the benefits are not immediately evident or easily evaluated. This lack of enthusiasm among elected officials is a relatively greater problem at the municipal level where the need for management development is not as well recognized and where financial and personnel resources for such activity are more limited.

Senior government employees have a long-term interest in the quality of public service management. Yet even among this group there is insufficient recognition of the necessity for management development. It is important that senior appointed officials persuade their political masters to support training and education programs and that these officials provide opportunities for their subordinates to participate in such programs. In some jurisdictions, however, there appears to be little interest in the adequacy of personnel to meet the demands of existing positions and no concern about planning for those managers required in the 1980's. The "hope and a prayer" method of operation, according to which governments trust that qualified personnel will somehow emerge when needed, is woefully inadequate. Some of the questions which senior officials should ask are these: Are existing managers well-enough qualified to perform their duties? Do they need training to update or improve their ability to do their jobs effectively? Will they be qualified to take on greater responsibilities at more senior levels in the future? What opportunities for management development are available?

A second major obstacle to the development of highly skilled and knowledgeable public service managers, even among those governments where the importance of management development is readily acknowledged, is the scarcity of financial resources. Training and education is a costly venture, not only in terms of the infrastructure required to make opportunities available but also in terms of the time lost from substantive work while staff members are taking courses.

Financial support for management development is related also to some aspects of what might be termed "the great training robbery." It is reasonable to ask whether a good case has been made for management training and education. Can it be shown that those who have completed some of the great assortment of available courses are better able to perform their present responsibilities or to take on new and more challenging tasks? Can a sensible program of management development be mounted if reasonably accurate management profiles and estimates of manpower needs are not available? How can we evaluate the numerous programs and courses offered by governments, by post-secondary institutions and by other organizations, including educational consultants?

A third impediment to effective planning for management development is the demands of career planning. Manpower planning would be a much simpler task if governments could treat present and future employees as automatons. Individuals could then be inserted into the appropriate slots in the administrative structure as they completed the prescribed forms of management development. However, career development does not always conform to organizational needs. Individuals have career goals, job preferences, and personal idiosyncracies which often run counter to the government's need for employees with particular qualifications. Individuals may not wish to accept positions for which they have the requisite skills and experience or they may not wish to engage in any management training and education, or in some forms of it.

Finally, the merit principle, as it is implemented through the mechanism of the merit system, conflicts in some respects with effective planning for management development. Under a merit system where staffing must take account not only of merit but also of such factors as the representativeness of candidates, the best managers are not always appointed or promoted. Moreover, since employee unions insist that positions be filled by a process of competition, the selection of persons for special management development and assignments are viewed as discriminatory.

III. MAKE AND/OR BUY?

Governments must not only determine as precisely as possible the number and quality of public service managers required but also whether the gap between the supply and the demand should be made or bought. The making of managers involves the provision of training and education by the governments themselves and on-the-job experience; the buying of managers involves recruiting graduates of management programs from post-secondary institutions, recruiting managers from other governments and non-governmental organizations, and sending government employees to post-secondary institutions for training and education.

The need for competent managers is so great that governments must make *and* buy the human resources they need. The relevant question then is the balance which each government should strike between developing its own managers and relying on other institutions for this task. The answer will depend largely on the financial and personnel resources available within governments for management training and education and on the capacity of non-governmental institutions to provide this service at an appropriate cost. Thus governments cannot give a well-considered response to the make or buy issue until their staffing needs have been identified and internal and external resources for management development have been assessed.

In discussing the respective roles of governments and external educational institutions, it is useful to identify the major components of management development, of which some can be provided only by governments and others only by post-secondary institutions. These components are:

1. graduation from a post-secondary institution
2. post-graduate university education
3. graduation from a post-secondary institution with specialization in management
4. post-graduate university education with specialization in management
5. graduation from a post-secondary institution with specialization in *public sector* management (or public administration)
6. post-graduate university education with specialization in *public sector* management (or public administration)
7. on-the-job experience in government during the course of one's formal, pre-entry education (e.g. internships)
8. on-the-job experience in government as a regular employee
9. on-the-job experience in non-governmental organizations
10. in-service management training
11. mid-career training and education in external education institutions, notably in post-secondary institutions.

Existing managers have acquired differing groups of these components during their educational and government experience: Some senior managers have attained their lofty positions solely on the basis of an undergraduate education supplemented by lengthy experience in government; others have post-graduate degrees in public management, on-the-job experience in government or other large-scale organizations, in-service training, and continuing education in post-secondary institutions. The present and future challenge of the management role means that increasingly important components in the preparation and development of a senior manager will be (1) post-graduate education in management, preferably public sector management and (2) continuing training and education, either in governments or in post-secondary institutions. These two components of formal management education and training, on a pre-entry and continuing basis, will bring the individual closer to what might be termed a "professional manager" as described earlier. The appropriate mix of these components in a manager's development will depend on the level of government at which he works, his position in the hierarchy and his particular responsibilities. This will affect in turn the extent to which governments and universities respectively contribute to his development.

It is evident that individuals can and do enter the process of management development at different points. For example, a university undergraduate who wishes to pursue a career in public management may seek a graduate degree in that field and then move on to other components of management development after he joins government service. In contrast, a professional scientist who aspires to a management position but who has no management training or experience will normally begin with in-service training.

The variety of points of entry to the management development process presents governments and post-secondary institutions with a difficult task. Opportunities for training, education and practical experience should, ideally, be made available in a comprehensive and coordinated fashion. At the same time, these opportunities, in the form of programs, courses, internships, rotations and educational leaves, must meet the needs of persons with widely varying education and experience. The creation and improvement of cooperative and consultative mechanisms by governments and educational institutions could improve significantly the overall quality and effectiveness of management development.[4]

21
Collective Bargaining in the Canadian Federal Public Service*

P.K. Kuruvilla

This essay briefly reviews the evolution and present status of collective bargaining in the Canadian federal public service. An account of the development of employer-employee relations in the public service is followed by an analysis of the Public Service Staff Relations Act and problems arising from its implementation.

---

[4]For elaboration on some of these mechanisms, see Kenneth Kernaghan, "Management Development for Canada's Public Services: Report of the Rapporteur," in Kenneth Kernaghan, ed., *Executive Manpower in the Public Service*, pp. 14-18.

---

*An original article written for this volume.

Canadian civil service associations which emerged in the late nineteenth century and pressed the government for improved conditions of employment did not make significant advances until the mid-1940s. In 1944 the government established the National Joint Council of the Public Service of Canada made up of representatives of the staff associations and senior officials representing the government as employer. The purpose of this body, as outlined by the government, was

> to provide machinery for regular and systematic consultation and discussion between the employer and employee sides of the public service in regard to grievances and conditions of employment, and thereby to promote increased efficiency and better morale in the public service.[1]

The Council served as a valuable consultative device between management and staff and as a forerunner to full collective bargaining. Among the many significant benefits it produced for employees were superannuation, medical insurance, travel regulations, the five-day week, and the check-off of membership fees. As an alternative to collective bargaining, however, the Council had major limitations: it lacked the authority to deal directly with the important issue of civil service salaries, and there was no provision for the settlement of disagreements between the staff and officials of the Council. As a result, the post-war decade was one of considerable ferment in public service staff relations.

The statutory right to be consulted on pay determination was extended to employee associations in 1961 by a new Civil Service Act. However, the consultative process was cumbersome because it obliged the associations to make representations to two bodies — the Civil Service Commission and the Treasury Board. Furthermore, the final determination of rates of pay and conditions of employment was still subject to unilateral decision by the Treasury Board. The demand by employee organizations for the right to negotiate directly with government without consulting intermediaries continued unabated until the promulgation of the Public Service Staff Relations Act in March 1967.[2]

This Act is unique in several respects. It grants public service associations the status of trade unions with the right to collective bargaining, compulsory arbitration, conciliation and even strike action. It also provides machinery through which employees with grievances about the terms and conditions of their employment have access to a formal grievance procedure permitting third party adjudication. Finally,

---

[1] J.L. Ilsley, Minister of Finace, referring to Order-in-Council P.C. 3676 of May 16, 1944, quoted in C.W. Rump, "Employer-Employee Consultation in the Public Service," *Civil Service Review*, XLV (June 1972), p. 8.
[2] Canada, *Statutes*, 1966-1967, Chapter 72.

the Act not only outlines the legal steps to be observed in the resolution of disputes but also sets up an administrative apparatus to enforce the Act's provisions. The Act is administered by the Public Service Staff Relations Board (PSSRB).[3]

Before an employee organization can negotiate with the government for a collective agreement, that organization must be certified as a bargaining agent.[4] The Public Service Alliance of Canada, which represents 170 000 employees, is the largest certified union. Other major public service unions include the Canadian Union of Postal Workers (23 000), the Professional Institute of the Public Service, (17 000), the Letter Carriers' Union of Canada, (16 500) and the Canadian Postmasters' Association (8200). Within a particular bargaining unit, all employees must be in the same occupational group. Each group belongs to an occupational category.[5]

Following the certification of an employee organization as a bargaining agent for a given bargaining unit, the bargaining agent must specify the process of dispute resolution it wants to follow in the event that negotiations are unproductive. There are two options: referral of the dispute to a conciliation board while retaining the right to strike, or referral of the dispute to an arbitration tribunal for binding award. Regardless which option is chosen, the Act requires that the choice be made before collective bargaining can begin and that it remain in effect until it is altered before another round of bargaining.

When conciliation is chosen, either party in the dispute may request the PSSRB to appoint a conciliator to assist in reaching agreement. The conciliator can only make suggestions; he cannot make binding directives. If the chairman of the PSSRB believes that a conciliator would not help to resolve the dispute, he may refuse to appoint one and proceed

---

[3]The Board is a politically independent body whose major responsibilities include defining bargaining units, certifying bargaining agents, investigating complaints alleging infringement of the Act, deciding on the lawfulness of strikes and making regulations on such matters as complaints, the hearing of questions of law and jurisdiction, the rules of procedure for its own hearings and for those of the Arbitration Tribunal and adjudication boards.

[4]Some unions act as bargaining agents for more than one bargaining unit with the result that, in 1976, fifteen bargaining agents represented eighty-one bargaining units.

[5]According to the present classification there are six occupational categories in the Canadian public service: Executive; Professional and Scientific; Technical; Administrative and Foreign Service; Administrative Support; and Operational. The Executive category does not come under the collective bargaining provisions of the Act. The Public Service Commission has the responsibility of specifying and defining the occupational groups in each of the five occupational categories that come under the collective bargaining provisions of the Act. So far, seventy-two occupational groups have been set up. These are:
twenty-eight occupational groups in the Professional and Scientific category;
thirteen in the Administrative and Foreign Service;
thirteen in the Technical category;
six in the Administrative Support category;
twelve in the Operational category.

directly to appoint a conciliation board. The chairman may also refuse to appoint a board and allow a lawful strike if he believes that a board would not help settle the dispute.

The Act stipulates that certain "designated employees" may not participate in a legal strike because their "duties consist in whole or in part of duties the performance of which at any particular time or after any specified period of time is or will be necessary in the interest of the safety or security of the public."[6] Thus, a conciliation board will not be established until the parties agree, or the PSSRB determines, which employees or classes of employees in the bargaining unit are essential.

The parties in a dispute are free to accept or reject the report of a conciliation board. If the report is unacceptable, the union has the right to declare a strike seven days after the report is received by the chairman of the PSSRB. The right to strike is clearly not an unconditional one. In addition to the constraints described above, no employee may strike when a collective agreement applying to his bargaining unit is in force, and no employee organization may declare a strike that would cause employees to participate in an unlawful strike. The officers or representatives of the organization are forbidden to counsel or procure the declaration of such a strike.[7]

When arbitration has been specified as the means of dispute settlement, an arbitration tribunal is appointed. The tribunal is composed of an impartial chairman and two members, one from a panel of employer representatives and one from a panel representing the employees. An arbitral award may deal with rates of pay, hours of work, leave entitlements, standards of discipline and other related terms and conditions of employment. However, no award may deal with "the standards, procedures or processes governing the appointment, appraisal, promotion, demotion, transfer, lay-off or release of employees, or with any term or condition of employment of employees that was not a subject of negotiation between the parties during the period before arbitration was requested in respect thereof."[8] Awards made by a tribunal are binding to both parties.

The Act also establishes a grievance procedure that permits third party adjudication. This procedure covers all employees, including those in managerial and confidential positions who are not allowed to belong to a bargaining unit. An employee may present a grievance on a wide variety of matters affecting the terms and conditions of his employment.[9]

6Public Service Staff Relations Act, Section 79.
7Ibid., Sections 101-102.
8Ibid., Section 70.
9Other important types of appeals in the public service are covered by the Public Service Employment Act (Canada, Statutes, 1966-1967, Chapter 71) and are administered by the Public Service Commission. These appeals relate to (1) appointment, including promotion;

Most grievances are settled within the employee's department. However, if the employee has exhausted his departmental remedies and is not satisfied with the result, he may refer the matter to adjudication by an adjudicator or an adjudication board. Most cases are heard by adjudication boards. The Governor-in-Council, on the recommendation of the PSSRB, appoints adjudicators, one of whom is designated the Chief Adjudicator. An adjudication board is composed of the Chief Adjudicator plus one member nominated by one party and one member nominated by the other party. The adjudication decision is binding on both the employer and the employee.

Public service employees have voiced several criticisms of the provisions and administration of the Act. One important source of dissatisfaction is the restrictions on matters deemed negotiable and arbitrable under the Act. Employees cannot negotiate on matters with as profound an impact on terms and conditions of employment as job security, classification and superannuation. The restrictions on arbitrable matters outlined earlier in this essay are even greater. The result is that only some matters subject to bargaining are arbitrable. Even if a matter is arbitrable, if it was overlooked originally as a subject of negotiation, the oversight cannot be rectified by placing the matter before an arbitration tribunal. Moreover, although agreement may have been reached on some non-arbitrable issues before an arbitration tribunal, once the employees choose arbitration as a means of dispute settlement, the employer is free to withdraw from the previous agreement. Employees have argued, therefore, that the scope of negotiable subjects should be expanded to cover all employer-employee problems which conceivably could lead to an impasse and that the existing distinction between matters subject to bargaining and matters subject to arbitration be erased.

A second major cause of employee dissatisfaction is that several classes of employees are specifically excluded by the Act from the collective bargaining process.[10]

A third contentious issue is the Act's provisions regarding the establishment of bargaining units and the certification process. The Public Service Commmission defines and specifies the occupational groups within each of the five occupational categories, and the establishment of bargaining units must be based on these occupational groups and not on the occupational categories. Employees argue that if bargaining units were based on occupational categories, bargaining could

---

(2) demotion or release because of incompetence or incapability; (3) dismissal for violation of provisions of the Public Service Employment Act dealing with political activity; and (4) revocation of appointment because of fraudulent practices during an examination conducted by the Commission.

[10]Section 2.

be simplified through negotiation of general contracts covering conditions of employment for each broad occupational category. Similarly, if certification of bargaining units was based on majority membership in an occupational category rather than a group, it would have been easier to enlist the necessary membership in each broad category and obtain bargaining rights on their behalf. Thus, employee organizations contend that the existence of over eighty bargaining units imposes an unnecessary burden as well as delays and complicates certification proceedings by causing excessive proliferation of bargaining units, organizational strife and costly legal battles.

Fourthly, employees contend that they have no manoeuvrability in the bargaining process: requirements dictate that they choose either conciliation-strike or arbitration before bargaining begins and that the method chosen must remain in effect until it is changed before the next round of bargaining. The employer, however, can manoeuvre by obliging unions to accept less in non-arbitrable areas to avoid going to arbitration in other areas. The employer can also force trade-offs in regard to non-arbitrable issues because, if non-arbitrable issues are in dispute, the unions have to accept trade-offs demanded by the employer or drop the issues entirely.

The conciliation-strike option also has drawbacks for the unions. This option is denied to such bargaining units as correctional officers, firefighters and hospital workers because all or the majority of their members are "designated employees". Also many of those who legally possess the right to strike may find they cannot exercise the right without risking serious consequences. Unlike the postal employees, many bargaining units find it difficult to mount a successful legal strike because their members are dispersed among various departments and their strike may not bring about immediate, serious and visible disruption of public services. Moreover, some unions and some employees cannot afford the cost and loss of income resulting from even a short strike.

During the late 1960s and early 1970s the trend in dispute settlement was towards negotiation and arbitration rather than conciliation and strike. Between 1967 and 1974, 322 collective agreements were reached without strikes; there were only 10 legal strikes although there were about 50 unlawful work stoppages lasting a day or more. In more recent years, there has been a shift toward conciliation and strike and a consequent rise in man-days lost through work stoppages. In 1973 to 1974, only 840 man-days were lost whereas in 1974 to 1975, not counting the postal strike, 84,130 man-days were lost. At the end of 1975, almost two-thirds of employees were in bargaining units that had opted for conciliation-strike.

Barnes and Kelly have concluded that this shift is a result of the following factors: (1) the replacement of older leaders in public service unions by younger, more militant leaders; (2) the adoption by arbitrators of a narrow, legalistic approach to the scope of arbitration as compared to the broader approach exercised under conciliation; (3) the lack of consistent criteria for making arbitral awards; (4) the excessive delays in handing down awards; (5) the suspicion of employees that arbitration has sometimes been subject to government influence; (6) the lack of confidence of employees in the pay research bureau's data on which arbitrators depend.[11]

While employee unions argue that the Act has stacked the cards against them, the public has developed

> a growing dissatisfaction with work stoppages in the public sector. . . . That means disaffection with the right to strike. . . . In increasing numbers of cases the withdrawal of services is exercised not against the prevailing or the countervailing power but against the public. . . . When the public interest appears to be victimized, private citizens are much more prone to conclude that they are being prejudiced by cynical manipulation and will urge a change in the system to provide the protection to which they feel they are entitled.[12]

Thus the government has been faced with the competing demands of employee unions for expansion of their collective bargaining rights and the public for uninterrupted public services. To obtain a basis for assessing the provisions and administration of the Act, the government, in April 1973, asked Jacob Finkelman, chairman of the PSSRB, to make recommendations on how the Act should be revised and improved. In his report,[13] submitted in March 1974, Finkelman concluded that the Act was basically sound and needed no drastic revision. The report, however, contained 231 recommendations for legislative change covering such aspects of employer-employee relations as the scope of collective bargaining; arbitration, conciliation and the right to strike; the grievance process; and the structure and powers of the PSSRB.

Although many proposals were of a technical nature, Mr. Finkelman did recommend some significant changes. For example, he proposed that the scope of arbitration be broadened to include conditions of employment and benefits normally referred to as "the compensation package". Secondly, he proposed that the classification of positions remain under the employer's authority but that provision be made for third party adjudication of classification grievances and for formal consultative machinery on classification standards supplemented by third party mediation in the event of a stalemate. Thirdly, he proposed a new set of procedures for the definition of management and confidential

---

[11]L.W.C.S. Barnes and L.A. Kelly, *The Arbitration of Interest Disputes in the Federal Public Service of Canada* (Kingston: Industrial Relations Centre, Queen's University, 1975).

[12]A.W.R. Carrothers, quoted in the *Globe and Mail*, October 27, 1972, p. B-4.

[13]*Employer-Employee Relations in the Public Service of Canada: Proposals for Legislative Change* (Ottawa: Information Canada, 1974) Part I, 301 pp. and Part II, 82 pp.

personnel in a bargaining unit. Finally, he proposed that the powers and responsibilities of the PSSRB in settling disputes be expanded. In regard to the right to strike, Finkelman stated that "to outlaw strikes by public servants at this juncture would be counterproductive. We should go to great lengths to make the bargaining process work better."[14]

The majority of the Finkelman proposals were generally acceptable to the unions. They continued to make representations to the government, however, with respect to substantive matters on which Mr. Finkelman did not support them or on which his recommendations did not go far enough. The views of the unions and other interested parties were then heard by a Special Joint Committee of the Senate and the House of Commons on Employer-Employee Relations in the Public Service.[15] This Committee, which was established to study and make recommendations on the Finkelman Report, reported in February 1976. The Committee agreed with Finkelman that the existing Act is basically sound and that the rights granted to employees should not be withdrawn merely to overcome inconvenience to the public and the government. Most of the Committee's 72 recommendations were similar to those of the Finkelman Report. However, in such areas as penalties for illegal strikes, voting procedures in the unions, and managerial and confidential exclusions, the Committee's recommendations were contrary to the unions' demands and went far beyond the Finkelman Report.

The Committee recommended more severe penalties against employees, employee representatives and employee organizations for unlawful strike activity. For example, Section 4 of the Act now provides a maximum fine of $150 against an employee organization for each day that an illegal strike remains in effect. The Committee recommended that this penalty be raised to a maximum fine of $10 000 plus $1000 for each day of unlawful strike activity. Where infractions involve designated employees, maximum penalties should be at least twice as high as those imposed on non-designated employees. (For designated employees the Committee recommended a maximum penalty of $25 000 plus $5000 per day.)[16]

In regard to union voting procedures, the Committee recommended that when a bargaining agent conducts a strike vote or submits a collective agreement to its membership for approval, the vote should be held by secret ballot in accordance with procedures set down by the PSSRB. Every member of the bargaining unit should be entitled to vote, and any act by a union or union official to prevent a member from voting should constitute an offence under the Act and be subject to penalty. The Committee also recommended that the number of managerial and

[14]Ibid., Part I, p. 125.
[15]See especially Report to Parliament, issue no. 47, February 26, 1976.
[16]Ibid., pp. 47: 18-19 and 47: 33-34.

confidential exclusions from the collective bargaining process be increased and that "health" be added to the criteria for determining essential services.

The employee unions have described these recommendations as grossly repressive and anti-union. In their view, the Committee gave the government almost everything it wanted and gave the unions very little. The government has not yet responded to the Committee's report but it seems likely that when the government does bring forth its long awaited amendments to the Act, they will be based on the recommendations of Mr. Finkelman and of the Joint Committee.

CASE REFERENCES

Canadian Cases in Public Administration
The Difficult Supervisor
The Health of Mr. Cole
Friends and Lovers
Robbery or Delusion?
The Auditor's Lament
Public Interest or Collective Interest?
The Minister and the Doctor

Case Program in Canadian Public Administration
The M.T.L. Simulation — Public Sector Collective Bargaining
A Conflict of Loyalties

BIBLIOGRAPHY

Archibald, Kathleen, *Sex and the Public Service.* Ottawa, Queen's Printer, 1970.
Baker, Walter, "Executive Manpower Requirements of the Canadian Public Services in the 1980's." In Kenneth Kernaghan, ed., *Executive Manpower in the Public Service: Make or Buy.* Toronto, Institute of Public Administration of Canada, 1975, pp. 39-62.
Bolduc, Roch, "Le perfectionnement des cadres." *Canadian Public Administration,* Vol. 17, No. 3, Fall 1974, pp. 482-94.
Callard, K.B., *Advanced Administrative Training in the Public Service.* Toronto, University of Toronto Press, 1958.
Canada, Civil Service Commission, *Report of the Preparatory Committee on Collective Bargaining.* Ottawa, Queen's Printer, 1965.
Canada, *Royal Commission on Administrative Classification in the Public Service, Report,* Ottawa, King's Printer, 1946.
Connell, J.P., "Collective Bargaining in the Public Service of Canada." In *Collective Bargaining in the Public Service.* Toronto, Institute of Public Administration of Canada, 1973, pp. 45-55.
Corson, John J. and Paul, Shale R., *Men Near the Top: Filling Key Posts in the Federal Service.* Baltimore, John Hopkins Press, 1966.
Crispo, John, "Collective Bargaining in the Public Service." *Canadian Public Administration,* Vol. 16, No. 1, Spring 1973, pp. 1-13.
Debanné, J.G., "Management Education for Tomorrow's Society." *Canadian Public Administration,* Vol. 14, No. 3, Fall 1971, pp. 354-72.

Duclos, G.G., "Executive Resources in the Public Services." In Kenneth Kernaghan, ed., *Executive Manpower in the Public Service: Make or Buy.* Toronto, Institute of Public Administration of Canada, 1975, pp. 63-74.

Frankel, S.J., *Staff Relations in the Civil Service: the Canadian Experience.* Montreal, McGill University Press, 1962.

Goldenberg, Shirley B., "Collective Bargaining in the Provincial Public Services." In *Collective Bargaining in the Public Service.* Toronto, Institute of Public Administration of Canada, 1973, pp. 11-43.

Golembiewski, R.T. and Cohen, M., eds., *People in Public Services: A Reader in Public Personnel Administration.* Itasca, Ill., Peacock, 1970.

Hodgetts, J.E., *The Biography of an Institution: The Civil Service Commission of Canada, 1908-1967.* Montreal, McGill-Queen's University Press, 1972.

Hodgetts, J.E. and Dwivedi, O.P., *Provincial Governments as Employers.* Montreal, McGill-Queen's University Press, 1974.

Hodgetts, J.E. and Dwivedi, O.P., "The Growth of Government Employment in Canada." *Canadian Public Administration,* Vol. 12, No. 2, Summer 1969, pp. 224-238.

Institute of Public Administration of Canada, *Collective Bargaining in the Public Service.* Toronto, Institute of Public Administration of Canada, 1973.

Kernaghan, Kenneth, *Ethical Conduct: Guidelines for Government Employees.* Toronto, Institute of Public Administration of Canada, 1975.

Kernaghan, Kenneth, ed., *Executive Manpower in the Public Service: Make or Buy.* Toronto, Institute of Public Administration of Canada, 1975.

Kernaghan, Kenneth, "Management Development for Canada's Public Services." In Kenneth Kernaghan, ed., *Executive Manpower in the Public Service: Make or Buy.* Toronto, Institute of Public Administration of Canada, 1975, pp. 1-18.

Kernaghan, Kenneth, "Perfectionnment des cadres de gestion dans la fonction publique au Canada." In Kenneth Kernaghan, ed., *Executive Manpower in the Public Service: Make or Buy.* Toronto, Institute of Public Administration of Canada, 1975, pp. 19-38.

Kilpatrick, Franklin P., *et al., The Image of the Federal Service.* Washington, D.C., The Brookings Institution, 1964.

Johnson, A.W., "Education and the Development of Senior Executives." *Canadian Public Administration,* Vol. 15, No. 4, Winter 1972, pp. 539-57.

Keenleyside, T.A., "Career Attitudes of Canadian Foreign Service Officers." *Canadian Public Administration,* Vol. 19, No. 2, Summer 1976, pp. 208-26.

Lapointe, Marc, "Règlement des différends du travail dans la fonction publique." In *Collective Bargaining in the Public Service.* Toronto, Institute of Public Administration of Canada, 1973, pp. 85-94.

Nigro, Felix, ed., "A Symposium, Collective Bargaining in the Public Service: A Reappraisal." *Public Administration Review,* Vol. 32, No. 2, March-April 1972, pp. 97-126.

Pertuiset, Dorothy, "Méthodes pédagoqiques au sein du governement et de l'université." In Kenneth Kernaghan, ed., xecutive Manpower in the Public Serivce: Make or Buy. Toronto, Institute of Public Administration of Canada, 1975, pp. 106-21.

Plunkett, T.J., "Municipal Collective Bargaining." In *Collective Bargaining in the Public Service.* Toronto, Institute of Public Administration of Canada, 1973, pp. 1-10.

Stahl, O. Glenn, *Public Personnel Administration.* 6th ed., New York, Harper & Row, 1971.

Stanley, David T., Mann, Dean E. and Doig, Jameson W., *Men Who Govern.* Washington, D.C., Brookings Institute, 1968.

Swettenham, John and Kealy, David, *Serving the State: A History of the Professional Institute of the Public Service of Canada, 1920-1970.* Ottawa, Le Droit, 1970.

Vaison, Robert A., "Collective Bargaining in the Federal Public Service: the Achievement of a Milestone in Personnel Relations." *Canadian Public Administration,* Vol. 12, No. 1, Spring 1969, pp. 108-22.

Warner, Kenneth O., ed., *Collective Bargaining in the Public Service: Theory and Practice.* Chicago, Public Personnel Association, 1967.

Warner, Kenneth O. and Henessey, Mary L., *Public Management at the Bargaining Table.* Chicago, Public Personnel Association, 1967.

Wilkins, T.J., "Wage and Benefit Determination in the Public Service of Canada." In *Collective Bargaining in the Public Service.* Toronto, Institute of Public Administration of Canada, 1973, pp. 57-84.

CHAPTER 6
POLITICS, POLICY AND PUBLIC SERVANTS

Earlier chapters in this book have examined the institutional and administrative milieu within which the public service operates and within which major management functions are performed. We proceed now to a consideration of the specifically political elements of public administration in Canada.

Most public servants are engaged to some extent in the determination of public policy and senior administrators are deeply involved in providing advice on policy to political executives. The essays in this chapter draw attention to the changing nature of bureaucratic influence in the contemporary political process in Canada. Taken together, they document the complex web of relationships between public servants and other participants in the political system.

Equally significant in a total assessment of bureaucratic power is the wide discretionary authority of a legislative and judicial nature exercised by public servants. The extent of this authority and the means available to control its exercise are examined in the next chapter.

Kenneth Kernaghan introduces this chapter by assessing the contemporary role of public servants in the political and policy processes. Then, William A. Matheson traces the evolution of relations between the Cabinet and the public service and describes the increasing power of Cabinet committees, the Privy Council Office and the Prime Minister's Office; A. W. Johnson draws on extensive personal experience in explaining the unique position of the deputy minister and his interaction with other participants in the policy process; S. H. S. Hughes explores the relations of public servants with legislators, the news media and the general public; James E. Anderson analyzes the formal and informal interaction of pressure groups and public servants.

22
Politics, Policy and Public Servants*

Kenneth Kernaghan

Theorists and practitioners of public administration have long acknowledged the inextricable links between politics, policy and administration and the consequent political role of public servants. It is important, however, not to exaggerate this role by replacing the myth of the public servant as 'political eunuch' with the fiction of the public servant as 'permanent politician.' The interface between politics and administration is a complicated and fluid one. The thesis of this essay is that the traditional model of political neutrality, which defines the relations between public servants and other actors in the political system is inadequate in its portrayal of the present nature and complexity of these relations.

In a parliamentary system of government, strict adherence to the traditional doctrine of political neutrality requires that the following conditions be met:

1. Politics and policy are separated from administration. Thus, politicians make policy decisions; public servants execute these decisions.
2. Public servants are appointed and promoted on the basis of merit rather than on the basis of party affiliation or contributions.
3. Public servants do not engage in partisan political activities.
4. Public servants do not express publicly their personal views on government policies or administration.
5. Public servants provide forthright and objective advice to their political masters in private and in confidence. In return, political executives protect the anonymity of public servants by publicly accepting responsibility for departmental decisions.
6. Public servants execute policy decisions loyally and zealously irrespective of the philosophy and programs of the party in power and regardless of their personal opinions. As a result, public servants enjoy security of tenure during good behaviour and satisfactory performance.

The sum of these several conditions constitutes a model in terms of which existing practices in a particular country may be assessed.

The failure of these conventional notions to depict accurately the

*Reprinted and substantially abridged by permission from Kenneth Kernaghan, "Politics, Policy and Public Servants: Political Neutrality Revisited," *Canadian Public Administration*, vol. 19, no. 3 (Fall 1976), pp. 432-456.

status of political neutrality in contemporary parliamentary governments is obvious. Some of the requisite conditions have never been met;
others have been altered to keep pace with changing political, social and
technological circumstances. The purpose of this essay, therefore, is to
assess the current status of the doctrine of political neutrality, with
particular reference to the Canadian federal public service. Central to
this inquiry is consideration of the extent to which the practices of the
public service adhere to or depart from the model outlined above. The
Canadian situation will be described and analysed in relation to each of
the six components of the model. Similar analyses could be conducted for
individual provinces in Canada and for parliamentary systems of
government in other countries.

POLITICS AND ADMINISTRATION

It is clear that any involvement by public servants in the political and
policy processes conflicts with the doctrine of political neutrality. The
model of political neutrality requires the 'depoliticization' of the
bureaucracy. However, abundant evidence points to the important
political and policy role of public servants in western democracies.

Recognition and acceptance of the political role of public servants is
very recent. With some notable exceptions, the public administration
literature before 1945 does not reflect the reality of the interface
between politics, policy and administration. The political neutrality of
public servants has traditionally rested on the possibility of a separation
between politics and administration and on a related distinction between
policy and administration. Frequently, the two dichotomies are treated as
synonymous — as if the terms 'politics' and 'policy' are interchangeable.
The scope of activity covered by the term politics is, however, much
broader than that embraced by the term 'policy'. R.J.S. Baker provides a
useful analytical distinction in his assertion that '*politics* is concerned,
throughout the sphere of Government, with the whole business of
deciding what to do and getting it done. *Policy* is decision as to what to do;
administration is getting it done.'[1] According to the politics-administration
dichotomy, political executives and legislators are concerned with the
formation of policy and public servants are concerned with its
implementation. Policy decisions are political; administrative decisions
are non-political.

The distinction between politics and policy on the one hand and
administration on the other has been central to the evolution of both the
study and the practice of public administration. From 1887 up to the end
of the Second World War, prominent writers on public administration in

---

[1]R.J.S. Baker, *Administrative Theory and Public Administration* (London: Hutchinson, 1972), p. 13.

the United States, especially the authors of the central texts in the field, wrote within a framework of a dichotomy between politics and administration. During the 1930s, however, writers on public administration who recognized the significant and growing political role of the bureaucracy lived uncomfortably with the textbook dichotomy between politics and administration.[2] The dichotomy came under increasing attack during the war years as many scholars gained practical administrative experience in government. Shortly after the war, a number of political scientists in the United States launched a devastating assault on the notion that politics and administration were or could be separated. British and Canadian writers demonstrated during this same period a growing recognition of the blurring of the traditional constitutional line between the politician and the administrator in the parliamentary system of government.

Since the political role of public servants is attributed primarily to their contribution to policy development, much attention in the literature has focused on the intermingling of policy and administration. The conventional view that a clear division may be made between policy and administration has always been a fiction but has become increasingly untenable with the continuing growth of government activities and of administrative power.

Despite the actual interweaving of politics and administration, of policy and administration, and of policy formation and execution, these distinctions serve an extremely useful analytical and practical purpose. They enable political theorists to distinguish — not in an absolute sense but as a matter of degree and emphasis — between the constitutional and legal functions of political executives and public servants. While the policy role of public servants has led some writers to refer to them as 'permanent politicians' and 'ruling servants,' they remain, in fact and in democratic theory, subject to the overriding authority of elected representatives and the courts. It is useful then to refer to the predominance of ministers in policy formulation and the predominance of public servants in policy execution while acknowledging that both ministers and public servants are involved in both policy formation and execution.

These dichotomies also serve a very practical end in that they enable politicians to preserve the appearance before the public that they, not the public servants, are the policy makers. Elected representatives have a stake in preserving the notion that public servants are neutral instruments of political masters. This notion in turn supports the

---

[2]See, for example, Luther Gulik's 'Politics, Administration and the New Deal,' *Annals of the American Academy of Political and Social Science*, 169 (1933), and Pendleton Herring, *Public Administration and the Public Interest*, 1936. Reprinted in 1967 by Russell and Russell, New York.

doctrine examined later in this essay that ministers must accept responsibility for the decisions of their administrative subordinates. Public servants have an interest also in preserving these convenient fictions so that they may retain their anonymity and be sheltered from public attack.

By 1960, the interdependence of politics and administration had been enshrined in the theoretical literature on public administration and accepted by the major actors in the political system. By this time, however, recognition of the reality of bureaucratic power in the political process led to suggestions that public servants should assume the task and the orientation of 'agents of social change.' To some extent, public servants were perforce already playing the role of social-change agents through their increasingly numerous contacts with various sectors of the public in an effort to explain and encourage participation in government programs. Public servants were encouraged to expand this role by promoting new and creative innovations and solutions in social policy, by aggregating and articulating the needs of unorganized and disadvantaged groups (for example, consumers, the poor), and by stimulating groups and individuals to make demands on government for remedies to their social and economic ills. It was clear that public servants who undertook such activities were likely to clash on occasion with those among their political and administrative superiors who did not perceive the proper role of public servants as active initiators of social change. The moot question was the extent to which appointed public officials could or should share with elected representatives the responsibility for stimulating and responding to social change.

Discussion of the role of public servants as social-change agents was intermingled with the movement for increased citizen participation in the making of government decisions. This movement brought both politicans and public servants into more direct contact and confrontation with the general citizenry.

In the United States, these developments culminated in the late 1960s in a loose confederation of scholars and practitioners seeking a 'new public administration.' Among the major concerns of the proselytes of this movement were social equity, sensitivity to and representation of disadvantaged minority groups, increased citizen participation in government decision-making, and new forms of public organization.

The direct relevance of the new public administration movement for the relation between politics and administration is that some of its spokesmen call for a reformulation of the traditional roles of politicians and public servants.[3] It is argued that public servants, because of their

---

[3]See especially, Eugene P. Dvorin and Robert H. Simmons, *From Amoral to Humane Bureaucracy* (San Francisco: Canfield Press, 1972) and Louis C. Gawthrop, *Administrative Politics and Social Change* (New York: St. Martin's Press, 1971).

special knowledge, training and experience and their close contacts with their various publics, are better qualified than political executives or legislators to determine the public interest. Public servants must, however, establish a value system with a focus on human dignity or administrative humanism; they should not simply reflect the values of thier political masters. Inplicit also is a rejection of political control over public administration. The new public administration movement draws attention to the actual and potential power of public servants and to the importance of their value system for decision-making in government; however, it does not resolve — indeed, it complicates — the issue of finding an appropriate balance between the power of public servants and that of elected representatives.

Thus, the scholarly literature on public administration records an evolution since 1945 from a situation where only a few writers recognized the necessary involvement of public servants in politics to the present situation where a few writers suggest that leadership in policy development rightly belongs to public servants rather than to politicians. This element of the new public administration movement in the United States has had little apparent spillover effect on the study and practice of public administration in Canada. Nevertheless, scholars and practitioners in Canada are acutely aware that the line between politics and administration has become increasingly indistinct as both politicians and public servants participate actively in policy development. Moreover, the line is also a fluctuating one, characterized by the expansion of administrative power and the gradual politicization of the public service.

POLITICAL PATRONAGE

A second essential component of the traditional doctrine of political neutrality is the practice whereby 'public servants are appointed and promoted on the basis of merit rather than on the basis of party affiliation or contributions.' Political patronage — the appointment of persons to government service on the grounds of contributions to the governing party — is a blatant violation of the doctrine of political neutrality. Indeed, the appointment is made on the basis that the appointee is *not* politically neutral but rather is politically partisan. Such appointments clash with the merit *principle* according to which

1. Canadian citizens should have a reasonable opportunity to be considered for employment in the public service.
2. selections must be based exclusively on merit, or fitness to do the job.[4]

The merit *system*, on the other hand, 'is the mechanism in use at any time

---

[4]R.H. Dowdell, 'Personnel Administration in the Federal Public Service,' in W.D.K. Kernaghan and A.M. Willms, eds., *Public Administration in Canada*, 2nd ed. pp. 282-83.

by which these goals are achieved.' It is 'an administrative device which can and should be adapted to changing circumstances.'[5]

The merit system established by the Civil Service Act in 1918 to reduce political patronage in the Canadian federal public service greatly diminished but by no means eliminated patronage appointments.

Available evidence suggests that by 1945 the number of patronage appointments had been cut to an acceptable (although not an irreducible) level and that there has been little change in the situation to the present day. However, a review of questions and debates in the House of Commons since 1960 shows that Opposition members are not satisfied that patronage has sufficiently succumbed to the application of the merit system. For these years, Hansard contains numerous charges and counter-charges, allegations and denials, regarding the use of patronage in staffing the public service. Most of the alleged patronage appointments have been to lower-level positions in the Post Office or the Department of Public Works. While such appointments may be a source of occasional embarrassment to the government, they appear to be so few in number and the appointees so far removed from policy development that their effect on the status of political neutrality in the public service is negligible.

Opposition parties, the news media and the general public have shown greater interest in senior positions which are filled by patronage appointees rather than on a competitive basis by persons from within or outside the public service. The cabinet has the authority to appoint, by order-in-council, deputy ministers, associate deputy ministers, heads and members of agencies, boards and commissions, ambassadors, high commissioners, consuls general and certain other diplomatic representatives, and federal judicial authorities.

Moreover, the Prime Minister selects the senior officials of his own office and individual cabinet ministers choose their assistants. All these appointments are exempt from the appointing power of the Public Service Commission.

Among the persons who may be, and frequently are, appointed to these exempt positions are retired legislators, defeated candidates of the governing party, and party supporters who have made significant financial or other contributions to the party's fortunes. Such appointments are often condemned on the grounds that they are made on the basis of partisanship rather than merit. Nevertheless, the government has the authority to make these appointments on whatever bases it deems appropriate. A measure of merit is achieved because the government is not usually willing to bear the embarrassment that the appointment of an incompetent partisan may bring.

Career public servants express more concern about patronage

---

[5]*Ibid.*, p. 283.

appointments to the senior echelons of departments and central agencies than about appointments to other categories of positions. Despite the partisan nature of some recent appointments at the deputy ministerial level, in the period since 1945 there has not been a significant increase in the number of such appointments to the most senior departmental and central agency positions.

Party supporters are more likely to find their reward in appointments to crown agencies, boards and commissions than to the regular departments of government. Defeated or retired cabinet ministers have enjoyed particular success in finding a comfortable niche in government service.

The expansion of the personal staff of cabinet ministers since 1960 has increased the importance of this group as a source of patronage appointments. The minister may choose his staff from among regular public servants or from party supporters or others outside the service.

Since the tenure of executive assistants is tied directly to the tenure of a minister, executive assistants are, like ministers, subject to the vicissitudes of partisan politics. A measure of employment protection is assured by the Public Service Employment Act which provides that a person who has served at least three years as an executive assistant, a special assistant or a private secretary to a minister 'is entitled, for a period of one year from the day on which he ceases to be so employed, to be appointed without competition . . . to a position in the Public Service, at a level at least equivalent to the level of private secretary to a deputy head, for which in the opinion of the Commission he is qualified" (section 37(4)). In reference to a similar provision in the 1961 Civil Service Act, J. R. Mallory observed that 'the Minister's Office has become a back-door into the higher civil service, untouched by the merit system.'[6]

The growth in the ministers' staff has been accompanied, especially since 1968, by a well-publicized expansion in the number of advisers appointed to the Prime Minister's Office from outside government. Arnold Heeney, Canada's first secretary to the cabinet, observed in his memoirs a tendency to institute in Ottawa 'a cadre of experts and confidantes devoted to particular policies and politicians rather than to the permanent service of the state.' He recognized that 'it is no longer likely that a professional Civil Service, however competent, can remain wholly in tune with the political and social situation of contemporary Canada.' He noted, however, the danger 'of a return to patronage, a bypassing of the carefully developed non-political service recruited on merit alone.'[7]

---

[6]'The Minister's Office Staff: An Unreformed Part of the Public Service,' *Canadian Public Administration*, 10, no. 1 (March 1967), p. 27.

[7]Arnold Heeney, *The Things That Are Caesar's Memoirs of a Public Servant* (Toronto: University of Toronto Press, 1972), p. 202.

The number of patronage appointments in each of the categories examined above is relatively small. Taking the appointments to all categories together, however, the number of senior positions in the federal public service filled by patronage appointees is substantial. The impact of these appointments on the status of political neutrality is difficult to measure with any precision. The appointment of such persons to public service posts without competitive examination and on grounds of partisanship violates the merit principle but not the merit system. Patronage appointees are on the whole likely to be less competent and less experienced than their counterparts in the career public service. The practice of patronage appointments also lessens the number of senior posts to which career public servants may aspire and thus has a detrimental effect on morale.

POLITICAL ACTIVITY

The tradition of political neutrality requires that public servants not 'engage in partisan political activities.'[8] During the first fifty years of Canada's political history, the issues of partisan activities by public servants and political patronage were intimately linked. Patronage appointments were rewards for service to the governing party. Many of the appointees sought to enhance their progress within the service by continuing their partisan support of the governing party after their appointment. Thus, when a new party came into power, it found these persons expendable and replaced them with their own supporters.

In an effort to eliminate this practice, legislators provided in the 1918 Civil Service Act that no public servant could 'engage in partisan work in connection with any . . . election, or contribute, receive or in any way deal with any money for any party funds.' Violations were punishable by dismissal. The penalty was so severe and so clearly stated that, with the exception of the right to vote, the impact of the Act was the political sterilization of Canada's federal public servants. Despite this effective weakening of the link between patronage and political activity, the rigid restraints imposed in 1918 remained virtually unchanged until 1967. The primary explanation for those enduring restraints was the desire to ensure the political impartiality of public servants as their advisory and discretionary powers gradually increased.

The Public Service Employment Act of 1967 liberalized the long-standing restrictions on political activity. Section 32 of the Act provides

---

[8]For a definition of political activity and an account of the arguments usually raised for and against the political activity of government employees, see Kenneth Kernaghan, *Ethical Conduct: Guidelines for Government Employees* (Toronto: Institute of Public Administration of Canada, 1975), pp. 26-28.

that a public servant, unless he is a deputy head, may stand for election to political office if the Public Service Commission grants him a leave of absence without pay for that purpose. The commission gives its permission if it believes that the usefulness of the employee would not be impaired by his being a candidate. With the exception of attendance at political meetings and contributions to the funds of a political candidate or political party, no employee may work for or against a candidate for election to a federal or provincial office or to a political party. The Act is unclear in regard to the extent to which employees not in senior or sensitive positions may participate in the wide range of political activities other than actual candidacy.

The decisons of the Public Service Commission suggest that roughly 90 per cent of all public servants will be permitted to seek election if they wish. This liberalization of restraints on political candidacy has not attracted a great horde of public servants to the hustings. Nevertheless, the number of public servants seeking election has gradually increased with each election since 1967 and this trend is likely to continue.[9]

The fact that most federal public servants may now stand for election and engage in a broader spectrum of political activities has heightened the general level of partisan activity and consciousness in the public service, especially among newer and younger recruits. However, officials in senior and sensitive posts are obliged to refrain from partisan activity; thus those officials most actively involved in policy formation and in the discretionary application of policy retain their impartiality. Moreover, it is probable that officials with many years of government experience will have difficulty overcoming their ingrained avoidance of political activity. Some public servants may also perceive overt partisanship as an obstacle to promotion to the senior ranks of the service. The broadening of the permissible limits of political activity has modified the traditional doctrine and practice of political neutrality but it has not had a rapid or revolutionary effect.

PUBLIC COMMENT

The admonition that public servants 'not express publicly their personal views on government policies or administration' is an integral component of the traditional model of political neutrality. The prime reason given by contemporary governments for restrictions on public comment is the need to preserve the confidence of the public and of political superiors in the impartiality of public servants.

The strict interpretation of this rule of official reticence requires

---

[9]See C. Lloyd Brown-John, 'Party Politics and the Canadian Federal Public Service,' *Public Administration* (U.K.), vol. 52 (Spring 1974), pp. 79-93.

that public servants not express personal opinions on government policies, whether they are attacking or supporting those policies.

Formal written guidelines on public comment are so sparse that considerable uncertainty exists as to the rights of public servants in this area. It is well established in the civil service legislation of modern democratic states that the role of public servants in policy development and implementation requires that they enjoy fewer political rights than other citizens. In the area of public comment, the difficulty is to strike an appropriate balance between freedom of expression and political neutrality.

The issue of public comment is much more complex than the conventional rule suggests. This rule does not take adequate account of the extent to which public servants are inescapably involved in public comment in the regular performance of their duties. In speaking or writing for public consumption, public servants may serve such purposes as:

1. providing information and analysis of a scientific or technical nature for consideration primarily by their professional colleagues within and outside government;
2. describing administrative processes and departmental organization and procedures;
3. explaining the content, implications and administration of specific government policies and programs;
4. discussing, within the framework of governmental or departmental policy, the solution of problems through changes in existing programs or the development of new programs;
5. discussing issues on which governmental or departmental policy has not yet been determined;
6. explaining the nature of the political and policy process in government;
7. advocating reforms in the existing organization or procedures of government;
8. commenting in a constructively critical way on government policy or administration;
9. denouncing existing or potential government policies, programs and operations; and
10. commenting in an overtly partisan way on public policy issues or on government policy or administration.[10]

This list moves from types of public comment which are generally expected, required or permissible to those which are questionable, risky or prohibited. Public servants have engaged in all these forms of public

---

[10]This classification is an expansion of that set out in Kernaghan, *Ethical Conduct*, p. 36.

comment but few have ventured beyond the first four categories. In regard to the fourth category, it is notable that public servants are more actively involved in consultation with persons outside government than is popularly believed. Discussions of possible remedies to problems with existing or proposed policies and programs often involve public servants in bargaining, accommodation and compromise on behalf of their political superiors. This process usually takes place in private, but public servants are sometimes required to make presentations and answer questions in public forums where a larger measure of risk exists.

Current demands for more openness in government and for a better-informed citizenry are accompanied by pressures to extend the permissible bounds of public comment. The Economic Council of Canada has argued that 'one of the central requirements for developing a well-informed electorate is that there must be an increasing willingness and competence *on the part of officials and politicians* to discuss basic policy issues in the public arena.'[11]

The extent to which Canadian public servants may venture beyond the first four categories of public comment either now or in the future is unclear. Placing an onus on public servants to 'discuss basic policy issues in the public arena' will raise problems of the appropriate limits of public comment, especially in the absence of formal guidelines in this area.

In view of the intimate links among politics, policy and administration described earlier, public servants unavoidably enhance understanding of the political and the policy process through their speeches and writings on the administrative process. The major burden of explaining the political system to the public is, however, likely to remain with politicians and academic scholars.

Public advocacy of administrative reform and constructive criticism of government activities may complement the public servants' information and conciliation functions. The participation of public servants in these forms of public comment is, however, restricted by their political superiors who bear public responsibility for the operations of government.

Denunciations and overtly partisan assessments of government policy or administration tend to be clearer than other forms of public comment in their manifestation and in the certainty of their punishment. Both the traditional admonition against public comment and recent decisions by administrative tribunals prohibit such activity unless public servants are on leave of absence to seek election.

Nevertheless, the unwritten rule against public comment, if stated without qualification and elaboration, is subject to varying interpreta-

---

[11]*Design for Decision Making*, Eighth Annual Review of the Economic Council of Canada (Ottawa: Information Canada, 1971), p. 85. (Emphasis added)

tions and applications in contemporary society. Public servants are now involved in forms of public comment not explicitly covered by the conventional rule and the nature of this involvement constitutes a significant departure from a position of political neutrality.

ANONYMITY AND MINISTERIAL RESPONSIBILITY

The traditional model of political neutrality requires that 'public servants provide forthright advice to their political superiors in private and in confidence. In return, political executives protect the anonymity of public servants by publicly accepting responsibility for departmental decision.s' In a parliamentary system of government, the anonymity of public servants depends in large measure on the vitality of the doctrine of ministerial responsibility. According to this doctrine, a minister is personally responsible to Parliament both for his own actions and for those of his administrative subordinates. Thus, public servants are not directly answerable to Parliament and their minister protects their anonymity.

The convention that ministers are responsible for the conduct of their subordinates is in a severely weakened state. A minister is not normally obliged to resign in response to revelations of maladministration in his department. In Canada, the writings of academic scholars and the practices of governments have demonstrated that a minister cannot be expected to have knowledge and control of all the activities of his officials.

The convention of ministerial defence of public service anonymity is in a comparatively healthy state. Ministers will not, however, invariably protect the anonymity of their officials by refusing to name or blame them publicly. Recent events have shown that there is disagreement among elected officials generally as to the present meaning of ministerial responsibility in relation to public servants.

For example, the report of the Public Accounts Committee on the refit of the aircraft carrier *Bonaventure* stated that disciplinary action might have to be taken against six senior officials named in the report.[12] Members of the Opposition suggested that the ministers of the two departments involved should be held responsible.[13] The ministers of both departments had changed since the events reported had taken place and the President of the Privy Council said that 'it is the minister currently holding the office in question who answers to the House for the acts and omissions of his public officials.' He noted that he had

---

[12]House of Commons, Standing Committee on Public Accounts, *Minutes of Proceedings*, no. 20, April 28, 1970.
[13]See, for example, House of Commons, *Debates*, June 8, 1970, p. 7868.

'carefully reviewed the evidence and the performance of the officials concerned' and had 'satisfied himself that there are no grounds for disciplinary action against the personnel involved . . . ' He also said, on behalf of his colleagues, that 'we regret this procedure of making specific attacks on individual public servants.'[14]

Then in 1972, a minister stated in public that a report researched and written by one of his departmental officials was 'a shabby piece of research' and that the official's conclusions were 'stupid.' When pressed by Opposition members in Parliament to retract his statements, the minister refused.

The Professional Institute of the Public Service, in a letter asking the minister to apologize to his official, argued that

> A Minister of the Crown assumes responsibility for the activities of his Department and the work of his employees . . . .[The] research was undertaken and [the] report released with the approval of senior officials in your Department. You cannot now avoid responsibility by engaging in personal attacks on your employee who is by virtue of his appointment in no position to defend himself. It is clearly detrimental to his professional reputation and career . . . .[15]

The doctrine of ministerial responsibility shields public servants from direct answerability for alleged maladministration. It does not, however, protect them from disciplinary action if they step outside the shelter of ministerial responsibility by engaging in public controversy over issues of government policy or its implementation. Public servants who criticize the government or their department embarrass their political and administrative superiors; public servants who vigorously defend the government undermine public confidence in their objectivity and put themselves in a difficult position in the event of a change in government.

The preservation of public service anonymity depends increasingly on factors other than the extent to which ministers adhere to the doctrine of ministerial responsibility. Departures from the traditional model of political neutrality in the areas of patronage, political activity and public comment also diminish the anonymity of public servants. The most threatening incursion on official anonymity is the expansion of public comment described earlier. Public servants interact more with specific 'publics' or clientele groups than with the public as a whole. These specialized relationships involve public servants in consultation, negotiation and accommodation and reveal to these various interest groups the nature of official involvement in policy development. The

---

[14]*Ibid.*, pp. 7863, 7866, 7864.
[15]'The Case of Dr. Usher,' *Professional Public Service* (May 1972), pp. 27-28.

cumulative impact of the growing information and conciliation functions performed by public servants is a gradual but significant decline in official anonymity.

Inroads on public service anonymity have been stimulated also by the changing role of public servants in their relations with parliamentary committees and the news media.

As a result of changes in the operations of parliamentary standing committees since 1965,[16] public servants now appear more frequently before these committees, either alone or in support of their ministers. They have thereby become more visible to those persons and groups with an interest in the outcome of the committees' proceedings, including interest groups and the news media. Public servants are expected to play an administrative, professional and supportive role by describing and explaining their department's policies. Ministers are responsible for the defence and debate of these policies. A. W. Johnson has written that when a senior public servant testifies before parliamentary committees, he 'must recognize . . . that he is the servant of parliament, without becoming servile; that he must be loyal to his minister, without becoming partisan; that he must present the whole of the truth without giving political advantage, or of betraying his first loyalty, that to his minister. Some feat, as any experienced public servant will tell you!'[17] Regardless of how adroitly public servants give testimony, the complexity of policies, the interweaving of policy and administrative considerations, and the fine line between the explanation and the defence of policies make it difficult for them to conceal completely their personal values and their likely contribution to policy development.

The pervasive role of the news media in contemporary society has been reflected in increased media coverage of the activities and identities of public servants. The media and public servants share a mutual desire to inform the public about government programs. Public servants utilize the media for public relations and publicity — to tell their department's story and to sell their department's programs. The media serve as excellent channels of communication to the public for officials who engage in forms of public comment requiring the description and explanation of government programs. The media in turn analyse the information received from public servants and comment on the purposes and personalities involved in the development and administration of programs. Moreover, journalists often strive to identify specific officials

---

[16]See Thomas A. Hockin, 'The Advance of Standing Committees in Canada's House of Commons: 1965 to 1970,' *Canadian Public Administration*, 13, no. 2 (Summer 1970), pp. 185-202.

[17]A.W. Johnson, 'Education and the Development of Senior Executives,' *Canadian Public Administration*, 15, no. 4 (Winter 1972), pp. 539-57.

as the source of their information and, whenever possible, to quote those officials.

The extent to which public servants are exposed to the public's gaze through the news media depends largely on the position they occupy, on current interest in their department's activities, and on their personal views and their minister's views on anonymity. Certain public servants (for example, the Deputy Minister of Finance) are better known because of the enduring importance of their position; others receive publicity during periods of public controversy in their sphere of responsibilities. Some public servants and ministers strive to preserve the tradition of anonymity; others are willing to sacrifice a measure of anonymity for more openness in government.

Although the tradition of anonymity remains strong among public servants, their visibility has been heightened by changes in political institutions and practices and by the media's response to demands for more public information. This gradual decline in official anonymity is likely to continue and to reveal the expanding role of public servants in the political process.

PERMANENCY IN OFFICE

The preservation of political neutrality requires that 'public servants execute policy decisions loyally and zealously irrespective of the philosophy and programs of the party in power and regardless of their personal opinions. As a result, public servants enjoy security of tenure during good behaviour and satisfactory performance.' Thus, in the event of a change in government, official neutrality helps to ensure continuity of administration by competent and experienced public servants as well as the provision of impartial advice on policy options and the enthusiastic implementation of policy decisions.

As public servants, especially at the senior levels, become more overtly or apparently political, the argument for political appointments to senior posts is strengthened. Thus, permanency in office depends largely on adherence to the elements of the political neutrality model already described. The merit system is designed to bring about a career public service by minimizing the number of patronage appointments and avoiding a turnover in personnel following a change in government. A legislative prohibition ensures that senior public servants refrain from any activity on behalf of political parties or candidates. Moreover, although public servants are obliged to engage in various forms of public comment, they are not permitted to engage in public or partisan criticism of government. Finally, the preservation of ministerial responsibility and of public service anonymity helps to protect officials from public identification as supporters or opponents of particular policies.

Despite these efforts to achieve the fact and the appearance of administrative impartiality, Opposition party leaders have frequently promised, if elected, to turf out senior officials because of their assumed contribution to government policies to which these leaders are opposed. Public servants must be able to demonstrate, therefore, the capacity to adapt quickly and effectively to the requirements of a new governing party.

When permanency in office for public servants has been combined with longevity in office by a particular political party, a change in government presents an especially difficult challenge to the capacity of public servants to serve impartially different political masters. It is understandable that senior officials who have worked closely with ministers in the development of existing policies should be apprehensive about the arrival of a new governing party.

Career public servants in Canada can normally expect security of tenure during good conduct and adequate performance so long as they maintain a level of impartiality acceptable to their political superiors and to Opposition political parties. The ranks of the career officials will continue to be supplemented, however, by such 'temporary' officials as political appointees to agencies, boards and commissions and to the staffs of the prime minister and ministers.

CONCLUSIONS

The present operations of the Canadian public service are not in accord with the traditional doctrine of political neutrality. Public servants are actively involved in the political process both by necessity in the areas of policy development and execution and by choice in the sphere of political partisanship.

It is widely acknowledged that a central challenge to modern governments is to ensure responsible administrative behaviour in the face of growing administrative power.[18] It is important therefore to assess the impact on the concept and practice of administrative responsibility of the expanding political role of public servants. An effort has been made in this essay to describe the current nature and extent of this role so as to facilitate the selection of the most appropriate means to promote administrative responsibility.

---

[18]For an examination of this question, see Kenneth Kernaghan, 'Responsible Public Bureaucracy: A Rationale and a Framework for Analysis,' *Canadian Public Administration*, 16, no. 4 (Winter 1973), pp. 572-603.

23
The Cabinet and the Canadian Bureaucracy

William A. Matheson

There are two theories regarding the relationship between the Cabinet and the civil service. One theory states that policy-making is the sole prerogative of the Cabinet, and it is the responsibility of the civil service to administer policy once it has been determined. This theory is derived to a large extent from government practice in Great Britain. According to one scholar, "The traditional view of British Government was that all decisions on matters of policy were taken by the Cabinet or by individual ministers so that the civil service merely carried out instructions."[1] The second, and possibly more popular theory, is that our society has become increasingly subject to administrative control, and the real initiative in policy formation has tended to pass from the hands of politicians to those of the civil servants.

It appears that each theory has an element of truth in it. The senior civil servant, in addition to his administrative duties, is involved in policy-making, and the more senior his position the more time he spends on policy matters. "... In fact the deputy (minister) spends as much of his time on policy advising and devising as he does on implementation."[2] It is, therefore, incorrect to assume that the business of government is conducted on two distinct planes, policy and administration, with the Cabinet or individual minister being responsible for the former and the civil service for the latter. It is equally erroneous to assume that the civil service dominates the policy-making process in Canadian Government.

It should be noted, however, that while the senior civil servant is involved in both administrative and policy matters, the converse is not quite true of members of the Cabinet since there has been a very strong tendency in Canada for the Cabinet to leave responsibility for administration almost exclusively to civil servants. Lord Bridges has noted that in Great Britain since "... no minister can do everything, he will rightly concentrate his main endeavours on policy and will leave its execution to others as far as he can...."[3] In Canada this tendency is reinforced by the pattern of recruitment of Cabinet Ministers; administrative ability seems to be one of the least looked for qualities in a potential minister.

---

[1]John P. MacKintosh, *The British Cabinet*, Stevens and Sons, London, 1962, p. 453.
[2]A.W. Johnson, "The Role of the Deputy Minister", *Canadian Public Administration*, Vol. iv, No. 4, December 1961, p. 363. Reprinted on p. 273.
[3]Rt. Hon. Lord Bridges, "The Relationship between Ministers and the Permanent Departmental Head", *Canadian Public Administration*, Vol. VII, No. 3, Sept. 1964, p. 271.

In the formation of a Cabinet an incoming Prime Minister is subject to very distinct limitations and restrictions. He is not free to choose ministers at his personal wish or will. Considerations of geography, of the size and total population of the provinces, as well as economic, racial and religious considerations, of total and party membership in the House of Commons and the special qualifications called for in the filling of certain portfolios are all among the factors of which full account should be taken.[4]

Since administrative capacity of the potential minister is clearly a minor consideration in Cabinet formation, concern for policy implementation has usually been left to the Ministers' administrative subordinates, i.e. the civil service. Indeed Mr. King once remarked in the House of Commons that: "...Different qualities are required for effective work as a Cabinet minister from those required in an administrative or executive post."[5]

The principle of having representatives in the Cabinet from various areas and groups within the country has become a rigid Canadian convention, and has been an important means of helping to maintain the unity of the country. It has also had considerable impact on the relationship between the Cabinet and the civil service.

The fact that the Cabinet is the significant federal body in Canada has made it necessary for it to function much more as a collegial body than Cabinets in other countries. A large number of matters have come up for discussion and decision at Cabinet level which could have been settled more efficiently at a lower level by individual Ministers and their senior advisors. "Almost every decision of a Minister, even of the most trivial importance is thus, at least in theory, brought before his colleagues for the purpose of obtaining their collective approval, which is necessary for its validity."[6] As a result, while civil servants have had considerable influence on policy formulation at the department level, i.e. influence over their Ministers individually, their influence has been sharply reduced at full Cabinet level. At this point their advice and recommendations have been subjected to the scrutiny of a large number of ministers. Sectional and group interests make it "...politically dangerous to give Ministers untrammelled authority over the policy of their departments. Each Minister tends to have a sort of veto of executive actions affecting the part of the country which he is known to represent in the Cabinet...."[7] This understanding was explicitly affirmed in an Order-in-Council, dated June 14, 1904, which stated that "In the case of members of the Cabinet, while all have an equal degree of responsibility in a constitutional sense, yet in the practical working out of responsible

[4]Mackenzie King to P.L. Hatfield, quoted in H. Blair Neatby, *William Lyon Mackenzie King, A Political Biography*, University of Toronto Press, Toronto, 1958, p. 172.

[5]*Debates*, Commons, July 8, 1940, p. 1400.

[6]Sir George Murray, *Report on the Public Service of Canada*, 1912, Sections 5, 6, 8.

[7]J.R. Mallory, "Cabinets and Councils in Canada", *Public Law*, Autumn 1957, p. 236.

government in a country of such vast extent as Canada, it is found necessary to attach a special responsibility to each minister for the public affairs of the province or district with which he has close political connections...."[8] This rule, which is similar to that of senatorial courtesy in the American Senate, has tended to limit the policy influence of Canadian civil servants.

Another effect of the representation principle in the Canadian Cabinet is that the immersion of the Cabinet in policy matters has tended to allow the civil service considerable autonomy in administrative matters. Time that a Minister might otherwise spend on administration has been spent on other matters in Cabinet, attendance in the House or on his political obligations. Moreover, the Minister's constitutional responsibility to Parliament and the public for everything done in his department has been somewhat vitiated by the Canadian tendency to resort to Orders-in-Council rather than to Ministerial directives for executive action. Since "Almost every ministerial act is covered by the authority of a Cabinet minute or order,"[9] it is often difficult to hold a particular minister responsible in cases of alleged maladministration. Consequently, it is even more difficult for Members of Parliament to single out administrative officials for criticism. Ministers greatly appreciate this custom; as Mr. Winters remarked "... it is a comfortable position for any minister to be in to be able to refer matters to the Governor-in-Council."[10]

A concomitant feature of Canadian government, at least in its first fifty years, was the tendency to have a larger number of departments than the business of government actually required in order to provide adequate representation for the various interests competing for Cabinet appointments. When the responsibilities of government grew, however, the creation of new departments would have made the Cabinet too large and cumbersome. An enlarged Cabinet would also have created problems in preserving sectional and group balance. Consequently, certain tasks were assigned to various departments more for expedient than functional reasons. Thus "... some departments have come to embrace a variety of ill-assorted functions simply as a means of housing what otherwise might become administrative orphans. The consequent problems of coordination through the Cabinet and other centralized agencies have been acute."[11] Again, this development has helped to increase the immunity of Cabinet members and the civil service from effective criticism. An exasperated Member of Parliament complained that:

---

[8]Canada, Sessional Papers, 1905, No. 13, p. 2.
[9]Mallory, op. cit., p. 236.
[10]Debates, Commons, June 18, 1956, p. 5126.
[11]J.E. Hodgetts, "Challenge and Response; A Retrospective View of the Public Service of Canada," Canadian Public Administration, Vol. VII, No. 4, Dec. 1964, p. 414.

We now have four ministers dealing with problems in respect of the wheat board.... The Minister of Industry, Trade and Commerce is still involved with problems of wheat sales. The new Minister without portfolio is charged with responsibility for the Wheat Board. We also have the... Minister of Transport... who is interested in moving grain. The Minister of Agriculture would naturally be interested in the welfare of the agriculture industry.[12]

The principle of representation tends to enhance greatly the role of the Prime Minister. The Prime Minister of Canada "... enjoys a pre-eminence other parliamentary systems seldom provide."[13] The Prime Minister is the *only* member of the Cabinet with a national constituency; all other members tend to be delegates from particular groups or areas. Thus, to a large extent, his considerably greater prestige and power "... are most obviously accounted for by the lesser lustre of his colleagues in Cabinet."[14] Ministers "... are dependent for leadership on the Prime Minister. They tend to recognize his paramount position and accept his leadership because their political survival in the Cabinet and in the House of Commons depends on him."[15] Since both Cabinet Ministers and Deputy Ministers are appointed by the Prime Minister, it is likely that his will prevails in cases of conflict over issues of policy formation or execution. The Deputy Minister's position as the appointee of the Prime Minister (and Prime Ministers have jealously guarded this prerogative) provides him with a measure of security in disagreements with his minister. In the event of conflict a Deputy Minister is not obliged to yield as a matter of course. If the Prime Minister must adjudicate such a conflict, the Deputy Minister can present his case from a position of relative strength.

It is important to note also that the nature of the Prime Minister's position demands that he possess, among other talents, a very specific capacity for reconciling the diverse interests and groups in Canada. "It was not by chance that the three Prime Ministers who had the greatest proclivity for holding on to office in Canada's history, Macdonald, Laurier and MacKenzie King had the ability to keep divergent interests together."[16] It is likely that in searching for Deputy Ministers a Prime Minister looks for individuals with the same ability. Consequently, there is less likelihood of conflict between ministers and their deputies.

It is true that prior to World War II, ministers were actively involved in both policy and administration. The limited functions of government and the consequent small size of the civil service made it possible for

[12]*Debates*, Commons, October 29, 1969, p. 254.
[13]James Eayrs, *The Art of the Possible*, University of Toronto Press, Toronto, 1961, p. 3.
[14]*Ibid.*
[15]R. Barry Farrell, *The Making of Canadian Foreign Policy*, Prentice-Hall, Scarborough, Ont., 1969, p. 13.
[16]Sister Teresa Burke, *The Canadian Cabinet 1867-1869 — An Analysis of the Federal Convention*, Ph.D. thesis (unpublished), Columbia University, 1958, p. 297.

ministers to closely supervise the work of their departments and still determine policy. Moreover, the inordinate number of ministers in the Cabinet resulting from the representation principle assured that no particular minister (with the possible exception of the Prime Minister) was overworked. The Cabinet was able to decide policy, defend it in Parliament, and in a general sense, oversee its implementation.

"Until 1939 the major and minor details of government policy were capable of being understood and actively considered by ministers and dealt with by the Cabinet."[17] The advent of World War II, however, completely changed the Cabinet's method of operation and affected its relationship with the civil service. The enormous number of decisions which had to be taken necessitated much more independence for the civil service. The volume of business conducted is illustrated by the fact that in the period 1939-1945 over 60 000 Orders-in-Council and over 60 000 Treasury Minutes had been passed.[18] This average of over 10 000 per year can be compared with the number for 1968, 2248 and 1234 respectively.[19]

While the influence of Parliament over policy-making had never been supreme, the emergency conditions of wartime hastened a shift of power into the hands of the executive—both Cabinet and civil service. "The public began to look to the Prime Minister and the members of the Cabinet. They and they alone came to be regarded as responsible for everything concerned with the war. This increased the prestige of the Cabinet and Government enormously and correspondingly decreased that of Parliament."[20] During this period Cabinet ministers could not possibly supervise everything carefully and much power was, of necessity, delegated to civil servants. "Operating collectively in large affairs the Cabinet's chief advisors became almost a second Cabinet, at times more potent than the first. A managerial revolution was under way and could never be repealed."[21] Thus, during this period, many policy decisions were determined largely by members of the civil service.

At the conclusion of the war, the deep involvement of civil servants in policy-making continued for a variety of reasons. The problems of post-war reconstruction and the continuing evolution of the welfare state imposed a heavy burden on the Cabinet and prevented a complete return to pre-war practices. Moreover, much of the planning for the post-war period was done, on the instructions of the government, by civil servants who thus acquired a great store of technical knowledge. This

---

[17]J.R. Mallory, "Delegated Legislation in Canada", *Canadian Journal of Economics and Political Science*, Vol. XIX, No. 4, Nov. 1953, p. 462.
[18]*Debates*, Commons, October 31, 1945, p. 1681.
[19]*Debates*, Commons, November 19, 1969, p. 985.
[20]C.G. Power, "Career Politicians: The Changing Role of the M.P." *Queen's Quarterly*, Vol. LXIII, No. 4, Winter 1956, pp. 488-9.
[21]Bruce Hutchison, *The Incredible Canadian*, Longmans Green & Co., Toronto, 1953, p. 266.

knowledge was indispensable to the Cabinet and it came to rely more and more on the civil service.

A second factor tending to enhance the power of the civil service was the long tenure in power of the Liberal party. A very close relationship grew up between ministers and senior civil servants. This was natural since: "The careers of many of these top public servants were administratively linked with long-serving cabinet members, not in a political way but as individuals working professionally on the same problems of government."[22] Cabinet members and senior civil servants came to share the same outlook and, as a consequence, civil servants became increasingly involved in matters formerly left to the politicians. One observer after looking over the 1957 Liberal platform commented: "A generation of Liberal politicians and a generation of presumably neutral senior permanent officials have worked hand in hand to create what is now described as a Liberal program."[23]

It is possible that this development had an adverse effect on the Liberal party. The lengthy term in office of the Liberal party brought about a situation where group and sectional influence was to a large extent neutralized. "A party long in power... apparently comes more and more to think exclusively in national terms particularly if most of the speculation and planning is done not by the party as such but by Ottawa based and Ottawa minded ministers assisted by Ottawa based and Ottawa minded civil servants."[24] Policy-making was left more and more to the civil servants, reaching its zenith under Mr. St. Laurent. "Most of the best ideas emanating from Ottawa during the latter part of the St. Laurent administration originated not with cabinet members but with senior civil servants. In fact, the functions of the two groups almost seemed to merge."[25] Thus it could be said about Mr. St. Laurent's regime that "even on important matters of policy, the cabinet appeared to take little initiative...."[26] It may be that the *national* type of thinking mentioned above contributed to the downfall of the Liberals in 1957.

Under Mr. Diefenbaker, who tended to distrust the civil service, the pendulum began to swing back the other way. There seemed to be little need for this distrust, however, as the civil service proved itself to be flexible and cooperative. Shortly after the Conservatives took office, Mr. Green remarked that "we have had the finest assistance from the

---

[22]Farrell, *op. cit.*, p. 27.

[23]J.E. Hodgetts, "The Liberals and the Bureaucrats", *Queen's Quarterly*, Vol. LXII, No. 2, Summer 1955, p. 176.

[24]John Meisel, "The Formulation of Liberal and Conservative Programmes in the 1957 General Election", *Canadian Journal of Economics and Political Science*, Vol. XXVI, No. 4, Nov. 1960, p. 573.

[25]Peter Newman, "Backstage in Ottawa", *Maclean's Magazine*, Vol. 70, No. 11, June 1, 1963, p. 3.

[26]Dale Thomson, *Louis St. Laurent, Canadian*, Macmillan, Toronto, 1967, p. 385.

members of the Canadian civil service."[27] In this period the Cabinet did assume more control over the policy-making process and the influence of the civil service was reduced.

The return of the Liberals to office under Mr. Pearson did not restore the civil service to its earlier pre-eminence. While the Pearson government contained several ministers who had been civil servants at one time, such as Mr. Sharp and Mr. Drury, the minority government situation under which the Liberals had to operate tended to prevent a return to the type of situation existing under Mr. St. Laurent. Thus the influence of the politician over policy continued. The Cabinet no longer was in control of the House of Commons and was continually in danger of defeat. The House was aware of this and members tended to display considerable determination in respect to influencing policy. "... With the minority situation and the length of sessions, ministers have never been more exposed to the influence of their own backbenchers.... In certain cases it is not an exaggeration to say that they meet private members more often than their own officials."[28] A major problem during the Pearson era was coordinating the implementation of Cabinet decisions by the various departments. There was no clear system of priorities and no mechanism to ensure coordination among the various departments.

Under the Trudeau government there has been another change in the relationship between the Cabinet and the civil service. The seeds of this change were sown during World War II when Mr. A.D.P. Heeney was appointed both Clerk of the Privy Council and Secretary to the Cabinet. Gradually a secretariat grew up which prepared an agenda for Cabinet meetings and followed up decisions taken at such meetings. A small staff was established in the Privy Council Office which was responsible directly to the Prime Minister and provided this service for the Cabinet and its committees.

Until the time of the Trudeau government all matters discussed in Cabinet committess were sent on to the full Cabinet for further discussion, i.e., the existence of a committee system, even a highly structured one as under Mr. Pearson, did not in any way detract from the collegial nature of the Cabinet's decision-making process. Under Mr. Trudeau, however, there has been "... a restructuring of the cabinet committee system which enables the cabinet to function more effectively."[29] Now, all matters which formerly came before the full Cabinet are sent first to a Cabinet committee, which is in effect a Cabinet in its own right with power to make its own decisions. At these Cabinet committee meetings (which departmental and other officials may attend on invitation) either a decision is reached or a recommendation is made to

[27]*Debates*, Commons, November 15, 1957, p. 1211.
[28]M. Lamontagne, "The Influence of the Politician," *Canadian Public Administration*, Vol. XI, No. 3, Autumn 1968, p. 268.
[29]*Debates*, Commons, February 27, 1968, p. 6015.

Cabinet. Those ministers not on the committee are immediately informed of any decision taken. If a minister disagrees with a Committee decision, he may, after advising the Prime Minister, raise the matter before the full Cabinet; otherwise the decision stands. The recommendations of Cabinet committees are discussed by the full Cabinet. The Cabinet secretariat, by providing secretarial service and research assistance for the committees and in following up decisions made by both the Cabinet and its committees, ensures a measure of coordination lacking in previous administrations.

Each committee has its own secretary who ranks as an assistant secretary of the Cabinet. The duties of the assistant secretary for the Cabinet committee on Priorities and Planning were outlined in the House of Commons as follows: "He is . . . responsible for the preparation, appropriateness and form of Cabinet materials concerning priorities and planning. His specific duties include developing the schedule of work for one of the Cabinet committees, preparing minutes of committee meetings and records of decisions."[30]

If a *department* wishes to submit a policy proposal, it is forwarded to the Cabinet secretariat in the form of a memorandum signed by the responsible minister. The Privy Council Office examines the proposal in the light of government objectives and then refers the proposal to the appropriate committee(s) for consideration or returns it to the department. It can be argued that the ability to make this decision has provided the officials in the Privy Council Office with considerable power. Given, however, the very senior position and role of the Cabinet committee on Priorities and Planning (composed of the Prime Minister and senior Ministers), it would appear that quite firm guidelines are provided, and that discretion regarding departmental proposals is limited. Nevertheless, the Privy Council Office is responsible directly to the Prime Minister, and its officials have access to information and suggestions coming from such sources as task forces and Royal Commissions, which also report to the Prime Minister. This type of information enables the Privy Council Office to provide advice independent of departmental influence and is an alternative and possibly a competing source of information to that of civil servants. The role of the department official will now, to a large extent, be restricted to:

(a) assisting in the preparation and development of policy proposals,

(b) advising ministers in Cabinet committee meetings (thereby eliminating many inter-departmental committees utilized since 1939),

(c) implementing Cabinet or Cabinet committee decisions.

It can be seen that this role more closely approximates the traditional role of the civil service.

---

[30]*Ibid*, June 11, 1969, p. 9984.

One innovation of the Trudeau government which has caused concern is the establishment of a major policy and executive centre in the Prime Minister's office (distinct from the Privy Council Office). By March 3, 1975, the size of the staff in the Prime Minister's office had increased from 39 persons under Mr. Pearson to 98, and according to a return tabled in the House of Commons, 24 of these individuals were appointed from outside the civil service. This means that most of the Prime Minister's staff are not civil servants in the conventional sense of that term but are political appointees. There is a great deal of evidence that these staff people are exercising considerable influence on policy, influence of a type formerly restricted to civil servants. This seems to confirm the contention that "... the decision-making system at the federal level is changing, with policy innovation now shifting back to the Cabinet and particularly to a strengthened Office of the Prime Minister."[31] It is alleged that the decision to reduce Canada's commitment to NATO and the decision to phase out the Department of Indian Affairs were taken counter to the recommendations made by the departments concerned. An outstanding example of a shift in influence was the decision to send Professor Ivan Head, one of Mr. Trudeau's personal assistants, rather than an official of the Department of External Affairs to negotiate with the Nigerian government regarding relief flights into Biafra. There has also been a proliferation of Royal Commissions and task forces designed to bring more persons outside the government into the policy-making process. Thus, in future the civil service must expect to share the responsibility for policy advice with other groups, a responsibility which until recently has been almost exclusively that of the civil service. This is the major change in the relationship between the Cabinet and the civil service brought about by the Trudeau government.

The chief reason for concern is the possibility that the experience and expertise of the departmental civil service may be overlooked or inadequately utilized in the policy-making process. To some extent this concern appears to be exaggerated in that Cabinet ministers will still have to rely heavily on the advice of their civil service advisors. The difference is that their advice will now be acceptable only on its own merits, rather that *qua* civil service advice. As a result, the situation will no longer exist that "... when the Establishment (i.e. the civil service) mind was united behind or against a certain policy its advice was accepted by the Cabinet...."[32]

It is clear then that since Confederation the Cabinet and the civil service of Canada have worked well together. The Cabinet has relied

[31]Fred Schindeler and C.M. Lanphier, "Social Science Research and Participatory Democracy in Canada," *Canadian Public Administration*, Vol. XII, No. 4, Winter 1969, p. 490.
[32]Lamontagne, *op. cit.*, p. 265.

heavily on the civil service for advice and information on policy matters but has, in the main, made the final decisions itself. The special circumstances of World War II resulted in greater responsibilities for the civil service and set a pattern which was difficult to dissolve in the post-war period. If it can be concluded that during this latter period the civil service exerted undue influence, the Cabinet, rather than the civil service, was responsible for this situation. Although in recent years there has been a reduction in the influence of the civil service on policy-making, this change has not resulted from the provision of poor advice or undesirable policies by the civil service; rather it has resulted from the government's desire to admit other groups to the decision-making process and to return the prime role in policy-making to the political executive. Some of the language used to describe recent changes in the government apparatus can be interpreted as questioning the quality of advice provided in the past by the civil service. There is no evidence to support this view, and Lord Morrison's remarks about the British civil service can be applied to Canada equally well. "What the reader can be sure of is that the British Civil Service is loyal to the government of the day. The worst that can be said of them is that sometimes they are not quick enough in accustoming themselves to new ideas...."[33] The civil service of Canada must now deal with new ideas regarding its role in the governing of Canada. In the past it has proved adaptable and flexible. It is being challenged to continue this tradition in the future.

24
The Role of the Deputy Minister*
A.W. Johnson

The role of the deputy minister is to create the conditions which make it possible for the minister and the cabinet to provide the best government of which they are capable—even better if either of them happens to be weak.

It might seem more exact to say that the Deputy Minister is responsible for implementing government policies. This is true, but to say only this might be to imply a certain differentiation between policy

---

[33]Lord Morrison of Lambeth, *Government and Parliament*, Oxford University Press, Oxford, 1954, p. 335.

---

*Reprinted and slightly abridged by permission from A.W. Johnson, "The Role of the Deputy Minister", *Canadian Public Administration*, vol. 4, no. 4 (December 1961), pp. 363-369.

formulation and policy execution, with the deputy minister responsible only for the latter. In fact the deputy spends as much of his time on policy advising and devising as he does on implementation.

What is more, despite the nice precision of saying what the deputy minister is responsible for, the plain fact is that he is not really responsible for anything. No matter how much he may feel responsible for what he does and what his department does, and no matter how much his minister may hold him responsible for departmental behavior, in constitutional fact only his minister is responsible.

I would argue, indeed, that it is incorrect to use entirely active verbs in describing the deputy minister's role. "Making something possible" is certainly less active than "doing" or "being responsible for." But this lack of precision is necessary. For the deputy minister must display a curiously two-sided nature in dealing with his ministers—sometimes active and sometimes passive, depending upon how firmly resolved they are to follow a certain course of action, or how actively involved they wish to be in doing so.

While it might be useful in describing the role of the deputy to employ the familiar administrative schema of policy formulation and policy execution, it would be misleading to do so unless one first were to describe the "uniqueness" that is characteristic of a deputy minister's job. It is true, of course, that the deputy minister is a sort of general manager. But it is equally true that his job has characteristics which are not likely to be found in most general manager's jobs.

BETWEEN THE PARTIAL POLITICIAN AND THE IMPARTIAL PUBLIC SERVANT

The key to this uniqueness is to be found in his position in the organization—sandwiched as he is between the "neutral" civil service on the one hand, and his "political" minister on the other. This is a relationship which is clothed with constitutional or organizational conventions—conventions which are supposed to clarify the relationship, but which sometimes seem to obscure it. And it is a relationship that is full of paradoxes.

First, the deputy minister is supposed to be impartial or politically neutral serving a political master. In fact it is extraordinarily difficult to be wholly neutral when it is one's profession to deal in public affairs. What is more, the deputy is exposed constantly to most of the pressures of public life—to members of parliament, to irate citizens, to interest groups—each of them arguing for some change in public policy. They do so with the expectation that the deputy has or will develop a point of view concerning the policy in which they are interested. And in fact he will. For one of his prime tasks is to try to develop an appreciation of long-run social and economic trends as they affect or will affect the policies of his department. And then he evaluates these policies in that context.

Despite this convention of impartiality most people would be quite surprised if any deputy turned out not to have a point of view concerning the policies of his department. Indeed, the public often seems implicitly to hold him responsible for his minister's policies. As for the minister, he would be more than surprised if his deputy seemed not to have a loyalty to his policies, or for that matter a taste for the "political facts of life."

The second convention is even more obvious than the first: the deputy minister, like all civil servants, must remain anonymous in everything he does. This is particularly so, of course, with respect to the advice he gives his minister. There is no paradox in this convention, but there are real difficulties. Frequently the senior public servant has occasion, with the approval of his minister, to discuss potential policies with people outside the civil service. In doing so he may unwittingly express a point of view in such a fashion as to make it clear when the ministerial decision is reached that he was not in accord with it. Participation in the policy formulating process makes difficult the achievement of this goal of anonymity where policy formulation involves more than civil servants, but the essence remains the same: the deputy minister must renounce any desire for public recognition of its efforts or for a personal identification with the government programs in which he has an interest.

The third convention concerns the so-called division between "policy" and "administration." The minister is responsible for framing policies and the deputy is responsible for implementing them. Now it is true that to most deputy ministers this convention is a useful one when they are put on the spot by an irate taxpayer. But I do not think any of us has any illusions about the existence of these two compartments or about the exclusive occupancy of one by the minister and the other by the deputy. In fact the convention is really useful only when one is trying to define the prime interests and concerns of a minister, or when trying to explain the primacy of the cabinet and of the elected representatives.

But even if there were two such compartments, administration is not uniquely characterized by impartiality nor policy formulation necessarily by partisanship. One cannot administer a program without developing some keen loyalties to it. Nor is it likely that ministers will evolve policies without an objective appraisal of their goals and implications—no matter how keen their sense for the political winds.

The final convention I want to mention concerns the loyalties of the deputy minister. Most people consider the deputy to have but a single loyalty—that to his minister. He is to express no disagreement with his minister's policies; in fact, if he fails to defend them in public he may expect whispers of a "rift" between him and the government.

Again, this is an oversimplification. The deputy minister has many loyalties. His first is to his minister, of course. But he also has a loyalty to the institution of parliament, and he feels a responsibility to assist members of parliament, on whichever side of the House they sit, when they seek his aid. He has a loyalty to the programs he administers, a loyalty which opposition members sometimes construe to be a political loyalty. He has a loyalty to his own profession and to his own conscience, a loyalty which causes him to speak out against certain policies, or remain silent about them, depending on whose company he is in. And both the talk and the silences are easily misunderstood.

This is the context within which one must evaluate the role of the deputy minister—indeed in some ways the context has already defined the role.

POLICY EXECUTION

But let me return to the schema of public administration and give you some of my personal impressions of the deputy minister's role, first in the field of policy execution, and secondly in that of policy formulation.

You will quickly discover that what I have to say is not particularly original and that it does not even apply exclusively to deputy ministers. A great many of the characteristics of a deputy's job are common to any senior civil service post. In many ways there is nothing unique about the deputy minister's role in implementing policy. He is like any other senior executive: he must create an appropriate organization and staff it well, then seek to employ all the arts of administration in directing and coordinating and controlling it. But there are some features about this part of the deputy's job which are unusual.

First, the deputy faces a special difficulty in creating that "climate of freedom" which characterizes really effective and dynamic organizations. Of course he must seek to achieve this, and by the usual administrative devices—notably the maximum delegation of responsibility. But in doing so he must face the fact that his is not the final decision as to how much shall be delegated. Ideally, public servants in the field should be given wide discretion in interpreting policy, and in applying it to circumstances as they find them. But they are not the architects of public policy—parliament is, and woe betide the civil servant who strays too far from what parliament intended.

What is more, what was delegated today may be withdrawn tomorrow—not by the deputy, but by the minister. And then it may be withdrawn only by implication. Policy may have been interpreted a certain way for five years, but if that interpretation is called into question by a citizen or an interest group, the minister is bound to review it. This inevitably creates uncertainty on the part of civil servants as to what lies within their competence, and as to when policy interpretations should be referred "up the line." What the minister and deputy may wish to leave to the man in the field may be different from what the taxpayer thinks should be left to him. And the line keeps shifting.

So it is the deputy's job somehow to maintain the desirable "climate of freedom" in the face of what harassed civil servants describe as "interference." In essence he is an "interpreter": he must try to interpret to his staff the rationale for ministerial forays into the day-to-day work of the civil service. Putting it another way, the deputy must seek to reconcile the political process with the administrative process.

He has the same sort of role when his staff encounters the impediments to freedom of action which are imposed—apparently capriciously—by central agencies of government. Of course, it is true that many of these treasury controls, public service commission controls, purchasing agency controls are unwarranted, and we who have some responsibility for central agencies should root them out. But the best run government will still have some such controls—if it has a parliament— and it is the deputy's job to interpret them to an impatient staff.

The Public Service Commission may be slow and meticulous in the recruitment of staff, but this is because parliament rightly insists upon every citizen having an equal right to try for a job. Appropriation and allotment controls may impose on field workers certain delays, but parliamentary control over expenditures is much more important than these minor inconveniences. The same applies to controls over individual expenditures: these must be reported in the Public Accounts in order that parliament might review them, and a good deal of "book-work" is justified in making this possible.

What I am trying to say is that there are some special problems in trying to create a climate of freedom in a department of government. The political process and the existence of parliament *do* impose impediments and these must be accepted by the civil service. The deputy's role, in common with that of all senior civil servants, is to try to communicate to his staff the dual loyalty which is necessary in the public service—one to the program and the other to the very processes of government which produce these frustrations.

My second comment about the role of the deputy in program administration concerns the development of what I might call a "pride of public service." No matter how idealistic one is about the public service one must recognize that there are areas of work which are boring, unrewarding, and repetitive. And the supervisors in these areas have no "profit motive" to move them to introduce work simplification, performance standards and the rest. But what there is in the civil service instead of the profit motive is a certain pride in effective public service. And this is the attitude which must prevail among departmental supervisors if optimum efficiency is to be achieved in these routine procedural operations. Again the role of the deputy and of the senior public servant is unique: he must not only engender a certain enthusiasm for efficiency, but he must seek and communicate a rationale for that enthusiasm.

There is a final impression about this part of the deputy's role upon which I would like to comment. It concerns the relationship of his department to the public.

It is true that in many ways the deputy minister is like an executive in any enterprise: he has a responsibility for maintaining good public relations. But in government this phrase has a very special meaning. The public is at one and the same time the involuntary recipient of the services the civil servants render, and their master. If the public does not have to buy your services you will likely develop a certain solicitude for their feelings: if it does, you may not. It is the job of the deputy and his senior people somehow to instill in the department a sense of public service, an understanding of public reaction to the impersonal and powerful forces of government, and, above all, a profound respect for what is paramount in every program: the rights of the citizen. Again it is a matter of diluting program enthusiasm with a second loyalty: that to the political process and the rights of the individual.

Beyond this is the other relationship between the public and the public service: what I might call the master-servant relationship. Obviously this is not a matter of obsequiousness on the part of the civil servant. Rather it is a matter of searching out the public reaction to the programs he is administering in order that a more mature evaluation might be made of their effectiveness.

Undoubtedly this is an everyday event in the lives of most civil servants, but to the deputy minister it is a matter of ensuring that he hears about the public reactions which his staff routinely receives. Similarly he must organize so as to solicit and receive from interest groups their views on the programs for which he is responsible to his minister. One might almost go so far as to say that he has a responsibility to seek out public advice on his area of government.

I hope I am not making the deputy minister sound like a "permanent politician." This, by the way, is how one political scientist describes senior civil servants.[1] In fact, I do not think any civil servant has the right to compete with the minister in his role of testing, sensing, reacting to public opinion. If he does he will find what an art it is, and what an amateur he is! But he must surely recognize that the public cannot react to elected representatives on every detail of program administration; consequently he should seek to "represent" to his minister the public

---

[1]"Their functional position is best described, perhaps, as that of permanent politician." J. Donald Kingsley, *Representative Bureaucracy*, The Antioch Press, Yellow Springs, 1944, p. 269.

view of the policies for which he is responsible. This is the sense in which I would agree with those who argue that the civil service should become a representative bureaucracy.[2]

POLICY FORMULATION

This discussion leads very naturally to an examination of the second major area of the deputy minister's job, that of advising his minister on policy. For it is as difficult to write separately about policy formulation and policy execution as it is to differentiate between them in one's day-to-day work.

Here the unique thing about the deputy minister's role and that of senior civil servants generally is that they *are* expected to advise their ministers on policy—that they are expected to do so despite the convention about the minister's policy role and the civil servant's administrative role.

One wonders, however, what the basis is for the wide acceptance of this policy role. Certainly the deputy has no "right" to advise his minister: he does so only at his minister's pleasure. And I hope that none of us takes himself so seriously that he agrees with this misleading but fairly prevalent view: "The real focus for the development of new policies is not the political process, but the civil service." Indeed the facts speak otherwise. It seems to me that the rationale for the deputy minister's policy role is to be found in the fact that a truly successful deputy minister—if there is such a thing—should possess three kinds of "authority." (I use this word in the sense in which it is employed in political theory.)[3]

First he enjoys the authority which derives from his post, not his person: the minister, the members of parliament and the public expect him to subject proposed new policies to critical scrutiny. His is the job of evaluating the ideas that emerge from the political process—considering their implications, examining the premises upon which they are based, evolving alternatives for achieving the same goals; in short, of ensuring an objective examination of every aspect of a proposal.

Secondly, the deputy is clothed—I do not say always rightly—with the authority of his profession. If his academic training and his experience in public affairs mean anything at all, they should mean that he possesses the ability to anticipate social and economic problems and find a solution to them. This is as much a part of the senior civil servant's job as simply evaluating the proposals put forward by others. For he is

---

[2]This point of view is most effectively expressed by C.J. Friedrich of Harvard University. See his *Constitutional Government and Democracy*, Ginn and Company, Boston, 1946.
[3]For a discussion of different kinds of authority see C.J. Friedrich, ed., *Authority*, Harvard University Press, Cambridge, 1958.

supposed to study these trends, he is supposed to identify emerging problems, he is expected to have some insight as to how these might be solved. A British political scientist puts it this way:

> Even though he must of course accept the minister's decision, he should always be thinking ahead of it, and he should always be ready to express his own views and to provide the information upon which they are based. For he is primarily concerned with the making of policy, and policy should not wait upon events.[4]

The third reason for this advisory role is the special relationship the deputy has with his minister. Each of them comes to know the other: his strengths and weaknesses, his interests and his blind spots, his insights and his obtuseness. So in the process of formulating policy each comes to look to the other to contribute those particular capacities and talents which he knows him to possess.

If there is some legitimacy to this role of policy adviser, what does it entail? Essentially it involves the initiation of policy suggestions without seeking to appropriate the initiative from the minister and the government; it involves inaugurating policy studies without usurping the minister's role. The cynics may suggest that this is power without responsibility: I suggest it is more akin to responsibility without power.

The principal task the deputy minister faces is trying to develop in himself and his organization that knowledge and perspective which makes possible an effective evaluation of social and economic trends, and their effect on the area of government in which he works. To do this he must make room for comtemplation and study, when all the pressures of events would rule these out. As Sir Edward Bridges, former permanent secretary to the British Treasury, puts it: "He must be a practical person, yet have some of the qualities of the academic theorist; his work encourages the longest views and yet his responsibilities are limited."[5]

The long view is particularly important in government. This is so not just by reason of the nature of government programs, and because of their impact on social and economic development, but also because the political view tends to be short. One might almost say that it tends to move in four- or five-year cycles. So the deputy always must try to find the longer view and introduce it, and to achieve a certain co-existence between it and the shorter view.

Secondly, the deputy minister must place a special emphasis on the development and maintenance of a dynamic department. This means that he must employ all of the arts he has developed—and they are never enough—for appropriate staffing, encouragement of ideas, rewarding the unusual, and so on. This is particularly difficult in government.

---

[4]H.R.G. Greaves, *The Civil Service in the Changing State*, George G. Harrap & Co., London, 1947, p. 48.
[5]Sir Edward Bridges, *Portrait of a Profession*, University Press, Cambridge, 1950, p. 28.

I say this not because civil servants are lazy, or because they lack enthusiasm for the public service. Quite the opposite is true, in my experience. But the civil servant is exposed to certain frustrations which are peculiar to work in government. When he enters the public service, he may be an unqualified enthusiast for his program—be it highway building or social welfare. But sooner or later he will meet with one or both of the frustrations which are typical of government.

First, he may find that despite the logic of his recommendations concerning his program, there are political factors to which his political masters give greater emphasis than they do to his logic. Alternatively, they may accept the validity of his proposals but decide in making their budgetary choices that some other program is more important. This will seem inconceivable to the program enthusiast but there it is.

How do you maintain enthusiasm in the face of these rejections? In business, if your idea will save money or increase sales you have a sporting chance of success. But in government the choices do not involve a single value system—more or less profit; they involve hierarchies of social values, all of which are subjective. And it is the elected representatives' value systems which are important, not those of the public servant. So it is up to the deputy to try to interpret to his staff the government's goals and its program emphasis, in order somehow to maintain their enthusiasm and dynamic.

Thirdly, the deputy minister must try to develop a certain talent for seeking out advice, without becoming the captive of those who give it. (If this is a problem for the deputy, by the way, how much more so it is for his minister. As a matter of fact I think this is part of the basis for mutual understanding between minister and deputy: in a sense they are in the same boat.)

The deputy and his minister need advice both from program specialists and from the interested public (or publics). In fact, one of the deputy's major jobs is to organize so as to ensure getting good advice of both kinds. Within the department he must organize so as to create foci of policy thinking and advice, tempered by the experience his people gain in policy execution. This means a certain kind of organization and an appropriate combination of "thinkers" and "doers." It means too that he must cultivate channels of communication which will facilitate a "feedback" or public reaction. Outside the department, the deputy will seek to develop the formal and informal consultations with the interested public that I have talked about earlier.

In all of this he must come to develop a sense of participation in policy formulation, without inducing a sense of paternity for ideas. After all, he is not himself formulating policies. This is a delicate position. For his staff will expect him to display a fighting loyalty to their ideas, if they are good ones, and will be disappointed if he seems not to go to bat for them with the minister. Interest groups, in turn, will seek to win him over to their point of view, or to cultivate in him a certain sympathy for their problems.

So the deputy minister finds himself in the curious position of being exposed to the political process, without at the same time being part of it. He must not permit himself the luxury of becoming too attached to ideas or positions. Somehow he must find a way of maintaining a cordial relationship with those who assist and advise him without ever losing sight of the fact that his first loyalty is to his minister. His first loyalty can never be to his staff or to the public affected by his minister's policies. To quote Sir Edward Bridges again:

> A civil servant has to combine the capacity for taking a somewhat coldly judicial attitude with the warmer qualities essential to managing large numbers of staff. Detached, at times almost aloof, he must be if he is to maintain a proper impartiality between the many claims and interests that will be urged upon him.[6]

Finally, the deputy minister must make a determined effort not to succumb to the ever-present temptation of merely anticipating ministerial will or political necessity, when framing policy recommendations. After all, the minister and his colleagues are subject to enough pressures to take the short-run view, without the deputy seeking to play in the same political league.

This is not to suggest that the deputy should evolve ideal systems which are clearly impractical in a given political situation. But it is one thing to evolve the ideal policy, then amend it, or have it amended on the basis of political necessity, and quite another merely to evolve courses of action which are based upon a civil servant's appraisal of what his minister wants.

Let the minister play his role, and the deputy his. It seems to me, in fact, that there are few enough areas in the political process where the broader span of time and events can be brought to bear in influencing policy, without the deputy minister abdicating his role in this regard. What is more, I think I can make a case for this view: given the broadest perspectives in decision-making the minister will make less "political" decisions, in the narrow sense of that word, than will a civil servant who is trying to "play politician."

This it seems to me is the role of the deputy minister in advising his minister on policy. He must seek out and then try to integrate what is suggested by social and economic trends, what is proposed by the academic theorists, what is propounded by the program specialists, and what is advocated by interest groups and the public. Having done this, he must then make an effort to adapt the ideal solutions to the practical difficulties his minister faces.

---

[6]*Ibid.*, p. 28.

25

The Public Official — Parliament, the Public and the Press*

S. H. S. Hughes

There is a salutary tradition of long standing in Parliament that civil servants are not to be called to account individually and by name for the actions which they perform under the authority of a minister of the crown, and only that minister (and perhaps his colleagues) can be assailed when things go wrong or legitimately acclaimed when things go right. There was a time when public officials were not afforded this protection; a time, needless to say, when ministers of the Crown were not yet responsible to Parliament, and in those far off days it was the custom, when either House felt that its prerogatives had been usurped or infringed, to call the offending functionary before its bar so that he might explain, apologize, and be admonished upon his knees. Many a modern antiquarian must have sighed over the passing of this golden age. It is hardly necessary to say that were this practice still followed, no minister could be impartially advised or efficiently served. None the less, this protection of the civil servant from specific and personal attack in Parliament is not always to his advantage. The very facelessness and namelessness of the men and women who conduct the day-to-day business of government have engendered the fear that legislative bodies are losing their grip upon administration, and that ministers no longer control the actions of their permanent advisers, but are themselves controlled by the views and the behaviour of the departmental officials, for whom they are responsible. This fear, like all fears, is of course partly the product of illusion. But it would be dangerously complacent to assume that by merely guaranteeing the independence of the civil service we have reached the promised land. If we as a people become convinced that the real power in the State resides in the permanent officials, and that electoral changes have no real meaning in terms of policy and administration, then a deadly blow has been dealt to our parliamentary institutions and we are on the brink of that disillusionment and cynicism which has assailed so many famous democratic states before the final fragmentation of their political beliefs has plunged them into totalitarianism. I say, therefore, with diffidence but with conviction, that it should be the abiding concern of civil servants to communicate with Parliament as fully and frankly as it is in their power to do within the

---

*Reprinted by permission from S.H.S. Hughes, "The Public Official — Parliament; the Public and the Press," *Canadian Public Administration*, vol. 3, no. 4 (December 1960), pp. 289-298.

compass of their authority, so that members of all parties may discharge their duties to the people whom they represent with the aid of the most complete information and the most disinterested advice required in any given situation.

I do not want to be understood as suggesting that the general rule of conduct of civil servants in these matters does not comply with the highest counsels of perfection. I think that most members of Parliament would agree that they are well served in these matters, but that they are sometimes baffled by an atmosphere of reticence which is likely to pervade government departments when called upon to answer enquiries. I shall have more to say on this subject when I come to refer to tendencies and trends which seem to be characteristic of the present-day relationship between the public and its employees. For the present it is sufficient to say that of all the means of communication with the public, Parliament — because of its great constitutional authority, its ability to require the production of papers and to have these and ministerial explanations submitted to the test of debate — is far the most reliable. The reporting of parliamentary proceedings has, none the less, had a strange history. In that period of our common British constitutional history before the principle of ministerial responsibility was established, no reporting was allowed, for the well-known reason that the House of Commons, at least, feared any form of royal surveillance which might result in reprisals taken against its members by the Sovereign and his servants. Later on, and particularly during the nineteenth century, the reporting of parliamentary debates became not only a matter of official approval but of the widest popular acceptance. Thereafter I think we can discern a tendency for the press to give increasingly less prominence to proceedings in Parliament and to adopt a less objective attitude towards parliamentary reporting. For example, a member of the House of Commons may ask a question which raises a matter of public importance. The question is often in a form which suggests that he is just as anxious to impart information as to receive it. It may be of a provocative nature, and if it is it is assured of receiving prominence in the press. But what happens to the answer? This may take some time for a minister to furnish, because enquiries must be made of his civil service advisers, who in their turn must secure all the relevant information. When the answer is at length given in the House, it may well receive so little prominence in the press that the purpose of giving it, which is really to inform the public through Parliament, is almost entirely defeated. Of course the parliamentary representatives of the press will have done their best. It is not for them to say where and how their material will be published, and newspaper editors will say that it is their business, in order to serve the material interests of their publishers and their advertisers, to supply the public with news that is fresh, stimulating and even alarming. I do not quarrel with this explanation, but I merely say that it appears to the public employee that the press is nowadays more interested in rumour than in fact, and that the public, if it gets any at all of parliamentary proceedings, has an impression of charge and counter-charge, and eventually of concealment.

It should not be assumed that members of the public services of Canada and its provinces tend, as a result, to undervalue the importance of the legislative bodies that represent the public which they serve. On the contrary, by the very nature of their duties, they are more appreciative of the representative function than most. Bu I do not think they are to be blamed if they have increasing recourse to direct communication with the public through all the media which are available, when the constitutional channels cease to be effective. We may expect an increasing reliance upon experts in the field of public relations, not only to deal directly with the press but to conduct costly and continuous advertising campaigns to attract public attention to departmental problems. This will result in the taxpayer having to pay to have his own elbow jogged, and I think it is fair to assume that the more often the jogging takes place the less sensitive his elbow becomes. We must not ignore the possibility that by the operation of some law of diminishing returns this type of communication will cease eventually to have any effect at all. However attractive speculation on this subject may be, I wish to consider with you for a moment the much more important problems involved in the day-to-day communication of public servants with men and women who come directly into contact with them, either personally or by correspondence.

We are all familiar with the paradox of public administration that being right 99 per cent of the time is no guarantee of success or even of safety. It is the hundredth or thousandth administrative process which, coming apart at the seams after a record of unbroken ease and tranquillity, threatens to condemn the whole system. In the field of communication about which we are speaking, there is nothing that succeeds like failure. Any casual acquaintance, so it seems, can wittily epitomize the civil service by giving you an example so exceptional in its circumstances and outlandish in its results that it is typical of nothing, but all the reasonable argument in the world will not serve to shake his conviction of its characteristic verisimilitude. This strange inversion of the law of averages is naturally encouraged by the press, which cannot be expected to resist news of the "man bites dog" variety. It is not surprising, therefore, that public officials become wary of giving anyone any more information that is absolutely necessary, and often much less than is desirable.

Here I think, in the public interest, certain simple rules can be laid down governing the direct relationships of civil servants with members of the public. First of all, a civil servant should be accessible, and wherever possible he should be at once available and not given to making members of the public wait simply to illustrate his intense preoccupation with other and more important matters. This rule can be applied to communication by letter by the simple expedient of ensuring that all letters from members of the public are at least acknowledged promptly, even if they cannot be answered immediately. We are all familiar with the delays that seem to overtake a great deal of official correspondence. A letter is received asking for information which the recipient does not have or cannot by himself supply. It is minuted from this person to that, and the assembling of information and the preparation of draft letters for signature by higher authority often takes a considerable time. When I was engaged in the practice of law I was irritated by the long silences which were apt to follow enquiries by letter from government departments, and was always agreeably surprised when my enquiries were promptly acknowledged, even though the information requested was not then forthcoming. I am still surprised, after experience of public administration in two jurisdictions, at the extent to which this simple and inexpensive form of courtesy is sometimes neglected. It is unnecessary to say that courteous and prompt replies go very far to creating a satisfied correspondent, even though the issue of his problem is not favourable to him. There is no doubt that the public service is improving in this respect, but I think it is still far from perfect.

In the second place, it is seldom possible to give too much information, provided that it is lawful to give it. This principle applies to internal communications within the service as well as contacts between the service and the public outside. The tendency to avoid candour, or to give too little information, is one of the most generally prevalent among public employees. I have heard various explanations of the reason for this lack of candour, and they all seem to stem from the apparent need for caution which an official feels must be observed in committing himself or his department in written dealings with the public or with other departments. This caution seems to reflect firstly the fear of being held responsible by superiors and secondly that of being held responsible by the law. It lies at the root of much that is unattractive and unglamorous about the public service and which gets departments of government described as inert and unenterprising. It is a great tribute to the resourcefulness of the legal profession that a letter from one of its members threatening to involve a government department or any of its members in legal proceedings frequently produces a gratifying state of perturbation, however empty the threat may be. I have had lawyers write to me and talk menacingly about Mandamus and Certiorari who clearly have about as much knowledge of the prerogative writs as I have about the theory of relativity. It is wise to remember that lawyers who have a case seldom tell you in advance where the lightning is going to strike. And since it is the law of libel which people seem to be afraid of when called upon to give information about the actions of individuals, it is also well to remember that telling the truth without malice is a good working rule of defence against the sometimes formidable weapons which that law makes available. When I was chairman of an administrative tribunal in Ontario which my colleagues and I had the great good fortune of establishing from the ground up, we were able to adopt as a principle, and implement in practice, the idea that all our files should be available to public scrutiny, and we even provided accommodation for the convenience of any member of the public who wanted to examine them. Needless to say, this attitude disarmed a great deal of curiosity and we were seldom troubled with many requests. Of course there will always be confidential papers which it will be constitutionally proper to make inaccessible, but as a rule of conduct as much information as can be given lawfully should be volunteered without hesitation, not only to establish good faith but also as a test of its accuracy and to separate rumour from fact. In personnel work particularly, it is easy to damage a man's character firstly by failing to test the accuracy of information which is apparently unfavourable to it and secondly by failing to divulge it and to allow the person affected to meet it with explanations. The inclination to conclude that it is better not to take a chance, and quietly close the file, is sometimes irresistible, but it is also an effective way of creating injustice.

The third rule of conduct which I would like to propound is that of consistency. I noticed recently in a magazine produced by a well-known manufacturer of business machines, among a number of other aphorisms, the following attributed to the latter-day American sage William Allen White, "Consistency", quoth he, "is a paste jewel which only cheap men cherish." The lot of the aphorist is a hard one, because so much sense has to be sacrificed to form, and wit and wisdom do not always go hand in hand. Making all the usual allowances for misquotation and removal from context, it would be difficult to find a more perverse observation, particularly when applied to the subject of administration. Consistency is as important in administration as it is in law, and a subject is as concerned with knowing how his rights will be interpreted as with what his rights are. Yet consistency has it drawbacks, as anybody who has the experience of being told "I cannot do this for you because if I did I would have to do it for everybody else" can testify. To each member of the public, his own problem is paramount, and it is of little comfort to him to be told that the requirements of consistency, in this respect, are all that stand between him and the beneficence of a warm-hearted civil servant who would otherwise be glad to help him. And yet here I think the public must be told emphatically that without consistency in administration there can be no real justice. A capricious, changing, unpredictable policy can only be a reflection of the minds of men who make it. It is only necessary to consider a situation where consistency is not observed, and which results in different treatment being given in individual cases where the facts and the law are the same, to realize that a position typified by the observation "I will do it for you but not for him" is indefensible. I labour this point because the cautious approach to so many questions which the need for consistency imposes upon members of the public service in all jurisdictions is one of the principal reproaches levelled at them by press and public alike.

Are there any special considerations applicable to communication with the public through the Press? I think it should be borne in mind that most of the trouble in this area—and for the civil servant it is frequently troublesome indeed—arises from the fact that the public official and the journalist often fail to speak the same language or think along the same lines. The official lives in a world where precision of thought and speech is valued for its own sake, and like the lawyer has developed conventions of expression which have significance primarily for his colleagues. The journalist is generally in a hurry and has been compelled, by the nature of his craft, to speak and write colloquially. He naturally distrusts the carefully-worded departmental press release and tries to instill some life into it with what he calls "background material," generally acquired directly from the official concerned with the business in question. The result of these communications, if not always a complete distortion of the facts, is often a perfunctory and incomplete reference to that to which the official has devoted considerable time and energy and thoroughly understands himself. The fact that he has taken the understanding of the journalist too much for granted and has perhaps failed to explain himself fully and exactly does not immediately occur to him and he indignantly claims that he has been misquoted, when at the worst he may only have been misunderstood. But it is certain that he will protect himself in the future by saying less, or perhaps nothing at all.

The result of this type of contretemps is that many government agencies will only communicate with the press through clearly defined channels, which the press will not always accept as either fully informed or completely candid. Another barrier is accordingly erected between the public and the Public Service—a barrier which mutual distrust will keep firmly in place. If public officials had some experience of journalism, and journalists of the Public Service, it is probable that the former would be more forthcoming and lucid and the latter more judicious in the provision and use of information respectively. There is, however, no easy solution to this problem, and I will have to be content with two observations. In the first place, the provision of information to the press in as full and complete a form as possible by officials should be encouraged by their superiors, even though it be occasionally misused or neglected, provided always that timely precautions are taken against indiscretions injurious to the State. Secondly, journalists, by curbing the tendency to be prescient in speculation at the expense of the facts as they have found them to be, may well confer even greater benefits upon the public than they now do.

If we can therefore summarize the foregoing rules for communication with the public by the slogan, "Courtesy, candour and consistency," there remain to be discerned, wherever possible, the trends in present day relationships between the public service and its employers.

No one will seriously contend that the influence of political patronage in the recruitment and selection of public employees is not on the decline. Even in those jurisdictions where there are no statutory safeguards against its operation, there is a general inclination to avoid it and at the very least to pay lip-service to the principle of appointment and promotion by merit. The reasons for this are not far to seek. A system of competitive selection administered by an independent government agency is surer to win public acceptance than one which depends upon the mere reward of political services and support, and the type of political support which is only given in the expectation of such reward is seldom of decisive influence in the determination of electoral contests. Over and above these considerations are those of the efficiency and quality of the Public Service, which no representative government can afford to neglect.

But as the independence and security of the service becomes more strongly rooted in the traditions of impartiality and loyalty to the State, free from partisan bias, they are apparently threatened by a new set of suspicions. The facelessness and namelessness to which I have referred appear to be more alarming as the complexity of administration increases. Lobbyists and pressure groups, to use terms which have acquired meaning on both sides of the Atlantic Ocean, are not as well recognized in the framework of our public life as in the United States, but the techniques which they employ have acquired a respectable seniority in Canada. It is inevitable that the public official, protected by constitutional safeguards and required to give impartial advice to his political head, should acquire serpentine characteristics in the eyes of advocates of special interests. My own experience in the regulatory field persuades me that the business community occasionally resents that type of regulation which it understands to be restrictive of free enterprise, and is inclined to regard those who are charged with the responsibility of designing and enforcing it with feelings akin to those felt by Sinbad for the Old Man of the Sea. It is hard indeed to dispel the feeling that the public service is indoctrinated with economic and social beliefs not necessarily acceptable to the nation as a whole.

Nothing, in fact, is so provoking to press and public alike as the silence which is imposed by custom upon the operations of public officials, but the measure of public acceptance of the course of conduct of which that silence is eloquent is illustrated by the general condemnation of the public servant who speaks out for himself on a question of policy for which he is not responsible to a legislative body. We are fortunate indeed in the moderation and sense of responsibility displayed by the press of Canada in dealing with this type of provocation. One has only to look at sections of the British and American press to see how the independence of the Public Service can be threatened by irresponsible agitation. We do not suffer here from the daily and envenomed use of the term "bureaucrat," and the compulsive malevolence of widely syndicated commentators earning reputations for fearlessness by abusing the "civil service mentality." Since we are still citizens of a comparatively small country, it is well recognized that the civil servant is like any other next-door neighbour who pays taxes to various public authorities, and pays them be it said withoqt recourse to those provisions of the law which lighten the load upon the shoulders of those of his brethren engaged in mercantile pursuits. It would be idle to pretend, however, that the practice of abusing the public service on general principles cannot be matched with sincerity in this country. Assuming, for the purposes of argument, that it does not deserve abuse, there is always that significant element in any group of human beings who cannot accept the proposition that they are the authors of their own misfortunes. We are all familiar with this phenomenon, and it is especially noticeable in the field of personnel administration. It is apt to be aggravated proportionately when those who are expected to realize that they are, in fact, the authors of their own misfortunes become convinced that they are not in reality the masters of their own destinies.

It would seem to be an arguable proposition that hostility towards an individual is easier and more natural to develop than hostility towards a class. The characteristics of an individual are easy to observe, and the consequence of injustice to one not as calamitous as injustice to many. But the lessons of history tell us that hostility towards a class, like the Spartan helots or the Roman publicans or the Russian kulaks, is equally easy to develop, if not easier, because of a human tendency towards broad generalization and the ease with which private virtues can be offset by submersion in a group or a common environment.

If we assume that the regulation of private activities by the State is increasing, and I submit that we are not justified in assuming the contrary, the tendency to attribute responsibility for its disagreeable aspects to those who administer and enforce regulations will increase correspondingly or perhaps disproportionately, depending upon the steps that are taken to excite public indignation. In a federal state like ours, with strongly established institutions of local government, the process may well be retarded, but the possibility of its development in advance cannot be ignored by anyone interested in public administration. We are accustomed to being told in this country that we are over-governed, that the increase in the numbers of public employees threatens our liberties and our finances, and that the size and number of government agencies must be reduced. We are well aware that many, if not all, of the same voices are raised in protest if any of the establishments complained about, or the services provided are actually reduced or curtailed. Government agencies are on all sides urged to do more, but to do it with less. It is easy to speak with feeling on this subject from the point of view of the Civil Service Commission of Canada, which has to satisfy the appetites of government departments in its recruiting function and so often to thwart them in that of organization and classification. In the course of a close, not to say rigorous, scrutiny of the Commission's operations early in 1959, the House of Commons Committee on Estimates recommended that the Commission embark on a course of action entirely commendable and salutary, which would, at a conservative estimate, have required the doubling of our personnel selection staff. Weighing the advantages of the recommendation against the propriety of a control agency indulging in such spectacular expansion, we had regretfully to decline, or at least postpone, contemplation of the course proposed. If we were wrong in this conclusion, we only succeeded in preventing or retarding a desirable development for the sake of an economy which may, in any event, be nullified by the external pressures of our national expansion.

Speaking generally, I forsee, as a concomitant of this expansion which is with us and around us at the present moment, a great increase in the duties and responsibilities of governments at all levels, accelerated perhaps by the inevitable tendency of our people to thrust more burdens upon them. I take my stand as firmly as anyone else on the side of free enterprise and the preservation of private rights, being always aware that never in our history have we been able to countenance enterprise in a state of perfect freedom or the ascendency of private rights over the eminent domain of public need. We live and move in a maze of contrivances, which could not by themselves and one by one survive the test of logic, at once as tenuous as the 49th parallel and as massive as the British North America Act. It follows, therefore, that there is no return for us to first principles of political theory, and that failing some inundation which will erase us as a nation from the pages of history, we must follow the current of our national life down ever-widening but pre-determined channels.

If such an increase in governmental responsibility and activity is inevitable, then I forsee a corresponding increase in the numbers and influence of the administrators and their executants who form the Public Service. There will be plateaux, as the doctors say, stages of temporary respite from this inexorable advance, and it will, I hope, be possible to preserve a just proportion between the enlargement of administrative function and the needs of a growing community. In consequence, there will be a very real danger that the tendencies which now seem to divide the public from its servants will become more marked and excite more feeling. I hope that the public and its great mentor, the press, will not take too lopsided a view of this process. There will always be safeguards against a "population explosion" among public employees. Legislative bodies and the executives which are responsible to them will no doubt continue to be concerned with the over-riding necessity of good husbandry in the raising and expending of public funds. Control agencies will continue to harry the empire builders. Enlightened statesmanship and a vigilant bench and bar will labour to preserve our characteristic and historic concern with the sanctity of private rights. In short, all the resources of democracy as we know it will be deployed against the advance of bureaucracy in the most invidious sense of that hard-worked word. We can only hope that the best traditions of public service will not be compromised in the struggle, and that a fully and fairly informed public will steadily survey the scene.

26
Pressure Groups and the Canadian Bureaucracy

J.E. Anderson

> "When I see members of Parliament being lobbied, it's a sure sign to me that the lobby lost its fight in the civil service and the Cabinet."
> "It's the deputy minister, not ministers, who are courted by most lobbyists, which suggests where the real power in Ottawa lies."
> "The actual rate of fiscal protection (tariffs) has become, in effect, a matter of departmental rather than parliamentary politics.... Thus, emphasis has tended to shift to influencing the policies and activities of government boards, commissions and departmental officials...."

These views of pressure group activity in Canada span a period of more than thirty years and carry the authority of an Ottawa lobbyist, a journalist for one of Canada's leading newspapers and a distinguished Canadian sociologist.[1] The significance of interaction between civil servants and pressure groups is widely, although many times only implicitly, recognized in studies of Canadian pressure groups. With very few notable exceptions, these studies allude almost incidentally to civil service-pressure group relations through description of the organization

---

[1]Respectively, an anonymous lobbist cited in F.C. Englemann and M.A. Schwartz, *Political Parties and the Canadian Social Structure*, Prentice-Hall, Scarborough, 1967, p. 105; Hugh Winsor, "A Primer for Innocents on the Art of Lobbying," *The Globe Magazine*, Toronto, February 27, 1971, p. 7; and S.D. Clarke, "The Canadian Manufacturers' Association: A Political Pressure Group," *The Canadian Journal of Economics and Political Science*, Vol. 4 (1938), p. 251.

or general activities of pressure groups.[2] The topic of this essay then, like many other subjects touching Canadian public administration, remains in that rough and preliminary stage of study that requires reliance on scattered references in scholarly writings, the rare statements of various actors in the political process and informed speculation based on the literature of comparative politics.

More detailed study has been difficult and rare, simply because the activities of pressure groups and civil servants occur so close to the core of government and politics. Much information is kept secret or is unavailable because consultation between civil servants and pressure group officials is often informal rather than formal or institutionalized. Moreover, the interaction process may be very complex. Any one civil servant or pressure group official moves in a web of relationships between people, parties, pressure groups, political leaders and civil servants. The individual is probably aware to some extent of these inter-relationships and acts in part at least in anticipation of the reaction of others; in part too, he may have very private and even idiosyncratic motives. We may assume, however, that the extent, variety and content of the interaction between administrators and pressure groups depend largely on the government leaders' perception of the proper role of civil servants. The range of civil service activities considered appropriate may include the initiation and evaluation of policy proposals, the administration and adaptation of existing policies, advice on the likely public acceptability of policies, the explanation or defence of policies before the public, and the education of public opinion for the acceptance of new policies. Civil servants may in turn consult with pressure group representatives on one or all of these aspects of the policy process.

The increasingly complex and demanding nature of modern society has obliged governments to utilize available sources of special knowledge and experience outside the public service. This need for expertise explains the development of bureaucratically organized pressure groups which accompanied the growth of public bureaucracies in this century. It also predetermined the close relations now existing between civil servants and informed pressure groups. The importance which civil servants attach to the expertise of certain pressure groups depends of course on the extent to which they must take account of alternative political resources possessed by other pressure groups, for example, votes and money. The care and frequency with which civil servants must make such calculations rests largely on political and constitutional factors. Civil servants become more politicized in a governmental system in which they have more than one constitutionally determined political

[2]Most of the published literature on Canadian pressure groups is identified in the bibliographies in F.C. Englemann and M.A. Schwartz, *op. cit.*, and W.D.K. Kernaghan, *Bureaucracy in Canadian Government*, Methuen, Toronto, 1973.

master and in which political leaders compete for bureaucratic support. Under these circumstances, civil servants tend to seek the independent political support of pressure groups, legislators and political executives. This situation creates a favourable milieu for the operations of organized special interest groups. Governments which are experiencing or have experienced this politicization of civil servants include the United States because of its separation of governmental powers and contemporary Italy, Third and Fourth Republic France and Weimar Germany because of their combination of powerful, stable legislative committees and unstable executives.

By way of contrast, under a Cabinet system with a reliable legislative majority, and particularly in the case of one-party dominance, the civil servants best promote their own interests by serving and defending their ministers and the government. Nevertheless, to a lesser extent than in the United States and the European regimes noted above, civil servants will calculate the effect on voting behaviour of widely beneficial social and economic policies on the one hand and the impact of campaign contributions from disadvantaged interest groups on the other. These considerations constitute at least part of what is meant by "political" advice to the government. It is difficult to appraise the political costs and benefits of pursuing widely beneficial policies, since governments can fail by cumulatively disaffecting small minorities. A Canadian Cabinet Minister, perhaps conscious of the difficulty of assessing the relative effects of choosing between general and particular interests, and perhaps hoping to escape the dilemma, has suggested to pressure groups that "the strategy area where the interests of the politician, or bureaucrat, and the lobbyist effectively overlap is that which concerns itself with the sensitivity to the common good".[3] In Canada, it appears probable that the long dominance of the Liberal Party and its peculiar independence of specific economic interests because of the reliability of its support from Quebec has encouraged civil servants to emphasize "the public interest". They have, therefore, recommended generally beneficial policies even when these policies affect specific pressure groups adversely. These conditions also suggest that in Canada the relations between civil servants and pressure groups are usually dominated by civil servants.

RECOGNITION OF PRESSURE GROUPS

Allen Potter defines recognition as a prescriptive right to receive "a response which is more than an acknowledgment," one which is an agreement, an argument or a request for additional information. He

[3]Honourable Donald S. Macdonald, "Notes for Remarks to the Twenty-Third Session of the Canadian Institute for Organization Management," President of the Privy Council Press Release, June 19, 1969.

notes also that "governmental [and other] requests for information from an organized group are a measure of its standing".[4] Where a pressure group already exists, recognition is manifested by the extensiveness of civil service replies or the frequency of their requests for information. In reference to the Canadian Better Business Bureaus' attempt to assume a leading role in consumer education, the Bureaus' president recognized that first

> the bureaus must achieve rapport with the government agencies working in the area of consumer protection and, more particularly, with the Consumer Affairs Department .... Recently, however, it [Consumer Affairs] has asked the BBB to distribute a circular dealing with misleading ads for hearing aids and department officials have been requesting information from the bureaus increasingly often ("I don't know if Mr. Basford knows how often") and it is possible that, as Mr. Dollard says, they will "come to depend on each other for exchange of information".[5]

It appears that civil servants grant recognition to interest groups primarily because these groups possess valuable knowledge and experience. One of the consequences of this emphasis on expertise is that civil servants will interact most frequently with those interests which must themselves be most diligent in producing and acquiring information in the ordinary pursuit of their own affairs, that is, with management more than with labour, with trading companies more than with farmers or consumers, and with self-governing doctors more than with salaried teachers. This bias in favour of relations with particular kinds of pressure groups may be corrected by the recognition of less expert groups. The purpose of this recognition may be a self-conscious pursuit of the public interest, an acknowledgment of the voting power of these groups or simply the creation of an illusion of countervailing powers. Whatever the purpose for their recognition, however, these less expert groups tend to remain of low status, to be prestige conscious and to be fearful of manipulation by government and civil servants. The recognition of pressure groups, then, is based most securely on expertise and the communication of this expertise to civil servants.

In granting recognition to a pressure group, public officials support it politically or, in some cases, maintain its sheer viability. Using a rational self-interest theory analogous to that of economics, Mancur Olsen has explained why many vocational and other economically concerned pressure groups need direct government aid or governmentally

---

[4] Allen Potter, *Organized Groups in British National Politics*, Faber and Faber, London, 1961, pps. 203, 190.

[5] Glenn Somerville, "Better Business Bureaus' president questions government techniques in handling consumer complaints," *The Globe and Mail*, Toronto, October 13, 1970, p. B3. (The article is from the *Globe's* "Man in the News" series, a particularly good newspaper source of current material on pressure group activities.)

determined status to ensure membership loyalty and thus survival.[6] This is one aspect of pressure group politics which has been relatively well studied in Canada. Accounts of the Canadian Federation of Agriculture and the Canadian Labour Congress emphasize the importance these groups attach to their annual presentation to Cabinet and to other formal relations with the government. It is probable that these presentations are most directly related to the need for status.[7] The Consumers' Association of Canada actually needs a direct governmental financial subsidy to survive.[8] These are examples of the *government's* decision to grant essential political support to pressure groups.

Much of this kind of political support, however, is channelled through *civil servants* who may go so far as to encourage the formation of pressure groups from unorganized but potentially useful interests. Long before the dramatic confrontation with a cabinet minister which led to the Canadian Federation of Agriculture's regular annual presentation, a civil servant appears to have been helpful in establishing the organization. H.H. Hannam, its first president, has related how the late Clifford Clark, then Deputy Minister of Finance, informally suggested the establishment of a national farm organization and how Hannam used Clark's prestige to enlist support for the organization of the Federation.[9] The viability of the Canadian Manufacturers' Association in its early days was very much aided by the decision of the Department of Railways and Canals to solicit the Association's views on rail rate changes.[10] Doubtless, many more instances of such bureaucratic initiative are unrecorded and civil servants rather than politicians made the supportive decision. Indeed, it may be inevitable that the public administrator be the agent most involved in the government's political support of pressure groups since that support is in large part just the obverse of the consultative, administrative relationship.

The importance of a pressure group's status with government also enables civil servants to exert counterpressure on a group. By looking

---

[6]Mancur Olsen, *The Logic of Collective Action*, Harvard University Press, Cambridge, Mass., 1965, esp. ch. 1 and 2. See also Ronald Manzer "Selective Inducements and the Development of Pressure Groups: the Case of Canadian Teacher Associations," *Canadian Journal of Political Science*, Vol. 2 (1969), pp. 103-117.

[7]See Helen Jones Dawson, "Relations between Farm Organizations and the Civil Service in Canada and Great Britain," *Canadian Public Administration*, Vol. 10 (1967), pp. 565-573; David Kwavnick, "Pressure Group Demands and the Struggle for Organizational Status: The Case of Organized Labour in Canada," *Canadian Journal of Political Science*, Vol. 3 (1970), pp. 56-72. For recognition of the same phenomenon in the United States see David Truman, *The Governmental Process*, Alfred A. Knopf, New York, 1951, esp. pp. 459-60.

[8]Helen Jones Dawson, "Consumers' Association of Canada," *Canadian Public Administration*, Vol. 2 (1969), pp. 103-117.

[9]H.H. Hannam, "The Interest Group and Its Activities," Institute of Public Administration of Canada, *Proceedings of the Fifth Annual Conference*, 1953, pp. 172-173.

[10]S.D. Clarke, *The Canadian Manufacturers' Association*, University of Toronto, Toronto, 1939, pp. 48-49.

elsewhere for information or for administrative assistance, civil servants can threaten pressure group officials and so achieve more compliance than the groups may otherwise be inclined to grant. Moreover, by means of a cool response or a disinclination to communication with a particular group representative, civil servants may sow discontent and discord among the group's leadership or even encourage part of the leadership to act as a more compliant influence within the group. If a group resists such pressure, civil servants may try to dilute its public influence. The Canadian Drug Manufacturers' Association was organized upon the suggestion of a civil servant and acted as a rival to the long established Pharmaceutical Manufacturers Association of Canada.[11]

POLICY MAKING

Pressure groups gain recognition more easily and more rapidly if they are frequently invited to provide expertise to civil servants. The provision of this special knowledge also gives pressure groups an opportunity to participate in policy formulation. By supplying information used in the creation of policy, a pressure group contributes to policy making in a "passive" sense. The government may ask a pressure group for comments on the potential effects of a proposed policy in such areas as future investment, employment, costs and prices. The government may also make a general request for suggestions as to how it might assist a group to contribute to economic development or the general welfare. Evidence that government invites groups to participate in policy making as a matter of course and that the main arena of such participation is civil service-pressure group interaction is provided by this statement of a Canadian Cabinet Minister:

> In the process of preparing legislation and also in considering general policy changes, the government requires as much information as possible about the areas to be affected and the possible implications of any proposed changes. In addition to all the other reasons why associations or organizations should be in continuous contact with government, this particular need for information and consultation to influence government policy is probably the most important. . . .
> What is of the greatest value is for the minister to be apprised of the impact of the legislation from the particular viewpoint of the group concerned. Legislation must of necessity speak generally, but there may be special cases which persons in a particular industry or group might recognize more easily than can someone in government, surveying industry or the community generally.
> Equally, it is of greater value to have positive alternative suggestions with respect to carrying out the general purpose of the statute rather than negative dissent only. . . .

[11]An interview conducted by the author.

> ... if there has not been ... general public discussion preceding legislation, it is important that the particular interest be brought to the attention of departmental officials so that it may be taken into account in policy formulation and it will be useful for the minister also to have these viewpoints so that he may raise them with officials.[12]

The minister's comments relate to policy advice on legislation. Pressure groups are also asked for advice on policy making which occurs in the drafting and amendment of regulations. Frequent illustrations of this type of policy making may be gleaned from the pages of a daily newspaper. For example, it was recently reported that:

> Mr. Ross [President of the Independent Petroleum Association of Canada] expects the federal government will invite industry inspection of new regulations and tax changes, as promised, before making its new policies public and binding.[13]

The participation of the Canadian Medical Association and the Canadian Federation of Agriculture in policy making at various levels has already been recounted.[14]

The relationships between the Pharmaceutical Manufacturers Association of Canada (P.M.A.C.) and the Food and Drug Directorate (FDD) of the Department of National Health and Welfare are typical of the relationships between interest groups and civil servants. In an address to the 5th Annual General Meeting of the P.M.A.C. in 1964, Judy LaMarsh, then Minister of National Health and Welfare stated that:

> Dr. Morrell (Director, Food and Drug Directorate), who is well known to all of you, would I am sure be the first to acknowledge that while he has in his Directorate able and qualified scientists, his task would be immeasurably more difficult if he did not have access to the combined knowledge of the industry and receive its support....
>
> The role of a responsible trade association, in my view, is the advice and assistance it can offer to government in carrying out its responsibility to the Canadian people.... In Canada, in the many associations with which we deal, we have learned to look to them, not only for the benefit of experience and knowledge, but also for support in carrying out the task for government. Your Association is no exception to this and we have received from you in the past valuable help and assistance in the development and administration of our drug regulations which are so essential.
>
> Many of you will recall that in the formulation of our present Act, committees of your Association met with officers of the Department and worked out matters which are now reflected in the provisions of

---

[12]The Honourable Donald S. Macdonald, *loc. cit.*
[13]Thomas Kennedy, "IPAC president praises know-how, Arctic effort, despite handicaps," *The Globe and Mail,* Toronto, March 25, 1971, p. B12.
[14]Malcolm Taylor, "The Role of the Medical Profession in the Formulation and Execution of Public Policy," *The Canadian Journal of Economics and Political Science,* Vol. 26 (1960), pp. 108-127, and Dawson Helen Jones, "Relations between Farm Organizations and the Civil Service in Canada and Great Britain," *op. cit.*

the law itself.... [The minister goes on to discuss three different sets of regulations, the problems involved in them, and the views of the government and of the P.M.A.C.]. I appreciate that these regulations do not go as far as some of the members of the Association would have wished....
... having paid deserved tribute to your Association..., I am sure that Dr. Morrell does not think for a moment that his problems will automatically disappear and life in his Directorate will henceforth be Utopian ... it is in the recognition that there may be different points of view and a willingness to reconcile those differences in the public interest that the success of peaceful coexistence in this area lies....
... I think it is well acknowledged that any aspect of our control which is unnecessary or unreasonable would be open to review.... I mention this as an indication of the willingness of government to take account of the views of a trade association and, to the extent that public interest makes it possible, to reflect those views in its administration.[15]

The minister's speech clearly indicates that civil servants and pressure group officials are "well known" to each other, that the P.M.A.C. influences policy making at various levels of the policy process and that formal arrangements for participation have been established. It is important to note that the government retains the right to invite or to refuse to engage in policy consultations with pressure groups. When the FDD was changing regulations on the distribution of drug samples to physicians, it did not seek advice or give forewarning since it expected great difficulty in reaching agreement with the industry. When the FDD does want advice on a regulation, it simply publishes an intention of amendment or a proposed amendment in the Trade Information Letter which it regularly circulates to the pharmaceutical companies and the P.M.A.C. The P.M.A.C. reaches a decision based on consultation with the companies in the industry and conveys that decision to the FDD. If, for scientific, administrative or economic reasons, the P.M.A.C. deems an amendment unworkable, it requests a meeting with the FDD to present its case. Depending on the nature of the problem, if agreement cannot be reached, the FDD will either proceed without agreement or yield to the industry's argument. Decisions to yield, however, may be accompanied by a clear warning that theere will be additional work on the problem and further attempts to reach a solution satisfactory to the FDD. Most communication occurs in such irregular meetings or in *ad hoc* study committees.

Conflicts between government and pressure groups may range from major disputes over general policy to disagreements over the day-to-day administration of a regulation. If the conflict centres on a detail of a regulation or on some other minor point that can be settled in private, the administrator must carry the major part of the burden of argument,

---

[15]Text of address. Permission to quote given by Miss La Marsh.

persuasion and cajolery. When a conflict arises over general policy, however, the political role of the administrator again comes into play.

If the decline of civil service anonymity, inferred above by Miss LaMarsh, continues, civil servants will in the future carry a larger part of the political defence of government policy. Civil servants are already expected to be helpful to members of the public and to provide information as a matter of course or on request to news reporters, pressure group officials and Members of Parliament. The decline of civil service anonymity, accentuated by the smallness and intimacy of the political community in Ottawa, will expose the civil servant to a growing number of such requests. He must constantly make judgments on the propriety of a response since the guidelines setting limitations on his discretion are so general. In supplying this information, the civil servant acts as a *de facto* source of political support for the government. This activity may be characterized as a "passive" political role because it occurs only in response to specific requests.

Civil servants play a more "active" and deliberately political role when they are allowed or even required by their ministers to act as publicists or propagandists to prepare public opinion for a policy change. Under these conditions, civil servants must take the initiative in providing information, especially the "right" information, to the public. This task can be accomplished primarily through civil service testimony in open hearings of royal commissions, government task forces and parliamentary committees. It may also be necessary, however, to take some initiatives to achieve the desired interpretation of this material even by those who are pre-disposed to support the government. To perform this information service effectively, civil servants are obliged to adopt techniques commonly used by professional public relations agencies. For example, in the case of drug prices, the likely policy was opposed by an established, competent pressure group before the government publicly and fully committed itself to a proposal.[16] Civil servants and pressure group officials then acted as the major protagonists and used similar methods to win public support. While the drug prices problem was being investigated by a special committee of the House of Commons, both civil servants and P.M.A.C. officials sought out Members of Parliament to provide them with selected information and refutations of their opponents' arguments. Moreover, both civil servants and pressure group officials gave special briefings to selected journalists who then assisted by presenting one of the sides of the argument and criticizing the other. This was an especially important

[16]The following account is based on a variety of documentary sources and on interviews conducted by the author with reporters, Members of Parliament, civil servants in several departments, and officials of several pressure groups. Each assertion here could be supported by a number of independent sources.

technique not only because of the readership enjoyed by reporters who wrote the original stories, but also because of the tendency of the press to reuse information and interpretations *ad infinitum*. In addition, both civil servants and P.M.A.C. officials sought out potential allies, encouraged them to testify before a Commons' Special Committee and provided them with the necessary information and arguments for their briefs. Indeed, it is likely that of those persons and groups not directly representing the pharmaceutical industry, only a very few who testified did so on their own initiative. It is only an example of rare candour that the Canadian Medical Association referred in its brief to information provided by the P.M.A.C.[17]

Such "cooperative lobbying" is well recognized among students of pressure groups.[18] What is more instructive to note is that the civil servants also constructed an effective cooperative lobby to testify before the Special Committee. The lengthy brief presented on behalf of the Province of Alberta was prepared after an especially thorough and extensive briefing of its author by civil servants. The Canadian Drug Manufacturers' Association, the creation of which had been suggested by a civil servant, did not give as effective testimony as some civil servants had anticipated. The Consumers' Association of Canada brief presented two quite separate arguments. The first, on drug safety, differed from the civil servants' assumptions, while the second, on drug prices, was largely similar to that of the civil servants. This second argument was added to the Association's brief only after civil servants had examined the proposed brief and, through informal channels, had contacted one of the vice-presidents of the Association to show him the arguments upon which civil servants had based their decisions. The attempts of civil servants to build a larger cooperative lobby with the aid of the Canadian Labour Congress and the Canadian Federation of Agriculture may be inferred from their frequently expressed regrets that these groups did not choose to present briefs on drug prices.

This discussion of the recognition of pressure groups and their interaction with civil servants in the policy process describes only part of the whole relationship. One important area, not explored at length here, is the delegation of administrative responsibilities by bureaucrats to pressure group organizations. When a group establishes standards for membership or rules for the self-regulation of its trade or profession, when it answers questions from its membership about the applicability of the law to a particular case, or when it publishes explanations of government policy in its trade or professional journal, it is performing a

---

17House of Commons, *Special Committee on Drug Costs and Prices, Minutes of Proceedings and Evidence*, No. 6, June 28, 1966, p. 413.
18Donald R. Hall, *Cooperative Lobbying — the Power of Pressure*, University of Arizona Press, Tucson, 1969 and Malcolm Taylor, *op. cit.*, p. 118.

task that otherwise might be required of civil servants.[19] Yet another significant aspect of the bureaucracy-group system is the etiquette or "rules of the game" accepted by both parties. These "rules of the game" include agreement as to when confidential materials may be exchanged and under what conditions the parties may agree to disagree. In every discussion of such rules of the game the emphasis is on privacy and confidentiality — in short on secrecy.[20] While such secrecy is convenient to the pressure groups, the civil servants and the government, it is probably the government which most demands and enforces it. Civil servants may lose their anonymity but the government insists on retaining its secrets.[21] As suggested earlier, the interaction of civil servants and pressure groups occurs in a context of other relationships; not least among these is the relationship between the government and its civil servants. It is that relationship which probably most effectively governs the interaction of the public and group bureaucracies.

CASE REFERENCES

Canadian Cases in Public Administration
> Public Interest or Collective Interest?
> The Kroeker Case
> A Sensitive Position
> The Foot and Mouth Disease Epidemic, 1952

Case Program in Canadian Public Administration
> A Draft Memorandum to Cabinet
> The Toronto Airport

BIBLIOGRAPHY

Altshuler, Alan A., ed., *The Politics of the Federal Bureaucracy.* New York, Dodd, Mead & Company, 1968.

Appleby, Paul H., *Policy and Administration.* University Ala., University of Albama Press, 1949.

Aucoin, Peter, "Pressure Groups and Recent Changes in the Policy-Making Process." In A. Paul Pross, ed., *Pressure Group Behaviour in Canadian Politics.* Toronto, McGraw-Hill-Ryerson, 1975.

Balls, Herbert R., "Decision-Making: The Role of the Deputy Minister." *Canadian Public Administration,* Vol. 19, No. 3, Fall 1976, pp. 417-431.

---

[19]The delgation of administration to a pressure group is described in more detail in Malcolm Taylor, *op. cit.*

[20]F.C. Englemann and M.A. Schwartz, *op. cit.,* pp. 103-104. See also Allen Potter, *op. cit.,* pp. 230-236 and the complaint against secrecy in S.E. Finer, *Anonymous Empire,* 2nd ed., Paul Mall Press, London, 1966, pp. 136-145.

[21]For example, after describing her unhappiness about the tactics of the insurance industry lobby against the Canada Pension Plan, Miss LaMarsh suggested to Cabinet that she "would hereafter hear all representations but only when the press was present. Pearson and all my colleagues were appalled." Judy LaMarsh, *Memoirs of a Bird in a Gilded Cage,* McClelland and Stewart, Toronto, 1969, p. 88.

Bellamy, David J., "Policy-Making in the 1970's." *Canadian Public Administration*, Vol. 15, No. 3, Fall 1972, pp. 490-95.

Berry, Glyn R., "The Oil Lobby and the Energy Crisis." *Canadian Public Administration*, Vol. 17, No. 4, Winter 1974, pp. 600-35.

Bryden, Kenneth, *Old Age Pensions and Policy Making in Canada*. Montreal, McGill-Queen's University Press, 1974.

Cronin, Thomas E. and Greenberg, Sanford D., *The Presidential Advisory System*. New York, Harper & Row, 1969.

D'Aquino, Thomas, "The Prime Minister's Office: Catalyst or Cabal?" *Canadian Public Administration*, Vol. 17, No. 1, Spring 1974, pp. 55-79.

Dawson, Helen Jones, "Consumers Association of Canada." *Canadian Public Administration*, Vol. 6, No. 1, March 1963, pp. 92-118.

Dawson, Helen Jones, "Interest Group: The Canadian Federation of Agriculture." *Canadian Public Administration*, Vol. 3, No. 2, June 1960, pp. 134-49.

Dawson, Helen Jones, "National Pressure Groups and the Federal Government." In A. Paul Pross, ed., *Pressure Group Behaviour in Canadian Politics*. Toronto, McGraw-Hill-Ryerson, 1975.

Dawson, Helen Jones, "Relations between Farm Organizations and the Civil Service in Canada and Great Britain." *Canadian Public Administration*, Vol. 10, No. 4, December 1967, pp. 450-70.

Deutsch, John J., "Governments and their Advisors." *Canadian Public Administration*, Vol. 16, No. 1, Spring 1973, pp. 25-34.

Doern, G. Bruce, "Recent Changes in the Philosophy of Policy-Making in Canada." *Canadian Journal of Political Science*, Vol. 4, No. 2, June 1971, pp. 243-264.

Doern, G. Bruce, "The Development of Policy Organizations in the Executive Arena." In *Structures of Policy-Making in Canada*. G. Bruce Doern and Peter Aucoin, eds., Toronto, Macmillan, 1971, pp. 39-78.

Doern, G. Bruce, *Science and Politics in Canada*. Montreal, McGill-Queen's University Press, 1972.

Dror, Yehezkel, "Muddling Through—Science or Inertia." *Public Administration Review*, Vol. 24, September 1964.

Dror, Yehezkel, *Public Policy-Making Re-Examined*. San Francisco, Chandler Publishing Company, 1969.

Dvorin, Eugene P. and Simmons, Robert H., *From Amoral to Humane Bureaucracy*. San Francisco, Canfield Press, 1972.

Dye, Thomas R., *Understanding Public Policy*. Englewood Cliffs, N.J., Prentice-Hall, 1972.

Etzioni, Amitai, "Mixed Scanning: A Third Approach to Decision-Making." *Public Administration Review*, Vol. 27, No. 4, December 1967, pp. 385-92.

Friedrich, Carl J., "Political Decision-Making, Public Policy and Planning." *Canadian Public Administration*, Vol. 14, No. 1, Srping 1971, pp. 1-15.

Gélinas, André, *Les parlementaires et l'administration au Québec*. Québec, Les Presses de l'Université Laval, 1969.

Hawkins, Freda, *Canada and Immigration: Public Policy and Public Concern*. Montreal, McGill-Queen's University Press, 1972.

Hodgetts, J.E., "The Civil Service and Policy Formation." *Canadian Journal of Economics and Political Science*, Vol. 23, No. 4, November 1957, pp. 467-79.

Hodgson, J.S., "The Impact of Minority Government on the Senior Civil Servant." *Canadian Public Administration*, Vol. 19, No. 2, Summer 1976, pp. 227-37.

Hoffman, David, "Liaison Officers and Ombudsmen: Canadian MP's and their Relations with the Federal Bureaucracy and Executive." In Thomas A. Hockin, ed., *Apex of Power*. Toronto, Prentice-Hall, 1971, pp. 146-62.

Hughes, S.H.S., "The Public Official—Parliament, Public and the Press." *Canadian Public Administration*, Vol. 3, December 1960, pp. 289-98.

Johnson, A.W., "Management Theory and Cabinet Government." *Canadian Public Administration*, Vol. 14, No. 1, Spring 1971, pp. 73-81.

Jones, J.C.H., "The Bureaucracy and Public Policy: Canadian Merger Policy and the Combines Branch, 1960-1971." *Canadian Public Administration*, Vol. 18, No. 2, Summer 1975, pp. 269-96.

Kernaghan, Kenneth, "Politics, Policy and Public Servants: Political Neutrality Revisited." *Canadian Public Administration*, Vol. 19, No. 3, Fall 1976, pp. 432-456.

Kernaghan, W.D. Kenneth, "The Political Rights and Activities of Canadian Public Servants." In W.D.K. Kernaghan and A.M. Willms, eds., *Public Administration in Canada.* 2nd ed., Toronto, Methuen, 1971, pp. 382-390.

Krislov, Samuel and Musolf, Lloyd D., eds., *The Politics of Regulation.* Boston, Houghton Mifflin Company, 1964.

Lalonde, Marc, "The Changing Role of the Prime Minister's Office." *Canadian Public Administration,* Vol. 14, No. 4, Winter 1971, pp. 538-55.

Lindblom, Charles E., *The Policy-Making Process.* Englewood Cliffs, N.J., Prentice-Hall, 1968.

Lowi, Theodore J., "Four Systems of Policy, Politics and Choice." *Public Administration Review,* Vol. 32, No. 4, July-August 1972, pp. 298-310.

Mainzer, Lewis C., *Political Bureaucracy.* Glenview, Illinois, Scott, Foresman, 1973.

Mallory, J.R., "The Minister's Office Staff: An Unreformed Part of the Public Service." *Canadian Public Administration,* Vol. 10, No. 1, March 1967, pp. 25-34.

Mallory, J.R. and B.A. Smith, "The Legislative Role of Parliamentary Committees in Canada: The Case of the Joint Committee on the Public Service Bills." *Canadian Public Administration,* Vol. 15, No. 1, Spring 1972, pp. 1-23.

Pickersgill, J.W., "Bureaucrats and Politicians." *Canadian Public Administration,* Vol. 15, No. 3, Fall 1972, pp. 418-22.

Pitfield, Michael, "The Shape of Government in the 1980's: Techniques and Instruments for Policy Formulation at the Federal Level." *Canadian Public Administration,* Vol. 19, No. 1, Spring 1976, pp. 8-20.

Porter, J., "Higher Public Servants and the Bureaucratic Elite in Canada." *Canadian Journal of Economics and Political Sciences,* Vol. 24, No. 4, November 1958, pp. 483-501.

Porter, J., "The Bureaucratic Elite: A Reply to Professor Rowat." *Canadian Journal of Economics and Political Science,* Vol. 25, No. 2, May 1959, pp. 205-7.

Pross, A. Paul, "Input Versus Withinput: Pressure Group Demands and Administrative Survival." In A. Paul Pross, ed., *Pressure Group Behaviour in Canadian Politics.* Toronto, McGraw Hill-Ryerson, 1975.

Pross, A. Paul, ed., *Pressure Group Behaviour in Canadian Politics.* Toronto, McGraw Hill-Ryerson, 1975.

Richards, Peter, *Patronage in British Government.* Toronto, University of Toronto Press, 1963.

Ritchie, Ronald S., "Policy-Making for the Long Term: The Need to do More." *Canadian Public Administration,* Vol. 16, No. 1, Spring 1973, pp. 73-82.

Robertson, Gordon, "The Changing Role of the Privy Council Office." *Canadian Public Administration,* Vol. 14, No. 4, Winter 1971, pp. 487-508.

Rourke, Francis E., ed., *Bureaucratic Power in National Politics.* 2nd ed., Boston, Little, Brown, 1972.

Rourke, Francis, ed., *Bureaucracy, Politics and the Public Interest.* Boston, Little, Brown, 1973.

Rowan, Malcolm, "A Conceptual Framework for Government Policy-Making." *Canadian Public Administration,* Vol. 13, No. 3, Fall 1970, pp. 277-96.

Rowat, Donald C., "On John Porter's Bureaucratic Elite in Canada." *Canadian Journal of Economics and Political Science,* Vol. 25, No. 2, May 1959, pp. 205-7.

Santos, C.R., Public Administration as Politics." *Canadian Public Administration,* Vol. 12, No. 2, Summer 1969, pp. 213-223.

Sharp, Mitchell, "Decision-Making in the Federal Cabinet." *Canadian Public Administration,* Vol. 19, No. 1, Spring 1976, pp. 1-7.

Sharp, Mitchell, "The Bureaucratic Elite and Policy Formation." In W.D.K. Kernaghan, ed., *Bureaucracy in Government.* Toronto, Methuen Publications, 1969, pp. 82-87.

Szablowski, George, "The Optimal Policy-Making System: Implications for the Canadian Political Process." In Thomas A. Hockin, ed., *Apex of Power.* Toronto, Prentice-Hall, 1971, pp. 135-45.

Taylor, Malcolm G., "Quebec Medicare: Policy Formulation in Conflict and Crisis." *Canadian Public Administration,* Vol. 15, No. 2, Summer 1972, pp. 211-250.

Tullock, Gordon, *The Politics of Bureaucracy.* Washington, D.C., Public Affairs Press, 1965.

Vickers, George, *The Art of Judgement: A Theory of Policy-Making.* London, Chapman and Hall, 1965.

Wade, Larry L., *The Elements of Public Policy.* Columbus, Charles E. Merrill, 1972.

Woll, Peter, *Public Policy.* Cambridge, Winthrop Publishers, 1974.

Wronski, W., "The Public Servant and Protest Groups." *Canadian Public Administration,* Vol. 14, No. 1, Spring 1971, pp. 65-72.

CHAPTER 7
ADMINISTRATIVE RESPONSIBILITY

This chapter explores the variety of means by which the exercise of administrative power can be kept within appropriate bounds and responsible administrative conduct achieved.

In the first essay, Kenneth Kernaghan provides a basis for discussion of subsequent essays by explaining conventional and contemporary theories of administrative responsibility and setting forth an analytical framework linking administrative responsibility to the concept of the public interest. The next essay, by Eric Hehner, explains the existing and potential means by which the delegated powers of public servants may be controlled. Then, Richard Schultz examines the problem of reconciling the independence of regulatory agencies with political control over these agencies. For an analysis of this issue as it bears on Crown corporations, readers should consult D.P. Gracey's essay in Chapter 2.

In the next three essays, Donald Rowat and Henry Llambias contend that the federal government should appoint an Ombudsman to help guard against administrative abuse of discretionary powers; the development, virtues and limitations of citizen participation in government decision making are discussed; and the major arguments relating to administrative secrecy in Canada are reviewed. In the final essay, Kenneth Kernaghan analyzes the value of codes of ethics for Canadian public servants and the relation of these codes to administrative responsibility.

27
Responsible Public Bureaucracy*

Kenneth Kernaghan

Public concern about responsibility in government has been stimulated in recent years by events ranging from political espionage and scandal to conflicts of interest and disclosures of secret information. Discussion of these incidents has revealed that both the general public and students of government are in disagreement as to what constitutes irresponsible conduct, who should assume blame in particular cases, and what penalty should be paid.

The scope and complexity of government activities have become so great that it is often difficult to determine the actual — as opposed to the legal or constitutional — locus of responsibility for specific decisions. Political executives are held responsible for personal wrongdoing. They are not, however, expected to assume *personal* responsibility by way of resignation for the acts of administrative subordinates about which they could not reasonably be expected to have knowledge. Yet it is frequently impossible to assign individual responsibility to public servants for administrative transgressions because so many officials have contributed to the decision-making process. The allocation of responsibility in government has been complicated even further by the interposition of political appointees or temporary officials between political executives and permanent public servants.

While the involvement of political executives and their appointees in dramatic and well-publicized events has drawn much attention to the issue of *political* responsibility, the status of *administrative* responsibility has also become a matter of increasing concern. Although elected officials make the final decision on public policy questions, administrative officials have accumulated vast powers to influence policy decisions and to affect the individual and collective rights of the citizenry. As a consequence, the longstanding interest of scholars and practitioners in the preservation of administrative responsibility has become more acute. This concern is shared in varying degrees by all major actors in the political system — whether legislators, political executives, judges, interest group and mass media representatives, or members of the general public. In an effort by all these individuals to promote what they perceive to be responsible administrative conduct, the decisions of public servants are subject to an almost bewildering assortment of controls and influences.

The primary purpose of this essay is to examine the meaning and

*Reprinted and substantially abridged by permission from Kenneth Kernaghan, "Responsible Public Bureaucracy: A Rationale and a Framework for Analysis," *Canadian Public Administration*, vol. 16, no. 4 (Winter 1973), pp. 572-603.

nature of administrative responsibility in contemporary democratic society. First, the conventional theory of administrative responsibility and challenges to this theory are described. Then, a distinction between objective and subjective responsibility provides a focus on the *sources* of administrative responsibility and on the *values* of public servants. These two elements are examined separately by means of an institutional and a value framework for administrative decision-making and the theoretical links between the two frameworks are demonstrated with reference to the concept of administrative responsibility.

MEANINGS AND INTERPRETATIONS

The Conventional Theory

The traditional concepts of administrative responsibility may be explained by reference to the celebrated debate between Carl Friedrich and Herman Finer during the period 1935-1941.[1] Both Friedrich and Finer correctly identified the source of burgeoning administrative power as the rapid expansion of government's service and regulatory functions. They disagreed severely, however, on the most effective means of guarding against abuse of administrative discretion so as to maintain and promote responsible administrative conduct. Their disagreement was in large part an outgrowth of their differing conceptions of the adaptive capacity of political systems and the proper role of public officials. In the defence of administrative responsibility, Finer placed primary faith in controls and sanctions exercised over officials by the legislature, the judiciary, and the administrative hierarchy. In his insistence on the predominant importance of political responsibility, he claimed that 'the political and administrative history of all ages' had shown that 'sooner or later there is an abuse of power when external punitive controls are lacking.'[2] Friedrich relied more heavily on the propensity of public officials to be self-directing and self-regulating in their responsiveness to the dual standard of technical knowledge and popular sentiment. While he admitted the continuing need for political responsibility, he argued that a policy was irresponsible if it was adopted

> without proper regard to the existing sum of human knowledge concerning the technical issues involved — [or] without proper regard for existing preferences in the community, and more

[1] Carl J. Friedrich, 'Responsible Government Service under the American Constitution,' in *Problems of the American Public Service*, New York, McGraw Hill, 1935, pp. 3-74 and 'Public Policy and the Nature of Administrative Responsibility,' in Carl J. Friedrich and Edward S. Mason, eds., *Public Policy*, Cambridge, Harvard University Press, 1940, pp. 3-24. Herman Finer, 'Better Government Personnel,' *Political Science Quarterly* (1936), pp. 569 ff. and 'Administrative Responsibility in Democratic Government,' *Public Administration Review*, vol. 1, no. 4 (1941), pp. 335-50. The most comprehensive statements of the opposing positions are found in the 1940-1 exchange of articles.
[2] Finer, 'Administrative Responsibility in Democratic Government,' p. 337.

particularly its prevailing majority. Consequently, the responsible administrator is one who is responsive to these two dominant factors: technical knowledge and popular sentiment.[3]

Friedrich contended also that 'parliamentary responsibility is largely inoperative and certainly ineffectual'[4] and that 'the task of clear and consistent policy formation has passed — into the hands of administrators and is bound to continue to do so.'[5]

Finer admitted the difficulty, but stressed the necessity, of remedying the several deficiencies of political control over administrative officials. He believed that the means and modes of legislative control should be improved.[6] He argued further that officials should not determine their own course of action. Rather, the elected representatives of the people should 'determine the course of action of public servants to the most minute degree that is technically feasible.'[7] Finer described the sum of Friedrich's arguments as *moral* responsibility as opposed to Finer's own emphasis on *political* responsibility.

An understanding of the Friedrich-Finer debate is an essential foundation on which to construct subsequent discussion in that it raises several of the major issues of administrative responsibility still being debated by contemporary scholars, albeit in a vastly different social and political environment. These issues are of perennial, enduring concern and continue to challenge the capacity of scholars to appreciate their dimensions and the ingenuity of practitioners to adopt institutional and procedural innovations to meet their demands.

The strength of Finer's approach lay in his recognition of the continuing need for political controls over the bureaucracy. Its primary weakness lay in his failure to anticipate the inadequacy of these controls to ensure administrative responsibility in a period of ever-accelerating political and social change. The strength of Friedrich's argument rested on his awareness of the deficiency of solely political controls. Its major weakness lay in the difficulty of reconciling conflicts between the two criteria of technical knowledge and popular sentiment.

Assault on Conventional Theory

During the past three decades, the Friedrich and Finer approaches have been subject to a number of critiques, and alternative interpretations have been formulated.[8] Their approaches have remained the dominant

---

[3]Friedrich, 'Public Policy and the Nature of Administrative Responsibility,' p. 232.
[4]*Ibid.*, p. 10.
[5]*Ibid.*, p. 5.
[6]Finer, pp. 339-40.
[7]*Ibid.*, p. 336.
[8]See, for example, the excellent summary and critique of five major interpretations in Arch Dotson, 'Approaches to Administrative Responsibility, *Western Political Quarterly*, vol. X (September 1957), pp. 701-27.

contending ones, however, and most writers on administrative responsibility have referred to their debate with a view to supporting, attacking, or updating one or both sides of the argument. Until recently, scholarly debate has been carried on within the context of these two conventional interpretations. In the past few years, however, these traditional notions of administrative responsibility have come under severe attack.

Michael Harmon, for example, has argued that both Finer and Friedrich, despite their differences, take a negative view of the nature of man and of administrative man in particular because they agree that 'without the checks provided by either the law or the processes of professional socialization, the resultant behaviour of administrators would be both selfish and capricious.'[9] Harmon looks to the existentialist's notion of self-development and self-actualization as a basis for a new theory of administrative responsibility. Officials are expected to become much more actively engaged in the initiation and promotion of policy. Harmon fails, however, to reconcile this increased participation with the conventional idea that administrators' decisions should be guided by the values and goals of elected politicians within the constraints of the law and the administrative hierarchy.[10]

Theodore Lowi's approach to administrative responsibility[11] is antithetical to Harmon's redefinition. Among what Lowi describes as 'proposals for radical reform' in the United States are suggestions which are reminiscent of the position articulated by Finer in the early 1940s. Lowi recommends that the Supreme Court declare 'invalid and unconstitutional any delegation of power to an administrative agency that is not accompanied by clear standards of implementation.'[12] This call to the legislature to specify the course of action of public servants in more precise terms is complemented by a plea for 'early and frequent administrative rule making.'[13] Rather than relying primarily on case-by-case adjudication under a statute delegating broad powers in vague language, bureaucrats should formulate rules which provide standards for the adjudication of cases under that statute.

The views and proposals of Lowi and Harmon offer a different but related version of the Finer-Friedrich debate.

Accompanying such recent redefinitions of administrative responsibility is the argument that the traditional focus on devising and altering

---

[9]Michael M. Harmon, 'Normative Theory and Public Administration: Some Suggestions for a Redefinition of Administrative Responsibility,' in Marini, ed., *Toward a New Public Administration*, p. 173.
[10]See John Paynter, 'Comment: On a Redefinition of Administrative Responsibility,' *ibid.*, p. 187.
[11]Theodore J. Lowi, *The End of Liberalism*, New York, North, 1969.
[12]*Ibid.*, p. 298.
[13]*Ibid.*, p. 299.

ways to promote responsible administrative behaviour has left us in a perilous position. We lack imaginative and innovative proposals to cope with the issue of administrative responsibility in an era of uncertainty and unprecedented rapid change. The complex and technological society to which we have so long alluded in a vaguely apprehensive and fearful manner is upon us with a vengeance.[14] The present and the anticipated effects of technical change on the structures and procedures of democratic government require that public administrative institutions keep the way open for rapid and perhaps radical reform.

OBJECTIVE AND SUBJECTIVE RESPONSIBILITY

In the face of recent attacks and new perspectives on conventional notions and practices of administrative responsibility, it is appropriate to seek a broader, more inclusive classification than the Friedrich-Finer categories. The two meanings of administrative responsibility set forth by Frederick Mosher meet this requirement admirably.[15] He asserts that *objective* responsibility 'connotes the responsibility of a person or an organization *to* someone else, outside of self, *for* some thing or some kind of performance. It is closely akin to *accountability* or *answerability*. If one fails to carry out legitimate directives, he is judged *irresponsible*, and may be subjected to penalties.'[16] *Subjective* or *psychological* responsibility, by way of contrast, focuses 'not upon to whom and for what one *is* responsible (according to law and the organization chart) but to whom and for what one *feels* responsible and *behaves* responsibly. This meaning is more nearly synonymous with identification, loyalty and conscience than it is with accountability and answerability.'[17]

In addition to postulating a valuable theoretical distinction between the broad concepts of objective responsibility and subjective responsibility, Mosher's classification serves two other important purposes. First, it draws attention to the *sources* from which one derives one's sense of responsibility, that is, the individuals to whom one *is* or *feels* responsible. The sources of administrative responsibility on which there is a substantial measure of agreement in scholarly writings include political

---

[14]See the following articles in Waldo, ed., *Public Administration in a Time of Turbulence* — Edward I. Friedland, 'Turbulence and Technology: Public Administration and the Role of Information-Processing Technology,' pp. 134-50; Orion White, JR., 'Organization and Administration for New Technological and Social Imperatives,' pp. 151-68; and Allen Schick, 'Toward the Cybernetic State,' pp. 214-33. See also Hubert Marshall, 'Administrative Responsibility and the New Science of Management Decision,' in C.S. Wallia (ed.), *Toward Century 21: Technology, Society and Human Values*, New York, Basic Books, 1970, pp. 257-68.
[15]Frederick C. Mosher, *Democracy and the Public Service*, New York, Oxford University Press, 1968, pp. 7-10.
[16]*Ibid.*, p. 7.
[17]*Ibid.*, p. 8.

executives, legislators, judges, administrative superiors, members of the general public, and interest group and mass media representatives. Secondly, by distinguishing between such values as accountability and answerability on the one hand and identification, loyalty, and conscience on the other, Mosher points to the significance for administrative responsibility of the official's value system.

Subsequent discussion will focus on these two central and related elements of administrative responsibility: (1) the institutional framework within which interaction between bureaucrats and other policy actors takes place, and (2) the value framework within which administrative decisions are made. Then, the inextricable links between these two frameworks will be explained with particular reference to the issue of administrative responsibility.

THE INSTITUTIONAL FRAMEWORK OF ADMINISTRATIVE DECISION-MAKING

The sources of administrative responsibility referred to above constitute the major policy actors who may exercise *power* over bureaucrats with a view to affecting the nature and content of administrative decisions. *Power* is defined here as 'the capacity to secure the dominance of one's values or goals.'[18] In the analysis to follow, power is viewed as the sum of *control* and *influence*. *Control* refers to that form of power in which A has authority to direct or command B to do something. *Influence* is a more general and pervasive form of power than control. According to Carl Friedrich, influence 'usually exists when the behaviour of B is molded by and conforms to the behaviour of A, but without the issuance of a command.'[19] Thus, when A orders or directs B to behave in a certain fashion, A exercises control over B. When B conforms to A's desires on the grounds of suggestion, persuasion, emulation, or anticipation, A exercises influence over B.

To exercise control, A must possess *authority* in the sense of having access to the inducements, rewards, and sanctions necessary to back up his commands. The possession of authority also gives A a formal, legal, or hierarchical status that enables A to exercise influence as well as control. The phenomenon which accounts in large part for this situation is 'the rule of anticipated reactions.'[20] Application of this general rule to the public bureaucracy is manifest in the innumerable instances in which an

---

[18]John M. Pfiffner and Frank P. Sherwood, *Administrative Organization,* Englewood Cliffs, N.J., Prentice-Hall, 1960, p. 77. I acknowledge the existence of many definitions of power which differ both from one another and from the definition used in this essay.
[19]Carl J. Friedrich, *Man and His Government,* New York, McGraw Hill, 1963, p. 200.
[20]The best single treatment of this concept may be found in Friedrich, *Man and His Government,* ch. 11.

administrative official 'anticipates the reactions' of those who have power to reward or constrain him. The official thus tends to act in a fashion that would be applauded — or at least approved — by those whose favour he seeks. Aside from the influence of anticipated reactions, those individuals or institutions with formally designated power may exercise that power not in the way of direction or supervision but by suggestion, insinuation, or intimation — that is, as an influence rather than a control.[21] It is important to keep in mind, therefore, that those individuals ordinarily perceived as exercising control (e.g., political executives) can also exercise influence by affecting a bureaucrat's decisions in an informal, unofficial — even in an unintentional — way. What distinguishes individuals with the capacity to exercise either control or influence from those possessing only influence is that the former have at their disposal sanctions and inducements *formalized by law and the organization chart.*

Influence then can be used to shape an official's conduct by those who do not have legally or formally sanctioned power to command and supervise. For example, interest group or mass media representatives may seek official favours by offering inducements (e.g., gifts) or imposing penalties (e.g., ostracism), but they have no legal or formal capacity to compel compliance to their wishes. This does not mean, however, that such influence may not be as effective as control or, in some instances, even more effective. An official may well grant special favours to interest group or mass media representatives despite formal directions to the contrary from his administrative superior. Thus, influence may be exercised by those without authority through a variety of means including persuasion, friendship, knowledge, and experience.

Clearly, the bureaucrat is subject to an enormous variety of controls and influences both from within and from outside the public service. It is important to note, however, that power relations between bureaucrats and other policy participants flow in two directions. Bureaucrats are not defenceless against pressures brought to bear on them. An examination of the real or potential impact of controls and influences over the bureaucracy must take account of the potent resources which bureaucrats may use to resist pressure and to exert power over others. Among the resources which bureaucrats possess to control and/or influence other policy actors are expertise, experience, budgetary allocations, confidential information, and discretionary powers to develop and implement policies and programs. Such resources may be utilized in various ways. For example, bureaucrats may prevail over political superiors by virtue of special knowledge of a policy area; they may feed selected bits of information to mass media representatives to enhance

---

[21]Some organization theorists distinguish between 'formal' and 'informal' controls. In the context of our definition of control and influence and throughout this essay, all controls are of a *formal* nature; informal controls are subsumed under the broad definition of influences.

support for a certain program; or they may disarm external critics by organizing them into advisory bodies.

There is clearly an enormous array of variables involved in interaction among bureaucrats and between bureaucrats and other participants in the political-administrative system. Yet even a comprehensive identification of controls and influences would be insufficient to explain the decisional behaviour of *the individual* bureaucrat. The various policy participants, whether they exercise power from within or from outside the public service, are forces *external to the individual*. The controls and influences by which a single bureaucrat is affected and the resources he employs to counter these forces depend to a very large extent on his *values*. Therefore, we now turn our attention from the multitude of controls and influences affecting administrative decision-making in general to the means by which the value system of the individual official is moulded.

THE VALUE FRAMEWORK OF ADMINISTRATIVE DECISION-MAKING

A value is defined here as 'an enduring belief that a particular mode of conduct or that a particular end-state of existence is personally and socially preferable to alternative modes of conduct or end-states of existence.'[22] Values 'are organized into value systems, which are hierarchical rank orderings of importance.'[23] An *administrative* value then is an enduring belief that, in administrative decision-making, a particular mode of conduct or a particular end-state of existence is personally or socially preferable to alternative modes of conduct or end-states of existence. The bureaucrat develops a value framework or value system in which various administrative values are ranked, admittedly very roughly, even unconsciously, in order of importance.

The bureaucrat seeking guidance as to the appropriate content of his administrative value system will find much advice, but little solace, in scholarly writings. Various authors single out different values for the 'ideal' or the 'responsible' administrator. There is substantial overlapping in the emphasis of different writers, however. Charles Gilbert, in his analysis of administrative responsibility in the United States, has distilled from the scholarly literature the values most frequently associated with the responsible administrator.[24] These administrative values are responsiveness, flexibility, consistency, stability, leadership, probity, candour, competence, efficacy, prudence, due process, and accountability.

---

[22]Milton Rokeach, 'The Role of Values in Public Opinion Research,' *Public Opinion Quarterly*, vol. XXXII (Winter 1968), p. 550.
[23]*Ibid.*, p. 551.
[24]Charles Gilbert, 'The Framework of Administrative Responsibility,' *The Journal of Politics*, vol. XXI (August 1959), pp. 373-407.

Situational Considerations

Since the list of values isolated by Gilbert is extrapolated largely from American literature, it is culture-bound in its application. The primary values affecting an official's decision tend to differ from one cultural setting and political system to another. The dominant administrative values of a society, which will be reflected in administrative performance, depend on the complex of political, economic, and social conditions extant in that society. Moreover, the relative importance of these values alters with changes in these conditions. For example, the administrative values of responsiveness and flexibility may become predominant during a period when the general public or the government feels that the interests of certain disadvantaged minority groups must be better represented and their needs and demands better understood and satisfied. During such a period, considerations of consistency and stability may be relegated to a secondary order of importance.

Factual Considerations

If an administrative issue is significant enough to require the formal or conscious preparation of alternative solutions and the evaluation of their possible consequences, each alternative will be an amalgam of what Herbert Simon refers to as the value and factual elements in any decision.[25] The mix of fact and value will, of course, vary greatly from one decision-making circumstance to another. Many decisions of a very routine and repetitive nature (programmed decisions) require little, if any, conscious value selection. Other decisions of a unique or novel nature (non-programmed decisions) may contain a substantial mix of value and factual elements. As Herbert Simon contends:

> Decisions are something more than factual propositions. To be sure, they are descriptive of a future state of affairs, and this description can be true or false in a strictly empirical sense; but they possess, in addition, an imperative quality — they select one future state of affairs in preference to another and direct behaviour toward the chosen alternative. In short, they have an *ethical* as well as a factual content.[26]

The Power of the Bureaucrat

Power was defined earlier as 'the capacity to secure the dominance of one's values or goals.' In this sense, administrative officials possess vast power by virtue of their role in policy development and execution. If the machinery of government could be so arranged that bureaucrats simply

---

[25]Herbert A. Simon, *Administrative Behavior*, New York, The Free Press, 1957, 2nd ed., pp. 45-60.
[26]*Ibid.*, p. 46.

implemented laws spelled out in very specific terms by the legislature, enforced judicial decisions interpreting these laws, and administered policies and programs under the close supervision of political executives and their senior administrative officials, few value problems would exist for most bureaucrats. The realm of policy and political considerations would belong to elected representatives and would be sharply delineated from the administrative sphere. The value issues in any situation would be worked out by others so that the bureaucrat's primary concern would be responsiveness to values emerging from the legislative, judicial, and senior executive levels of government.

The historical record shows that an era of such bureaucratic innocence has never existed in modern democratic states. There is in reality a considerable area of discretion where the official's value preferences determine the nature of the decision made. Given the complexity of contemporary government and the interweaving of political, policy and administrative issues, it is unrealistic to assume that any combination of controls and influences could so diminish the scope of administrative judgment that no room would remain for the injection of personal values into public policy formation and implementation.

Writers on bureaucratic power have long recognized the enormous influence of bureaucrats in the initiation and development of new policies. Senior officials in particular make significant discretionary decisions as to the policy alternatives to be set before their political masters. Moreover, in the formulation and presentation of policy proposals, these officials are expected to be attuned to the *political* as well as the administrative and technical implications of their recommendations.

Discussions of the policy role of the bureaucracy must also take account of the impressive discretionary powers which officials wield in the implementation of both new and on-going policies and programs.

Sources of the Bureaucrat's Values

A focus on the bureaucrat's values is especially important in that decisional behaviour may be explained or interpreted in terms of the interplay (1) among the individual bureaucrat's values, and (2) between the bureaucrat's values and the values of those with whom he interacts. Before an individual joins the public service, his general value system, as well as his particular attitudes and orientations toward the public service, are moulded by powerful and enduring forces. This is accomplished through the process of socialization, i.e., 'an individual's learning from others in his environment the social patterns and values of his culture.'[27] The socializing 'agencies' involved in this process include family, peer

---

[27]Kenneth P. Langton, *Political Socialization*, New York, Oxford University Press, 1969, p. 3.

groups, schools, prior employment, and adult organizations. As a result of this socialization experience, an individual does not take up government employment with a *tabula rasa* so far as values relevant to bureaucratic decision-making are concerned. In varying degrees, the several socializing agencies continue to affect the bureaucrat's values during his public service career.

The focus of our analysis is the sources of values impinging on the individual as a consequence of his employment as a bureaucrat and of his occupancy of a particular bureaucratic position. The individual's personal values and his perceptions of the public service are altered by a process of *organizational socialization* which begins the very day he is recruited for a public service position. *Organizational socialization* refers to the process (*a*) through which the individual learns the expectations attached to the position he occupies in the organization, and (*b*) through which he selectively internalizes as values certain of the expectations of those with whom he interacts.

The bureaucrat is located at the focal position or core of a network of counter positions occupied by such other policy actors as political executives, legislators, and administrative superiors. Each policy actor manifests certain expectations as to how the bureaucrat should behave in his official position. These expectations, in the form of commands, directions, guidelines, standards, and suggestions, express the values of the policy actor, and the bureaucrat is expected to reflect these values in his decisions.

The Crucial Link

It is precisely at this juncture that the theoretical link between the value framework of administrative decision-making and the institutional framework described earlier may be demonstrated. The bureaucrat is expected to be responsive to the values of the various policy participants as these values are expressed through the exercise of specific controls and influences.

Since various policy participants pursue different, and sometimes mutually exclusive, ends in their relations with bureaucrats, the official occupying a certain position will be the object of conflicting expectations and pressures as to his behaviour. The purpose of each participant's interaction with the bureaucrat will usually be the dominance of the participant's particular values and goals over those of both the bureaucrat and other participants. The problem for the bureaucrat is clearly posed — how can he be responsive to the multiplicity of values expressed?

The linkages between the institutional and the value frameworks help to explain the means by which the number and assortment of variables impinging on the bureaucrat may be reduced to more manageable proportions.

Over a considerable period of time and in a variety of bureaucratic positions, an official might conceivably interact with virtually the whole range of policy participants and be subjected to a wide variety of controls and influences. As the incumbent of a specific position over a shorter period, he will, however, only interact with and be subjected to the power resources of a limited number of actors. The range of these actors will be confined to those with a stake in the activities of the occupant of a particular position or in the issue at hand. For example, a deputy minister of Consumer and Corporate Affairs is the object of much greater pressure from outside the public service (e.g., interest group and mass media representatives) than a deputy minister of Supply and Services. More important, during the process of organizational socialization, the bureaucrat learns what kinds of decisional behaviour will bring reward or punishment from various policy actors and what values they are seeking to realize. The bureaucrat's value system is usually most directly moulded by the values of those hierarchical associates on whom he relies most heavily for approval and reward, that is, his political and administrative superiors and his peers and subordinates. He is also expected, of course, to be responsive to the values of such other policy actors as legislators, interest group representatives, and the general public. Faced with complementary, conflicting, and contradictory expectations issuing from various sources, the bureaucrat inculcates certain of the values manifested by those with whom he interacts.

Value Conflict

Despite all efforts to minimize the number of variables involved in any given decision-making situation, a condition of value conflict is a frequent one, especially for senior bureaucrats. Herbert Simon contends that

> at the lower levels of the hierarchy, the frame of reference within which decision is to take place is largely given. The factors to be evaluated have already been enumerated, and all that remains is to determine their values under the given circumstances. At the higher levels of the hierarchy, the task is an artistic and inventive one. New values must be sought out and weighed; the possibilities of new administrative structures evaluated. The very framework of reference within which decision is to take place must be constructed.[28]

The major categories of value conflicts which the bureaucrat encounters are those. (1) between personal values and administrative values; (2) between and among administrative values; and (3) between administrative values and the values of other policy participants. The resolution of value conflicts involving personal and administrative values

---

[28]Simon, *Administrative Behavior*, p. 217.

(e.g., ambition *v.* accountability or avarice *v.* integrity) depends on the personality and character of the particular bureaucrat. There is no escape from the reality that 'most officials are significantly motivated by self-interest when their social function is to serve the public interest.'[29] From among Anthony Downs's typology of 'purely self-interested officials' (i.e., climbers and conservers) and of 'mixed-motive officials' (i.e., zealots, advocates, and statesmen), we may for analytical purposes utilize the 'statesmen' type. Statesmen are 'motivated by loyalty to society as a whole and a desire to obtain the power necessary to have a significant influence upon national policies and actions. They are altruistic to a high degree because their loyalty is to the "general welfare" as they see it.'[30]

Although the statesman — the least self-seeking and most public-oriented of bureaucrats — has comparatively little difficulty in reconciling personal and administrative values, he is occasionally obliged to choose between and among administrative values he holds equally dear (e.g., accountability *v.* integrity or accountability and consistency *v.* responsiveness and efficacy). Similarly, the bureaucrat's values come into conflict with the values expressed by those with whom he interacts (e.g., accountability *v.* responsiveness to an interest group's request or accountability *v.* competence expected by a professional colleague).

Depending on the factual and contextual elements of any decision-making situation and on the character of the bureaucrat, it is evident that he may conceivably pass through one, two, or all three stages of value conflict. In practice, of course, these stages are not chronological; rather they overlap and interact with one another. Thus, a choice between the administrative values of accountability and responsiveness is likely to be made in conjunction with and to be affected by controls and influences reflecting the values of other policy actors.

Value Conflict Resolution

The following analysis is based on the premise that the weight of evidence supports the existence of a concept of *the public interest* which has both theoretical and practical utility. The numerous, often brilliant, debates on the issue will not be reviewed here.[31] It is clear, however, that no interpretation of the public interest has won universal acclaim as

---

[29]Anthony Downs, *Inside Bureaucracy*, Boston, Little Brown, 1967, p. 87.
[30]*Ibid.*, p. 88.
[31]See especially Pendleton Herring, *Public Administration and the Public Interest*, New York, McGraw Hill, 1936; Frank Sorauf, 'The Public Interest Reconsidered,' *Journal of Politics*, vol. XIX (November 1957), pp. 616-39; Glendon Schubert, *The Public Interest: A Critique of a Political Concept*, Glencoe, The Free Press, 1960; Carl J. Friedrich (ed.), *Nomos V: The Public Interest*, New York, Atherton Press, 1962; Herbert J. SToring, 'The Crucial Link: Public Administration, Responsibility and the Public Interest,' *Public Administration Review*, vol. 24 (March 1964), pp. 39-46; and Richard E. Flathman, *The Public Interest*, New York, Wiley, 1966.

relevant and appropriate in all contexts. One interpretation of the public interests—as the best possible accommodation of conflicting particular interest—provides an essential element of specificity. This interpretation requires some refinement, but offers a promising base for the formulation of a definition of the public interest.

The adjustment of the claims of special and private interests connotes a power struggle among competing groups, each possessing approximately equal access to the decision-maker and devoting roughly equivalent resources to the struggle. In reality, both access and resources in money, organization, supporters, and research capacity are uneven among various groups. Moreover, the interests of some sectors of the population may not be represented because these sectors are underprivileged, uneducated, uninformed, inarticulate, unorganized, or simply uninterested. Even if the whole range of relevant special interests is taken into account, our definition is still incomplete. Public interest theorists commonly assert that the public interest is not the mere sum of special interests, no matter how evenly and equitably these interests are represented.

The critical contribution to the determination of the public interest comes from the decision-maker. But the avenue to some decisions runs through a myriad of conflicting and complementary values. Among the obstacles along the road is the temptation to succumb to personal or particularistic interests when a decision in the broader interest of the general public or of substantial sectors of the general public is required. The fact that the bureaucrat, whether consciously or unconsciously, follows a multi-stage route of value conflict resolution does not guarantee the 'best' decision at the end of his journey. Nor does it ensure that the occasional public servant, like other human beings, will not stray from the well-trodden path into the mire of self-interest.

Except in situations where the bureaucrat has been given complete discretionary authority, he may be able to shift the burden of choice among contending values to his hierarchical superior. *Hierarchy* in administration is a prime safeguard to administrative responsibility in that it forces 'important decisions to higher levels of determination or at least higher levels of review where perspectives are necessarily broader, less technical and expert, more political.'[32] At the highest policy-making levels of government, it may be argued that in the final analysis the determination of the public interest is the task of the elected representative. Constitutional and political imperatives do not, however, permit the official to escape the responsibility of providing his political master with the best possible advice. Moreover, if only in the cause of personal survival, the official cannot evade the responsibility of pointing

---

[32]Mosher, *Democracy and the Public Service*, p. 212.

out the political, economic, and social costs and benefits of selecting one course of action over another.

The voluminous writings on the public interest demonstrate the difficulty of establishing specific and immutable criteria for its determination in any given situation. The public interest may fruitfully be viewed as a dynamic concept. Its content changes from one situation to another and depends in large part on the values of both the decision-maker and the interests whose claims are considered.

No one expects the bureaucrat to proceed through a detailed checklist of the great variety of pressures in his decision-making environment. Few will deny, however, the necessity for the official to step back on occasion to examine the value premises on which he has been acting. 'In general,' the public interest 'is a spur to conscience and to deliberation.'[33]

An important distinction may be made between a *passive* as opposed to an *active* pursuit of the public interest. The official who considers the claims only of *organized* special interests and whose range of values is narrow and inflexible is passive in the search for the public interest. By way of contrast, the official who seeks the views of *all relevant interests* and whose value framework is comparatively broad and flexible is in active pursuit of the public interest. No judgment is made here as to the desirability of one orientation over the other. Each has its virtues and drawbacks at various levels of the organizational pyramid.

ADMINISTRATIVE RESPONSIBILITY AND THE PUBLIC INTEREST

The passive and active orientations toward the public interest may be linked with our earlier distinction between objective and subjective (psychological) responsibility. In a brief and admittedly oversimplified fashion the main characteristics of two hypothetically extreme types of bureaucrat — the objectively responsible and the subjectively responsible official — are suggested here.

The objectively responsible bureaucrat feels responsible primarily to the legal or formal locus of authority and takes a passive approach to the determination of the public interest. His most prominent characteristic and value is accountability to those who have the power to promote, displace, or replace him. The controls and influences which he internalizes in the form of administrative values are those expressed by his hierarchical superiors. In making and recommending decisions, he anticipates and reflects the desires of his superiors. It is they who have

---

[33]J. Roland, Pennock, 'The One and the Many: A Note on the Concept of the Public Interest,' in Friedrich (ed.), *Nomos V: The Public Interest*, p. 182.

legitimate authority and who may most easily threaten or impose penalties to ensure compliance. This type of bureaucrat does not actively seek the views of policy actors other than those of his superiors unless he is required or directed to do so. For example, he consults certain interests about impending regulations affecting their activities only if such consultation is required by law or expected by his superiors. His foremost administrative values include answerability and efficiency. He does not take initiatives or risks which may get him or his superiors into trouble. He prefers, if possible, that others, notably his political and administrative superiors, resolve any value dilemmas and determine the content of the public interest for him.

The objectively responsible bureaucrat is ultimately responsible to the general public through the administrative hierarchy, the political executive, and the legislature. His behaviour is based on the possibility and the desirability of separating policy and administration — even at the senior levels of the public service. In Finer's terminology, he is therefore, 'politically', responsible.

The subjectively responsible bureaucrat is a striking contrast. He feels responsible to a broad range of policy participants and is active in the pursuit of the public interest. His most outstanding characteristic and value is commitment to what he perceives to be the goals of his department or program. Since he views the expectations of a variety of policy actors as legitimate, the sources of his administrative values are numerous and diverse. Tension and conflict between the subjectively responsible official and his superiors are frequent, but he is minimally concerned by the threat of negative sanctions. He seeks the views of interests affected by his decisions and recommendations in the absence of, and even in violation of, any legal or formal obligation to do so. His primary administrative values include responsiveness, effectiveness, and flexibility. He is innovative, takes risks, and bends the rules to achieve his objectives. He urges his superiors to follow certain courses of action and is prepared to resolve by himself the value dilemmas he encounters in his search for the public interest.

The subjectively responsible bureaucrat rejects the possibility and desirability of separating policy and administration — especially at the senior echelons of the bureaucracy. To use Finer's language again, this type of official is 'morally' responsible in that he looks to his own conscience rather than to 'external punitive controls' for guidance.

Neither the purely objective nor the purely subjective type is appropriate as a model of the responsible bureaucrat. Some characteristics of both types produce conduct which scholars and public officials generally view as undesirable. Undue emphasis on certain elements of objective responsibility may lead to behaviour which is inflexible, unimaginative, unresponsive, or ineffective. At the other extreme, too great emphasis on particular aspects of subjective responsibility may bring equally undesirable results in the way of behaviour which is unaccountable, inconsistent, or unpredictable.

If the public service 'writ large' is composed predominantly of either objectively or subjectively responsible officials, it will tend to manifest the same objectionable features. The 'ideal' situation, then, is a public service in which each official strikes that balance between the objective and subjective elements of responsibility which is appropriate to his level in the hierarchy and to the requirements of his particular position. The determination of the 'appropriate' balance for all positions would, however, be a Herculean and impracticable task. In every instance, the determination would involve a personal judgment as to the optimum blend of objective and subjective values and orientations.

CONCLUSIONS

The issue of administrative responsibility cannot be separated from that of administrative power. Indeed, the essence of the debates between Friedrich and Finer and between their intellectual descendants is the most effective means of constraining administrative power in democratic states. The literature abounds with proposals for new and improved institutional and procedural means (e.g., an ombudsman, strengthened legislative committes) by which administrative power and administrative responsibility may be reconciled. The aim of such proposals is to attain a larger measure of objective responsibility by holding bureaucrats more accountable for their decisions.

On the basis of the preceding analysis, however, it may be argued that policy actors should devote more attention to bringing about an environment in which subjective responsibility may be fostered. Since external policy actors will continue to rely on institutional and procedural devices to control and influence administrative conduct, the task of encouraging subjective responsibility falls on senior officials within the public service itself. Senior administrators have traditionally endeavoured to instill in their subordinates a commitment to organizational and program goals through their personal influence and example. The scale and complexity of the public service are now so great, however, that other means to the same end must be utilized. Evidence now available in Canada, for example, suggests that to stimulate administrative responsibility — indeed, to avoid disruptive dissent — senior officials must break through the hardrock strata of the administrative pyramid. They must permit and encourage participation in the policy process by those highly educated, articulate, and restless officials in the middle to upper ranks of the hierarchy.

Despite the multitude of external controls and influences over the bureaucracy, the preservation and encouragement of responsible administrative conduct requires vigorous and sustained effort by the public servants themselves. At a time when the pace of administrative reform is already hectic and unsettling,[34] some officials may reasonably be expected to resist further change — even if it is justified on grounds of administrative responsibility. Nevertheless, there is cause for optimism both in present reform efforts in the public service and in J. E. Hodgett's contention that 'among our major political institutions the public service has given more attention to and shown the greatest willingness to experiment with adaptations in form and procedure.'[35]

Changes not only in structures and procedures, however, but also in values and modes of thought are required. By striving to meet the challenge, the public service can ensure that the power of the bureaucrat will be more evenly matched by his sense of responsibility — to his superiors, to the public, and to his own conscience.

28
Growth of Discretions—
Decline of Accountability*

Eric Hehner

The functions of the public service have changed in a fundamental way which requires re-appraisal of the positions of Parliament and of the courts of law. This change has happened so quietly that its extent, its basic nature, and its significance to our system of government have not yet been widely recognized. The administrator has gained vastly wider powers and the legislature is losing both knowledge of, and effective control over, the way in which the powers it has conferred are exercised. This has created a new relationship between the individual and the state, and over a period of many years has progressively contributed to the sterilization of Parliament.

Parliament, the public service, and the courts of law were designed

[34]H.L. Laframboise, 'Administrative Reform in the Federal Public Service: Signs of a Saturation Psychosis,' *Canadian Public Administration,* vol. XIV, no. 3 (Fall 1971), pp. 303-25 and Walter Baker, 'Administrative Reform in the Federal Public Service: The First Faltering Steps,' *Canadian Public Administration,* vol. XVI, no. 3 (Fall 1973), pp. 381-98.

[35]J.E. Hodgetts, *The Canadian Public Service: A Physiology of Government, 1867-1970,* Toronto, University of Toronto Press, 1973, p. 353.

*Eric Hehner, "Growth of Discretions — Decline of Accountability" (updated from an unpublished address delivered to the Ottawa Regional Group of the Institute of Public Administration of Canada on November 24, 1965). Mr. Hehner is Chairman of the Board, Corporation House Limited, Ottawa. The editor extends appreciation to Mr. Hehner for his work in updating this selection.

for limited functions of government. The ideal of legislation was to be definitive and precise, and to leave little to the imagination or to opinion. Our forefathers undoubtedly fell far short of this ideal, but the ideal was there. The public service performed administrative and service functions. The courts were adjudicators of facts and defenders of injured individuals from other individuals or from the state. Judicial decisions were made under a rule of law with the rules fixed beforehand and equally applicable to all.

Government today is expected to offer direction and to execute policies of a positive nature—to be an active participant in economic and social affairs, not just a writer of rules and an umpire. Had our economic and social structures and the technology on which they in part rest been relatively static, a rule of law as known in the past might have provided an adequate mechanism to enable government to play an increased role. However, the expansion of the scale of economic processes has been great enough to produce differences of nature, not just of size. It has made necessary the use of discretions by governmental authority, which cannot be exercised by Parliament itself.

The activities of government have changed to meet the needs of the times, but our political and legal structure for many years failed to keep pace. There has been increasing delegation of authority by Parliament to the Cabinet, to departments and boards, and to nameless public servants. Since the government is playing a more active and positive role at a time of rapidly changing technology, changing patterns of domestic and international trade, and changing social viewpoints, it cannot spell out in statutes all the provisions and exemptions needed to look after the innumerable variations of modern requirements. Our need for greater flexibility in administration has been growing, and the location of responsibility for executive, legislative, and judicial functions has become somewhat vague. The activities of departments of government are no longer separable into neat, mutually-exclusive areas of interest. As the functions and direct participation of government have extended, the machinery of administration has become more complicated and has ceased to be merely administrative.

We have changed the activities of government to an extent that makes even more discretionary powers inevitable. We have provided for many such powers, and at an accelerating pace. However, instead of entering wholeheartedly into the creation of discretions with our eyes open to its implications and needs and simultaneously providing machinery to prevent the abuse of discretionary powers, we tried to pretend that there had been no basic change. We left discretions to be exercised as much in the shadows of secrecy as possible. It has become more difficult to tell where lawmaking stops and administration starts. It has become harder to place responsibility for actions (or lack of them) among the multiplicity of government agencies now involved. Even greater use of discretionary powers may be essential but these powers carry with them potential for abuse unless there are surrounding safeguards.

It became the norm for a statute to delegate authority to make regulations to achieve objectives which have been expressed in very general terms. If regulations extend only to details of mechanical procedures, no real discretionary powers are delegated. However, where the statutory provisions are only a skeleton and it is left to regulations to say "what, where, when, why, how and who," then we have created meaningful discretionary powers and should examine the mechanisms available to review the exercise of these powers. When regulations are issued by the Governor-in-Council, or even by a minister of the Crown, there is at least a degree of accountability for this first step. Where the power is conferred upon a board or commission, review of its exercise becomes more difficult and remote. However, if the discretions have been consciously delegated to a named body directly responsible to the legislature, there is at least a placing of responsibility. If persons or bodies possessed of delegated powers re-delegate them, we come to a state that may be described as "dispersed discretions". When discretionary judgements are not the result of a conscious act which has placed the responsibility upon a named person or body, but are the results of pretending that matters of opinion are matters of fact, we are farther into an area of trouble.

The courts have been the traditional safeguard for the rights of one individual against another or against the state, but the courts were designed to adjudicate matters which at least purport to be issues of fact in relation to pre-established law. Courts lack both the powers and in most cases the capacity to substitute their judgement for opinions which others have been empowered to express. In essence, the traditional courts are incapable of playing a constructive part in the newly developing functions of government, where exercise of discretions is required. For this reason positive action was freqently taken by legislatures to exclude the exercise of delegated discretions from the jurisdiction of the courts, if it was found or suspected that the courts might be in a position to intervene.

The magnitude of the developments described has been generally unrecognized. Most people still think that Parliament makes the laws except for small details; that public servants just administer; and that those exercising delegated discretions are accountable for their actions in fact as well as in theory to the elected representatives of the people. In fact, the rule of law as we knew it until World War II has just about gone and effective accountability to Parliament has been lost over a wide area of governmental activity.

These are not just impressionistic statements. Let us look at some specific examples of this continuing process of growth of discretions. It would not matter what year's legislation we look at. The pattern has been the same session after session. The following examples are taken from the Acts of the third session of the 28th Parliament (October 8, 1970—January 12, 1972) which continued the process of legislating in generalities, leaving the substance to be prescribed by regulations to be administered beyond the control of Parliament. There were 65 public bills introduced in that session which subsequently became law. Many of these were of a mechanical nature such as redefining electoral boundaries and repealing the Leprosy Act, or formalisms such as proclaiming "Pollution Awareness Week", and similar measures of limited interest and content. Of the bills which affected the public at large, the majority conferred new discretionary authority.

Under the Consumer Packaging and Labelling Act (Bill C-180), full power to exempt goods from the application of the Act is delegated to the Governor-in-Council. The labelling requirements that are to apply to goods are to be prescribed by regulations. Thus, in passing the Act, Parliament prohibited the sale or import of goods not packaged in compliance with regulations that had not yet been made and were therefore unknown to Parliament. Similarly, the Act delegates the power of entry without warrant and the seizure of goods at the sole discretion of inspectors in order to enforce regulations made under the Act and therfore unknown to Parliament when the Act was passed.

It should not go unnoticed that the Statutory Instruments Act (Bill C-182),[1] "to provide for the examination, publication and scrutiny of regulations and other statutory instruments", itself created new discretionary powers by authorizing the Governor-in-Council to prescribe by regulation that regulations or classes of regulations need not be examined, published or scrutinized. This the Governor-in-Council subsequently did, in the Statutory Instruments Regulations.[2]

Another example is the Clean Air Act (Bill C-224). "Air quality objectives" are left to be "prescribed by the Governor-in-Council". What are to be regarded as "air contaminants" are left to be prescribed by regulation. Those types of operations to be subject to regulation are left to be "specified by the Governor-in-Council". Powers to decide who should be required to conform to standards, who should be exempted, and what the standards should be are also delegated to the Minister. Discretionary enforcement powers are delegated to "inspectors", to be exercised according to what the inspectors "may reasonably believe" to be the facts, or as an inspector "deems necessary".

The Act to amend the Canada Labour (Standards) Code (Bill C-228) had 24 sections. Thirteen of these delegate discretions by reference to "as prescribed by regulations" or the use of similar phrases.

---

[1]Canada, *Statutes* (1971).
[2]SOR/71-592, P.C. 1971-2485, November 9, 1971.

The Unemployment Insurance Act, 1971 (Bill C-229) is an outstanding example. The definition of "insurable earnings" was left to be "prescribed by regulation". What are "excepted employment" and "insurable employment" were left to be defined by regulations which might be general, or restricted to areas in the country, groups of persons, or even applicable only to individual persons. Unemployed persons can be disentitled to benefits by regulation. Wide powers to make regulations are given to the Minister, and the Minister is given power to authorize others to exercise his powers. The Unemployment Insurance Commission is not only given wide powers to issue regulations, but is empowered in turn to delegate its powers to any employees it desires. There are close to 75 references in the Act to the power to make regulations, or requirements to comply with regulations. Without the regulations the Act is hollow.

In addition to legislative acts of this nature, there is the whole area of "Rules, orders, regulations, by-laws or proclamations which are made by regulation-making authorities in the exercise of a legislative power"— commonly known as Statutory Orders and Regulations. In any year these are numbered in the thousands, and not only delegate authority but frequently re-delegate it.

For example, the powers to make regulations provided by the Unemployment Insurance Act, 1971, were promptly and frequently exercised. Authority to exercise judgements and make determinations was extended through the use of such phrases as "in the opinion of the Commission", "approved by the Commission", "in the manner set out in the instructions from the Commission", "may be determined by the Commission". Regulations redefine significant words and phrases from meanings given to them in the statute. There is redelegation of powers, through such phrases as "Where it is established to the satisfaction of an officer of the Department of National Revenue, Taxation. . . ." The Unemployment Insurance Act, 1971, came into effect on various dates starting in June 1971. In the following 12 months the Unemployment Insurance Regulations were amended 12 times, and the revisions took up about 90 pages of small type in the Canada Gazette. One can appreciate a comment of Mr. Stanley Knowles, M.P., when this series of amendments had barely started:

It is our experience in Parliament time and time again to think we knew what we passed when we gave final approval to a piece of legislation, only to find months later that things were being done or restrictions were being imposed of a kind we did not believe appeared in the bill at all. When we try to find out what happened, we discover that we had given authority to the Governor-in-Council to make regulations for the carrying out of the purposes of the act and that under this authority restrictive regulations were passed, or restrictive definitions introduced of such a nature as to produce quite a different result from the result we thought had been intended. I

> could give a number of examples.... let me give just one, not in order to be contentious, but merely to make my point. Take the new Unemployment Insurance Act. Because we gave the Governor-in-Council the power to define "earnings" we found that things were happening which we did not expect and that in many cases benefits were greatly reduced.[3]

The statutes and regulations used as examples have the merit of being published documents. In addition, there is a large area of unpublished Orders-in-Council and Ministerial prescriptions. There is also the broad field of so-called administrative decisions (or lack of decisions) which are equally exercises of discretion. These are by nature difficult to deal with in public, because they frequently involve decisions relating to private and confidential affairs of individual persons or companies. One can only learn of the details through a confidential relationship to those affected. However, these unpublished Orders-in-Council, Ministerial prescriptions, or administrative decisions are frequently of general application and remain unknown to many persons affected by them because they are not published.

In the last few years it has been more widely recognized that this problem exists, and the first steps towards doing something about the problem have been taken.

The Parliamentary Special Committee on Procedure and Organization which reported in December 1964, recognized the joint problems of growth of discretions being exercised by appointed officials and loss of effective control by Parliament. It attempted to deal with the situation by recommending that there be established a Standing Committee on Delegated Legislation. The purpose of this Standing Committee was described as follows:

> The function of this Committee would be to act as a watchdog over the executive in its use of the powers conferred by statute, with the duty of reporting to Parliament any tendency on the part of the executive to exceed its authority. The committee's terms of reference should exclude it from considering the merits of or the policy behind delegated legislation, but it would be expected to draw the attention of Parliament to any regulations or instruments which impose a charge on public revenues, which confer immunity from challenge in the courts, which have an unauthorized retroactive effect, which reveal an unusual or unexpected use of a statutory power, or which otherwise exceed the authority delegated by the parent statute.[4]

This recommendation was not accepted by the Government. The flood of unregulated regulations continued and burgeoned.

With the Trudeau administration, there came a change on a number of fronts simultaneously. In September 1968, the House of Commons appointed a Special Committee on Statutory Instruments

---

[3]*Debates* (Commons), October 4, 1971, p. 8,681.
[4]*Debates* (Commons), December 14, 1964, p. 988.

... to consider and, from time to time, to report on procedures for the review by this House of instruments made in virtue of any statute of the Parliament of Canada.[5]

In July 1969, the scope of the powers of this Special Committee was extended to permit it, also

to consider and, from time to time, to report on the adequacy of existing statutory authority for the making and publication of Statutory Instruments and on the adequacy of existing procedures for the drafting, scrutiny and operational review of such instruments, and to make recommendations with respect thereto.[6]

This special Committee did not have powers to review the exercise of delegated authority—merely to recommend what, in its opinion, should be done to deal with this problem.

The report of the Special Committee on Statutory Instruments, presented October 22, 1969, reiterated the importance of the area of delegated legislation, using such phrases as:

... public knowledge of governmental activities is the basis of all control of delegated legislation. For parliamentary democracy is a system of government which requires that the executive be responsible to the legislature and that both be accountable to the people, and there can be neither responsibility nor accountability where there is no knowledge of what has been done....

Your Committee can agree with the view of Dr. D.C. Rowat that the general tradition of administrative secrecy is based on an earlier system of royal rule in Britain that is unsuited to a modern democracy in which the people must be fully informed about the activities of their government....

Your Committee's contention is, therfore, that there should be, as a general rule, public knowledge of the processes of delegated legislation, before, during, and after the making of regulations, and that any derogation by government from this rule requires justification.[7]

The Committee made extensive recommendations (23 in number). Some were subsequently accepted by the Government, others were not. Among those *not* accepted was that the Committee "be reconstituted in the next session to allow further consideration of certain matters referred to in this Report". Of those recommendations that were accepted, it can be said that the period of gestation between acceptance in principle and subsequent action was lengthy, and in some cases the offspring were stillborn.

It took eight months before there was a government statement on the Committee's recommendations which had been tabled in the House of Commons in October 1969. In June 1970 the President of the Privy Council stated government policy and intentions as follows:

---

[5]*Ibid.*, September 30, 1968.
[6]*Ibid.*, July 10, 1969.
[7]Canada, *Third Report of the Special Committee of the House of Commons on Statutory Instruments,* October 22, 1969.

> Due to the nature of the committee's recommendations it is not practical, nor is it reasonably possible, to proceed with their implementation by any one means. Rather, implementation of the committee's recommendations will require action of three different kinds: first, legislative action by Parliament to replace the existing Regulations Act by a new statutory instruments act; second, a number of cabinet directives to implement several of the recommendations which cannot be dealt with by general legislation and, third, amendment of the Standing Orders for the purpose of establishing a scrutiny committee to review regulations.
>
> The government accepts fully the principle that both Parliament and the public are entitled to be fully informed of, and to have convenient access to, regulations and other instruments made under the authority of Acts of Parliament. The legislation and other measures that will be proposed by the government will be guided by this paramount principle, and only demonstrably necessary and carefully defined exceptions to the general requirements of the law relating to the examination, registration and publication of such instruments will be permitted.[8]

There had already been a positive step in a related area through the introduction in March 1970, of a bill to establish the Federal Court of Canada, to replace with extended powers the Exchequer Court. This measure, which was proclaimed effective June 1, 1971, repealed provisions in many statutes which had specifically prohibited appeals to the Courts against procedures, or from findings, of a number of semi-judicial boards and tribunals. This measure now affords protection against arbitrary action and the failure of such boards or tribunals to proceed in a judicial manner. However, it does not, of course, empower the court to substitute its judgement for that of the bodies empowered to exercise discretions.

In November 1970, Bill C-182, "to provide for the examination, publication and scrutiny of regulations and other statutory instruments" was introduced, and in January 1971, it was referred to the Standing Committee on Justice and Legal Affairs. The Hon. John Turner, then Minister of Justice, restated government intentions as being those previously stated by the President of the Privy Council:

1. To issue Cabinet directives "to deal with departmental directives and guidelines and the conferring by legislation of regulation-making powers".
2. To replace the existing provisions for scrutiny and publication of regulations by a new and broader Statutory Instruments Act.
3. To provide a parliamentary committee to review statutory instruments.

The Cabinet directives are said to have been issued, but what they said cannot be reported. When a question on this matter was addressed to

---

[8]*Debates* (Commons), June 16, 1970.

the Privy Council office, access to them was denied. The official reply was that they are confidential, "They are not in the public domain".

Bill C-182 received Royal Assent May 19, 1971, and came into force January 1, 1972, together with regulations made thereunder. Adequate commentary on the Statutory Instruments Act and the regulations thereunder is not possible within the scope of this article. However, a few major points should be noted. It would be an error to think that the requirements of the Act extend to all of the many Orders-in-Council, rules, orders, regulations, by-laws, proclamations, prescriptions—call them what you will—that affect the rights and responsibilities of individuals. The Statute applies only to certain "regulations" and "statutory instruments" as defined in the Act. The definitions are both restrictive and obscure in their wording. They make broad provision for exemptions from requirements of inspection before issuance, registration, publication or public access—even access by Parliament. A large area of the exercises of administrative discretions has been left outside the scope of the Act.

The Act also applies only to those regulations and statutory instruments (as defined, and not then excluded) made subsequent to its passage. It leaves untouched the thousands of pre-existing "regulations" and "statutory instruments", as well as the mass of other provisions considered to lie outside these narrowly defined phrases. The provisions of the Statutory Instruments Act did not, and do not, carry out stated government policy, namely that "... both Parliament and the public are entitled to be fully informed of and to have convenient access to regulations and other instruments" and that "... only demonstrably necessary and carefully defined exceptions to the general requirements of the law relating to the examination, registration and publication of such instruments will be permitted". In fact, the provisions are a mockery of these statements of principle.

With respect to the "scrutiny committee" the Act did provide that certain types of statutory instruments (as narrowly defined) after the coming into force of the Act:

> ... shall stand permanently referred to any Committee of the House of Commons, or the Senate or of both Houses of Parliament that may be established for the purpose of reviewing and scrutinizing statutory instruments.

Motions to establish a Standing Committee on Regulations and Other Statutory Instruments as a Joint Committee of the House of Commons and Senate were introduced in October 1971, but it was not until March 1972 that the Senate and the House of Commons named its members. Then there was silence. The powers of the Committee were not specified. It was not instructed to do anything. All it was empowered to do under the Statutory Instruments Act was to look at these new statutory instruments (as narrowly defined) which were not withheld from its inspection. What the Committee could or should do after such a review was not stated. In spite of repeated inquiries and references to inaction from government as well as opposition members, when the 28th Parliament dissolved September 1, 1972, and its Committees died with it, the Joint Committee on Regulations and Other Statutory Instruments had never met.

The Joint Committee was re-established when the 29th Parliament opened in January 1973. Its Joint Chairmen were Gordon Fairweather, M.P. and Senator Eugene Forsey. An organization meeting was held on March 1, 1973, and a further meeting took place in April 1973 at which the Joint Committee considered how to find out what it was supposed to be investigating. The Committee was not voted any funds to carry on its work, and these two meetings ended the work of the Committee for 1973. In the first few months of 1974 it obtained its first staff (borrowed from the Library of Parliament), held two more meetings and once again ceased to exist when Parliament was dissolved on May 9, 1974. The staff nucleus, however, continued to work.

The 30th Parliament met on September 30, 1974, and the Joint Committee was again re-established in October, this time under the Joint Chairmanship of Robert McCleave, M.P. and Senator Forsey. It met promptly and, for the first time, three years after its initial creation, the Joint Committee came alive. In the next year and a half, up to the summer recess of Parliament in 1976, it held 59 meetings in relation to its function under the Statutory Instruments Act. (In December 1974 the House of Commons referred two other matters to the Joint Committee— Guidelines for the Production of Papers and Bill C-225, the proposed Freedom of Information Act. The Committee held over 20 other meetings to deal with these matters.) It heard many witnesses, amassed much material and scrutinized and commented upon a multitude of statutory instruments. It was denied access to material deemed outside the scope of "statutory instruments"—the phrase that governs the Committee's jurisdiction under the Statutory Instruments Act.

At the time of writing only formal reports have been rendered. However, the first substantive and comprehensive report is now in draft form and, hopefully will be issued early in 1977. It may deal strongly with the subject of what is a statutory instrument and therefore properly before the Committee. It may also give examples of the fetters under which the Committee has been operating. It is expected to refer to statutory instruments which the Committee has reviewed and found objectional. The frankness of the report and its reception by the Government may determine whether the activities of this Joint Committee will be steps towards parliamentary control over government by bureaucratic fiat, or whether the activities of the Joint Committee will be smothered and we will continue on the course of decline of accountability.

Perhaps what has happened has been inevitable; it may even be desirable—but not as long as we pretend that nothing has really happened to change the old order. If we permit the proliferation of powers—dispersed discretions—without setting up an effective mechanism to supervise the exercise of these powers, a free community will not long survive. Unless we find some way of bringing Parliament back into the picture, its individual members, legislating only in generalities and without effective means of seeing how their servants are acting, are reduced to comparative impotence.

Delegated legislation is sufficiently significant that it deserves a special mechanism for review of its exercise. Unless members of Parliament fulfil this function, Parliament as we have known it will become relatively impotent. Some public servants have questioned whether members of Parliament can be expected to approach review of the exercise of discretions in a non-partisan manner. They seem to feel that politicians will refuse to distinguish between the essentially political acts of determining policy and voting for legislative programs, and the essentially non-partisan function of studying how powers delegated by legislation are being exercised. Perhaps the question might be phrased, "Can members forget party politics long enough to be objective in protecting the rights of the individual to the end that there is equal justice for all, and efficient, non-discriminatory application of the law?" This is a function which the courts cannot fulfil in relation to the exercise of delegated discretions. If members of Parliament cannot, or will not, do this job through committees established for this purpose, then we should at least abandon the pretence that they are able to do so now, even with the new Statutory Instruments Act.

29
Regulatory Agencies and the Canadian Political System

Richard Schultz

"The question of delegation to an independent regulatory authority," according to one commentator, "is a settled one in Canada. It has not excited the passions of Canadian political scientists and politicians to the extent that it has in the United States."[1] If this is an accurate assessment, it can be argued that the question is "settled" not because of extensive analysis and appraisal but because of inertia and neglect. This is

---

*An original article written for this volume.
[1]Ronald G. Penney, "Telecommunications Policy and Ministerial Control," *Canadian Communications Law Review,* 1970, p. 14.

unfortunate because regulatory authorities are not at the "fringe" of the public sector in Canada but are primary instruments of social, economic and political control.[2] Moreover, they constitute a major institutional innovation in the Canadian parliamentary system inasmuch as they involve a transfer of power from elected representatives to appointed officials. In an era of government by discretion, it is no longer acceptable that the role of regulatory authorities in the political system be settled by default.[3] This essay, which admittedly is an introductory overview, attempts to encourage greater attention to such bodies.

A recent survey suggested that there were over one hundred federal regulatory agencies[4] and much work needs to be done to establish a useful classification of them.[5] This essay will not attempt such a task but will limit itself to a discussion of some of the central problems of what may be called economic regulatory agencies from the perspective of public administration. The scope of this essay, then, is limited to the six federal regulatory agencies which, because of the nature of their functions, may be described as the most important of our regulatory bodies. The agencies in question are the Anti-Inflation Board (AIB), the Atomic Energy Control Board (AECB), the Canadian Radio-Television and Telecommunications Commission (CRTC), the Canadian Transport Commission (CTC), the Foreign Investment Review Agency (FIRA) and the National Energy Board (NEB). These agencies all share one common characteristic: they are entities that exist outside traditional departmental structures. Three of them, CRTC, CTC and NEB, also share another and more important attribute: they are, in varying degrees, independent. The nature of this independence, which is the central concern of this essay, will be discussed below.

Although these agencies account for a small proportion of government employees and government expenditures, they perform some of the most important functions of government—functions that are critical to individual welfare and social and economic development. The Canadian Transport Commission, for example, can have a tremendous impact on the transportation system in view of its power to "co-ordinate and harmonize" the operations of all federally regulated

---

[2] The "fringe", according to Desmond Keeling, is "Whitehall jargon" to describe regulatory and other "quasi-governmental agencies" in Britain. See Desmond Keeling, "Beyond Ministerial Departments: Mapping the Administrative Terrain," *Public Administration* (London), 54 (1976), p. 161.

[3] The Law Reform Commission of Canada recently estimated that there were some 15 000 discretionary powers that have been conferred on public authorities by federal statutes. See Philip Anisman, *A Catalogue of Discretionary Powers in the Revised Statutes of Canada 1970* (Ottawa: Information Canada, 1975).

[4] Canadian Consumer Council, "Inventory of Provincial and Federal Regulatory Agencies," Ottawa, 1971.

[5] For two useful starting points, see André Gelinas, *Les organismes autonomes et centraux* (Montreal: Les Presses de l'Université du Quebec, 1975) and D.C. Hague *et al.*, *Public Policy and Private Interests: The Institutions of Compromise* (London: Macmillan, 1975), esp. Appendix III.

modes of transportation.[6] In the communications field, the impact of the Canadian Radio-Television and Telecommunications Commission has been widely felt because of its broad interpretation of its responsibilities to "supervise and regulate all aspects of the Canadian broadcasting system".[7]

Given their importance as instruments of governing, regulatory agencies — especially those that are independent — should interest the student of Canadian public administration because these agencies have a special degree of delegated power in the political system. Moreover, this delegation is unique because it transforms the traditional lines of responsibility governing the relations between politically accountable authorities and the bureaucracy. The Canadian parliamentary system is governed by the principles of ministerial responsibility, both individual and collective, to Parliament.[8] Ministers, however, are only partially, and in some cases not at all, responsible to Parliament for the actions of independent regulatory agencies. The student of public administration must determine the justification for the existence of agencies, the reasons for the independence of some of them, the nature of their powers and the consequences of transferring political power.

ORIGINS OF REGULATORY AGENCIES

Regulatory agencies are, in Hodgetts's phrase, "structural heretics" in the Canadian political system because of their non-departmental form.[9] Given, as Hodgetts also states, that such departures from the departmental norm to varying extents do "violence to the constituted system of ministerial responsibility,"[10] one needs to determine why such agencies have been created. Moreover, the question is not simply one of historical curiosity, because a host of regulatory activities in areas such as food and drug protection, health and safety standards and working conditions are performed by the traditional departments. This argues that there must be exceptional circumstances to justify the creation of "structural heretics".

The exceptional circumstances are to be found in the nature of the function common to all the agencies considered in this essay: the function of economic regulation. By economic regulation we mean government intervention by regulatory instruments into those areas traditionally reserved in a market economy for private economic decision makers — the owners and managers of firms and industries. More specifically, economic regulation entails a government role in the setting

---

[6]National Transportation Act, (NTA), *Revised Statutes of Canada*, Section 21, Chapter N-17.
[7]Broadcasting Act, *Revised Statutes of Canada*, Section 15, Chapter B-11.
[8]J.E. Hodgetts, *The Canadian Public Service* (Toronto: University of Toronto Press, 1973), pp. 48-51.
[9]*Ibid.*, Chapter 7.
[10]*Ibid.*, p. 141.

of prices, the controlling of entry into particular sectors of economic activity and the establishment of standards of service. Economic regulation by government is a "halfway house" between an unfettered market and public ownership in an economy based primarily on private enterprise. In general, regulation is intended to be a surrogate for the competitive forces of the marketplace when competition is deemed either not possible or not practicable.[11] Moreover, regulation traditionally has been the means by which Canadian governments have imposed public social objectives on sectors of the economy such as transportation and communications to supplement the economic objectives of private decision makers.

The nature of economic regulation, it is argued, provides the reasons for establishing agencies outside the traditional departmental structures. It is important to emphasize, however, that the creation of regulatory agencies, notwithstanding the reasons to follow, has not been the result of a coherent, well-defined philosophy. In general, there are three basic reasons cited in defence of the creation of separate agencies. In the first place, economic regulation is a highly complex responsibility and requires a type of expertise not usually found in government bureaucracies. Secondly, traditional structures cannot provide the flexibility or continuity of policy necessary for the experimental and innovative needs of economic regulation.

Before turning to the third reason, it should be noted that the reasons already cited were far more compelling in an earlier era of governmental activity in Canada — when the civil service was based primarily on patronage rather than on merit and was far less dependent on specialized knowledge than it is today. The fact that the majority of members of the recently created Anti-Inflation Board, for example, were seconded from other government departments would suggest that the argument regarding specialized knowledge is no longer convincing.

The third traditional argument — and the only one that remains convincing today — is that a separate agency is required to insulate the function of economic regulation from political pressures. Inasmuch as regulation involves either public interference in the exercise of traditional private proprietary rights (as in the transportation and energy sectors) or competing private applications for control of sections of the public domain (as in radio and television licences), impartiality must be exercised to ensure that there is no partisan interference in the regulatory process. This has been a particularly telling argument in Canada and the United States. In Britain, however, regulation

---

[11]On the functions of economic regulation, see Roger Noll, *Reforming Regulation* (Washington: Brookings Institution, 1971); Clair Wilcox, *Public Policies towards Business,* 4th ed. (Homewood, Ill., Irwin-Dorsey, 1971), and Michael J. Trebilcock, "Winners and Losers in the Modern Regulatory State," Paper read at the 1975 Meeting of the Institute of Public Administration of Canada, esp. pp. 14-15.

traditionally has been performed within government departments and there has been less concern with political interference.[12]

THE CONCEPT OF REGULATORY INDEPENDENCE

The concern for impartiality also explains the independence of some regulatory agencies. A non-departmental identity was not deemed sufficient in Canada to ensure that economic regulation would be "taken out of politics." To reinforce an impartial nature, some agencies were made independent. It is important to note that independence was not extended to all regulatory agencies despite the similarity of their functions. The appointed regulators were granted a quasi-judicial status: they serve, not like deputy ministers or the heads of Crown corporations, "at pleasure" but on condition of "good behaviour" and can be removed only for "cause".

Notwithstanding this general statement of the rationale for agency independence, the concept of independence requires substantial clarification. It is unclear, for example, why some regulators are independent and others are not. Why are the members and administrator of the AIB or the Commissioner of the FIRA not independent while members of the CTC or CRTC are? The administrator, for example, may make binding orders similar to those made by the CTC or CRTC, yet he serves at pleasure.

The second aspect of regulatory independence that requires clarification is the fact that the independence of some regulators does not necessarily mean that the whole of the regulatory process must be impartial. It may only mean that the regulators' role in the decision-making process is governed by the principles and requirements of impartiality. The position of the NEB best illustrates the significance of this comment. The members of the NEB are so independent that they cannot be removed before the end of their terms except by a joint address of the House of Commons and the Senate. Yet the overwhelming majority of NEB decisions require Cabinet approval. Cabinet, in making its decision on a particular application, is not governed by any requirement that it act impartially because it is permitted to exercise its discretion and make its decision on any grounds it sees fit. It is important to realize, therefore, that it is the appointed regulators who must act impartially and it is they who are granted a special degree of independence but the ultimate decisions need not be impartially determined. The significance of this distinction will become clearer if we turn to a discussion of the nature of the powers of regulatory agencies.

---

[12]On the British experience in air transport regulation, see Sir Ronald Edwards, Chairman, *British Air Transport in the Seventies*, Report of the Committee of Inquiry into Civil Air Transport (London, HMSO, 1969).

THE POWERS OF REGULATORY AGENCIES

The independent status of regulators can be viewed as a protective shield enabling them to ward off interference, partisan or otherwise, in exercising their impartial discretion. As such, the quasi-judicial status of regulators is concerned with the question, "independence from what?" It is equally important to ask "independence for what?" because, unless we assess the significance of the functions of regulatory agencies, the independence that is granted to regulators may not be of much significance. This section is concerned, therefore, with the nature and scope of independent regulatory decision making. Again, it is important to remind the reader of the difficulties in making general statements of equal validity for all agencies because of the variety among agencies. Indeed, it should be remembered that some regulatory agencies, although outside the departmental norm, do not possess an independent decision-making capacity. The AIB and the FIRA, for example, are not decision makers but are primarily negotiating and advisory agencies.

The powers of decision-making agencies can be divided into two general categories, adjudicative and legislative. The former is the power to decide on individual applications for licences, routes, tariffs, standards of service, etc. The latter is the power to make policy principally by means of a regulation-making power. In some instances there are problems in distinguishing between legislative and judicial functions because the distinction between the two activities is not always clear. Yet the statement that one cannot draw the line between them has generally gained credence through repetition rather than sufficient examination. The problems, in fact, appear to have been overstated.

In this paper we need not attempt to resolve the issue. It is precisely because policy can emerge from both adjudicative and legislative decisions that attention to the political control of such functions is needed. An analysis of independent policy making by regulatory agencies is appropriate for an appreciation of the extent to which such bodies do "violence to the constituted system of ministerial responsibility." What emerges from such an analysis is the ironic fact that, despite the rationale of impartial decision making invoked to justify the creation of such bodies, independent exercise of the adjudicative function appears to be subject to greater control than independent exercise of the legislative function. This varies, as will be shown, with the individual agency.

The political controls on adjudicative decision making can be assessed from two viewpoints. They can be positive or negative, active or passive. Positive-negative refers to whether politically accountable authorities can substitute their own decisions for regulatory decisions or whether they are limited to rejecting such decisions. Active-passive refers to political power to initiate a review of regulatory decisions. This power is an active one if politically accountable authorities can review at their own discretion; it is passive if the review is dependent on an appeal from an interested party.

There is no uniform system of political control of regulatory decisions. Cabinet exercises active control over NEB decisions, for example, in that all major decisions on certificates and licences require Cabinet approval before they are valid. Yet this control is also negative in that Cabinet cannot substitute or vary a decision made by the NEB but can only reject it. With respect to the CTC the situation is somewhat confused in that Cabinet has both active and positive power over CTC decisions[13] while the Minister of Transport, who exercises control on his own, has positive but passive control over CTC licensing decisions.[14] The CRTC, on the other hand, appears to have the most discretion in terms of independent decision making because Cabinet exercises only negative and passive control over CRTC decisions.[15]

One need not attempt to explain the haphazard nature of political control of regulatory adjudicative decisions. What is significant, at least in formal terms, is the extent to which such decisions are subject to political control. As suggested earlier, this is somewhat unusual in that the primary rationale for an independent regulatory agency was the need for an impartial decision-making body. The Canadian situation is fundamentally at odds with the American in this regard because for comparable agencies in the United States, there is no process of appeal to political authorities nor do such authorities have the right to veto or substitute adjudicative decisions.[16] The only existing appeal with respect to American independent regulatory agencies is to the courts. The extent to which the political controls are exercised is, of course, far more significant than their existence in the statutes. This is an area where a great deal of research is required to assess the utility and practice of such controls.

There is another aspect of political control of adjudicative decisions that merits comment. Regulatory agencies are created in principle to implement government policy in particular sectors of the economy. The quality of the statutory policy statements as guides for regulatory decision makers is therefore an important consideration in any assessment of regulatory policy making. From this perspective we find that, in general, the potential of regulatory policy making is great because of the vague and general nature of statutory policy statements. Some regulators have little more to guide them than the requirement that applications be assessed in terms of "present and future public

---

[13]NTA, Section 64.
[14]*Ibid.*, Section 25.
[15]Broadcasting Act, Section 23.
[16]Noll, *op. cit.*, p. 5.

convenience and necessity."[17] For others, such as the CRTC, the statements of policy are so widely and vaguely drawn that anything can be read into them.[18] In the case of the CTC, the difficulties are compounded because of the nature of the statement of "national transportation policy" which calls for an "economic, efficient and adequate transportation system."[19]

The lack of definitive statements of statutory policy to guide regulators has major consequences for independent agency policy making. The inevitable consequence, to paraphrase Lowi, is that such "broad discretion makes a politician out of a regulator."[20] Regulatory agencies are not restricted to what Currie, in the case of the Board of Transport Commissioners, suggested they do best, namely regulating "in fields where parliamentary direction is reasonably precise."[21] Rather, they become intimately involved in the resolution of political issues that cannot possibly be resolved solely—or even primarily—on technical, impartial grounds. From our perspective the issue lies in the transference of the political process from Parliament, to which Ministers are accountable, to independent agencies, which have often proven themselves singularly incapable or unwilling to manage that process. The more important problem is that the normal principles of accountability no longer apply because the resolution of highly political issues is entrusted to non-accountable authorities.

Given the lack of specificity in policy statements, one must question the ability of politically accountable authorities to clarify any policy confusion or fill any policy vacuum that may develop. Once again there is no uniform set of political controls that exist. Under the Atomic Energy Control Act, the designated Minister may issue directions to the AECB with respect to the carrying out of the purposes of the Act and the Board is required to comply with such directions.[22] Under the Broadcasting Act, there is a provision for such directions on three specific matters.[23] There are no comparable controls with respect to the CTC or the NEB. As a consequence, short of rejecting individual regulatory decisions of these bodies or legislative amendments, there is no opportunity for elected officials to develop or clarify the policy that regulators are mandated to

---

[17]See, for example, the Aeronautics Act, *Revised Statutes of Canada*, 1970, Section 16 (3), Chapter A-3.
[18]Broadcasting Act, Section 3.
[19]NTA, Section 3. On this point see Hudson Janisch, *The Canadian Transport Commission* (Ottawa: Law Reform Commission of Canada, forthcoming).
[20]Theodore Lowi, *The End of Liberalism* (New York: W.W. Norton & Company, 1969), pp. 300-301.
[21]A.W. Currie, "The Board of Transport Commissioners as an Administrative Body," in J.E. Hodgetts and D.C. Corbett, eds., *Canadian Public Administration* (Toronto: Macmillan, 1960), p. 239.
[22]Atomic Energy Control Act, *Revised Statutes of Canada*, 1970, Section 7, Chapter A-19.
[23]Broadcasting Act, Section 22.

implement. Furthermore, even if individual decisions are rejected on policy grounds, there is no guarantee that the policy considerations will set precedents with regulators for future decisions.[24]

Policy making by regulatory agencies, it has been argued, is an "inevitable concomitant of judicial power,"[25] although the scope for such activity is dependent on the degree of specificity of the agency mandate and the opportunity for binding supplementary political policy directives. It is important, therefore, to recognize that policy may emerge from adjudication and to provide for adequate safeguards on the exercise of such power. It is unlikely, however, that an independent legislative function will be delegated to regulatory agencies.

Not all agencies possess legislative power and this, in itself, is an interesting comment on those agencies that do. The Governor in Council must approve all policy regulations—as opposed to "house by-laws"—of the AIB, the AECB, the FIRA and the NEB before such regulations can take effect. There is no similar control over CTC or CRTC regulations.

Why should an independent regulatory agency possess an independent legislative power? Professor Hodgetts suggests the reason may be that regulatory agencies are expected to perform "functions which called for both adjudicative and law-making operations which were substantially different from those traditionally associated with conventional departments."[26] Yet excluding the AIB and FIRA, which are not independent, this does not explain why the CRTC and CTC can make regulations independently while a comparable body, the NEB, cannot. Moreover, such law making may cover technical matters which in other cases are the responsibility of the departments. The CTC, for example, is responsible for railway safety regulations while the Minister of Transport is responsible for aircraft safety. What is particularly ironic in this situation is that, unlike the CTC, the Minister requires the approval of Cabinet for his regulations.

There is obviously no logical explanation for the fact that some agencies have an independent legislative function while others do not. However, more is involved than a question of abstract institutional logic. Regulation making is an important power in the arsenal of regulatory authorities because agency regulations are not necessarily limited to technical matters. The CRTC regulation on the deletion of American commercials on cable television is a major policy issue and has involved Canada in a serious international dispute with the United States. Similarly, the CTC has brought about a major intergovernmental

---

[24]Janisch, *op. cit.*
[25]Louis L. Jaffe, "The Independent Agency — A New Scapegoat," *Yale Law Journal,* 65 (1955-56), p. 1070.
[26]Hodgetts, *The Canadian Public Service,* p. 144.

dispute involving Alberta's purchase of Pacific Western Airlines. This dispute was specifically a result of a CTC regulation that extended the scope of a section of the National Transportation Act.[27] There can be no argument, furthermore, that the drafting of regulations, as opposed to their individual application, should be done impartially. This follows from the conclusion of Chief Justice Laskin of the Supreme Court in the Marshall Crowe case: while the NEB's quasi-judicial function must be discharged "in accordance with the rules of natural justice . . . to a degree that would reflect integrity of its proceedings and impartiality in the conduct of those proceedings," this was not "a prescription that would govern an inquiry" under the relevant sections of the NEB Act.[28] By inference, impartiality would not govern regulation-making sections. It is only the adjudicative function that must be performed impartially. There is no justification, therefore, for granting a direct legislative function to an independent regulatory agency. Yet the existence of a power to make public policies not subject to political controls constitutes a fundamental breach of the principles of political accountability and responsibility in the Canadian political system.

SUMMARY AND CONCLUSIONS

In this essay it has been impossible to deal with all the major aspects of regulatory agencies in the Canadian political system. Consequently many important issues have been ignored. Attention has been concentrated on the questions of regulatory independence and political control and accountability.

Although regulatory agencies are not the only "structural heretics" in the bureaucratic system, they may be the most important. They are a major institutional innovation in that they are granted a policy-making responsibility over which there may be minimal or non-existent political controls.

An analysis of the nature of regulatory independence reveals that an appropriate degree of independence must be granted without conflicting with the traditional principles of political accountability. There is a need to ensure impartiality and objectivity, insofar as the regulatory adjudicative functions are involved, and there can be no serious challenge to this position. The problem is that the adjudicative function may give regulatory bodies a powerful defence against political intervention in the regulatory process not only where such intervention is unacceptable but

---

[27]On this aspect of the regulatory process, see Richard Schultz, "The Regulatory Process and Federal-Provincial Relations," in G. Bruce Doern, ed., *The Regulatory Process in Canada* (Toronto: Macmillan, 1977).

[28]Majority Reasons for Decision, *The Committee for Justice and Liberty v. The National Energy Board*, Supreme Court of Canada, p. 16.

also where it is desirable and necessary. Independence, then, must be balanced with responsiveness and accountability.

The basic thesis of this essay is that regulatory agencies "should not have more independence from the political process and more opportunity to apply expertise to non-technical decisions than is consistent with effective, democratic government."[29] Existing political controls over some regulatory agencies suggest that such agencies in fact do have a degree of independence that is inconsistent with the principles of democratic government. Politically accountable authorities should be able to issue binding policy directives to all, and not just some, regulatory agencies. Granting such a power to elected officials is based on the recognition that there cannot be, nor should there be, "a detailed, once-for-all list of... objectives crystallized in statute."[30] Consequently, political authorities must possess the necessary power to provide amplification and interpretation of statutory objectives and the means to implement them in order to keep regulatory policy in accordance with current political needs. Similarly, there should be a consistent set of controls over independent policy making by regulation of regulatory agencies. An independent legislative function is not a necessary attribute for effective impartial regulation.

There is no logic in a regulatory system where some agencies are subject to extensive and effective political controls while other similar agencies are not. The issue involves not only logic, however, but also a fundamental principle—ministerial responsibility in the parliamentary system. As Hodgetts has stated, "the Canadian system of parliamentary government can only impose responsibility on Ministers of the Crown."[31] When ministerial responsibility is diluted or non-existent, effective democratic control over the instruments of governing is lessened. The "question of delegation to an independent regulatory authority" must no longer be considered "settled".

---

[29]Lloyd N. Cutler and David R. Johnson, "Regulation and the Political Process," *Yale Law Journal*, B4 (1975), p. 1406.
[30]Sir Ronald Edwards, *op. cit.*, p. 13.
[31]J.E. Hodgetts, "The Public Corporation in Canada," in W. Friedmann and J.F. Garner, eds., *Government Enterprise: A Comparative Study* (London: Stevens & Sons), p. 226.

30
The Ombudsman in Canada*

Donald C. Rowat
Henry F. Llambias

Canada shares the general characteristics of the parliamentary system that exists in the Commonwealth countries. Among its main features are: a union of executive and legislative powers in a politically dominant Cabinet, a single-member, single-vote electoral system that often throws up a huge parliamentary majority which gives obedient support to that Cabinet, a tradition of secrecy that permeates the whole administrative structure, and severely limited opportunities for the appeal or judicial review of administrative decisions. All of these lend support to the proposition that the citizens and Parliament need the help of an Ombudsman in any attempt to get at the facts regarding a complaint of maladministration or arbitrary administrative action.

In fact, there are good grounds for believing that the need for the Ombudsman institution in Canada is more pressing than in many other Commonwealth countries. As in the United Kingdom, the liberties of the subject are not entrenched in a written constitution. But Canada has fewer administrative tribunals, where decisions can be made in a judicial manner, and no Council on Administrative Tribunals. Also, she has inadequate legislative prescription of administrative procedure; many regulatory boards and commissions with power to decide cases but no provision for appeal to the courts; antiquated laws on Crown privilege, expropriation and liability; weak arrangements for free legal aid to needy citizens; and no formal procedures in either Parliament or the provincial legislatures for settling the grievances of individuals. In addition to all this, the federal division of powers means that the provisions protecting the citizens' rights against administrative action are worse in some provinces than in others, and that the administration of justice varies because it is divided between the federal government, which appoints and pays the judges, and the provinces, which appoint all magistrates and control the organization and civil procedure of provincial and lower courts.

Throughout the Commonwealth countries there seems to be a general attitude of complacency about the protection of the citizens' rights, perhaps engendered by the strength of the tradition of the 'rule of law'. People do not realize that due to the modern growth of administrative powers the meaning of this tradition has lost much of its content. In Canada, one of the most frequently voiced objections to the

---

*Reprinted by permission from D.C. Rowat, ed., *The Ombudsman* (Toronto: University of Toronto Press, 1965).

Ombudsman proposal is that it is not needed: citizens' rights seem to be adequately protected already, and one doesn't 'hear about' very many cases of persons who have been dealt with unfairly by the administration. The objectors do not appreciate that, since administrative action is secret, the great majority of such cases do not come to light. Only some of the most serious ones are revealed and, since they concern isolated individuals, often they are not widely publicized by the press and are soon forgotten by the public.

To meet this objection, the authors of this essay have made it their business to collect cases of maladministration, arbitrariness and outright injustice which have been publicly reported within the past few years and which were not adequately handled by existing machinery. These reveal a bewildering variety of examples of bureaucratic bungling at all three levels of government — federal, provincial and local; they range from simple (but none the less serious) cases of red tape such as failure to answer an inquiry or make a decision, to heart-rending stories of sane persons incarcerated for years in the cockroach-ridden mental wing of Montreal's Bordeaux jail.[1] We have collected about 60 such cases, most of which occurred in a three-year period. In all of them an Ombudsman could have improved the situation for the complainant, usually by finding out the true facts at a much earlier date, by obtaining either redress or a change in the decision, and by doing so with far less injurious publicity. In several, he would no doubt have secured administrative and perhaps even legislative reforms.

These cases, however, are ones that, by good fortune or the strenuous efforts of the complainant, happen to have been revealed. There are countless others that are never brought to light and in which the aggrieved persons may suffer years of heart-breaking frustration. This was demonstrated by the numerous letters that Professor Rowat received from aggrieved citizens when he wrote a magazine article and spoke on radio and television about the Ombudsman idea. Their cases are of much the same type that the Ombudsmen receive and investigate. Another indication of the volume of unsatisfied complainants is the number of cases handled by a voluntary organization called Underdog, organized in Toronto to help mistreated persons. In Underdog's first eighteen months of operation there were 173 cases involving government officials. Of these, 69 had to do with the federal government, 84 were provincial and 20 were municipal.[2]

On the basis of the Scandinavian experience, one can estimate that the total case-load for Ombudsmen at all levels of government in Canada

---

[1]Henry F. Llambias, "Wanted—An Ombudsman", *Edge*, No. 2, Spring 1964, pp. 81-91; D.C. Rowat, "We Need a New Defense Against So-Called Justice", *Maclean's*, Vol. 74, January 7, 1961, pp. 10, 82-83.
[2]Robert McKeown, "Why Canada Needs an Ombudsman", *Weekend Magazine*, January 11, 1964, p. 24.

might be about 7000 per year, with perhaps 3000 at the federal level alone. Even using the low Danish figure of about 10 per cent that require some kind of corrective action, this would mean that the number of cases of uncompensated administrative injustice in Canada must be at least 700 per year. However, these figures may be far too low because of the earlier-mentioned inadequacy of Canada's protections against arbitrary administration. Also, the federal division of the country into two levels of government causes administrative conflict and delay, and creates confusion for the citizens, who are likely to complain to the wrong level of government at first, thus increasing the total case load at both levels. Another significant difference from the Scandinavian countries is Canada's higher level of post-war immigration and the accompanying administrative problems of eligibility for admission and citizenship.

While opponents may admit that most of an Ombudsman's cases could not be handled by the courts in Canada, they frequently object that with the single-member district it is the job of the member of Parliament to handle such cases for his district. In effect, they say, Canada already has 265 Ombudsmen at the federal level of government, to say nothing of those at the lower levels. To investigate this argument — to find out how many and what kinds of complaints MPs receive, how they handle them and whether they think an Ombudsman would help — Mr. Llambias sent a questionnaire to all members of the House of Commons in the spring of 1964, and received 80 replies. Nine of these were refusals of information, of which two were from Ministers who declined to express any opinion for fear that this might be interpreted as Government policy. Although the remainder is probably a biased sample, in the sense that only the most interested and sympathetic MPs replied, it does reveal some interesting facts.

The MPs were asked to estimate 'how many complaints about some aspect of governmental administration in relation to individuals' they received per month from constituents, and there was a surprising scatter in the replies. Thirty-six MPs estimated they had fewer than 10 complaints per month while twelve said they received more than 30, and two indicated that they were burdened with as many as 65. The difference in the number of complaints seems to depend mainly on the rural or urban character of the constituencies and their total populations, which at present vary tremendously. The average number of complaints received by the forty-four MPs who replied to this question was about 15. Extending this average to all MPs would mean that in total they received an estimated 4000 per month, or nearly 50 000 per year. Even if we assume that it was mainly the overburdened MPs that replied, and that an average for all MPs would be closer to 10 per month, this would still mean a total of 32 000 complaints per year. The replies indicated that a surprising number of complaints concern provincial or local government and even non-governmental bodies. Only about 70 per cent relate to federal departments or agencies, so that complaints of the latter type may total about 32 000 per year.

To a question on whether the complaints concern the personality of officials, the manner of proceeding or the substance of the action taken, there was considerable variation in the replies. However, most of the MPs thought that about 10 per cent concern personalities, 35 per cent the manner of proceeding, and that a majority are directed to the substance of the action. It is likely that many of the latter deal with the reasonableness of a decision or the effect of a law or policy. These matters an Ombudsman would not ordinarily investigate. MPs would continue to handle such cases, as well as requests for help and information and demands for change in the laws or regulations.

When the MPs were asked to identify the areas of governmental activity into which complaints mainly fell, they named 41 different areas, departments and agencies. However, there was a heavy concentration on certain areas. Decisions regarding pensions seemed to cause the most trouble, appearing in 20 questionnaires. The next most common areas of complaint were citizenship and immigration, income tax, health and welfare, unemployment insurance, and veterans' affairs.

Questions were also asked on the efficacy of the existing procedure for handling complaints. It is interesting that there was considerable disagreement about whether being on the Government or Opposition side of the House made a difference to the success of a complaint, although a majority of the MPs felt that it made no difference. Perhaps the reason for this disagreement, as one stated, is that being on either the Government or Opposition side has advantages and disadvantages. While access to information is easier for Government MPs, they are reluctant to ask the Minister a question in the House for fear of embarrassing the Government. As one MP wrote, 'No questions to the Minister, as I am on the Government side!' An Opposition MP, on the other hand, is free to publicize a case and to press an attack on the floor of the House.

A crucial question was: 'Do you ever handle complaints which are settled in a manner unsatisfactory to you and/or the complainant?' To this the great majority (55 out of 63) answered yes, and many said that half or more of their complaints were settled unsatisfactorily. Various reasons were given for the shortcomings of the existing system. One stated bluntly, 'Insufficient time and secretarial assistance to deal with each complaint' Another felt that the basic inadequacy of the system was the 'weakness of individual MPs who are unwilling to intercede on behalf of constituents'. A third believed that not all MPs had the 'experience or training to deal with some of the issues which arise', while two MPs pointed out that in most cases they could only obtain information at second-hand from the Minister or civil servant, since they lacked access to the files.

The MPs were then requested to describe one or more typical cases, or cases in which they felt that the Minister's explanation and or the department's action was unsatisfactory. Although many MPs felt that they could not take the time to do this, the others went to the trouble of presenting a great variety of interesting and sometimes shocking cases. While space does not permit an analysis of these cases here, it is clear that many of them would fall within the competence of an Ombudsman.[3]

To the final question, whether they thought that a Parliamentary Complaints Commissioner (Ombudsman) would be of help, 53 MPs answered yes, 13 said no, and 2 were doubtful. Of this sample of 68, then, the proportion in favour of the Ombudsman exceeded three to one.

Because of the large number of unsatisfied grievances against administrative action in Canada, and the inability of members of Parliament to deal with them adequately as revealed by the questionnaire, interest in the Ombudsman proposal has been rising — especially since New Zealand's adoption of the scheme in 1962. It is important to recall, however, that the jurisdiction of an Ombudsman created under federal law in Canada could not extend to the provinces or municipalities. For this purpose each province would need to provide its own Ombudsman. Realizing this, a number of provincial bar associations and legislative representatives have become interested in the idea, and several provincial Governments are considering it. Indeed, it is very likely that an Ombudsman will be established in one of the provinces of Canada before it is adopted at the federal level.[4] But this is perhaps as it should be. One of the great advantages of a federal system is that an experiment with a new idea or constitutional form can be tried on a small scale in one of the states or provinces first. If it is successful there, it will then spread to the others and can safely be adopted by the central government.

The needs at the provincial level, however, are different, and therefore the provincial and federal offices should not be mere carbon copies of one another. Because the provincial governments are smaller, an Ombudsman would get to know the senior officials personally so that he would be less likely to criticize them. The Cabinet's control over the administration is more direct, party patronage exerts a greater influence, and provincial Governments frequently have very large majorities in the legislatures for long periods of time. For these reasons, stronger provisions will be needed to ensure the Ombudsman's independence from the executive. Moreover, while there may be grounds for exempting the higher courts from an Ombudsman's supervision, the situation regarding the lower courts, which the provinces control

---

[3]Mr. Llambias has analyzed and outlined some of these cases in his MA thesis, "The Need for an Ombudsman System in Canada", Carleton University, Ottawa, 1964.

[4][Editor's Note] The authors' prediction has been realized in that the office of the Ombudsman has been established in 8 of the 10 Canadian provinces.

completely, is different. The Chief Justice of the Supreme Court has some disciplinary control over the judges of the higher courts but any disciplining of magistrates must be initiated by a provincial Gtvernment. Because of the tradition that the executive should not interfere with judicial independence, provincial Governments rarely undertake to do this. Yet magistrates are often inadequately trained and inexperienced, and, because of the large volume of cases they must consider, frequently make decisions involving civil liberties that are too hasty, or delay making decisions so long that the delay amounts to a denial of justice. Theoretically, the appeal system should take care of such faults, but it is in the lower courts that the real 'underdog' most frequently appears — with no education, no money, no counsel, and no thought of appeal. The case for including the lower courts in a provincial Ombudsman scheme is therefore strong.

Another difference between the federal and provincial governments is that the latter control the local governments. Hence a provincial Ombudsman would need to have jurisdiction over decisions made by municipal officials. Indeed, it may be that the largest city corporations, such as Montreal, Toronto, and Vancouver, should each have an Ombudsman of their own. On the other hand, the federal government controls the armed services. There is plenty of evidence that cases arise within them which need the aid of an Ombudsman. But perhaps the nature of military organization and the laws governing service personnel are sufficiently different to justify a separate office for military cases, as in Sweden, Norway and Western Germany. Although in most provinces a single Ombudsman may be adequate to handle the volume of work, one wonders whether this would be true at the federal level. The countries in which the Ombudsman system now exists all have small populations. A plural Ombudsman, in the form of a Complaints Commission, would probably meet the need more adequately in larger countries like Canada.[5] Sweden, the biggest of the Scandinavian countries, is itself seriously considering this idea, now that the work of the Ombudsman and his Deputy is growing so rapidly.

Whatever adjustments may be required to make the institutions coincide more neatly with conditions at the federal and provincial levels, there is no doubt of the need in Canada for an institution like the Ombudsman. Yet it is important to realize that such an institution cannot cure all administrative ills. It will work successfully only in a country, province or state that is already reasonably well administered. Where an administration is riddled with political patronage or corruption, the problem is too big for an Ombudsman, and a reform of the

[5]For further comments on the adjustments needed to fit Canadian conditions, see D.C. Rowat, "An Ombudsman Scheme for Canada", *Canadian Journal of Economics and Political Science*, Vol. 28, No. 4, November 1962, pp. 554-556.

whole system is required. Even where this is not the case, the need for additional protections against arbitrary administrative action is now so great in most Commonwealth countries that other reforms will be needed if the institution is not to become overloaded. Canada, like other Commonwealth countries, is now living on its past reputation for 'the rule of law'. We are like the dog in the anonymous rhyme:

> There was a dachshund, one so long
> He hadn't any notion
> How long it took to notify
> His tail of his emotion;
> And so it was that, though his eyes
> Were filled with tears and sadness,
> His little tail went wagging on
> Because of previous gladness.

Faced with our failure to solve the problem of protecting the rights of the citizen in the modern administrative state, and with the progress made in solving this problem by other democratic countries, our eyes are 'filled with tears of sadness'. But our tails go wagging smugly on, because of previous gladness.

31
Citizen Participation*

Committee on Government Productivity

The participation phenomenon is pervasive. It springs from a variety of socio-economic strata — middle-class homeowners, students, business-men, the aged, Indians, the poor. It affects not only governments but also such institutions as businesses, labour unions, universities and voluntary associations. Demands for participation come both from employees of these institutions and groups external to them.

Increasing numbers of people seem more eager to make their own decisions about what is best for them, less willing to delegate decision-making power, more distrustful of elected officials and more aggressive in making their views known to decision makers. The new tactics adopted by many individuals and groups are, perhaps, the most striking evidence of this change of attitude. Traditional political processes — joining political parties, voting, writing to elected representatives — are

---

*Reprinted and substantially abridged by permission from *Citizen Involvement* (a working paper prepared for the Committee on Government Productivity), Toronto, April 1972, pp. 1-29.

no longer sufficient for many people. Mass demonstrations and angry confontations with both elected and appointed officials, now common-place events, are gaining a new legitimacy.

A second and related change of attitude is reflected in an increasingly jaundiced view of expertise and professionalism. Some contend that people directly affected by a specific problem are often better informed about its nature and implications than are the so-called experts. Others question the notion that expertise is neutral, objective or value-free. It is argued that underlying any set of recommendations advanced by an expert are a set of value judgements and such judgements are no better or worse than those of non-experts.

Aside from the well-publicized confrontations between citizens and governments, new bonds of co-operation are beginning to develop. Some examples are worth citing.

At the municipal level, the Toronto Planning Board approved the two million dollar first phase of the Trefann Court Urban Renewal Scheme in June 1971. This plan was developed by a working committee composed of local politicians and citizens who had hired their own planner. City council had approved the creation of the working committee several years earlier after local residents protested an earlier urban renewal plan which called for the expropriation and demolition of their homes.

At the provincial level, the Community Development Branch in the Ontario Ministry of Community and Social Services exists for the purpose of assisting individuals and community groups to identify and achieve the priorities and goals of their communities. The Branch provides funds to help establish citizen groups working to increase participation in community affairs and counsels Ontario government ministries and agencies wishing to involve citizens in their decision processes.

At the federal level, Opportunities for Youth and the Local Initiatives Program both indicate a new relationship between citizens and government. Traditionally, government job-creating programs have been of the winter-works variety where jobs were both designed and administered by a government agency. In more recent programs, the federal government has assumed a new role, providing the resources but leaving the design and administration of job-creating schemes to individuals and groups in the community.

There are several factors contributing to the new demands for participation. First, the massive investment by governments in education may have produced a public which is better educated and therefore more critical and anxious to participate in political activity. The public is also exposed to a wide variety of information through the news media.

Secondly, as a result of the increasing size, complexity and power of modern governments and other institutions, many people feel they are losing control over the direction of their lives. Some citizens regard large institutions as being remote and impersonal and seek participation to ensure that *somebody* deals with issues affecting them. The expanding scope and complexity of institutions have placed enormous burdens on top-level decision makers. Politicians can deal with only a limited number of issues at a time and cannot possibly consider all the implications of each decision. Thus, individuals organize to ensure that their interests are not overlooked.

A third factor is the belief that governments and other institutions base their decisions on a narrowly defined view of what constitutes human well-being. According to this argument, most institutional decision making is based on the assumption that scarcity is mankind's central problem. Therefore, the primary objectives of all governments are economic development and growth. Considerations of quantity supercede those of quality. For example, our economic cost accounting system often fails to consider the impact of technological change on our environment. More people realize that by organizing and participating they can oblige decision makers to take account of such elements as beauty, diversity, human relationships within a given community and a pleasing environment.

Finally, the accelerating rate of change in society, much of which is based on technological innovation, contributes to demands for participation. As traditional institutions such as the family, the church and the neighbourhood become less important, people feel the need to establish new communities. For some people the new community groups satisfy a basic need for support and companionship. Citizens are also exposed to such disruptions to their way of life as wider roads, more traffic, intensified noise, increased building development and new airports. Many people participate simply to protect their vested interests against these disruptive developments. Authors such as Alvin Toffler and Donald Schon have pointed out one further problem: changes are occurring so rapidly that existing institutions simply don't have the capacity to digest and adjust to them. Thus, pressures for participation can be seen as both a cause and an effect of this incapacity to deal with rapid change.

Although governments are beginning to devise new programs for citizen participation, it is important to consider whether or not they should encourage and extend them.

There are three major reasons given for constraining or discouraging citizen participation: the contentment of the large majority of Canadians with the present system of government; the incompatibility of participation with new trends in public administration stressing comprehensive anticipatory planning; and the potentially inefficient and manipulative nature of participation.

It is often argued that the dominant orientation of citizens is not participatory; that Canadians on the whole are conservative, complacent and show little desire to depart from established political norms. Thus, while demands for participation from a minority of citizens may gather momentum, the response of political decision makers, according to this view, should be low-keyed and consistent with the views of the majority who are opposed to participatory politics.

It appears also that we are entering a new era in public administration and decision making. This era is characterized by a belief that analytical and technological capabilities will transform the decision-making process and improve the quality and effectiveness of decisions. Many people believe that interdependence and complexity of events will impose progressively heavier burdens on government politicians and administrators. It is suggested that if we do not anticipate events and plan comprehensively, we may permanently eliminate many potentially desirable results and leave only second-rate alternatives for our children. The central values underlying the public decision-making process will be efficiency, rationality, comprehensiveness, control, planning and anticipation. It is argued that the structures and decision processes spawned by these values and the public attitudes required for them to work will be incompatible with any valid participatory decision-making process.

It is often argued that too much participation would reduce government's effectiveness. It would be incapable of acting quickly, its decisions would be watered-down compromises and please no one, and false expectations would be raised. One author has written that

> groups of laymen — and especially groups of poorly educated laymen with little or no administrative experience — have particular handicaps as decision-makers. They have little time to devote to consideration of the issues; their concerns are selfish and immediate; they lack technical competence; they are both timid and suspicious. . . . If policies are ever adopted, they tend to be extremely short run and conservative — giving each interest a little bit more of what it already knows and values. As the typical citizen values effective government more than he values participation, however, the results of trying to involve and please everyone may be to please no one.[1]

It is notable also that participation might increase, rather than counteract, political inequalities in our society. Those who already know will know more; those who already express their opinions will express them more effectively. Participation can also be manipulative, especially when middle-class people act as catalysts in poor working-class districts.

On the other hand, two reasons are most often cited for actively encouraging participation: pressures for participation will intensify, and positive values inherent in participation should be fostered.

---

[1]Alan A. Altshuler, *Community Control* (Washington: Urban Institute, 1970), p. 45.

The new linkages between citizens and government will set important precedents. Citizens, politicians and officials will insist on adoption of some of these linkages to enhance their own effectiveness. Also, pressures for participation noted earlier may intensify. Levels of education are bound to increase. The news media will provide us with more information on the participation efforts of our fellow citizens. Organizations will become larger and more complex as governments show no signs of decreasing their involvement in our lives. The rate of technological change will probably continue to accelerate. Young people entering the work force will bring new ideas and attitudes to bear upon our institutions.

Both theorists and practitioners of politics and public administration justify citizen involvement by reference to the positive effects on the individual and society. These effects include education, self-development, integration, political equality, the acceptance of decisions, efficient and cost-effective decision making.

It has been suggested that participation can promote education and self-development in the following ways:

— by broadening the individual's intellect through exposure to new and challenging ideas and to different classes and groups of people.
— by enhancing the individual's self-esteem as others respond to his needs and desires and as he perceives the tangible results of his contributions to a decision.
— by promoting independence as a result of the individual's prerogative to judge what is best for him.
— by challenging the initiative of the individual through encouraging him to "do his own thing."
— by promoting a feeling of fellowship and a sense of community with others.

Participation can have an integrative effect by forcing individuals involved in decision processes to consider the interests of others. Individuals gradually expand their perspectives beyond the bounds of their own interests and then beyond the bounds of the interests of their organization.

Advocates of participation often argue that participatory government offers greater political equality to such groups as the Indians and the poor who traditionally have had little influence on decisions affecting their lives. Moreover, the greater the number of citizens who participate in government and the greater the amount of time spent by each individual in political activity, the more remote the possibility that substantial political power will rest in the hands of a few.

It is important to recognize also that individuals are more likely to accept decisions when they know that they have influenced them. This principle has been expounded by such administrative theorists as Robert Blake, Jane Mouton and Chris Argyris and has been widely accepted by managers in large organizations.

Two current administrative techniques emphasize the importance of involving employees in the decisions which affect them. The first, management by objectives, employs a formal system wherein managers and their superiors and subordinates up and down the corporate hierarchy meet to "discuss their goals." Broad company-wide goals come from above, but individuals are expected to propose what they themselves intend to accomplish. The objectives, large and small, are then meshed into a presumably coherent plan.[2] A second technique, known as Organizational Development (O.D.), also involves employees in decision making, but on a group rather than on a superior-subordinate basis. It takes such forms as T-groups, encounter groups and sensitivity training; it attempts to develop interpersonal competence, teamwork and group dynamic skills. O.D. gains effectiveness and adaptability by helping to overcome the limitations of highly structured organizations. Its purpose is to incorporate employee participation and collaborative decision making in problem solving.[3]

By applying the logic of these techniques to political involvement, there is a strong basis for arguing that participation will facilitate the implementation of public decisions.

A final reason for encouraging participation is that participation may be the most efficient and cost-effective way of making decisions. Frederick Thayer has argued the point as follows:

> While conventional wisdom argues that participation slows down decision processes, adds to the overall cost and design of implementation, and introduces a host of irrelevant factors, participation may do precisely the opposite. Most decision-making studies never examine the costs of overcoming consequences not foreseen in advance. There can be no better way of discovering these unforeseen consequences, long a problem of administration, than by involving in the decision processes those likely to be affected by them. A slower decision can become economical over the long term. Participation in other words may be cost effective through cost-avoidance, something that may be widely accepted in a few years.

The successful introduction of new forms of participation will depend primarily on the willingness of people inside and outside government to assume new roles and experiment with new ideas. For politicians and public servants, this will mean placing greater emphasis on facilitating and enabling roles than on directive leadership.

---

[2]Richard Todd, "Notes on Corporate Man," *Atlantic*, September 1971.
[3]William B. Eddy, "Beyond Behaviouralism, Organizational Development in Public Management," *Public Personnel Review*, July 1970.

32
Administrative Secrecy in Canada*

Task Force on Government Information Services

Canada has inherited some cherished traditions of parliamentary democracy and, along with them, the tradition of administrative secrecy. This tradition is a major barrier between the citizen and his Federal Government, and it has a great deal to do with the atmosphere in which the government performs its information functions. Canadian scholars are aware of the basic conflict between administrative secrecy and the fact that publicity services are indispensable to a modern, participatory democracy. Professor James Eayrs, wrote: "All bureaucracies are secretive, some more so than others. Canada's is more secretive than most. Totalitarian capitals apart, only official Canberra comes close to matching that special air of furtive reticence which marks the Ottawa mandarins off from other men."[1] Professor Donald C. Rowat argues that there is a strong tradition of administrative secrecy in all countries that have inherited the British parliamentary system, and that the tradition is a legacy from the time of absolute monarchy.[2] In Canada, as in these other countries, it is the accepted principle that all administrative activities and documents must be secret until the government chooses to reveal them. Rowat argues that "any large measure of government secrecy is incompatible with democracy." Yet, the decisions at the very apex of our political system are made secretly in Cabinet by Ministers who swear to "keep close and secret all such matters as shall be treated, debated and resolved on in Privy Council." Moreover, Ministerial decisions are carried out by what Rowat terms an "anonymous, faceless and impervious" public service, which has traditionally been more than eager to restrict access to information.

The press, the public, opposition political parties, and even government back-benchers frequently find that they have only the most inadequate means for getting information about the administrative activities of the government. Without adequate knowledge of what is going on, Parliament and the public cannot hope to call the government to account; and the administration's monopoly of information ensures that many members of Parliament are unable to offer informed criticism.

Opposition members, and government supporters as well, have provided several examples of their difficulties in gaining access to

---

*Reprinted and abridged by permission from *Task Force on Government Information Services*, Vol. 2 (Ottawa: Queen's Printer, 1969), pp. 25-34, 43.
[1] *The Toronto Star*, July 8, 1969.
[2] Donald C. Rowat, "The Problem of Administrative Secrecy", *International Review of Administrative Sciences*, Vol. 32, No. 2, 1969, pp. 99, 100.

government information. One Opposition spokesman said that getting information about research conducted for ARDA "is like pulling teeth." Another complained that he had been refused access to the reports on which the government based a decision to alter ways of spending on Indan health services, and said, "too often we're cut off from the reasoning behind government decisions."

A Liberal Member offered an illuminating example of previous government thinking when he recalled the fate of the Minister of Industry, Trade and Commerce's suggestion — made when he was a member of the Pearson Cabinet — that supporting papers, sent up to Cabinet at the time of policy formulation, should be published. The Member understood that the objection to the Minister's suggestion was that the publication of such papers would reveal the steps taken in making decisions. This brings us back to the strong tradition of administrative secrecy in countries with a parliamentary system of government, where ministerial responsibility goes hand in hand with public service neutrality and anonymity, and both are accepted as essential parts of the system.

Complaints about restricted access to government documents also come from many people who are not Members of Parliament. There are the representatives of the news media who, as Rowat says, "work in a crazy world of illicit purveyors of official information, who, like gossipers, give them a story but insist either that they must not tell anybody, or that if they print it, they must not give its source."[3] Scientists complain that the wall of military security prevents the free flow of information essential to scientific development. Social scientists have access to public records only in a limited sense and often at the sole discretion of the Dominion Archivist: they have no "right" of access.

Apart from the Official Secrets Act, Canada has no Statutory provisions that either forbid or permit access to government records. An Order in Council is currently in preparation to spell out details of access to records. Until now, Canadian governments have relied upon departmental discretion. In cases where Canadian documents might contain information from other countries, the government has adhered meticulously to the rules regarding access in the relevant country, but it has no guidelines of its own. There is, however, an accepted degree of classification in three main areas: correspondence concerning our relations with other countries (External Affairs and Defence); personnel records; and security and intelligence records. In other areas, government departments vary in their approaches.

The files of the Department of External Affairs include so many documents originated by other governments that the Department has felt obliged not to release these files until the governments concerned

---

[3] Ibid.

release their foreign correspondence. Until recently, British and American diplomatic records remained closed until they were 50 years old. But the 30-year period has now been adopted by the United States in relation to State Department records, and by the United Kingdom in relation to most documents including Cabinet papers, but excluding security and intelligence records.

On May 1, 1969 the Prime Minister of Canada announced[4] that Canada, also, plans to adopt the 30-year rule "to make available for research and other public use as large a portion of the records of the Canadian government prior to July 1, 1939 as would be consistent with the national interest." Certain records will be exempted from public access — "particularly those whose release might adversely affect Canada's external relations, violate the right of privacy of individuals, or adversely affect the national security."

With these exceptions, all departmental records over 30 years old will be transferred to the Public Archives; and, in addition, departments and agencies "will be encouraged to transfer to the Archives records less than 30 years old, insofar as this would be consistent with the efficient operation of departments or agencies involved." These records will remain under the control of the Ministers concerned and will be made available to the public under terms to be established by the Minister responsible in consultation with the Dominion Archivist. In no case will Cabinet documents be made available until they are 30 years old.

The recent *Report of the Royal Commission on Security, (Abridged)* offers little encouragement to those who looked forward to a greater sense of freedom and openness than there is now in matters of access to administrative records.[5] The Royal Commission has only just reported and it is too early to know the government's response to its detailed recommendations in this field. The report does say that the absence of a government policy has been "a serious handicap" to historical and other research but, at the same time, the Commission sees no alternative to the 30-year rule. Indeed, from the point of view of security, the Commission feels that there is some material which "for a variety of good reasons should not be made public even after thirty years, and adequate arrangements must be made to strip files of such material before the files are made available to the public."

Rowat's suggestion, made in 1965, was that a much shorter period, perhaps 12 years, should be adopted as the norm, with the government retaining clear authority to keep sensitive documents longer than this, and discretion to release non-sensitive documents earlier. Many western countries, including Britain and the United States, have shown concern

[4]*Debates*, Commons, May 1, 1969, pp. 8, 199-200.
[5]*Royal Commission on Security* (Abridged), Ottawa, Queen's Printer, 1969, p. 80.

in recent years over unduly restricted access to administrative documents. But the *Report of the Royal Commission on Security, (Abridged),* apart from suggesting that the classification "Restricted" be abandoned because it is superfluous and misleading, recommended no changes in classification procedures. The Commission was not sympathetic to what it termed "the current concern about overclassification" and said that "it would appear to us that very compelling arguments would need to be advanced for making major changes in the present system."[6] Indeed, the Commission thought some tightening-up necessary, and said that more attention should be paid to the "need-to-know" principle, that classified information should be disseminated no further than necessary for the conduct of business. Rowat believes the most sensible scheme would be to apply the American declassification system, whereby the great bulk of unimportant documents can be made available immediately. The *Report of the Royal Commission on Security (Abridged)* suggested that departments should be constantly reminded of the value of down-grading the security classification of documents and that officers should seize any opportunity to amend the classification of papers. But, it added, departmental judgment must be permitted to play a large role in declassification.

Reactions to the Royal Commission's recommendations were mixed. Roger Champoux, writing in *La Presse,* summed up the general press view when he said many of the recommendations were "exagérées dans leur rigueur."[7] Professor Eayrs' comment on the *Report of the Royal Commission on Security (Abridged)* was that "it has pushed us back into the murk of administrative secrecy of which other countries are working free."[8] Administrative secrecy is an important element of the atmosphere in which government operates. It is a matter of considerable concern in several other democratic countries.

For almost 200 years the assumption in Sweden has been that all government documents are public unless legal provision has been made for them to be withheld. In effect, a Swedish official who is drafting a document does not assign a security classification to it. All documents, except those in certain defined areas, are considered "unclassified" up to the time they are requested to be produced for public examination. Any citizen may ask for a document. It is up to the official responsible (or his superiors) to say whether or not it can be produced but, if he refuses access, he must be able to give adequate reasons that conform to the regulations.

The Swedish Constitution provides limitations to access: "To further the free interchange of opinion and general enlightenment, every Swedish citizen shall have free access to official documents....

---

[6]*Ibid.,* p. 74.
[7]*La Presse,* June 28, 1969.
[8]*Toronto Star,* July 8, 1969.

This right shall be subject only to such restrictions as are required out of considerations for the security of the realm and its relations with foreign powers, or in connection with official activities for inspection, control or other supervision, or for the prevention and prosecution of crime, or to protect the legitimate economic interests of the State, communities and individuals, or out of consideration for the maintenance of privacy, security of the person, decency and morality."

The Constitution goes on to say that the specific cases in which official documents are to be kept secret shall be "closely defined" in a special statute. This law, the Secrecy Act, spells out an impressive list of matters that must be kept secret.

The principle of open access, however, has extensive application. It applies to public documents both prepared and received by all sorts of administrative agencies, from government departments to the police, administrative tribunals and local governments. Even Parliament comes under the rule; citizens can demand to see the minutes of its committees. Moreover, a person who asks to see public documents does not have to show that he has a legal interest in them. He does not even have to say why he wants them. The Constitution provides that a requested document shall be "made available immediately or as soon as possible." The courts in their judgments have taken this rule seriously.

As Rowat has indicated, the list of exceptions covers all the circumstances that are traditionally used as arguments against free access to administrative information. But in general, the right of free access is to prevail, and this right is limited only by the listed exceptions.

In the Secrecy Act itself, and in other government regulations, the secrecy of documents is valid only for a specified period of time, and the restrictions are not valid for documents preserved in the courts. Where documents of the Foreign Office and the armed services are concerned, the Secrecy Act carefully enumerates those that may be temporarily kept secret. Most of the regulations for secrecy do not refer to documents containing administrative decisions.

The principle of open access is upheld by the Ombudsman who handles questions about the classification of documents with regard to publicity, by the courts and by regulations requiring special arrangements to facilitate easy access to documents by scholars, the press and by any interested members of the public.

Open access makes it possible for the interested Swedish public to participate in the formation of policy. Citizens have a chance to criticize and discuss proposals before the government makes decisions, often using the same documentation as the experts. In Sweden, draft bills are made public. They are widely discussed among interested groups before their presentation to the legislature. This overcomes one of the disabilities of the Canadian parliamentary system, in which the government has no easy way to seek public reaction to a measure before it is presented to Parliament in a form that is almost final. The most important effect of publicity, according to Canadian scholar Jacques Prémont,[9] is that any decision taken by government and administration is under public scrutiny and therefore control.

The Report of the Royal Commission on Security (Abridged) acknowledged the fact of the Swedish system of open access but it did not approve of the principle behind the system:

> We would view suggestions for increased publicity with some alarm. We think the knowledge that memoranda might be made public would have a seriously inhibiting effect on the transaction of public business. We believe that the process of policy-making implies a need for wide-ranging and tentative consideration of options, many of which it would be silly or undesirable to expose to the public gaze. To insist that all such communications must be made public would appear to us likely to impede the discussive deliberation that is necessary for wise administration.[10]

The Royal Commission saw no reason why controlled access to specific Canadian Government files should not be arranged on an *ad hoc* basis, when a genuine requirement can be established.

The Swedish system of open administration may be admirable but it is not necessarily easily adaptable to Canadian conditions. Nor is there much evidence that the real results for the public — in improved quality of information or lack of suppression of essential documents — are notably different from the results in the Canadian or United States systems.

Rowat, however, is convinced that Canada should follow the Swedish example because "the principle of open access to administrative information is essential to the full development of democracy."[11] He was challenged by K.W. Knight in an exchange of articles published in *The Canadian Journal of Economics and Political Science* in 1965 and 1966. Knight felt that making official files available to the public might "induce such a degree of administrative caution as would seriously inhibit the effective functioning of government." He foresaw officials "completely avoiding the risks of putting pen to paper," or "writing with an eye to history by recording only favourable information." Full access to working papers might lead to the officials being "forced to the hustings" to "engage in public controversy" allowing "political capital to be made." Under such circumstances Ministers of the Crown "might be tempted to fill senior posts with their political sympathizers...."[12]

[9]J. Prémont, "Publicité de Documents Officiels," Canadian Public Administration, Vol. 11, No. 4, Winter, 1968, pp. 449–453.

[10]*Report of the Royal Commission on Security* (Abridged), Section 223, p. 80.

[11]Rowat, *op. cit.*, p. 105.

[12]K.W. Knight, "Administrative Secrecy and Ministerial Responsibility," *Canadian Journal of Economics and Political Science*, Vol. 32, No. 1, February 1966, p. 78.

In reply,[13] Rowat suggested that, rather than taking a defeatist position on the first points, the public should ensure that such things did not happen. In Rowat's view, Knight's fears were "largely false" because the great bulk of administrative information is required to be recorded, and this requirement could easily be extended by legislation. Under the existing system, Rowat believes that "officials and governments are free to put out only favourable publicity. Access to records which are required to be kept would prevent them from doing this." Rowat argued that, in the Swedish experience, the open access principle had produced an attitude in officials which worked against any wholesale tendency to evade the requirement of putting pen to paper. In any case, he was not advocating complete access to information and documents at all times. His proposal would still be compatible with an appropriate measure of secrecy in administration. "There will always be the problem of drawing a line between the government's need to deliberate confidentially and the public's need for information. It is simply a question of emphasis."

Rowat agreed there was a possibility Ministers "might be tempted to fill senior posts with their political sympathizers" but suggested the temptation need not be satisfied. In Sweden not only are all public service jobs publicly advertised, as they are in Canada, but the press and the general public has the right to examine the list of applicants after an appointment has been made. In several Western European countries, senior officials have considerable freedom to express their views publicly. In the United States, the whole top level of the civil service is politically appointed. Rowat believes such a system has "certain advantages, such as the top officials' commitment to and enthusiasm for the government's programmes, as compared with the cold neutrality of permanent officials under the Commonwealth parliamentary system ... other workable arrangements exist and they may even be superior to our own."

This argument went to the root of Knight's doubts about the principle of open access. Knight believes the principle is basically incompatible with the parliamentary democratic system practised in Commonwealth countries. He wrote: "In questioning the need for administrative secrecy we are casting doubt on notions that not only have some constitutional support, but also represent a significant element in our general ideology of government. It may be that we have been believing (or acting as if we believe) in a myth. Perhaps we should completely abandon the doctrines of ministerial responsibility and public service anonymity and neutrality; based as they are on the doubtful idea that a clear distinction can be made between policy-making and

---

[13]D.C. Rowat, "Administrative Secrecy and Ministerial Responsibility: A Reply" loc. cit., pp. 84-87.

administration. If this is to be the approach, however, the issues must be presented clearly."[14]

Canada has lagged behind other countries — and particularly Britain, the United States and Sweden — in opening administrative practices to the public, Members of Parliament, and the "public watch-dog" of the news media.

In Canada, as in all Commonwealth countries with a common-law tradition, it is left to the discretion of the various courts of the land to decide whether the public interest is better served by revealing sources or concealing them. Customarily the Canadian courts give admonitions or suspended sentences to journalists who refuse to divulge their sources. But judgements differ.

A secrecy-oriented society is unlikely to produce the atmosphere that is necessary for public participation in the democratic process. But an open administration is only one of the requirements for a participatory democracy. If participation is to mean anything, citizens must be fully informed of their government's purposes and activities and, to get this information, they are largely dependent on their government's information services.

33
Codes of Ethics and Administrative Responsibility*

Kenneth Kernaghan

Revelations and allegations of unethical conduct involving government officials quickly arouse public concern and, usually, public displeasure. Indeed, members of the general public seem to find a special fascination in incidents of real or apparent wrongdoing in government. This interest is often initiated, stimulated, and sustained by representatives of the news media who perceive the discovery and exposure of official misconduct as one of their prime duties. Moreover, the government's opponents understandably tend to revel in the political advantage they can gain from fanning the flames of public outrage over unethical conduct.

During the past few years, there has been unusually strong public demand in Canada that the federal, provincial, and municipal govern-

---

[14]Knight, *op. cit.,* p. 84.

---

*Reprinted and abridged by permission from Kenneth Kernaghan, "Codes of Ethics and Administrative Responsibility," *Canadian Public Administration*, vol. 17, no. 4 (Winter 1974), pp. 527-541.

ments devise means to ensure the ethical conduct of public officials. This concern has arisen in large part from disclosures and charges that ethical offences have been committed by government officials not only in Canada but also in the United States, Great Britain, and France.

In Canada, the most widely publicized and politically damaging incidents have been conflict-of-interest situations and 'leaks' of confidential government documents in which both elected and appointed officials have allegedly been involved. There has been much debate also over the extent to which government employees should engage in partisan political activity or express publicly their personal views on government policy and administration. These issues have, in varying degrees, plagued all levels of government in Canada. Elected officials as well as employees of regular government departments and of agencies, boards, and commissions have become entangled in ethical problems.

RECENT CANADIAN EXPERIENCE

During the period since World War II there has been a recurring pattern in the exposure and disposal of cases of unethical conduct in Canadian governments. An accusation or allegation of unethical conduct has been made; public indignation has been expressed; political advantage has been taken; demands for legislative remedies have been heard; blame has occasionally been laid; and a penalty has occasionally been imposed. Then, there has been a rapid decline in public interest as the rush of new events has blocked out yesterday's news from public consciousness. These cycles of rise and decline in public concern have been accompanied by demands for laws and regulations to help ensure that similar incidents do not occur in the future and that appropriate sanctions are available to punish abuses. As public concern has subsided, however, so has the sentiment for formal action to guard against future offences. Although most of the publicity on ethical conduct has surrounded the activities of politicians, there were until very recently few statutes, regulations, or guidelines relating to the ethical conduct of elected officials.[1] The extent to which appointed officials have been subject to constraints and directions in this area has varied greatly from one department or agency and from one level of government to another.

In the past few years there has been a dramatic break with this traditional pattern. Several governments have responded to the public's outcry against unethical behaviour by drafting and promulgating laws, regulations, and guidelines on various aspects of ethical conduct, especially on conflicts of interest. There has been a 'chain reaction' as one

---

[1]For a discussion of the ethical conduct of members of Parliament in the sphere of conflict of interest, see *Members of Parliament and Conflict of Interest*, Sessional Paper No. 291-4/61, 1st Session, 29th Parliament. July 1973.

government has followed another in issuing formal statements on ethical conduct. There has also been a 'spillover effect' as anxiety about the proper conduct of elected officials has spread to apprehension about the ethical standards of all public officials, including government employees. Moreover, this concern has been extended not only to employees of regular government departments but also to employees of agencies, boards, and commissions.

The recent departure from the conventional ebb and flow of public concern about ethical conduct may be explained in large part by three factors, namely, the activities of the mass media of communication, events in other countries, and changing public expectations about the level of morality in government.

The news media have become increasingly vigilant in seeking out and exposing actual or potential cases of misconduct in government. Investigative reporting and continuing coverage by the news media reveal ethical problems that might not otherwise come to light and help to discourage government employees from yielding to temptation. The current public concern about ethics in government may have arisen less from the commission of new sins than from the greater publicity being given to the old ones. The news media have contributed substantially to the public attitude towards ethics in government by reporting instances of official misconduct in other countries. For example, 'Watergate' has become a collective term embracing a variety of illegal, unethical, and questionable activities on the part of elected and appointed officials in the United States. Thus, international coverage has helped create a widespread climate of opinion in several countries, including Canada, against unethical conduct in government.

During the post-war years there has been a gradual but substantial modification in the public's view of what standards of conduct are appropriate for government officials. The pace of this change has accelerated in very recent years and has been an important factor in disrupting the traditional pattern of response to instances of unethical behaviour. Certain kinds of official conduct that used to be tolerated or mildly disapproved are now considered unacceptable and punishable, especially in the area of conflicts of interest. The seriousness of even a *potential* conflict of interest was recognized in a recent decision made under the federal Public Service Staff Relations Act.[2] The adjudicator upheld the suspension of a federal employee who established a company offering services that could lead to a conflict of interest with his official duties. The Board found that the appearance of conflict was enough to establish a conflict of interest. According to the adjudicator, 'it is not sufficient for the public servant or his associates to be convinced of their

---

2'Public Service Staff Relations Act Decision, Between Maurice Dudley Atkins, Grievor, and Treasury Board (Ministry of Transport), Employer,' 21 March 1974, File 166-2-889.

own innocence and integrity. Nor is it necessary to prove that they have been disloyal to the employer. Even in the absence of evidence of wilful wrongdoing, a conflict of interest or the appearance thereof can be easily recognized by an intelligent citizen as contrary to public policy.'[3]

VALUE OF CODES OF ETHICS

Scholars and practitioners are by no means unanimous in their support for codes of ethics. Opinions on the value of codes range from the view that they are virtually worthless, or at best unnecessary, to the view that they serve as effective controls over administrative action. It is certainly unrealistic to portray codes of ethics as a cure-all for violations of the public trust. It is suggested here, however, that codes may provide preventive medicine against the malady of unethical conduct and a distasteful dose of medicine for an employee who contracts the disease. The extent to which a code of ethics has value depends on whether the code is written or unwritten, on its acceptance by the public and by government employees, and on its form, content, and administration.

Written Versus Unwritten Codes

The weight of evidence points to the desirability of a code of ethics as a formally written document rather than an 'unwritten' code composed of traditions, practices, and understandings. Some public employees assert that a code of ethics is unnecessary because they know what standards of conduct are expected of them. They contend further that they share allegiance to an 'unwritten' code of conduct based on customary practices and informal understandings. Opposition to a written code is also based on the fact that the standards of a code are sometimes difficult to apply to specific cases, especially in the conflict-of-interest area. Advocates of a written code, however, do not claim that it provides easy solutions to the great variety of ethical problems that may arise; rather, they seek clarity through written guidelines and recognize the need for flexibility and judgment in the interpretation of these guidelines. Critics of a written code appear to offer no alternatives to the status quo, namely, reliance on unwritten understandings and practices. It is important to note also that employees may develop informal, unwritten agreements on unethical as well as on ethical practices.

Unwritten codes have distinct disadvantages when compared with formal, written codes. In the first place, the activities and comments of public employees at all levels of government have demonstrated that they do not agree on what kinds of behaviour are permissible or

---

prohibited. Moreover, conduct perceived as generally acceptable by one individual, group, or department is often quite different from that acceptable to others. Employees require a common set of standards — in written form — applicable to the administrative unit within which they are working.

Secondly, the extent to which a public employee will adhere to an unwritten code will depend on his personal judgment or the opinion of his colleagues. Heavy reliance must be placed on the conscience of the individual employee. However, an employee's conscience, unencumbered by a statement of written guidelines, may in some situations be his best accomplice. This is not to suggest that appeals to conscience based on traditional practices may not be effective in preserving a high level of ethical conduct but to argue that an employee is less likely to violate written standards than he is to depart from unwritten understandings and practices subject to debate not only on their interpretation but on their very existence. A related disadvantage of an unwritten code is that it is difficult to enforce because penalties cannot easily be attached to unwritten ethical guidelines.

Finally, dependence on an unwritten code of ethics made more sense when the scope of government responsibilities were smaller, when government operations were less complex and technical, and when government employees were less numerous. Certainly there is still an enormous range in the size and activities of administrative units — from huge federal departments at one extreme to a few clerks in tiny rural municipalities at the other. In large cities, in provincial governments, and in the federal government, however, expanding discretionary powers are exercised by a larger number of more highly educated employees dealing with increasingly complex and technical matters. Administrative control over one's subordinates used to be more direct and more personal — and based on more adequate understanding of the subject matter at hand. It has become a difficult task for political and administrative superiors to be aware personally of the vast number of decisions taken by their subordinates, much less to know whether some subordinates have made private gain from certain of these decisions.

A written code of ethics also serves a number of important purposes both for the general public and for government employees.

Codes of Ethics and the Public

The public demands that government employees maintain high standards of ethical conduct. They insist that there not be situations where public office can actually or potentially be used for private, personal, political, or pecuniary gain — or for any combination of these benefits. The public seems to expect a higher level of morality among government employees than among their counterparts in private business and to be in general agreement also that the level of ethical conduct in government is in fact higher than that found in the private sector of society. There is an apparent tendency for some citizens to expect a public official to adhere to a loftier set of standards than that to which they themselves aspire in their personal lives. The 'public' element of public administration gives taxpaying citizens some motivation to be vigilant and indignant about violations of the public trust. The public's vigilance sometimes also seems prompted by envy of officials who are in a position to use their government office for personal gain.

High standards of ethical conduct in government bring more tangible benefits to the public than mere satisfaction that public office is not being misused. High ethical standards may help to promote a greater measure of efficiency in the implementation of government programs. For example, when an official awards a contract to a firm from which he has received a gift, the work may be of lower quality (and higher cost) than if another firm had been awarded the contract on the sole basis of competitive bidding. High standards of ethical conduct will also help to ensure that citizens receive uniform and consistent treatment from impartial and objective government officials. Members of the public do not expect to receive less generous service because others have developed a special, secret, mutually beneficial relationship with government employees. The exposure of abuses committed by a few officials can have an impact out of all proportion to their number and gravity. An undiscriminating public tends to tar all officials with the same brush. Thus, any significant number of reported or alleged abuses of the public trust may lead to severe criticism and pessimism about the quality of all public officials and undermine faith in political and administrative institutions generally.

The reaction of the public to instances of official misconduct shows that citizens are confused and disagree among themselves about what kind of behaviour is unethical and what penalties should be imposed for offences. A written code informs the public of the level of ethical conduct expected from government employees. It thereby provides citizens with a set of standards by which they may assess the conduct of public employees and helps to sustain their confidence in the integrity of government and in particular of appointed officials.

Codes of Ethics and Public Employees

The ethical standards of public employees are in large part a reflection of the standards prevailing in society generally. Since government employees are members of the general public when they are not acting in their official capacity, it is not surprising that they are influenced by the level of ethical standards of their fellow citizens. Nor is it surprising that government employees, like their fellow citizens, have differing perceptions of what constitutes unethical conduct.

A code of ethics, then, provides government employees with criteria by which they may evaluate their own behaviour as well as the behaviour of their administrative colleagues — whether their peers, superiors, or subordinates. A code is especially valuable in the education of new recruits. It furnishes a guide to which all officials may refer when in doubt about the propriety of their own actions or the actions of others. They have a document that states, with varying degrees of clarity and specificity, that certain kinds of behaviour are not only inappropriate for public employees but are forbidden on the pain of disciplinary action.

With the passage of time, some, if not all, provisions of a code tend to become internalized by many employees as a means of self-discipline — a kind of automatic regulating device. For example, an experienced employee will, in the normal course of events, without conscious thought and deliberation, avoid conflict-of-interest situations and maintain the confidentiality of government documents. The role of senior officials is especially important in this process. They must not only keep employees well informed about ethical standards but also by exemplary behaviour provide a model to be emulated by other officials. The senior official should strive to become a personification of the code he has the responsibility of enforcing. Another very important pressure encouraging employees to maintain high ethical standards is the expectations of their peers. A climate is created wherein all those in a work group or section of a department or agency come to share a common view as to what constitutes proper behaviour. This is more likely to occur and the standard of ethical behaviour is likely to be higher if there is a written code serving as a criterion for performance.

There are employees, of course, who are influenced only slightly or not at all by the exhortations of codes of ethics and by the high ethical standards of their superiors and peers. For these employees a code of ethics may serve as an instrument of administrative control. Senior officials may utilize the code as a means of judging whether an employee has acted properly in a given situation and as a basis for disciplining an employee who has acted improperly. With a written code of ethics in their possession, supervisors will no longer be obliged to admonish employees by making reference to vague and uncertain conventions and understandings. Moreover, the means of preventing and punishing unethical conduct will be set out for the direction of all employees. If a code is to have value as a basis for administrative control, it is helpful, although not essential, to spell out the penalties for unethical behaviour in the code itself.

It is not necessary for all employees to 'get religion' in the sense of being converted to strong adherence to the tenets of the code. What is especially important is that those in formal positions of authority or in informal positions of influence accept the code as one standard by which an employee's conduct is assessed in connection with promotion and other rewards. The employee will be expected to achieve certain ethical standards as well as technical standards. If the employee does not 'get religion,' he may at least 'get the message' that occupational success and congenial relations with fellow employees depend in part on his demonstrating appropriate ethical standards. Thus, a code may be used both as an instrument of control and a means of influence over administrative action.

ETHICAL CONDUCT AND ADMINISTRATIVE RESPONSIBILITY

Ethical conduct has traditionally been a central component of the larger concept of administrative responsibility. For scholars and practitioners concerned with the preservation of responsible administrative behaviour, the importance of the subject of ethical conduct has been enhanced by the current high level of public and governmental interest in the ethical standards of government employees. Students of government have tended to concentrate on the design and adaptation of institutional and procedural means to check bureaucratic abuse of power and so to promote administrative responsibility. This emphasis has been to the detriment of thought and writing about the ethical climate within which public employees work. It is suggested here that ethics in government will be a continuing and increasingly important concern in the foreseeable future. Whether or not the public's interest in the matter enters its customary decline, it seems appropriate for government employees, academic scholars, and mass media representatives to retain their interest in stimulating an ethical sense of responsibility in government.

The development of codes of ethics is one potentially effective means of achieving this end. The relationship of codes of ethics to administrative responsibility may be demonstrated by reference to two major interpretations of administrative responsibility, namely, objective and subjective (psychological) responsibility. Objective responsibility connotes the responsibility of a person or organization to someone else, outside of self, for some thing or some kind of performance. It is closely akin to accountability or answerability. If one fails to carry out legitimate directives, he is judged irresponsible and may be subjected to penalties. Subjective or psychological responsibility centres not upon to whom and for what one *is* responsible ... but to whom one *feels* responsible and *behaves* responsibly. This meaning is more nearly synonymous with identification, loyalty and conscience than it is with accountability or answerability.'[4]

A written code of ethics may be used to promote both types of administrative responsibility. To help achieve objective responsibility in the sense of accountability, a code should be much more than a brief list of platitudes. To serve as an instrument of control over administrative action, a code should be as specific as possible while allowing for flexibility in its interpretation; provision should also be made for its effective enforcement.

However, in view of the difficulty of holding public employees responsible solely through the threat or imposition of penalties, it is desirable to have a code of ethics become as self-enforcing as possible. A written code provides a common set of standards. If it is accepted by an employee's superiors, peers, and subordinates as a model for behaviour, adherence to its provisions will gradually be internalized in the value-system of many employees. Through this process, a code may serve as a means by which government employees may influence rather than control the ethical conduct of their colleagues. The forces at work will be conscience and organizational loyalty rather than fear of punishment. In this fashion, a significant measure of subjective or psychological responsibility may be elicited and, thereby, a fuller measure of responsible administrative conduct achieved.

CASE REFERENCES

Canadian Cases in Public Administration
    Reality or Appearance?
    The Renfrew Group
    The Minister and the Doctor
    A "Miner" Problem
    The Resigning Engineer
    The Foot and Mouth Disease Epidemic, 1952

Case Program in Canadian Public Administration
    A Conflict of Loyalties

BIBLIOGRAPHY

Appleby, Paul H., *Big Democracy*. New York, Alfred A. Knopf, 1945.
Appleby, Paul H., *Morality and Administration in Democratic Government*. Baton Rouge, Louisiana, Louisiana State University Press, 1952.

---

[4]Frederick C. Mosher, *Democracy and the Public Service*, New York, Oxford University Press, 1968, pp. 7-8. See also Kenneth Kernaghan, 'Responsible Public Bureaucracy: A Rationale and a Framework for Analysis,' *Canadian Public Administration* vol. 16, no. 4, Winter, 1973, pp. 572-603.

Cheffins, R.I., *The Constitutional Process in Canada*. 2nd ed., Toronto, McGraw-Hill, 1976, Cahpter 3.

Courtney, John C., "In Defence of Royal Commissions." *Canadian Public Administration*, Vol. 12, No. 2, Summer 1969, pp. 198-212.

De Smith, S.A., *Judicial Review of Administrative Action*. London, Stevens & Sons Limited, 1959.

Douglas, Paul H., *Ethics in Government*. Cambridge, Mass., Harvard University Press, 1952.

Dussault, René, Relationship between the Nature of the Acts of the Administration and Judicial Review: Quebec and Canada." *Canadina Public Administration*, Vol. 10, No. 3, September 1967, pp. 298-322.

Dussault, René, *Le contrôle judiciare de l'administration qu Quebéc*. Quebec, Les Presses de l'Université Laval, 1969.

Dussault, René and Bernatchez, Roger, "La fonction publique canadienne et québecoise." *Canadina Public Administration*, Vol. 15, No. 1, Srping 1972, pp. 74-159 and Vol. 15, No. 2, Summer 1972, pp. 251-374.

Fera, Norman, "Review of Administrative Decisions Under the Federal Court Act." *Canadian Public Administration*, Vol. 14, No. 4, Winter 1971, pp. 580-94.

Finer, Herman, "Administrative Responsibility in Democratic Government." *Public Administration Review*, Vol. 1, No. 4, Summer 1941, pp. 335-50.

Gawthrop, Louis C., ed., *The Administrative Process and Democratic Theory*. Boston, Houghton Mifflin Company, 1970.

Gellhorn, Walter, *Ombudsmen and Others: Citizens Protectors in Nine Countries*. Cambridge, Mass., Harvard University Press, 1966.

Great Britain, *Committee on Administrative Tribunals and Enquiries, Report*. London, Her Majesty's Stationery Office, 1957.

Great Britain, *Committee on Ministers' Powers, Report*. London, His Majesty's Stationery Office, 1932.

Harris, Joseph P., *Congressional Control of Administration*. Washington, D.C., The Brookings Institution, 1964.

Herring, Pendleton, *Public Administration and the Public Interest*. New York, Russell, 1967. Reprint of 1936 edition.

Hewart, G.H., *The New Despotism*. London, Ernest Benn Limited, 1929.

Kernaghan, Kenneth, "Codes of Ethics and Administrative Responsibility." *Canadian Public Administration*, Vol. 17, No. 4, Winter 1974, pp. 527-41.

Kernaghan, Kenneth, "Responsible Public Bureaucracy: A Rationale and a Framework for Analysis." *Canadian Public Administration*, Vol. 16, No. 4, Winter 1973, pp. 572-603.

Kersell, J.E., *Parliamentary Supervision of Delegated Legislation: The United Kingdom, Australia, New Zealand and Canada*. London, Stevens & Sons Limited, 1960.

Kersell, J.E., "Statutory and Judicial Control of Administrative Bheaviour." *Canadian Public Administration*, Vol. 19, No. 2, Summer 1976, pp. 295-307.

Knight, K.W., "Administrative Secrecy and Ministerial Responsibility." *Canadian Journal of Economics and Political Science*, Vol. 32, No. 1, February 1966, pp. 77-84.

Krislov, Samuel, *Representative Bureaucracy*. Englewood Cliffs, N.J., Prentice-Hall, 1974.

Mosher, Frederick C., *Democracy and the Public Service*. New York, Oxford University Press, 1968.

Peel, Ray V., ed., "The Ombudsman or Citizen's Defender: A Modern Institution." *The Annals of the American Academy of Political and Social Science*, Vol. 377, May 1968.

Redford, Emmette S., *Democracy in the Administrative State*. New York, Oxford University Press, 1969, Chapter 6.

Rourke, Francis E., *Secrecy and Publicity*. Baltimore, Johns Hopkins Press, 1961.

Rowat, Donald C., *The Ombudsman Plan*. Toronto, McClelland and Stewart, 1973.

Rowat, Donald C., "Administrative Secrecy and Ministerial Responsibility: A Reply." *Canadian Journal of Economics and Political Science*, Vol. 32, No. 1, February 1966, pp. 84-7.

Rowat, Donald C., "An Ombudsman Scheme for Canada." *Canadian Journal of Economics and Political Science*, Vol. 28, No. 4, November 1962, pp. 543-56.

Rowat, Donald C., "How Much Administrative Secrecy?" *Canadian Journal of Economics and Political Science*, Vol. 31, No. 4, November 1965, pp. 479-98.

Rowat, Donald C., *The Ombudsman*, 2nd ed., Toronto, University of Toronto Press, 1968.

Sharp, J.M., "The Public rvant and the Right to Privacy." *Canadian Public Administration*, Vol. 14, No. 1, Spring 1971, pp. 58-64.

Williams, Roger and Bates, David, "Technical Decisions and Public Accountability." *Canadian Public Administration*, Vol. 19, No. 4, Winter 1976, pp. 603-632.